As We Wave You Goodbye

As We Wave You Goodbye

Australian Women and War

Edited by Jan Bassett

Melbourne
OXFORD UNIVERSITY PRESS
Oxford Auckland New York

This project has been assisted by the Commonwealth Government through the Australia Council, its arts funding and advisory body.

OXFORD UNIVERSITY PRESS AUSTRALIA

Oxford New York
Athens Auckland Bangkok Bogota Bombay
Buenos Aires Calcutta Cape Town Dar es Salaam
Delhi Florence Hong Kong Istanbul Karachi
Kuala Lumpur Madras Madrid Melbourne
Mexico City Nairobi Paris Port Moresby
Singapore Taipei Tokyo Toronto Warsaw

and associated companies in
Berlin Ibadan

OXFORD is a trade mark of Oxford University Press

First published 1998

National Library of Australia
Cataloguing-in-publication data:

As we wave you goodbye: Australian women and war.

Bibliography.
Includes index.
ISBN 0 19 554086 7.

1. War—Literary collections. 2. Australian literature—Women authors. 3. Women and war. 4. War in literature. I. Bassett, Jan, 1953– .

A820.80358

Edited by Katherine Steward
Text design by Anitra Blackford
Cover design by Anitra Blackford
Typeset by Solo Typesetting
Printed by Kyodo Printing, Singapore
Published by Oxford University Press
253 Normanby Road, South Melbourne, Australia

CONTENTS

	List of illustrations	viii
	Introduction	ix
	Editor's acknowledgments	xvii
	List of abbreviations	xviii
PART ONE	BOER WAR	
	Miles Franklin (1879–1954)	3
	Gertrude Fletcher (dates unknown)	5
	Julia Anderson (dates unknown)	7
PART TWO	GREAT WAR	
	Kathleen Mangan (1906–)	17
	Ethel Cooper (1871–1961)	20
	Hilda Freeman (1885–1937)	22
	Louise Mack (1870–1935)	24
	Ethel Turner (1872–1958)	28
	Martha Coxhead (dates unknown)	29
	Evelyn Davies (dates unknown)	32
	Mabel Brookes (1890–1975)	36
	Joan Dugdale (1943–)	40
	Emily Dunbar (dates unknown)	42
	Mabel Brookes (1890–1975)	46
	Mary Grant Bruce (1878–1958)	49
	Mary Edgeworth David (1888–1987)	51
	Margery Ruth Betts (dates unknown)	54
	Lesbia Harford (1891–1927)	55
	Mollie Skinner (1876–1955)	61
	Olive King (1885–1958)	64
	May Tilton (1884–1964)	69
	Mary Marlowe (1884–1962)	72
	Mary Gilmore (1865–1962)	77
	Gladys Hain (1887–1962)	78
	Vida Goldstein (1869–1949)	82
	Gwen Kelly (1922–)	84
	Adela Pankhurst (1885–1961)	88

Katharine Susannah Prichard (1883–1969) 90
Grace Ethel Martyr (dates unknown) 94
Alice Davies (dates unknown) 96
Gertrude Moberly (dates unknown) 97
Ruth Park (1923–) 99
Dorothy Hewett (1923–) 102
Aileen Young (dates unknown) 104
Nettie Palmer (1885–1964) 105
Mary Grant Bruce (1878–1958) 106
Angela Thirkell (1890–1961) 109
Zora Cross (1890–1964) 113
Jessie Traill (1881–1967) 116
Katharine Susannah Prichard (1883–1969) 117
Shirley Hazzard (1931–) 121

PART THREE SECOND WORLD WAR
Helen Light (?–) 125
Mary Kent Hughes (dates unknown) 127
Meta Maclean (?–) 129
Faith Richmond (1935–) 131
Neilma Gantner (1922–) 132
Jessie Street (1899–1970) 135
Dorothy Elmes (1914–42) 139
Betty Jeffrey (1908–) 140
Jessie Simons (1911–) 142
Judith Wright (1915–) 145
Katharine Susannah Prichard (1883–1969) 146
Elyne Mitchell (1913–) 150
Kylie Tennant (1912–88) 154
Patsy Adam-Smith (1926–) 157
Eleanor Dark (1901–86) 158
Katharine Gallagher (1935–) 162
Gwen Harwood (1920–95) 162
Ethel Turner (1872–1958) 164
Ola Calderala (?–) 166
Geraldine Halls (1919–96) 167
Jean Sims (1922–) 169
Nancy Wake (1912–) 170
Jean Devanny (1894–1962) 174
Dymphna Cusack (1902–81) and Florence James (1904–93) 178
Anonymous 182
Marjorie Barnard (1897–1987) and Flora Eldershaw (1897–1956) 183
Elizabeth Kata (?–) 185

Lily Brett (1946–) 188
Susan Varga (1943–) 191
Ramona Koval (1954–) 192

PART FOUR KOREAN WAR
Olwyn Green (1923–) 197
Katharine Susannah Prichard (1883–1969) 199
Mary McFadzean (1928–) 204

PART FIVE VIETNAM WAR
Susan Terry (?–) 209
Dorothy Auchterlonie (1915–91) 212
Gayla Reid (1945–) 214
Judith Wright (1915–) 221
Jane Ross (1947–) 222

PART SIX GULF WAR
Jan Pearce (?–) 229
Pamela Bone (1940–) 232
Jennifer Maiden (1949–) 235

Bibliography 237
Sources and acknowledgments 239
Index 243

ILLUSTRATIONS

Ann Midgley, *The departure of the first Queensland contingent for South Africa*, 1899. 6

Iso Rae, *Football game*, 1915. 27

Hilda Rix Nicholas, *A mother of France*, *c*. 1916. 44

Iso Rae, *German prisoners working*, 1917. 59

Vida Lahey, *Rejoicing and remembrance, Armistice Day, London*, 1918. 75

Dora Meeson, *Departure of the last Australian hospital ship from Southampton, England*, 1919. 89

Evelyn Chapman, *Ruins of the church of Villers-Bretonneux*, 1919. 101

Hilda Rix Nicholas, *A Man*, 1921. 107

Barbara Hanrahan, *Poppy Day*, 1982. 120

Grace Cossington Smith, [*Interior with flag*], 1941. 138

Christine Miller (Aldor), *Searchlights*, 1942. 152

Stella Bowen, *Bomber crew*, 1944. 165

Nora Heysen, *Sister Minnie Goldstein working in the blood bank, Alexishafen*, 1944. 180

Sybil Craig, *Chargewoman Stasia McGillivray*, 1945. 190

Olive Bishop, *Wash and war, General*, 1978. 202

Mandy Martin, *Vietnam*, 1975. 220

Roslyn Evans, *All the fine young men: In the middle of 1990 as Saddam and Bush rattled their sabres*, 1992. 231

All illustrations are of works of art held by the Australian War Memorial. The editor and publishers are grateful to the Memorial and other copyright holders for permission to reproduce them here.

INTRODUCTION

A single, vivid, red fabric poppy leaps out from its black background on the front cover of my battered copy of Vera Brittain's *Testament of Youth* (first published in 1933, reissued by Virago in 1978), now lying on my desk. 'One woman's unforgettable record of the First World War — a haunting elegy for a lost generation' underlies, and underlines, the poppy. On the back cover is a photograph of Brittain, a young Englishwoman, dressed in a Voluntary Aid Detachment nurse's uniform. The only flowers that I ever have on my desk, I have just realised, are a bunch of similar red fabric poppies. They are, of course, symbols of Remembrance Day (originally Armistice Day), sometimes called Poppy Day, which was founded to commemorate the ending, on 11 November 1918, of the Great War, now more commonly known as the First World War. An old Cypriot woman, living in a place where real poppies splatter the countryside every spring, once told me that when she was a little girl people used to tell her that they were the blood of Christ.[1]

'Your battle wounds are scars upon my heart', Vera Brittain wrote in a poem to her soldier brother in mid-1918, several days before he was killed in action. His death followed those of Vera's fiancé and two of her closest friends. Her words were used as the title of a British collection of women's First World War poetry, *Scars Upon My Heart*, edited by Catherine W. Reilly and published by Virago in 1981. Reilly went on to compile a companion volume for the Second World War, *Chaos of the Night* (1984), also for Virago, which has since published Jenny Hartley's collection of British women's writing on the Second World War, *Hearts Undefeated* (1994).[2]

After reading *Testament of Youth* in 1979, and subsequently most of Brittain's other works, I began searching for her Australian counterpart, a strange pursuit for someone who does not consider that she has spent much of her life as a captive of cultural cringe. My search says more about the impact that Brittain's life and works had upon me than it does about my opinions of the relative merits of English and Australian literature. I hoped to find an Australian woman who could combine personal and political experiences of war on paper.

Had an Australian Vera Brittain existed, she would have been lucky to have got a guernsey in the Australian anthologies of war (or anti-war) literature that proliferated in the 1970s and 1980s. The best known of these is J. T. Laird's *Other Banners* (1971), comprising poems, short stories, and other extracts about the First World War written between about 1914 and 1939. Of more than thirty people represented in this volume, four are women. The 'anti-war anthology' edited by Shirley Cass, Ros Cheney, David Malouf, and Michael Wilding, *We Took Their Orders and Are Dead* (1971), has almost eighty writers represented in it, of whom twelve are women. Four of the thirty-odd poets published in *Vietnam Voices* (1973), a special issue of *Overland* compiled by R. H. Morrison, are women. The proportions are similar in *Shadows from Wire* (1983), in which Geoff Page juxtaposes recent poems about the Great War, some of them his own, with historic photographs. He had originally intended using poems written during the war rather than photographs, but changed his mind because he found the former to be of 'depressingly low' quality. One wonders whether he considered the impressive poems of people such as Zora Cross.[3]

'No other anthology traces the poetry written about a century of wars in which Australians have been involved', runs the blurb of Chris Wallace-Crabbe and Peter Pierce's *Clubbing of the Gunfire* (1984). 'It represents the responses in verse of Australians, whether participants or civilians, to the strangely varied wars in which this country has taken part, from the Sudan Campaign of 1885 to the recent war in Vietnam.' Four of almost sixty poets whose work appears in it are women. In his foreword to Carl Harrison-Ford's *Fighting Words* (1986), Osmar White claims that here 'is an anthology of excerpts from books by Australians who served as combatants, non-combatants or professional observers in the great wars of the twentieth century'. Two of the seventy-plus writers in this volume are women.[4]

Nor do women fare especially well in Laird's final anthologies, *The Australian Experience of War* (1988) and *On All Fronts* (1989). The first collects together what are said to be the best war literature, poems, stories, vignettes, and extracts from novels and memoirs, relating to the Boer War, First World War, Second World War, and Vietnam War. Six [illegible]e more than sixty people appearing in it are women. Nineteen people are represented in the second of these anthologies, a collection of Australian stories of the Second World War, of whom five are women. To be fair, however, one should note that Laird's earlier Great War bibliographies are very comprehensive.[5]

Given that countless Australian women have recorded their views about war, in a variety of genres, lack of available resources does not explain women's absences from these anthologies. Nor can their work have been excluded on grounds of literary merit, or lack thereof, since many examples of the anthologised men's writings, to put it charitably, must be described as being of greater historical significance than literary quality. The most likely explanation for the gender imbalance in these works is that the anthologists were working with very traditional, very masculine definitions of war, focusing on battles rather than bereavement (or both). They seem, in a sense, to have not seen the wood for the trees. In this anthology I have attempted to redress the balance, providing a range of Australian women's war writings from the Boer War to the Gulf War.

Throughout the period of European settlement of Australia, men's and women's expectations, experiences, and views of war have been markedly different. Most of the small number of Australian women who have served close to battlefronts have been nurses, such as May Tilton, who recounts her Great War experiences in her book, *The Grey Battalion* (1933). A handful of adventurers have carved out roles for themselves, including Olive King, who drove ambulances in the same war. Here she gives her account of the 'Great Fire' that destroyed much of Salonika in August 1917. Australian women's wartime involvement did become more direct and more diverse during the Second World War, a fact that is reflected in the words of women such as Jean Sims, who served as a land girl.[6]

Even when men's and women's experiences have overlapped, especially after total war made a mockery of the distinction between combatants and non-combatants, perceptions have differed according to gender. 'A keen sense of shame [...] distinguishes the personal war narratives of the men who did not fight from those who did', writes Robin Gerster in his brilliant study of Australian war literature, *Big-noting* (1987). 'This is particularly evident in the memoirs of the men of the Second A.I.F. who became prisoners-of-war.' There is no such sense of shame in the classic personal narratives of the prisoner-of-war army nurses, Betty Jeffrey's *White Coolies* (1954), and Jessie Simons' *In Japanese Hands* (1985), which was first published as *While History Passed* (1954). On the contrary, these women are considered to be the most heroic of the already heroic breed of army nurses.[7]

The perennial problem of sorting fact from fiction looms large when one considers war literature. Gertrude Moberly, the author of *Experiences of a 'Dinki Di' R.R.C. Nurse* (1933), was an actual army nurse with a genuine Royal Red Cross from the Great War. Her book appears to be made up of real letters written during the war to her fiancé, Peter, and was accepted as such by the writer of its foreword and contemporary reviewers. However, as Moberly admits in her personal papers, she rewrote her war diary in this form, despite not having met her fiancé until after the war, because she thought that this would be the simplest method of writing her first book. And what of Emily Dunbar, one of whose letters is reproduced in these pages? Was she a real person? Or was she, after all, an 'ANZAC "Ern Malley" hoax' or 'an "Emily Malley" fantasy or fabrication'?[8]

Many women have drawn upon their own experiences for their war novels. Mabel Brookes does so blatantly, attempting to add authenticity to the first of her Great War novels, *Broken Idols* (1917), by using her own photographs as illustrations and by writing in the novel's foreword: 'I was fortunate enough to visit Egypt during both these phases of her existence [before and during the war], and this book contains incidents taken from each. Many of the scenes described I have witnessed personally. The characters are, for the most part, drawn from life with certain necessary changes to disguise any possible chance of identification.' One does not need to be a genius to identify the character in this extract as Banjo Paterson. Mollie Skinner, best known for *The Boy in the Bush* (1924), which she wrote in collaboration with D. H. Lawrence, claims that all the characters in her second Great War novel, *Tucker Sees India* (1937), are fictitious, but that all the incidents in it 'are at the same time facts or rather a retailing in sequence of events that did happen during the Great War'. I have spared readers an excerpt from this unlikely sounding tale of the adventures of Tucker Smith, an Australian digger who seems to be a forerunner of Indiana Jones, although I was tempted to include a chapter entitled 'Tucker the Midwife'. Instead, I have included a piece from her earlier novel, *Letters of a V.A.D.* (1918), published under the pseudonym 'R. E. Leake', which is also based partly upon her own experiences. Other semi-autobiographical novels from which excerpts are taken include Geraldine Halls' wonderfully titled novel, *The Last Summer of the Men Shortage* (1976), one of numerous novels that incorporate descriptions of 'the Yanks' in Australia during the Second World War.[9]

I have played somewhat fast and loose with my definition of 'Australian' literature, in order to include the final chapter of Englishwoman Angela Thirkell's satirical novel, *Trooper to the Southern Cross* (1934), originally published under the pseudonym 'Leslie Parker'. I have rationalised this decision on the grounds that the book's content is Australian (it is based on Thirkell's hideous trip to Australia at the end of the Great War with her newly acquired digger husband) and that the book is listed in bibliographies of Australian literature. But my real reason for including it is that it is too delicious to leave out. As Gerster observes, this book is 'the most comprehensive debunking of the Digger during the inter-war period'. The subject matter, fact or fiction, of the Australian writers represented here is not always Australian, as can be seen most readily in the cases of people such as Ethel Cooper and Elizabeth Kata. And one of the most quintessentially Australian scenes in the anthology comes from the expatriate writer Shirley Hazzard's great novel about two expatriate Australian women, *The Transit of Venus* (1980). As will become apparent later in this anthology, for many women boundaries between countries have often seemed meaningless. Despite that, I suspect that poor Angela Thirkell would object very strongly to the thought of being dubbed Australian.[10]

Like the prose extracts, the poems that I have included vary in quality. Aside from the problem of finding a publisher foolish enough to take it on, I have long thought that it would be very easy to compile a solid tome entitled 'Dreadful Doggerel of the First World War'. I have tried to keep to a minimum the number of poems that would be eminently eligible for such a work. I have retained one or two because they do capture something of the flavour of their times. On the other hand, there are some fine poems here about the Great War and other wars, written by women such as Mary Gilmore and Judith Wright.

In line with my two earlier anthologies, *Great Southern Landings* (1995) and *Great Explorations* (1996), I have deliberately tried to make this collection as eclectic as possible. This time, however, I have not restricted my selection to published works. Indeed, some of the most poignant pieces in the book have not been published previously. The contents of some pieces are deeply moving, as in the artist Jessie Traill's evocative description of an empty frame in France in the 1920s. The contexts of others are enough to make them tragic. Dorothy Elmes's rather scrappy little letter to her friend 'Dear Old Smithy' takes on a terrible significance when one realises that it was written several weeks before she was machine-gunned to death on Banka Island during the Second World War. Another vivid scene reproduced here comes from a published book, the actress Mary Marlowe's little-known autobiography, *The Fragile Hour* (1990). It involves the death of a soldier during the Great War, who becomes Marlowe's 'ghost in November'. As the beautiful lyrics of the song 'Bui-Doi', from the musical *Miss Saigon*, say, 'some pictures never leave your mind'.[11]

In some ways, the bereavement during the Great War of the Australian artist Hilda Rix Nicholas painfully parallels that of Vera Brittain. When the war began, Hilda Rix was in France with her sister and mother. They soon went to England, where her sister died in September 1914 and her mother in March 1916. In October 1916, Hilda married a fellow Australian, Major George Nicholas, in London. Returning to the front three days later, he was killed in action the following month. I cannot look at her painting of an idealised soldier, *A Man* (1921), in a uniform that is much too big for him, without thinking of her sadly brief honeymoon. She is one of a number of Australian women artists whose works illustrate and illuminate this anthology. Like Hilda Rix Nicholas, some of them were represented in the Australian War Memorial's exhibition entitled *Through Women's Eyes: Australian Women Artists and War 1914–1994* (Canberra, 1994–95), which 'was developed to redress the balance at the Memorial of galleries dominated by the works of male artists'. In the exhibition's catalogue, curator Lola Wilkins listed some of the issues that she hoped the exhibition would raise. 'What motivated women artists to depict war? What are the themes of women's art? Do women see war differently from men? Why were the official war artists predominantly men?' I hope that this anthology inspires similar questions about women's war writings.[12]

Although most of the extracts in this collection do not contain 'fighting words', and are not boastful in the 'big-noting' style that Gerster argues characterises much of the Australian men's war literature, there are some gung-ho pieces. Two of Australia's most famous children's writers both rapidly became involved in voluntary war work, and in writing war novels, during the Great War. As Brenda Niall says, 'so intense was the commitment to the war of Ethel Turner and Mary Grant Bruce that their work took on the immediacy of a newspaper report and the direct moral appeal of a recruiting poster'. (It is interesting to compare the different tone that Turner employs in a letter written to her prisoner-of-war son during the Second World War.) But there is a considerable distance between their words and those of Hilda Freeman in her work of anti-German propaganda, *An Australian Girl in Germany* (1916). Despite my deep distaste for the latter, I have included an extract from it, as part of a process of presenting a range of views.[13]

Obviously it would be ridiculous to assume that there has been only one Australian women's perspective on war from the Boer War to the Gulf War. If there is, however, one major theme that runs throughout much of the writing by Australian women about war, it is, to borrow the words of artist Roslyn Evans, 'a lament that war occurs'. It is not surprising, although it was not intentional on my part, that the first and last pieces in this anthology are anti-war ones. The book opens with an extract from one of two novels by Miles Franklin which involve the Boer War. The book ends with a powerful poem by Jennifer Maiden about an actual act committed by American troops during the Gulf War that would rival any atrocity that Hilda Freeman could have imagined German people capable of three-quarters of a century earlier. Some of the most heated words in this collection are those of the pacifist Vida Goldstein, who founded the Women's Peace Army in 1915, and her sometime colleague Adela Pankhurst, one of the 'fighting Pankhursts', who had come to Australia in 1914 after falling out with her family.[14]

There are less overt ways in which some Australian women have sought peace in war. Women seem often to have empathised with 'the enemy' as well as with their 'own sides'.

The letters of the Australian musician Ethel Cooper, who remained in Germany throughout the Great War, reveal little of the bigotry that blights Freeman's writings. The poet Lesbia Harford, who was a member of the radical Industrial Workers of the World during that war, wrote an interesting novel considering the plight of foreigners and dissidents within Australia during the war years, *The Invaluable Mystery* (1987). Written in the 1920s, this book failed to find a publisher for more than sixty years. Gwen Kelly and Joan Dugdale have also drawn sympathetic portrayals of Germans in Australia during that war, in their recent respective novels, *Always Afternoon* (1981) and *Struggle for Memory* (1991).[15]

Some women have also been well aware of war's continuing presence in times of peace. To quote another few words from 'Bui-Doi', 'War isn't over when it ends'. Artist Jessie Traill is one of a number of Australian women who have helped to rebuild war-torn places; others include Olive King and Ethel Cooper. Novels allow one rare glimpses of the havoc that war creates in families, insights that otherwise might only be gained if one ploughed through bundles and bundles of bureaucratic files. Surely one of the saddest imaginable aftermath stories is that surrounding Katharine Susannah Prichard's novel *Intimate Strangers* (1937).[16]

As history books inevitably and inexorably replace personal memories as the main way in which people know about the major twentieth-century wars, there is a growing public interest in wartime experiences and meanings, evident in changes such as increasing Anzac Day attendances. There is also more acknowledgment of a phenomenon that can be described loosely as 'intergenerational transmission' of war. The Gulf War caused Roslyn Evans to turn to war as a subject for her art. Talking about her mixed-media, six-part work *All the fine young men* (1992), in a statement for the *War & Memory* exhibition held in Canberra to coincide with the official unveiling of the Vietnam Veterans' National Memorial in 1992, she said: 'The theme of "War and Memory" has allowed me to research my family's particular history over the last 50 years. This research and the subsequent making of the work has led me to the understanding that although I have had no direct war experience I still carry the memory or imprint of war. My narrative is a paradigm for the experiences of all Australian families of the 1940s ... there is always a father, brother, uncle or mate who never came back or who did but was irrevocably changed.' Other women who have explored similar deeply personal themes include Susan Varga in her non-fiction book *Heddy and Me* (1994), and Ramona Koval in her novel *Samovar* (1996), in which she asks her deceased mother, 'Can the dead speak for the living, what do you think, Mother?' Another is the poet Lily Brett in poems such as 'Possession'.[17]

The function of Remembrance Day has been broadened, no longer being linked only to the Great War. As the Governor-General, Sir William Deane, said in his Canberra address on 11 November 1996, it 'is now a day on which Australia and Australians pause and remember the sacrifice of all those who have died or suffered in Australia's cause in any war or conflict in which Australia, as a nation, has been engaged'. Given the writings of women such as Varga, Koval, and Brett, it seems likely that 'November's ghosts' will continue to haunt Australians well into the twenty-first century.[18]

Jan Bassett

NOTE TO READERS

Original spellings have generally been retained in these extracts. Some footnotes and other technical detail have been deleted.

NOTES

1 See Vera Brittain, *Testament of Youth: An Autobiographical Study of the Years 1900–1925*, Virago, London, 1978 (first published by Victor Gollancz, London, 1933).

2 See Catherine W. Reilly (ed.), *Scars Upon My Heart: Women's Poetry and Verse of the First World War*, Virago, London, 1981; Catherine W. Reilly (ed.), *Chaos of the Night: Women's Poetry and Verse of the Second World War*, Virago, London, 1981; and Jenny Hartley (ed.), *Hearts Undefeated: Women's Writing of the Second World War*, Virago, London, 1994.

3 See J. T. Laird (ed.), *Other Banners: An Anthology of Australian Literature of the First World War*, Australian War Memorial and the Australian Government Publishing Service, Canberra, 1971; Shirley Cass, Ros Cheney, David Malouf & Michael Wilding (eds), *We Took Their Orders and Are Dead*, Ure Smith, Sydney, 1971; R. H. Morrison (comp.), *Vietnam Voices: A Retrospect*, special issue of *Overland*, no. 54, Autumn 1973; and Geoff Page (ed.), *Shadows from Wire: Poems and Photographs of Australians in the Great War*, Australian War Memorial, Canberra, 1983, especially p. 9.

4 See Chris Wallace-Crabbe & Peter Pierce (eds), *Clubbing of the Gunfire: 101 Australian War Poems*, Melbourne University Press, Carlton, 1984; and Carl Harrison-Ford (ed.), *Fighting Words: Australian War Writing*, Lothian Books, Melbourne, 1986.

5 See J. T. Laird (ed.), *The Australian Experience of War*, Mead & Beckett, Sydney, 1988; J. T. Laird (ed.), *On All Fronts: Australian Stories of World War II*, University of Queensland Press, St Lucia, 1989; J. T. Laird, 'A Checklist of Australian Literature of World War I', *Australian Literary Studies*, vol. 4, no. 2, October 1969, pp. 148–63; and J. T. Laird 'A Checklist of Australian Literature of the First World War' (rev. edn), *Australian Literary Studies*, vol. 12, no. 2, October 1985, pp. 275–87.

6 See May Tilton, *The Grey Battalion*, Angus & Robertson, Sydney, 1933. Full details of all the sources from which the extracts in this anthology are taken, including those by Olive King and Jean Sims, are given in the list of sources and acknowledgments at the end of the book.

7 See Robin Gerster, *Big-noting: The Heroic Theme in Australian War Writing*, Melbourne University Press, Carlton, 1987, p. 225; Betty Jeffrey, *White Coolies*, Angus & Robertson, Sydney, 1954; and Jessie Simons, *In Japanese Hands: Australian Nurses as POWs*, William Heinemann, Melbourne, 1985 (first published as *While History Passed*, Heinemann, Melbourne, 1954).

8 See Gertrude Moberly, *Experiences of a 'Dinki Di' R.R.C. Nurse*, Australasian Medical Publishing Company, Sydney, 1933; re Moberly's admission see Gerster, *Big-noting*, p. 126, and La Trobe Library, State Library of Victoria, MS 7960, Moberly Papers; and re Emily Dunbar see Irene MacDonald & Susan Radvansky (eds), *Arthur and Emily: Letters in Wartime*, McPhee Gribble/Penguin Books, Ringwood, 1984, p. 2.

9 See Mabel Brookes, *Broken Idols*, Melville & Mullen, Melbourne, [1917]; D. H. Lawrence & Mollie Skinner, *The Boy in the Bush*, Martin Secker, Great Britain, 1924; M. L. Skinner, *Tucker Sees India*, Martin Secker & Warburg, London, 1937, p. 6; 'R. E. Leake' [Mollie Skinner], *Letters of a V.A.D.*, Andrew Melrose, London, [1918]; and Geraldine Halls, *The Last Summer of the Men Shortage*, Wakefield Press, Kent Town, 1995, rev. edn (first published by Constable Books, London, 1976).

10 See Angela Thirkell ('Leslie Parker'), *Trooper to the Southern Cross*, Sun Books, Melbourne, 1966 (first published by Faber & Faber, London, 1934); quote from Gerster, *Big-noting*, p. 166; and see Shirley Hazzard, *The Transit of Venus*, Penguin, New York, 1980.

11 See Jan Bassett (ed.), *Great Southern Landings: An Anthology of Antipodean Travel*, Oxford University Press, Melbourne, 1995; Jan Bassett (ed.), *Great Explorations: An Australian Anthology*, Oxford University Press, Melbourne, 1996; and Mary Marlowe, *That Fragile Hour: An Autobiography*, Angus & Robertson, Sydney, 1990.

12 See Avenel Mitchell, 'Emily Hilda Nicholas', in *Australian Dictionary of Biography*, vol. 11, Melbourne University Press, Carlton, 1988, pp. 20–1; and *Through Women's Eyes: Australian Women Artists and War 1914–1994* (exhibition catalogue), Australian War Memorial, Canberra, 1994, for both of the quotes about this exhibition.

13 See Gerster, *Big-noting*; quote from Brenda Niall, *Seven Little Billabongs*, Melbourne University Press, Carlton, 1979, p. 146; and Hilda M. Freeman, *An Australian Girl in Germany: Through Peace to War (January–October 1914)*, The Specialty Press, Melbourne, [1916].

14 Roslyn Evans's quote from *War & Memory* (exhibition catalogue), Canberra Contemporary Art Space, Canberra, 1992.

15 See Lesbia Harford, *The Invaluable Mystery*, McPhee Gribble/Penguin Books, Ringwood, 1987; Gwen Kelly, *Always Afternoon*, Collins, Sydney, 1981; and Joan Dugdale, *Struggle of Memory*, University of Queensland Press, St Lucia, 1991.

16 See Katharine Susannah Prichard, *Intimate Strangers*, Arkon Edition, Angus & Robertson, Sydney, 1981 (first published by Jonathan Cape, London, 1937); and Ric Throssell, *Wild Weeds and Wind Flowers: The Life and Letters of Katharine Susannah Prichard*, Angus & Robertson, Sydney, 1975.

17 I have borrowed the term 'intergenerational transmission' from Yael Danieli, 'Treating Survivors and Children of Survivors of the Nazi Holocaust', in Frank M. Ochberg (ed.), *Post-Traumatic Therapy and Victims of Violence*, Brunner/Mazel, New York, 1988, pp. 278–94, although of course I am using it in a general rather than psychiatric sense; Roslyn Evans's quote is from the *War & Memory* catalogue; Susan Varga, *Heddy and Me*, Penguin, Ringwood, 1994; and Ramona Koval, *Samovar*, Minerva/Reed Books Australia, Melbourne, 1996, especially p. 6.

18 William Deane's quote from 'The Meaning of Remembrance Day', address by Sir William Deane, Governor-General of the Commonwealth of Australia, on the occasion of Remembrance Day, Australian War Memorial, Canberra, Monday 11 November 1996, copy of speech supplied by the Australian War Memorial Director's Office, 3 October 1997.

EDITOR'S ACKNOWLEDGMENTS

I should like to thank Olga Abrahams, Irene Alexandrou, Margaret Beadman, Beryl Beaurepaire, Anitra Blackford, Janette Bomford, Nicholas Bomford, Gary Boulter, Jude Bourguignon, Debra Burgess, Gillian Cardinal, Sue Coffey, David Collins, John Collins, Geraldine Corridon, Jill Davies, Felicity Edge, Robin Gerster, Ron Gilchrist, Michael Green, Yvonne Greenberg, Daniella Interligi, Frank Lyons, Una Lyons, Jean McAuslan, Peter McCormick, Marcia McGrath, Richard McGregor, Cheryl McKenzie, Lex McKenzie, Michael McKernan, Ross McMullin, Neil McPhee, Peter McPhee, Richard McPhee, Alan Mason, David Preston, Sue Preston, Carolyn Rasmussen, Maggie Richardson, Peter Rose, Richard Samson, Katherine Steward, David Stockley, Louise Sweetland, Elly Symons, Red Symons, Jeff Trounce, Harry Unglik, Robyn Unglik, Gill Upton, Chris Wallace-Crabbe, Beth Whiting, Lola Wilkins, Dorothy Wilson, and Peter Wilson for their much appreciated assistance. The late Lloyd Robson taught me much about the infinite suffering caused by war. Andrew Demetriou has taught me much about life.

ABBREVIATIONS

AAH	Australian Auxiliary Hospital
AAMWS	Australian Army Medical Women's Service
AANS	Australian Army Nursing Service
AGH	Australian General Hospital
AIF	Australian Imperial Force
ALSG	Australian Logistical Support Group
ANZAC	Australian and New Zealand Army Corps
ARVN	Army of the Republic of Vietnam
ASC	Army Service Corps
ATS	Auxiliary Territorial Service
AWAS	Australian Women's Army Service
Bn	battalion
C of E	Church of England
CCS	Casualty Clearing Station
CNN	Cable News Network
CO	Commanding Officer
DMS	Director of Medical Services
GHQ	General Headquarters
GI	a United States serviceman
HQ	headquarters
IWW	Industrial Workers of the World
MASH	mobile army surgical hospital
MO	Medical Officer
NCO	non-commissioned officer
NLF	National Liberation Front
OC	Officer Commanding
PAVN	People's Army of Vietnam
POW	prisoner of war
QM	Quartermaster
QMG	Quartermaster-General
RAAF	Royal Australian Air Force
RAANC	Royal Australian Army Nursing Corps
RAF	Royal Air Force
RAMC	Royal Army Medical Corps
RAR	Royal Australian Regiment
RC	Roman Catholic
RRC	Royal Red Cross
RVN	Republic of Vietnam
SOE	Special Operations Executive
SVN	South Vietnam
URTI	upper respiratory tract infection
VAD	Voluntary Aid Detachment
VC	Victoria Cross Viet Cong
WAAAF	Women's Auxiliary Australian Air Force
WAAC	Women's Army Auxiliary Corps
WPA	Women's Political Association Women's Peace Army
WVS	Women's Voluntary Services

Part One

Boer War

MILES FRANKLIN

(1879–1954)

Writer. After spending the first ten years of her life in the Monaro region of New South Wales, Miles Franklin moved with her family to a smaller, poorer property near Goulburn. Her first novel, My Brilliant Career *(1901), was an immediate success. She writes of the Boer War in two novels,* My Career Goes Bung *(1946) and* Cockatoos *(1954), the latter originally being published under her pseudonym 'Brent of Bin Bin'. Written in 1901 and 1902, they were initially rejected by publishers. The cockatoos of the second book's title are cockies, or cockatoo farmers, attempting to scratch a living from the soil. In this significant scene from the novel, the rebellious Ignez Milford discusses the war with would-be poet Dick Mazere and, as Shirley Walker has pointed out in her article on Boer War literature, equates martial imperialism with sexual imperialism. Despite Franklin's loathing of war, she later served with the Scottish Women's Hospitals in Macedonia for several months during the Great War.*

IMPERIALISM

Another week and all the good-bye parties were past. Sylvia was leaning from a first-class carriage at the Goulburn Railway Station. Her chiffon picture hat was stowed on the rack, and her hair gleamed in the gaslight. All the children were seeing her off. Dick had brought her luggage in the spring cart, leaving the buggy for the others. The halt for refreshments in the smallest hours of the morning was expiring; passengers swallowed black boiling tea frantically and bolted to their seats with scalded gullets to the sound of the slap-to of the doors and the warning bawling of the wily old porter, so adept in receiving the tips prohibited by the Government that employed him.

Blanche's eyes were swollen with weeping. Sylvia was the one creature whom she could love with self-abandonment and joy, and Sylvia probably was the one creature who warmly loved Blanche.

'Oh, Sylvia, how can I live now? It's been heavenly with you at home.'

'When I'm married you can stay with me altogether.'

'Mother couldn't spare me.'

'Philippa will soon be a dabster housekeeper.' Sylvia beamed upon the little girl.

'I could do it all now if Blanche would let me.'

'It's going to be deadly dull with none of the men who pretended to be so fond of us to lend us horses and guns any more,' lamented Allan. 'I wish I was old enough to go to the war.'

Sylvia leant out to snatch a last kiss and then was sucked out of sight in the chasm of the railway station. Dick persuaded Ignez to share the spring cart with him on the return journey. Only the rumble of a couple of cabs made a noise in the town as it lay asleep under a thin veil of mist in its basin of foothills. The two little towers of the post office rose like sentry boxes in the long main street, which ran empty in the moonlight to the south horizon, marked by imported pine-trees, and miles away to the north were the ranges still clothed in primeval gums.

'Nothing lovely seems to last,' said the girl as they reached the Great Southern Road and extinguished their lantern. 'That night after the concert everything was wonderful and happy. Now it's as flat as a pancake.'

For the last six months the young people's work had been arranged to accommodate the social activities inspired by Sylvia's visit. Dick and Ignez travelled silently. Ignez's being was set to a rhythm of escape with the Southern Mail, racketing on through the splendid night. Rushing between embankments draped with sage brush and the fairy blackthorn, snaking round turns, steadying over culverts and crossings, disturbing the stock resting in peace and plenty near the steel tracks that gleamed like long rivulets in the moonlight, shaking the fettlers comfortably a-snore in their box-like cribs, scaring the plovers from the cool damp flats—on, on, by gully and spur, through hop scrub and cherry, she-oak and box, gum and pine, stringybark and wattle, across the plains and over the ridges in the eternal enchantment of night.

'Wouldn't it be lovely to be ricocheting in the train, on to Melbourne and then to London? I'd like always to be leaving and then I should not have to suffer the dreadful pangs of being left behind.'

'But it must hurt like beggary to leave others behind.

> And what is our life but greeting
> and parting and long regret?

'You see what living here comes to—just drifting about from day to day like cockatoos. If we don't work like fury to escape we'll be just like the people of the Ridges—the women pot-washing and the men pottering. Have you written any poetry lately?'

'I don't think poetry'll take me very far. Poets all seem to have to get drunk and be half mad, and everyone but our sort despises them. If I could get to the war I'd really have something to write about.'

'I hate this killing. Hypocrites, going to free the Uitlanders, and they haven't given their own women votes yet!'

'Yes, but don't you think all the men'll have to be freed first and then the women?'

'No! England should practise what she preaches and free her own women first. I despise soldiers. Even that silly old Cowpens can be a soldier.'

'But don't you think a man would be a puling creature if he didn't take up his gun to defend his women?'

'It might be different if the Boers were coming here, but they're not even threatening to. At any rate, I'd never marry a man who had been slaughtering other men. It would make me creepy.'

This was some comfort to Dick. 'As soon as you leave here I'm going, too.'

Cockatoos (1989 edition, first published 1954)

GERTRUDE FLETCHER

(dates unknown)

Nurse. New Zealand-born Gertrude Fletcher grew up in Australia and trained as a nurse in Sydney. Nursing in England when the Boer War began, she served in South Africa with the British Army Nursing Service Reserve from March 1900 to March 1901. During the Great War, she served in war hospitals in England and Italy. For some unknown reason, she uses the pseudonym 'Marian Horner' and writes of herself in the third person in her quaint autobiography, Some Memories and Extracts from the Life of a Nurse *(no date given), although she published the book under her own name. In this extract from it, she talks of some of her South African experiences.*

'INVASION OF CAPE COLONY BY THE BOERS'

At last we have fallen upon exciting times. Yesterday was full of excitement, sensations, and alarms. For some days we have been hearing rumours of the Boers having advanced into Cape Colony, and yesterday morning brought us word that they were within a few miles of us.

As we have large quantities of stores, besides a great many firearms and ammunition belonging to the patients, it would be quite worth their while to make a raid on us if there was any rising among the Dutch here.

On getting word that they were so close to us, two of our medicos were despatched in hot haste to two of the outlying farms to give warning to the loyal farmers there and offering protection to the women and children. One of our messengers returned in a couple of hours, while the other kept us in a state of anxiety for half the day. It appears that he ran right into a party of Boers close to the farm to which he was going. They called to him, 'Hands Up,' and announced to him that he was their prisoner, but he objected, calling attention to the Red Cross on his arm. At this critical moment the farmer appeared, and saved the situation by saying, 'Good morning, Doctor, you have come to see my sick Kaffir I suppose?' to which he of course at once agreed. The Boers were very suspicious and insisted upon four of their number going with them to the sick Kaffir; fortunately there *was* a sick Kaffir, so our man was merely detained till the Boers moved on.

While they were still there, a man drove up in a Cape cart whom they also detained until he satisfactorily explained his presence. After their departure he showed our messenger two revolvers under his coat and said that he had with him £5,000; he was the Bank Manager from Britstown. A narrow escape!

In the meanwhile, in the camp things were humming. We were all set to work making the regulation white armlets with the red cross for the men on the Staff, while we hunted out our own — so long discarded as unnecessary. While in the midst of this, a Sister rushed breathlessly in saying that a party of Boers were advancing over a hill. With an air of great presence of mind and composure, my companion whipped off her belt to which was attached a silver buckle and match box, and hid it! We had previously hidden our money and valuables, sewing them into various portions of our clothing.

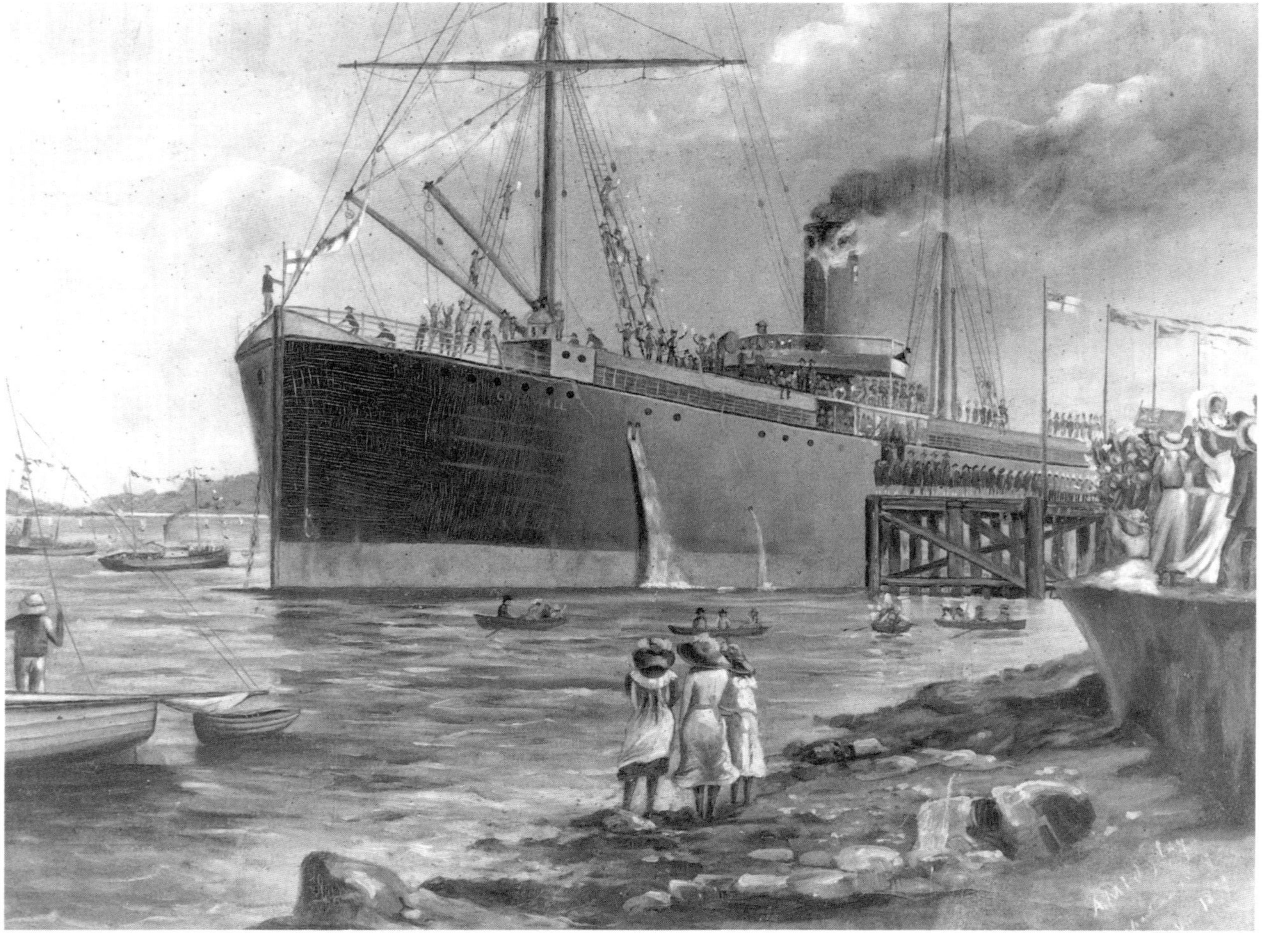

Ann Midgley (1866–1943), *The departure of the first Queensland contingent for South Africa*, 1899, oil on academy board, 47 x 62.1 cm. Purchased in 1986. (AWM 50111).

The advancing Boers turned out to be returning scouts.

The bugle call 'To Arms' was answered by a wild rush of patients, fit and unfit, all ready for action, and in a remarkably short time two hundred were equipped and armed. Stretcher bearer companies were formed, field dressings got ready; the camp was seething with excitement when a telegram came from headquarters saying that we were not to attempt to defend ourselves and that all fit men, all arms, and ammunition were at once to proceed to Beaufort West by the train then in our station which had brought up mounted scouts and others.

The scouts were dashing in and out adding to the general stir and feeling.

Of course the presence of armed men and the red cross flying was incongruous. The fact that we had arms and ammunition in the camp at all was a source of danger to us, and I believe that the very fact of their presence was enough to legalise any attack the Boers might make upon us, in spite of our flag; so it was with great relief that we saw them depart.

Needless to say, we Night Sisters got no sleep that day. At night a mounted patrol of nine men were out and we fed them on their return in the small hours. One party of men saw a man in a Cape cart who said that he was the Postmaster from Britstown and that all his telegraphing plant had been destroyed; he was coming to get instructions, so of course they brought him in.

To-day a party of one hundred and twenty armed men have arrived to protect the water tank (our original guard having been withdrawn some time ago).

There are twenty-five men on the kopje [hill] I climbed, and twenty-five on the kopje nearer the station, guarding the narrow nek which leads up into what *we* call The Upper Valley, another plain encircled by kopjes just like this one on a slightly higher level.

There is great unrest between this and Cape Town; troops are collected at Beaufort West and Richmond, at both of which places there has been great uneasiness for some time past now. Martial Law has been proclaimed in twelve districts in the Colony. We are in the Richmond district.

Will this letter pass the Censor? I wonder. It is very doubtful.

No trains are travelling at night now, and everything is very disorganised.

Some Memories and Extracts from the Life of a Nurse (n.d.)

JULIA ANDERSON

(dates unknown)

Nurse. After training at St Vincent's Hospital, Sydney, in the early 1890s, Julia Anderson nursed at North Sydney Hospital, the Women's Hospital in Melbourne and privately, before becoming the first head nurse at the Queen Victoria Hospital, Melbourne, when it opened in 1899. She was one of ten nurses who sailed on the Euryalus *with the Third (Bushmen's) Contingent from Victoria in March*

1900. The British government paid these nurses' fares and employed them under British Army Nursing Service Reserve conditions and rates of pay. Anderson later wrote this article about her time in South Africa for the journal of the Victorian Trained Nurses' Association, Una, *which took a keen interest in the activities of the Boer War nurses.*

'SOME EXPERIENCES OF A VICTORIAN NURSE IN SOUTH AFRICA'

On arriving at Cape Town our lady superintendent found orders awaiting us to proceed to Bloemfontein that night. However, as our Bushmen's contingent was going round to Beira without any nurses, we had the option of going with them, and decided that we would not desert our own men, although we were warned that Rhodesia was not a fit place to send women to, and that there were no arrangements made for nurses to accompany the troops.

Beira was our next port, after another week's voyage. It is the capital of the Portuguese settlement, and the Bushmen's was the first contingent to land there. We stayed for nine days, which were taken up with balls, garden parties, lunches, and afternoon teas given by the Portuguese governor, instead of the stern realities which we had come out to face. We then started off with 200 troops, leaving the rest behind with the horses, for Rhodesia. The troops went in horse boxes, as there were no railway carriages, but the owner of the line put on his own carriage for us to travel in, so we were very comfortable, and enjoyed the land trip after our long voyage. It was like a huge picnic, and the travelling very slow. Mr L— telegraphed to each station to have meals ready for the sisters; at one station we arrived at 10 p.m., and a dinner of three courses was waiting, and sent down to the train with eight Kaffirs. We slept in the train and travelled on like this for three days, and then our carriage had to go back for Sir Frederick Carrington, and we then had an open truck fitted up with chairs and covered with an awning.

At Umtali we got a great reception, 'three cheers for the sisters.' The residents would not allow us to sleep in the train, so some of us went to a house provided by Cecil Rhodes for passing visitors, and the others with some of the townspeople. We then had a delightful hot bath, the first fresh bath since leaving Melbourne.

Umtali is a very pretty place, surrounded by lovely green hills, covered with vegetation, in fact the scenery the whole way from Beira was beautiful.

From Umtali we went to Marandellas, and then on to Salisbury, where quarters were provided for us, and from there we dispersed for work at last.

We spent an expensive fortnight there, the Imperial Government paying 15s. a day at the principal hotel for each of us.

We met there a very interesting character in Mother Patrick, of the Benedictine Order. She was one of the first white women in Rhodesia, going out from Ireland with three other nuns ten years ago, to establish a hospital and mission station. She was the person of the greatest influence in the district, everyone looking to her for advice and help; men and women of all denominations and creeds going to her. On all sides we heard of her great goodness and self sacrifice, and were told how she came out a beautiful woman, and had quickly faded away under the hardships she had to encounter at first. She was dying of phthisis, but stuck to her post till the last, and we heard of her death before leaving South Africa. Although not an army nurse, Mother Patrick was the possessor of the Royal Red Cross, presented for her great services during the rebellion. Some few of the sisters followed the march as far as Zeerust, and nursed in Kaffir huts and under all sorts of difficult conditions.

Imagine being left alone on the veldt in a Boer farm with your patient, far from any assistance, hearing no news, and knowing nothing of what was happening. I was detailed for such duty and sent to nurse an officer lying ill with pneumonia in a farm, consisting of a cluster of huts belonging to an English farmer. His wife was the only white woman I saw for eight weeks. There were hundreds of Kaffirs, practically slaves to this man for whom they worked, from whom they bought their wives, bringing from one to three head of cattle in payment, according to the rank of the bride, the daughter of an Induna bringing the highest price.

My hut was built of clay, round, with a mushroom-shaped roof of reeds, in which the patient lay on a fairly comfortable bed. I was rather fortunate in having plenty of fresh milk and eggs (at 16s. a dozen) and stimulants from an hotel and store belonging to the farmer. There were no drugs other than I had with me, and no medical aid available.

The poultices were original — tar and axle grease on brown paper, left on for three or four days, and were very efficacious in relieving the pain and assisting expectoration. This is a Dutch method and universally used. One did not expect to learn how to make a poultice in South Africa, but no other material being at hand one had to adopt strange methods. At all events the patient, though very ill, made a splendid recovery under the treatment, which I adopted again.

All treatment was left entirely in my hands, and I had to do the best I could. I used my whole stock of phenacetine, quinine, and strychnine. My number of patients rapidly increased, as each detachment of troops trekking down left me a few too ill to take on to the next hospital thirty miles away.

Altogether I had thirty patients at Charter, and thirteen at one time. Seven in one small tent on the ground with a mackintosh sheet underneath. The cases were pneumonia, double pneumonia, broncho-pneumonia after measles, concussion, malaria, and dysentery. Fortunately no deaths.

Night work under these circumstances was rather awful; the yelping of wild dogs and jackals making night hideous, and once the terrible roar of a lion, which carried off four pigs from the farm. I always carried a light from hut to hut as lions will not come near a light; at the same time, reassuring as this fact was, my relief was great when I entered the next hut. A little Dutch boy was very much concerned at my not getting any sleep, and wanted to do the night duty, 'Sister, I'll watch and call you.' The only rest I got was an occasional snatch at night, when things were at all quieter. It was impossible in the daytime, as I had all the cooking to do, the farmer's wife being ill with malaria most of the time.

The cooking was very funny, as the Kaffirs couldn't speak English, and I had to wait for the farmer to interpret. He made the bread and the butter, which were very successful. I tried to make a stew the first day, and taking off the skin and fat, wanted the Kaffir to throw it away, but he considered that was waste and put it in the pot, making rather a greasy result. The Kaffirs were very suspicious of any new modes of cooking, and watched me most carefully, jabbering incessantly till they saw the completed dish.

Some English ladies of rank travelled through on a hunting expedition to the Zambesi with their escorts. They were wearing rational dress and smoking cigarettes, which was a source of great amusement to the Kaffirs, who squatted on their haunches all day watching them, and could not be induced to do any work until after their departure.

After eight weeks most of the troops had passed through Charter, and leaving my convalescents with the officer in charge of the remount camp, which was just established there on account of an outbreak of glanders, I took coach to Buluwayo to join the base hospital of the Rhodesian field force.

The coach was like one of the old mail coaches in Australia, which used to be stuck up by the bushrangers, and reminded me of an old survival on which I once travelled in the Australian bush. It was drawn by ten mules, which were outspanned every ten miles, and we travelled for two days and nights on a rough unmade road, into and out of spruits [small streams or water courses]. Very few women travel by coach, they always trek comfortably in their own waggons.

I was not sorry to see the lights of Buluwayo at eight o'clock at night. Buluwayo is quite a fine township, about the size of Ballarat or Bendigo, with mostly English inhabitants.

The civil hospital was quite up to date, a theatre on aseptic principles, glass tables, revolving lotion stands, sterilizers, built in memory of the officers who fell in the rebellion in 1892.

One could write a long description of this hospital, so far superior to what one would expect in South Africa, but the chief point of very melancholy interest to us is that there one of our sisters died of an attack of pneumonia contracted in devotion to duty. She was quite alone with as many as twenty-six patients at one time, no possibility of assistance or relief, and without sufficient nourishment. The kindness of the people at Buluwayo at this sad time will never be forgotten by the Victorian sisters. The Bushmen and her fellow sisters erected a marble cross to her memory at Buluwayo.

The army authorities commandeered the athletic club as a base hospital, and it was fitted up very comfortably. There were 600 troops in camp at Hillside, two miles from the hospital. At that time the base hospital was to have been there, and the troops conveyed from Tuli and Petersburgh, when the Boers were expected but never came. Plans were altered, and Zeerust was proposed as base, so the position was given up, and patients were sent to Hillside camp hospital, a collection of huts, with untrained orderlies and sergeant-in-charge, no nursing sisters.

At this time we went on a visit to the Buluwayo hospital, where our quarters were paid for, and we had nothing to do but amuse ourselves. We had a coach or van with four mules, or more if required, to drive about. We went to the Matopo Hills and camped at night, visiting Cecil Rhodes' farm. It was interesting to see the animals on this farm, all kinds of deer, elands, zebra, and others, and about 200 ostriches. The huts were all surrounded with orange trees, imported from Australia.

As the patients at the camp hospital increased in number and sickness, the services of the orderlies were very inadequate, and the men insisted on having the sisters to nurse them. We were only waiting for the opportunity, and were delighted to return to work. The surgeon-captain in charge of the camp had a great prejudice against the colonial-trained nurses, having been unfortunate in his experience, but before long he admitted that we had converted him, and gave the fever patients entirely into our charge, and we have to thank him for helping us in every way possible.

Camp life, when we had our own quarters and hospital tents, was not at all unpleasant. Duty was fairly severe, but a little pleasure used to creep in, in the form of picnics on the veldt, drives in Cape carts, riding, and other relaxations. People seemed to make it their business to be hospitable and kind in every way to the nurses.

Let me describe an average day in a camp hospital. The quarters consisted of a messroom and two bedrooms, which we had to divide between six, and another room for two. Tubs and a bucket of water were brought every morning by a Kaffir. We had two Kaffirs to wait upon us. The cooking was done at the hospital and was very good for a time, until our cook was succeeded by an ambulance man who would not make puddings. He did not come out to do 'fancy cooking.' We had a paraffine stove on which we did our fever patients' cooking. This was made much easier by the luxuries provided by Mr Richard Chamberlain, who sent calvesfoot jellies, all kinds of essences, tea tablets, and all manner of useful small things.

We were more fortunate than most camps, in being able to get plenty of fresh milk, meat for broths, and fresh vegetables.

The huts each held four or five beds, good spring hospital beds, with comfortable mattresses and plenty of blankets and bed linen, for which we also had to thank Mr Chamberlain. There were plenty of good bed garments sent from New Zealand. The boxes of handkerchiefs from Victoria were very useful indeed. Unpacking a case was a scene of great excitement, each sister grabbing all she could for her patients. We were usually assisted in this work by any of the doctors or officers who found time hanging heavily on their hands.

Bed tables were provided by long planks laid right along the length of the hut — no other furniture — and an earthen floor, very uneven, which made it no easy task to carry a glass of water unspilt. The walls were limed inside and looked cool, but the huts were very hot and dusty, though, fortunately, they cooled quickly at night.

The huts were in the barrack square, and stood in two rows. In the summer time verandahs were added to the front row and the roofs were thatched.

The day's work commenced at 6.30 a.m. and usually went on till 9 p.m. One sister then took charge, with orderlies to help or hinder her, an orderly not being trained to keep awake at night. One who was placed to watch a very bad patient was found rolled up in his blanket fast asleep. There were exceptions, of course, to the rule, but the best orderlies we had were the volunteers from the Australian troops and the Yeomanry. There were many medical students among these, who were of the greatest assistance. From what I have seen of army nursing, I think the orderly system is not by any means to be commended. The men who take this work up are not as a rule of sufficient training or education to appreciate, as a trained nurse can, the gravity of the work. The camp hospital was at first carried on by only three sisters, but later the superintendent, Sister Rawson, and the other sisters returned from Mafeking, where they had been sent to join the army corps.

The work then became much easier, and there was a little time for social relaxation, such as going to a garden party at Government House in a tip dray, with two mules, and to the races in the same conveyance. Afterwards we were provided with a Cape cart and four mules, and had many pleasant jaunts in it.

We also had three side saddles and several horses. The commanding officer occasionally had field practice for the men in camp, some miles from town on the kopjes, and this nearly led to a fatal accident, as one afternoon, when there was a large party out to witness the practice, two of the sisters chose the wrong kopje for their point of vantage and only discovered that they were beside the target in time to beat a hasty retreat.

We were fourteen months at Hillside camp, and during that time we had 500 patients, out of which number there were seven deaths.

Most of the cases were enteric — all those who died were — and arrived in very bad condition, the poor fellows being jolted to pieces in the rough ambulances drawn by oxen, and coming from long distances. They could only travel at a slow pace and in the cool hours of the day. They would outspan from 10 a.m. till 4 p.m., then go on till 10 p.m., outspan again till 4 or 5 a.m. Imagine the tediousness and discomfort of this travelling. Sometimes a doctor and properly equipped ambulance corps would be in charge of the party, and did their best to relieve the suffering. One poor trooper was found ill, and almost unconscious, having been lost on the veldt for four days. He had gone off shooting and lost his way. An officer and trooper remained behind looking for him, and brought him on with the next ambulances. Marvellous to say he recovered after two or three relapses.

During the fourteen months, the sisters were sent away on many expeditions, some to Mafeking when the troops were transferred to Lord Methuen's command, some to join the RAMC hospital at Springfontein, some to Tuli; but it was my fortune to remain in Buluwayo, so that I did not have any experience of the regular army nursing.

The troops had rather a monotonous time here, as there was no active service, and only drill for an hour or two every day. The chaplain tried to keep them out of mischief by getting up reading rooms, concerts, etc., helped by the ladies of the town.

Plenty of amusement was provided for the officers, in which we were always invited to join, when off duty and not too busy; but as we had usually about 60 patients, mostly enteric, there was plenty to do. We generally contrived to have afternoon or evening off alternately, and always had some recreation awaiting us. A favourite amusement was listening to the British South African Police Band, which played every Sunday evening for an hour after church, in the town square. There were 300 chairs hired at 6d. each, and people drove and rode in from the surrounding country to hear the band, which played all the latest music, and to see their friends.

After the enteric (of which I unfortunately came in for a share) had subsided, our services were no longer required at the camp, one sister only being left in charge of the remaining invalids.

We had our choice of being transferred to the south or returning home, and chose the latter. We were quite sorry to leave the place where we had made many friends, who saw us off at the station, laden with all sorts of good wishes, and more substantial proof of friendships, in the shape of provisions enough to last us till we arrived at Cape Town. Our route lay through Cape Colony, and we arrived after four days' journey.

We travelled in ordinary trains with sleeping cars arranged fairly comfortably, but could not travel at night as it was not safe. We had the escort of two armoured trains from Mafeking to De Aar, one in front and one behind, with about six trains between — quite a procession.

We stayed one night at Mafeking, and saw some of the damage done by the siege, the holes in the convent walls made by the shells.

Between Mafeking and Kimberley we crossed the Fourteen Streams, where the bridge had been blown up by the Boers, and we arrived just in time to witness the opening of the new bridge, waiting on the other side while it was opened by the commanding general.

We spent a night at Kimberley, but left too early to see much. We next passed through Magersfontein, and saw the scene of the battle, a peaceful enough scene at that time, with only the trace of the past horrors shown by the cluster of tombstones erected to the fallen. A little further on was the Modder river, with more tombstones. Then came Grasspan and Belmont, with their wrecked and dismantled homes, both garrisoned. Passing the hospital at Beaufort West, the sisters caught sight of our red capes on the train, and came and carried us off to breakfast. This is a pretty township, the streets lined with fruit trees. We spent some hours there, and arrived in Cape Town at seven in the morning, finding to our disappointment that our passages had been taken in the steamer leaving that day, so we said farewell to South Africa with mingled regret and anticipations of home.

Una (July 1903)

Part Two

Great War

KATHLEEN MANGAN

(1906–)

Memoirist. Kathleen McCubbin (later Mangan) was the youngest child of the artist Frederick McCubbin, one of the founders of the Heidelberg School, and his wife Annie. When the Great War began, the family was living at 'Carlsburg', South Yarra. Many years later, Kathleen Mangan recalled that time, in these words from her charming memoirs.

'4 AUGUST 1914'

Sunday used to be our At Home day. From early morning onward our house was a hive of activity. Each member of the family, apart from me, had various chores to attend to while mother made preparations for the evening meal.

It was not unusual for twenty or more guests to sit down at our supper table on Sunday evening. Artists, musicians, visiting celebrities, friends and relatives would start arriving from early afternoon and by five-thirty there would be groups of people in father's studio, in the music-room or out in the garden if the day were fine.

I used to look forward to Sunday because there were always good things to eat on that day: chicken, hams, cold roast beef, green salads, delicious fruit salad, trifle—smothered with whipped cream—and the various spiced sweets that mother used to make.

After supper our guests would retire to the music-room for coffee and conversation before being entertained by a singer accompanied by a pianist. Occasionally there was a violin soloist or perhaps an aspiring poet reciting poems with much feeling.

I was invariably packed off to bed when supper was over and, I must admit, I preferred the chirruping of crickets and the croaking frogs in Como swamp to the singers and musicians who entertained my elders. Even the distant sounds of singing and laughter from passengers on a motor-boat on its way down the river to Princes Bridge were preferable to baritones and sopranos singing their hearts out in our music-room.

One particular Sunday that I vividly recall was 4 August 1914. It began like any other Sunday with the family bustling round the house getting the place ready for the influx of guests. As usual I was sent out into the garden to keep myself amused until it was time to come in for lunch. It was a crisp kind of morning with bursts of sunshine and cloud-shadows and when I became bored with my usual games I retired to the swing to await the summons for lunch.

About noon a man on a bicycle came racing up our driveway and dismounted at our front porch. He was a neighbour from further down our road and he seemed impatient, keeping his hand on the bell until he was greeted and admitted by my brother Louis.

I was still swinging lackadaisically back and forth some ten minutes later when the neighbour reappeared with father, both looking very serious. They stood for a few seconds in earnest conversation before our neighbour pedalled off again down the driveway. Neither father nor he had laughed or smiled. And this was unusual, especially for father who always farewelled his friends with a cheerful goodbye. Something was wrong. Though I was very young, some instinct warned me that father had been given bad news.

The smell of jonquils, daffodils, the first violets and the haunting, cloying perfume of the early wattles were all reminders that winter was drawing to an end and warmer days were not too far away. But on that August day I felt suddenly chilled as a cloud passed over the sun and cast its gloomy shadow over the landscape. I slipped off the swing and ran inside.

All through that Sunday afternoon guests arrived with newspapers. Newspapers with giant, scary headlines which, though I could not read them, carried a threat. That it was bad news was soon obvious from the expressions on our visitors' unsmiling faces. I would never forget that grim procession of friends who did not laugh any more.

Usually the people who visited our home made a fuss of me or brought a gift. But on that particular day they scarcely noticed me at all so I crawled under the grand piano and munched some cake while I watched the feet of our guests — the elegantly-shod feet of the women and the heavier boots and shoes worn by the men. One man in particular, who wore grey spats over his dark shoes, could not keep still. It occurred to me that he must be very worried about the news everyone was discussing.

'The bloody Germans', I heard father groan. 'This has been coming ... this war ... for years. The Germans must rule, must be top-dog!'

That was the beginning. From that time forward a day never passed without mention of war, of what was happening 'over there' and of people who had been hurt or killed. Day after day, week after week, month after month, there was war and talk of war. It was endless.

In father's collection of *Nation Pictures* there were lots of coloured prints of soldiers at war. I used to browse through these prints and study the battle scenes: soldiers on horse back galloping into battle with standards raised and cannons firing, knights in armour charging at each other with fearful-looking weapons, Romans with shields and raised swords, British soldiers in red coats firing at the enemy on a war-torn battlefield. They were there before my eyes in a great pageant and I studied them with avid interest because I wished to understand the fear and misery that so plagued the minds of my elders.

Feelings against the Germans were strong and anything with a German-sounding name became an embarrassment. Soon after the outbreak of war, father changed the name of our house from Carlsburg to The Studio.

'Dirty Germans', one of my playmates sneered when he saw my collection of lead soldiers. 'Girls don't play with soldiers, anyway.'

I felt so mortified by this taunt that I put the soldiers into a paper bag, took them outside and buried them deep in the garden. And there they lay for the duration of the war because I was never brave enough to dig them up.

At first it was like a game the grown-ups played: talking about war and the effects of war and who would be next to enlist. 'First it was George, now it's my husband. Father and son!

Oh dear, where is it all going to end?' I overheard one of mother's friends say. Each week the list grew longer and more and more men appeared in uniform. The city was full of soldiers and sailors and men marching.

The war bounced right into our house one evening. Mother had invited two of her co-helpers from the soldiers' canteen on St Kilda Road to supper; two women who were dedicated to their work and very patriotic. Father had also invited a guest to supper that evening, a young student from the National Gallery whom he believed to be very talented. When we sat down at the supper table father informed everyone, 'This young man is one of my most promising students.'

Our two women guests smiled bleakly at the young man but made no comment. Mother, sensing some embarrassment, immediately drew the two ladies into a long conversation about the canteen. Did they enjoy working with Mrs Deakin? What a fine woman Mrs Deakin was, and so on.

I cannot remember how it came about but at some stage during that rather strained meal one of mother's canteen friends launched a scathing verbal attack on father's young student friend.

'Tell me, young man', she asked, quite suddenly, 'why are you not in uniform?'

He made no attempt to answer her question but she persisted. 'Are you not ashamed?' she asked, fixing her eyes on him from across the table. 'Playing around with art while better men are dying for their country?'

'What this young man does with his private life is no concern of yours, Mrs Taylor', father announced, glaring at the woman. 'No concern whatever!'

'This is so embarrassing', the young man burst out. 'Please, sir …'

'You see, Mr McCubbin, he is pleading now', Mrs Taylor announced triumphantly. 'Shirkers always plead for their lives.'

'Madam!' father exclaimed, thumping the table with his fist. 'You have gone far enough. I'll not tolerate such insults to a guest in my house.'

Having launched her attack, however, Mrs Taylor was not to be put down. 'Your husband, Mrs McCubbin, is obviously pro-German', she said, turning to address mother with a sweet-sour smile. 'Very obviously so.'

Further accusations were cut short by the young student. Rising from his place at the table he threw down his serviette and hastened from the room. His footsteps echoed along the empty main hallway then the front door slammed as he went outside.

After his sudden departure an ominous silence fell upon the gathering. Even I could feel the tension, so whilst my elders were sorting out their ruffled feelings I decided to slip quietly away from the table and go outside. I was curious to know what had become of our vanished guest.

There was no sign of the young man out in the garden. I thought he must have gone home, then the sound of coughing from the direction of the lilacs at the side of the house caught my attention and I hastened round to see what was happening.

The moment I saw him I felt ashamed. The poor young man was vomiting his heart out and this made me wish that I had not been so curious. Fortunately he did not see me and I stole quietly away.

The episode of the student was a lesson to me; my first enlightenment on the vileness of war, the cruelty of people to one another when each thought they had right on their side and their cause was absolutely just.

'You behaved so badly last night', I overheard mother say to father next day. 'You must remember that Mrs Taylor has been very emotional since she lost her son. I can understand her feelings when she believes that some men are not doing their bit.'

'Does that give her the right of attack?'

'No, not really. But I appreciate her point of view.'

I heard father gasp and this meant his anger was rising. 'Hang it all!' he exploded. 'People should get their facts right before they attack. That poor fellow has been rejected twice. He has a heart condition. You tell her that, will you, next time you see the old bitch.'

The matter of the accused student was dropped after that but whenever I overheard my elders discussing white feathers or men still in civilian clothes, the unfortunate student came to mind and I recalled his great mental and physical distress. It made me think about it all and wonder what war was all about.

Daisy Chains, War, then Jazz (1984)

ETHEL COOPER

(1871–1961)

Traveller and musician. Ethel Cooper was born and educated in Adelaide, where she began studying music. She furthered her studies in the German city of Leipzig from 1897 to 1906, before returning to Adelaide, but went back to Germany in 1911. She remained in Leipzig until late 1918. Throughout the war, she wrote weekly letters to her sister Emmie, some of which were smuggled out, others posted from England by Ethel at the end of the war. Decie Denholm, editor of a published volume of those letters, wonders whether Ethel Cooper was actually a spy. She certainly had many eccentricities, one of which was keeping a pet crocodile, Cheops, in Leipzig, until, sadly, he caught a chill and died. Back in Adelaide in 1921 and 1922, Cooper then returned to Europe where she worked with Quaker relief teams in Poland and Salonika. A fellow worker in Poland, Australian-born Joice NanKivell Loch, later described her in the following memorable terms: 'She was an Australian; frail and very ancient [she was in her early fifties], and she had been sitting, legs crossed, in badly-cut riding kit. One cigarette after another drooped in turn from her thin lips, hanging under a bony nose. Before lighting them she stroked them in turn with the cork from a tiny bottle containing some drug.

Then her heavy drooping eyelids slowly raised themselves, and her perfectly shocking old eyes peered out.' After further travels, Ethel Cooper eventually settled in Adelaide with Emmie in 1936.

CROWDED HOUSE

14.8.1914

My dear Emmie,

The week has dragged by somehow — it ought to go quickly, for one is busy from morning till night, but one is inwardly waiting for the next telegram to be shouted in the street, and the time seems endless. I have the house full — in the bathroom a man called Bennie from Melbourne, a mathematician who arrived this week — he came to do a year's work at the University! I took him in because he has only a pound or two in his pocket, but this afternoon he is moving on to Fraulein Ludicke's, who will welcome anyone with open arms in these desperate times. He is a nice creature too, but terribly silent — capable of sitting for three hours at a stretch and not uttering a word. When one is alone with him he is just a trifle better, but in any sort of society he might be dumb and one would not notice any difference. Then I have a Mrs Page on the sofa in the dining room — she is really a brick, does no end of housework, is always in a good temper, and is really a pleasure to have in the house. She was a nurse once, but is married now to a doctor in London. And on the sofa in the writing room is a little public school teacher from Manchester, a Miss Hancock — a silly little goose, with a much painted face and an awful north country twang. She has lost her head entirely, and spends much of the day in tears — I think I told you last week that I had offered to take in some of the dancing girls, but we found it was cheaper to take a room and give them a shilling or two a day to get their own food. And they are getting along alright for as long as the money that we managed to raise for them holds out — and each of them seems to have picked up a young man somewhere or other, so they are not on one's mind at all. A much more hopeless case is that of six wretched negroes, with a few wives and children. They were in restaurants, music halls, selling nuts in the street and so on — from Jamaica, Honduras, Zanzibar. They were absolutely on the street and starving, and as you can imagine, nobody is inclined to take in such people. Willy was awfully good and gave one of them a shake-down for two nights — I can't pretend that I was anything but relieved when my landlord said he must draw the line at black people! But then an English teacher here collected £4 among her acquaintances, so I am doling it out at 1/- per day — they can't starve on that.

The press censure is very strict now — we have heard nothing official since Liege fell, except that a German boat laid mines in the mouth of the Thames, and was sunk by the 'Amphion', who then went down on one of the mines. And tomorrow the last reserve is called out.

The police came here today — they were quite civil, but forbad one to telephone in English, to speak English in the streets or to leave the town — an unnecessary precaution, for at every railway station one is obliged to show one's pass, and every bridge and highway is guarded, so that it is impossible for a foreigner to pass.

Sandor wants to come back, but I hope he will decide to stay on quietly in Arad. He writes and telegraphs every few days that he has not heard for over a fortnight now, so my letters are evidently being stopped, though they are in German and absolutely harmless. I am getting Willy and Dr Knopf to write for me. Only one passenger train a day is running, and stops at every village on the way, and has to wait for military trains to pass it, and all other trains are in military hands. Fraulein Sander came back from Berlin on Sunday—the usual expresses run through in 2 hours, and it took her 13 hours.

A card has just come from Pepi—he is in Czernowitz in Galizia, quite near the border, but not fighting yet. Indeed reports say that the Russians have drawn back into Russia proper, and left all Poland undefended. And Poland will certainly welcome the Austrian troops with open arms, as deliverers—anything rather than Russia or Germany. England declared war against Austria yesterday [12 August], and one waits every hour for news of the fleet in the Mediterranean, but nothing has come into print yet.

Today we have had a washing day, and tomorrow we shall do the ironing. Mrs Page is splendid and can turn her hand to anything—Miss Hancock teaches sewing in her school, and darns beautifully, and is now coping with all the darning. It would all be rather a joke, if there weren't such a tragedy as the reason of it all, and if one hadn't the terrible fear that one's own country may be the greatest sufferer by it. That England could be beaten has always been to us an impossible idea, but that anything can conquer the iron organization of this country now seems to me equally unthinkable.

My letter to you of a fortnight ago has just been returned to me—I have numbered it No. 1, and put it aside to send with the others some day.

Very much love to you from your loving
ETHEL

Behind the Lines, ed. Decie Denholm (1982)

HILDA FREEMAN

(1885–1937)

Propagandist. Hilda Freeman was in Germany from January to October 1914, during which time she wrote a diary. She used it as the basis for her blatantly propagandistic book, An Australian Girl in Germany *(1916). In her foreword, she claims 'that every event and dialogue in the book are literally true, and in no way polished up for effect'. A difficult statement to believe. She goes on to say that, 'Under other circumstances, if publishing a story of my life in Germany, I should not have given the actual names of the people I met there, but I am advised that the present conditions absolve me from any charge of a breach of good taste.' Using people's real names would seem to be one of the lesser breaches of good taste in this horrid work.*

LIES

Sunday was very peaceful. The church bells rang joyously, and everybody hurried to church. The German people have become completely metamorphosed since the war began. There is not a man or woman who does not attend church at least twice a week.

I rather dreaded meeting the Herr Pastor at dinner, as I knew him for a hot-blooded politician. As we assembled in the drawing-room before dinner, he came forward, with many congratulations on my recovery. I felt relieved. It is dreadful to be always expecting insults, when you've really done nothing to deserve them. At dinner, they toasted, 'Success to the troops,' and, of course, *'Der Kaiser.'* The whole conversation centered on Paris.

'Our Crown Prince, our dear Crown Prince, has done so wonderfully well. We are so proud of him,' said Frau von Klinggraeff. 'The Kaiser is also at the front. He is such a wonderful example to us all, and to other nations.'

'The King of the "Cultured Nation" (England), takes good care not to come within range of the bullets,' said the Baron sarcastically. 'Albert of Belgium has fought with his troops, but he will soon fly to England.'

The Herr Pastor leaned his arms on the table and flourished his hands. 'Yes! Albert of Belgium will soon be there, and the King of Portugal, and the President of France, and probably the Tzar of Russia; when we have bottled them up, we shall walk over at our ease and take them.' He laughed in the great, hearty way so characteristic of him.

'Shall we go to Bordeaux after we take Paris, or —?' Ulric hesitated, and looked at me. I went quietly on with my dinner.

'I think,' said his father, 'that our great love for the old Aunty on the Thames, will induce us to cross the water.'

'But, if we take the French Seat of Government, then we shall have France at our mercy.'

'My dear boy,' laughed Herr Pastor, 'that Seat of Government is as elusive as — er — well, honour among the enemies, or — truth in England.'

'Yes! Or truth in England!' The Baron spoke meditatively. 'Is it not remarkable, that a nation, which has always been so noted for its — well, stolidity, reserve, and honour, should be capable of the flights of imagination so characteristic of it at the present moment.'

'Imagination!' grunted Herr Oberlehrer in his downright way. 'Lies! lies! horrible lies! I had not dreamt that any modern nation could have manufactured such a tissue of lies. Lies, without the slightest foundation of truth. Surely the world at large recognises the fact that they are lies. Surely the neutral nations acknowledge them to be lies.'

The Baron lifted his wine glass, and looked critically through it; then he spoke in his cynical, slow way. 'If we win, they will be acknowledged as lies; if we lose —' he shrugged, 'they will be truths.'

'Then we shall win. Are we not already thundering at the gates of Paris? Are we not nearing the English coasts? Shall we not show their proud Navy that it is helpless, once we reach their coast?' The Herr Pastor declaimed with hands and voice and shoulders.

'We will arrive in time to interrupt the last game of football,' said the Baron, 'they cannot give up their sport, unfortunately for themselves.'

'Did you see that they have brought their footballs into the field with them?' eagerly asked the Baroness.

'So! Then we shall disturb their game, or perhaps, invent a new one. Was?'

'A new one!' exclaimed the Baroness, energetically peeling a peach. 'We don't mix war with sport.'

'No, *Liebling,* but I thought we would introduce a game with a great number of balls.'

'Bullets! Shells!' cried Ulric. 'Yes! That is the game for us.'

'Have you seen that those blasphemous creatures have been laughing at our *deutscher Gott*?' asked the Herr Pastor indignantly.

'Laugh! Do they?' the Baroness answered, her face hard and angry. 'We will show them that our *deutscher Gott* will help us to be victorious over them. He will lead us to victory. We will conquer. Every child, every man is prepared to give his best, to sacrifice his life, property and comfort, to that end. The women are already doing their part; everywhere they are taking the place of their men folk and thus freeing them for their country's service.'

She nodded to Karl to open the doors, and we rose from the table and went into the music-room. As I kissed Frau Grossmutter's hand, she patted my cheek. '*Mahlzeit,* my love! But, still pale cheeks and shadowed eyes! Why do you not regain strength? It is so strange.'

But I do not think it strange.

An Australian Girl in Germany (1916)

LOUISE MACK

(1870–1935)

Writer. Louise Mack was born in Tasmania, but grew up in South Australia and New South Wales. Before going to England in 1901, she wrote for the Bulletin *and published several novels. She remained overseas after the publication of her book* An Australian Girl in London *(1902), living variously in England and Italy. Mack is considered to have been the first woman war correspondent, having written from Belgium in 1914 for the English* Evening News *and* Daily Mail. *She subsequently published* A Woman's Experiences in the Great War *(1915). Returning to Australia in 1916, she made a lecture tour in 1917 and 1918, raising funds for the Red Cross. According to her niece, the author Nancy Phelan, she was 'a genuine Bohemian'.*

'DEATH IN LIFE'

What is it I've been saying about gaiety?

How could one ever use such a word?

Here in the heart of Brussels one cannot recall even a memory of what it was like to be joyful!

I am in a city under German occupation; and I see around me death in life, and life in death. I see men, women, and children, with eyes that are looking into tombs. Oh those eyes, those eyes! Ah, here is the agony of Belgium — here in this fair white capital set like a snowflake on her hillside. Here is grief concentrated and dread accumulated, and the days go by, and the weeks come and pass, and then months — *then months!* — and still the agony endures, the Germans remain, the Belgians wake to fresh morrows, with that weight that is more bitter and heavier than Death, flinging itself upon their weary shoulders the moment they return to consciousness.

Yes. Waking in Brussels is grim as waking on the morn of execution!

Out of sleep, with its mercy of dream and forgetfulness, the *Bruxellois* comes back each morning to a sense of brooding tragedy. Swiftly this deepens into realization. The Germans are here. They are still here. The day must be gone through, the sad long day. There is no escaping it. The Belgian must see the grey figures striding through his beloved streets, shopping in his shops, walking and motoring in his parks and squares. He must meet the murderers in his churches, in his cafés. He must hear their laughter in his ears, and their loud arrogant speech. He must see them in possession of his Post Offices, his Banks, his Museums, his Libraries, his Theatres, his Palaces, his Hotels.

He must remain in ignorance of the world outside. Worst of all! When his poor tortured thoughts turn to one thought of his Deliverance, he must confront a terror sharper than all the rest. Then, he sees in clear vision, the ghastly fate that may fall upon the unarmed Brussels population the day the Germans are driven out. The whole beautiful city may be in flames, the whole population murdered. There is no one who can stop the Germans if they decide to ruin Brussels before evacuating it. One can only trust in their commonsense — and their mercy!

And at thought of mercy the *Bruxellois* gazes away down the flat, dusty road — away towards Louvain!

The peasants are going backwards and forwards to Louvain.

Little carts, filled with beshawled women and children, keep trundling along the road. A mud-splashed rickety waggonette is drawn up in front of a third-rate café. 'Louvain' is marked on it in white chalk. On a black board, in the café window, is a notice that the waggonette will start when full. The day is desperately wet. There is a canvas roof to the waggonette, but the rain dashes through, sideways, and backwards and forwards. Under cover of the rain as it were, I step into the waggonette, and seat myself quietly among a group of peasants. Two more get in shortly after. Then off we start. In silence, all crouching together, we drive through the city, out through the northern gateway; soon we are galloping along the drear flat country-road that leads to the greatest tragedy of the War. It is ten o'clock when we start. At half-past eleven we are in Louvain. On the way we meet only peasants and little shop-keepers going to and from Brussels.

Over the flat bare country, through the grey atmosphere comes an impression of whiteness. My heart beats suffocatingly as I climb out of the waggonette and stand in the narrow Rue de la Station, looking along the tram-line. The heaps of débris nearly meet across the street.

The rain is falling in Louvain; it beats through the ruined spaces; it does its best to wash out the blood-stains of those terrific days in August. And the people, oh, the brave people. They are actually making a pretence of life. A few shops are opened, a café opposite the ruined theatre is full of pale, trembling old men, sipping their byhr or coffee; Louvain is just alive enough to whisper the word '*Death!*'

But with that word it whispers also 'Immortality.'

In its ruin Louvain seems to me to have taken on a beauty that could never have belonged to it in other days. Those great fair buildings with gaps in their sides, speak now with a voice that the whole world listens to. The Germans have smashed and flattened them, burnt and destroyed them. But the glory of immortality that Death alone can confer rests upon them now. Out of those ruins has sprung the strongest factor in the War. Louvain, despoiled and desolate, has had given into her keeping the greatest power at work against Germany. Louvain, in her waste and mourning, has caused the world to pause and think. She has made hearts bleed that were cold before; she has opened the world's eyes to Germany's brutality!

Actually, in Africa, Louvain it was that decided a terribly critical situation. Because of Louvain, many, many hesitating partisans of Germany threw in their cause with the Allies.

Ah, Louvain! Take heart! In your destruction you are indestructible. You faced your day of carnage. Your civilians bravely opposed the enemy. It was all written down in Destiny's white book. The priests that were shot in your streets, the innocent women and children who were butchered, they have all achieved great things for Belgium, and they will achieve still greater things yet.

Louvain, proud glorious Louvain, it is because of you that Germany can never win. Your ruins stand for Germany's destruction. It is not you who are ruined. It is Germany!

❧ ❧ ❧

I wander about. I am utterly indifferent to-day. If a German officer took it in his head to suspect me I would not care. Such is my state of mind wandering among the ruins of Louvain.

I am surprised to find that in the actual matter of ruins Louvain is less destroyed than I expected.

Compared with Aerschot, the town has not been as ruthlessly destroyed. Aerschot no longer exists. Louvain is still here. Among the ruined monuments, houses and shops are occupied. An attempt at business goes on. The heaps of masonry in the streets are being cleared away. With her interior torn out, the old theatre still stands upright. The train runs in and out among the ruins.

The University is like a beautiful skeleton, with the wind and rain dashing through the interstices between her white frail bones.

Where there are walls intact, and even over the ruins, the Germans have pasted their proclamations.

Veuve D. for insulting an official was sentenced to ten years in prison.

Jean D. for opposing an official, was shot.

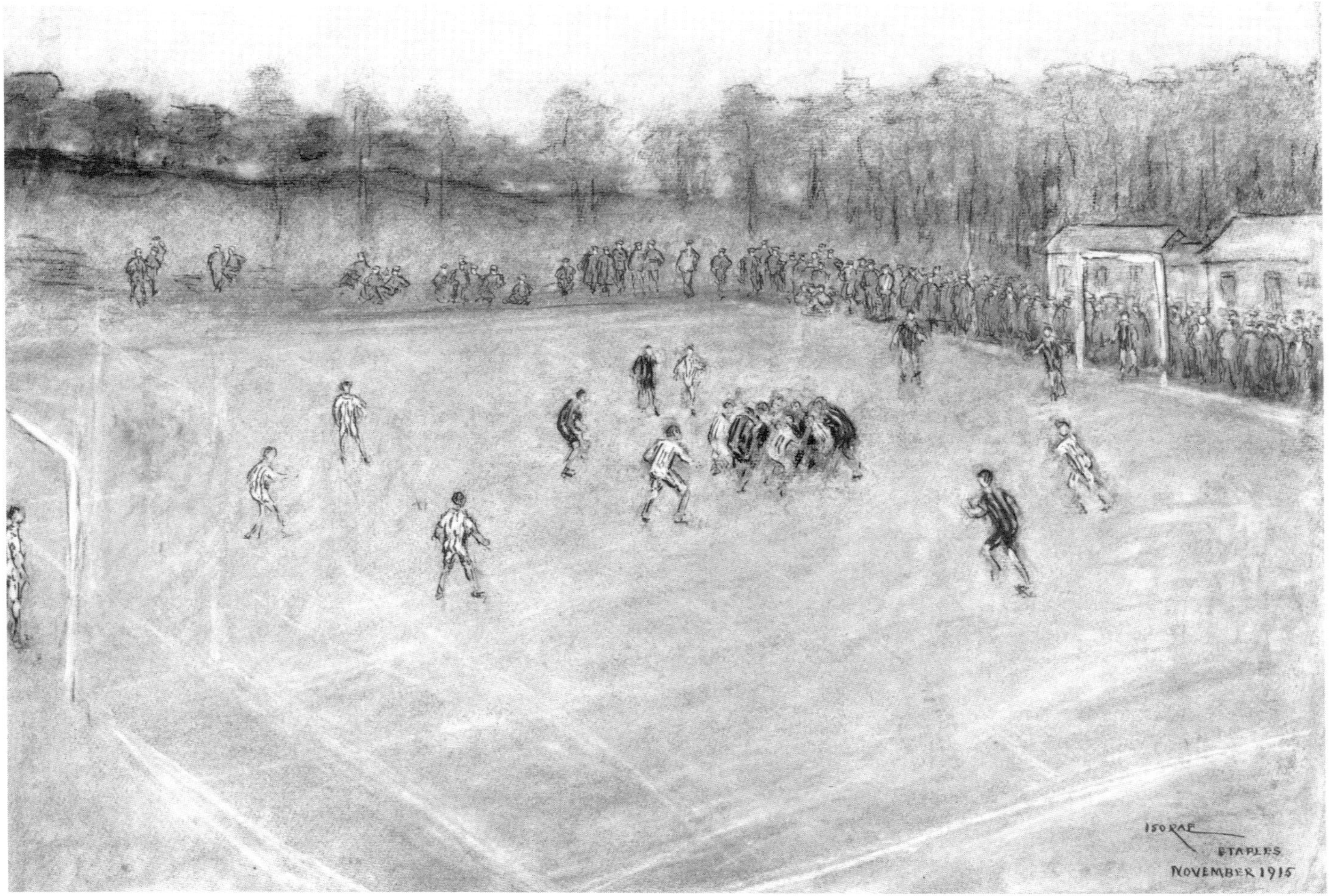

Iso Rae (1860–1940), *Football game*, 1915, pastel, 47.3 x 61.9 cm. Purchased in 1978. (AWM 19595)

And in flaunting placards the Germans beg the citizens of Louvain to understand that they will meet with nothing but kindness and consideration from Das Deutsche Heer, as long as they behave themselves.

I step into a little shop as a motor car full of German officers dashes by.

'How brave you are to keep on,' I say to the little old woman behind the counter. 'It must be terribly sad and difficult.'

'If we had more salt,' she says, 'we shouldn't mind! But one must have salt. And there is none left in Louvain. We go to Brussels for it, but it grows more and more difficult to obtain, even there.'

'And food?'

'Oh, the English will never let us starve,' she says. 'Mon Mari, he says so, and he knows. He was in England forty years ago. He was in the household of Baron D., the Belgian Ambassador in London. Would you like to see Mon Mari?'

I went into the room behind the shop.

Mon Mari was sitting in a big chair by the window, looking out over some rain-drenched purple cabbages.

He was a little old Belgian, shrivelled and trembling. He had been shot in the thigh on that appalling August day when Louvain attempted to defend herself against the murderers. He was lame, broken, useless, aged. But his sense of humour survived. It flamed up till I felt a red glow in that chilly room looking over the rain-wet cabbages, and laughter warmed us all three among the ruins, myself, and the little old woman, and Mon Mari.

'Yesterday,' he said, 'an American Consul was coming in my shop. He was walking with a German Colonel. The American says: "How could you Germans destroy a beautiful city like Louvain?" And the Alboche answered, "We didn't know it was beautiful"!'

And the old woman echoes ponderingly:

'*Didn't know it was beautiful!*'

A Woman's Experiences in the Great War (1915)

ETHEL TURNER

(1872–1958)

Writer. Ethel, her elder sister Lilian, and their twice-widowed mother came to Australia from England in 1879. Both girls were educated at Sydney Girls High School, where Ethel was friendly with Louise Mack. Ethel Turner eventually published many books for children, the best known being Seven Little Australians *(1894), now a classic. During the Great War, she worked energetically for patriotic causes and campaigned for conscription. In addition to co-editing* The Australian Soldiers' Gift Book *(1917), Turner wrote a war trilogy about a boy nicknamed 'the cub' and a girl named Brigid. The trilogy comprises* The Cub *(1915), from which this piece comes,* Captain Cub *(1917), and* Brigid and the Cub *(1919).*

SOCKS

In the billiard-room at Wahgunyah, upon the three-hundred-pound table, upon the Chesterfield lounges, upon the mantelpiece made of polished jarrah, were pyjamas—two hundred and forty pairs of them to be precise. And even that is not precise, for not yet were they in pairs at all; they stood in unwieldy parcels just as they had come from the machine-cutters; one parcel held backs, two hundred and forty backs; another fronts—four hundred and eighty fronts. There were four hundred and eighty sleeves; four hundred and eighty legs; each collar was in four parts; there were nine hundred and sixty collar pieces.

In the drawing-room, the drawing-room whose scheme of silvery grey and purple had been so intensely satisfying to the artistic sense of Brigid, in the drawing-room were stacks of sober-coloured skeins of wool, stacks of empty kit-bags, and heavy rolls of grey flannel shirting.

In the drawing-room sat knots of women, fashionably dressed, unfashionably dressed; many a hat there was just unpacked from Paris; many a hat was three seasons' old, and of suburban origin at that.

In the breakfast-room sat a group of seven ladies—rather a pathetic group if one happened to be looking for pathos. It was constituted of six 'society' persons with all the frills beloved of society persons, and one person with a plain skirt—it was the day of tunics—and a plain high-necked blouse—it was the day of open-throated blouses.

But the one person, so long an absolutely negligible quality in trams and on the streets, had come into her own. She sat enthroned, and the six sat or stood humbly around her, watching her slightest movement, drinking in the words that fell from her lips. She was an expert knitter of the old school, and she was teaching the six the highly technical process of turning the heel of a sock.

The Cub (1915)

MARTHA COXHEAD

(dates unknown)

Poet. In the foreword to the collection in which the following paean of praise to the original Anzacs appears, Martha Coxhead observed that, 'I have not made any endeavor to soar to heights above my powers ...' It might have been better had she done so. Perhaps her powers were limited. But the heights that she reached in this book ensured that there was no risk of the wax on her wings melting. Less inspired poems in the volume include 'The Brave British Cyclist', 'The Haunted Castle at Maribyrnong' (complete with photograph), and 'Lines on Hearing of the Queen's Illness'.

'HEROES OF ANZAC'

25th April, 1915.

Faint comes the sound of cheering
Across from Mudros Bay;
The Austral troops are nearing—
They're hastening on their way.

Long have they been in training
Through months of arduous work;
In skill and muscle gaining
To grapple with the Turk.

And now their goal they're sighting—
Their hearts are beating high;
Their eager eyes are lighting
In hopes that skill to try.

Oh, brave young heroes hasting
Across the heaving tide!
The name they've earned is lasting,
Their fame has travelled wide!

Now, as the beach they're gaining,
The foe their greetings send;
And shot and shell are raining,
And cheers and curses blend.

The boats, their full freights bearing,
Deep down to gunwale weighed;
The shrapnel round them tearing,
Its dreadful havoc made!

Some overboard were leaping,
While bullets round them roar,
And death makes fearful reaping,
Long ere they reach the shore!

For in that awful landing
The noblest of our sons—

Brave, manly, true, upstanding—
Fell 'neath the Turkish guns!

Those who escaped, defying
The foe's incessant fire,
Were bent upon replying
In manner, swift and dire.

Straight onward then advancing,
They rushed, with hearts aflame;
Their bayonets, brightly glancing,
On to the charge they came!

Forward, with lusty shouting,
They dashed with dripping blade;
No time for pause or doubting,
The Turks, they fled, dismayed.

Up, up, where rocks were barring
Their way as on they went!
Up, ever upwards faring,
On victory intent!

Behind them, comrades cheering
Above the Maxims' roar,
Where cliffs their steep sides rearing
Stood up against that shore!

With purpose fixed, unheeding
The perilous ascent—
Up, ever upwards speeding—
Our bold young warriors went!

The bullets, thickly teeming,
Checked not their onward rush;
With sweat and blood drops streaming,
On, onward! still they push!

Ah! many a score were lying
In death's cold, silent sleep;

The wounded and the dying
Bestrewed that awful steep!

Yet, nothing daunted, braving
The screaming leaden rain,
They dashed — no thought of saving
Themselves from death or pain!

With fortitude unswerving,
And courage, keen and rare,
'Mid sights and sounds unnerving,
And horrors past compare.

With heroism thrilling
They taught the foe that day,
Australia's sons were willing
'Their little part' to play.

Oh! valiant lads are sleeping
Upon that shell-swept shore;
And eyes are dim with weeping
For those they loved of yore.

While with grief our hearts are swelling
For the gallant souls who sleep,
The whole wide world is telling
Of their charge on Gaba Tepe!

Lost a Continent! (1917)

EVELYN DAVIES

(dates unknown)

Army nurse. Evelyn (Tevie or Tev) Davies went overseas with the Australian Army Nursing Service in May 1915. She subsequently served on Lemnos, and in Egypt, England, France, and India, before her appointment was terminated in January 1920. While away, she wrote frequently to her widowed mother, who lived on the outskirts of the Victorian town of Healesville. The following letter was written after five difficult months at Mudros, on the Greek island of Lemnos (the closest place to Gallipoli that Australian army nurses were based). Tevie begins by describing the soldiers' evacuation from Gallipoli ('the Peninsula').

EVELYN DAVIES

LIFE ON LEMNOS

Hospital Ship 'Oxfordshire'
Mudros Bay
Aegean Sea
Jan. 15th 1916

My Dearest Mum

I started a letter for you last week but in the excitement of moving I have mislaid it and cannot find it anywhere but maybe it will turn up before we again come to a Post Office.

You have heard all about the evacuation of the Peninsula no doubt how successfully it was accomplished there only being 3 casualties. Mum it was wonderfully arranged the Turks were quite unaware that the Australians were leaving, they had fixed rifles on the Parapets of trenches and with water in tins perforated and allowing water to gradually fill another tin which was attached to the trigger of the rifles and the requisite weight to fire off the Rifle, altogether it was well thought out. I shall never forget the Suspense watching for boats to come in during the night, and also listening for bombardment, it took in all about five days, it was quite a relief to see boats creeping stealthily about the Harbour, and see the Shadowy form of a barge laden with men then when daylight appeared to see the poor weary boys making their way to the Camp which was on the opposite side of the small Gulf from our Hospital it was about 3 miles round to walk but by boat took five minutes.

On the Sunday there were 12 000 troops on Lemnos really one could see them at all points, how pleased we were to see them safe before Xmas day, for although there wasn't much doing, still there were constant casualties from 'Beachey Bill' that terrible gun of the Turks that did such deadly work. It does seem sad to leave the Peninsula after so many valuable lives being lost and having to leave them behind for their Resting places perhaps to be desecrated Mum Dear it must hurt those Brave Women who let their Men come out. The saddest part of all is to hear the men talk about their Mates who have fallen, I didn't think men became as fond of each other as they really do, they are fine even the roughest of them. Have you heard of the man named Simpson belonging to the Field Ambulance who did such excellent work rescuing the wounded under fire with the aid of a donkey, Mum he was a 'White man' as the Boys say, he worked night and day going from the firing line down to the Beach taking two patients sometimes on the Donkey and perhaps supporting two or three others he wouldn't pause even for meals the men would try and get him to take tea he would take a few sips and then get back to work, he worked two Donkeys resting them alternately he seemed to have a charmed life and did most daring deeds and was known as 'The Man with the Donkey' however he at last was Killed by a Sniper poor fellow every man on the Peninsula Knew and mourned his loss. His grave was decorated beautifully and a cross erected inscribed with 'The Man with the Donkey' and 'Greater love hath no man than this etc.' he was one of the many Heroes who deserve but do not get Victoria Crosses.

At Xmas time we had a happy though mild time, I was on night duty the men were so funny on Xmas eve they all hung up their Socks, we had issued a tin filled with all sorts of things sweets, handkerchiefs, Cards etc. I had to sneak round at 3am and give them round, two men saw me and said 'Santa Claus has a white cap and gown on', there was great excitement in the morning when each tin was opened. On Xmas day we rose early and entertained friends at Afternoon tea, Harry Sawyer and a friend of his came, and everyone seemed to enjoy themselves very well. The Patients had Plum Pudding and various Sweets Jellies etc. Poor Old Chaps I am afraid they had rather a slow time. On Sunday we had our Xmas Dinner it was fine. Turkeys roasted, and all sorts of goodies which upset several of the Sisters after our plain fare, however there was a festive air surrounding the whole place, everyone participated therein, and the weather was perfect. On New Year's Eve Gertie's Birthday (I thought of her all day) well we went to Castro the Capital of the Island which is about fifteen miles from Our Camp we drove in a Gharry (a Phaeton like contrivance) drawn by two ponies and driven by a Greek man clad in the baggiest of trousers and a plush Cap on his head. I sat on a high seat beside him right in front, and in attempting to pull up the Rug I pulled his pants one time, much to my embarrassment.

It was awfully foggy when we started, but as the day wore on the fog lifted and we had a fairly clear day after all, the driver knew a little English and I knew less Greek so we misunderstood each other a good deal, however by gesticulations we understood fairly well. About half way is a place named Therma where there are hot Springs and for the Sum of 2/- one is enabled to indulge in the luxury of a bath, as it was my first in five months I enjoyed it to its full I can tell you. You enter a small room to disrobe in, then pass into another room with a marble floor over which constantly flows hot water, sitting on the floor you soak yourself all over then pour beautifully soft hot water (32° Centigrade) over yourself from a marble sink into which the water flows before going over the floor, then the next performance is to plunge into a marble bath of hot flowing water right up to our necks, Mum is was lovely we didn't like getting out, three had to go in together, still we enjoyed it. Castro is a dirty place much the same as other villages but larger and right on the water's edge, they have rather a fine Fort with a Turreted Castle-like appearance, it is quite a steep climb to the top and one passes under Moorish arches and up old steps past the queerest old guns fenced in with rows and rows of old Cannon balls some of which were in halves joined together with 2 links about six inches in length the object is for them to spread when fired and encircle masts or Rigging of ships and thence do a great deal of damage, then we visited the Dungeons. Mum they were fearful places just dens right down under the ground, it seems too awful to think of people living there.

We picnicked right up on the cliff and it was beautiful, the air was so clear and refreshing. Down in the Town everything was changed, the streets are narrow, winding, and unclean and Simply thronged with children who demanded 'Buksheesh' at every turn, such dirty little varmints too, the prices demanded in the shops were exorbitant. About 2 miles from Castro there is a village on the hillside, right up on the brow of the hill are about 10

Windmills the effect was most striking, some of them had sails and were very picturesque. We reached home at about 7 p.m. after a perilous drive the road way was cut into the hill-side in places and in others was raised about four feet and barely wide enough to allow another vehicle to pass. I just wish you could come here Mum to see all the different places and people, for I cannot do them justice really. I have a great admiration for Donkeys since coming here the poor wee patient beasts are cruelly treated, such loads the Greeks pile on them, and adding insult to injury by climbing up on its tail then they goad the poor beast on with a pointed stick. I have seen them just staggering under heavy loads of fruit in Panniers so that they cannot stand up straight. I am afraid you will have had to wait a long time for this letter Mum Dear but during the Evacuation we were for a month and couldn't write at all, and now there is a further delay I know you'll feel worried too, if I thought you were getting all my letters I wouldn't mind a scrap, but so many go astray one way and another. I am separated from Ida Mockridge & Kitty McNaughton now, they have gone away on another Hospital Boat to 'Goodness Knows where', but we may possibly meet again, but there is some talk of them rejoining their own units in Cairo, as No 2 Hospital go near the firing line. We do not Know ourselves where our destination is, but I do hope it isn't Western Africa, anyhow we shall soon know. We are enjoying life on this Boat although still in the Harbour, the food is just lovely to what we have been used to lately, besides which we have china crockery, table linen, and nice cutlery, it will spoil us for rough living once more but we'll settle down I suppose if necessary, anyhow we can't have worse times than we had the first two months on Lemnos. Still I never regret going there, it must be awfully 'flat' to settle in England and live a humdrum life, one could do that any time. I am wonderfully well Mum, I haven't been as stout for years, the life seemed to agree with most of us in fact it would be difficult to elicit sympathy, and people wouldn't believe we ever have had hard times from our present appearances. As time hangs rather heavily on our hands now I set to and developed four spools of films today, some are rather good but others are a failure I am getting the book ready to fill and you ought soon to have it Mum, only I wish they were clearer. We sail tomorrow 18th and then my troubles begin, I know you can sympathise with me, every time it is the same I never seem to get used to the sea at all.

No doubt you have seen quite a lot of Mrs Norris & Billie by now. You will love having Her again. I often think of her goodness to me in London, how lost I would have been otherwise, it is wonderful how we have fallen on our feet in most places, most people have been exceedingly Kind, and on this boat the Sisters cannot do enough for us.

One of our Sisters Daley by name was married out here and consequently is to be sent back to Australia her name now is Lawrence and her people live in St Kilda, I am sending a parcel by her which she has promised to deliver either by post or rail, but she will drop a line to let you know when to expect it. When we go to Egypt that is if we stay there. I hope Daley will be able to go up & see you, she would be able to tell you all about us and our doings, I wish it was myself going home too, but suppose it will much nicer to return when this War is all over. Mum Dear won't it be nice to see Port Melb. again

I get excited when I think of it, no one Knows the longings for familiar faces that come over us at times.

We sailed yesterday and I was sick in the afternoon & evening but feel much better today, but not happy. I do dislike the Boat, even when the passage is comparatively smooth I get sick.

It is much warmer today and I daresay we shall find it almost hot there anyhow we have missed the Blizzards of Lemnos it rained 5 inches in a few hours last week some of our people were on Shore and had a terrific time, tents blew down, huts leaked and the mud was terrific, some of the Camps were flooded out and the men took refuge in our empty huts, still with it all we did not like the idea of coming away, the Evacuation was a sad business for us all.

In the book of Snaps I'm sending is a view of Kondia a Greek village near which the Horse figuring in the 'Siege of Troy' was supposed to have been made, altogether the place is very historical. Wasn't it on Lemnos that Vulcan was supposed to land after being cast out of Heaven? I do wish I knew more ancient history. You can do what you like with the Photos but hang on to them Mum don't let any one 'pinch' them. I'll write again shortly Mum when we know 'what' and 'where' for the present I'll close Much love to your Dear Self, Treg and Rupe

from your loving
TEV

Evelyn Davies Papers

MABEL BROOKES

(1890–1975)

Voluntary war worker. Mabel Brookes, later to become 'Melbourne's leading society hostess', wrote three war novels, Broken Idols *(1917),* On the Knees of the Gods *(1918), and* Old Desires *(1922). The first and third are set largely in Egypt, where Brookes spent some time during the war, accompanying her husband, Norman Brookes, Australia's first great international tennis player, who was working there as a Red Cross commissioner. The unnamed poet officer in this extract is based upon Banjo Paterson, the author of 'Waltzing Matilda', who served as an ambulance driver in France and as a remount officer in the Middle East during the Great War.*

'AN UNPRECEDENTED FEAT'

One of their last expeditions to be planned in the precious fourteen days of leave remaining to John was a visit to the Remounts Camp, where many bush friends of his were quartered in charge of the horses, and the Hares, ever keen to inspect new horse-flesh of any kind, be it Arab or waler, went with them, using their big motor to convey the whole party. It was among the gum-trees of Meadi, and there are many of them on the edge of the desert that the Remounts established their quarters. Where once the pale shifting sands ebbed and flowed in obedience to the caprice of the wind, soon lines of restless animals stood tethered, trampling the desert into a million dimples.

Tents sprang up like mushrooms in the night with here and there in front of them a few feeble attempts at a garden. Immediately before the Officers' quarters facing the roadway lay a large map of Australia picked out in white stones. Beyond the Lybian hills faded into the pink of an evening sky and Napoleon's Watch Towers frowned down upon the invaders of their solitude.

The Nile wound round the foot of these hills, bearing its burden of white sailed feluccas, the water reflecting each outspread sail in intense blackness. Across the river, a few miles away, stood the Pyramids of Dahshur, cut as in ebony against the sunset, and beyond them lay the Sahara Desert.

But the hardworking Remounts possessed no spare time to gaze upon the scenery. A considerable number of exceedingly wild horses had been committed to their charge, the gentle attentions of which were being felt by many of the men. These horses arrived practically unbroken. Months of idleness while their riders fought on foot at Gallipoli had returned them to their wild state, and at first regular buckjumping exhibitions were the order of the day. But as the Remounts possessed in their ranks the champion horsemen of Australia, these contests soon ceased. Apart from this they also had the welfare of some hundreds of Argentine mules to consider.

Of all this the little party of sightseers was duly informed. They marvelled at the tidiness of the camp, which appeared to them wonderful as a mushroom city grown up in a night from out of the desert sand. They admired the precision of the horse lines where the animals stood drowsy and content, and visited the mules, whose restless ears and shifting eyes betokened more uncertain feelings than their quieter cousins. As the sun neared the horizon and the visitors prepared to return to the city the sleepy calm was disturbed by the arrival of 400 more of these animals, sweating, dusty and tired, and at Ellen's request they lingered a while to watch them. Behind, rode sixteen men, and all the trappings of the soldier failed to hide the fact that they hailed from the bush. They sat loosely in the saddle, tunics unbuttoned, plumed hats well back and each held the coils of a long business-like stock whip, while over everything lay a heavy coating of dust. The men seemed well pleased. They had just performed an unprecedented feat in driving, unaided, this mob of 400 animals through the crowded streets of Cairo. The officer in charge dismounted wearily and wiped the powder-fine dust off his face. Then he caught sight of the visitors and greeted them warmly as he shook hands, chatting the while about the Remounts and of the day's work. He was tall and slender with grizzled hair and keen sighted brown eyes, a typical son of Australia, and as it happened, one of her best-known poets, beloved of the bushman and the 'Bulletin'. He told them that earlier in the day he and his men had ridden the fifteen miles to Abbasiya to take delivery of their new charges. On arrival, the officer in command, who happened to be an Englishman, explained at some length the impossibility of so few men handling the number, and considered that the only method of getting the mules to Meadi was to lead them. He gazed at the Australians more in sorrow than in anger when they intimated that they intended to drove them all the way, and offered to lay a heavy bet that half the animals escaped. This the Australian Captain immediately took.

The camp turned out to see them depart and at the gentle persuasion of sixteen stock whips the cavalcade made for the road at a hand gallop and soon were on the way to the City of the Dead. Here they cavorted merrily over the tombs of various respectable deceased Arabs, and diligently explored all the cross roads which abound in that part of the city.

Dust rose in a dense cloud. It hung on the eyelashes of the men and coated their hair with a white powder, while the mules were smothered in it. The mosques and the deserted tomb-houses disappeared as behind a veil and it floated high in the warm still air behind them.

They swept past the huts of the silkweavers which have gathered in picturesque confusion under the shadow of these tombs. One mule burst into an open doorway with an earnest and profane Australian in hot pursuit while the inmates scurried to safety. Down past the walls of the Citadel they went, past the mosque of Sultan Hassan (of which the sides still show the scars of Napoleon's guns) and into the winding streets of Old Cairo. Here the crowds melted before them as if by magic. Sweetmeat sellers, sherbet vendors and mendicants ceased plying their trades and fled for shelter while the Arabs' donkeys and a confused collection of camels and vehicles crowded on the footpath to escape destruction. Never in all its years of varied history had Old Cairo seen anything like this before.

Things had calmed considerably by the time the procession reached the Meadi Road, and eventually it was a very orderly procession that turned into the Remounts Camp. The visitors walked over the sand and inspected the mules at length. They appeared to be big upstanding animals about 15 hands high and seemingly in no way injured by their long sea voyage from the Argentine or their adventurous journey from Abbasiya.

Ellen's attention was then caught by the ever enthralling sight of a camel string appearing over a rise of desert. It swayed with a measured tread towards the road, each camel almost hidden by its burden of berseem. Beside them walked some blue-robed fellahin while others rode astride the sweet smelling loads. On the first of them sat a woman completely hidden by her black robe and heavy yashmak. Along the bridge of her nose lay the piece of bamboo so affected by her class, and round her ankles and arms hung many bangles of colored glass and silver.

They stopped by a little canal of fresh water, and, one by one, with many grumblings the camels telescoped themselves into a sitting position, their thin quarters and attenuated necks being all that was visible beneath the emerald green fodder.

Some bareheaded soldiers in shirt-sleeves came out of a tent and sauntered over to have a closer inspection, and there was an interchange of 'Sa-ideh;' 'Very good, very nice camel;' and the usual conversation in which the AIF and Arab indulges when wishing to be polite. The woman pulled her black robe closer round her with dirty henna-stained fingers and squatted with the animals on the sand, while they swayed their ever restless necks and snarled at the soldiers. The East and West stood strangely intermingled and that hint of mysticism which so imperceptibly surrounds all things oriental, vanished before the breezy modernity of the Australian. Ellen sighed as she watched, realizing its limitations, for she well knew that once stripped of that halo the East loses its most potent charm while its garishness becomes paramount. The effect is like a ray of sunlight shining on a painted face. As she turned to follow the others, the smell of cigarette smoke oddly mixed with the sweetness of berseem drifted to her nostrils and she heard the sound of laughter. The Captain had left the party to telephone of his arrival to Abbasiya, and then to have a much needed bath. By this time the mules had rolled luxuriously in the warm sand, and now rested content. In the evening light their ears seemed abnormally large.

In the distance the horse lines stood out clear cut like a cameo against the sky, and a faint breeze from the river carried over sounds of men's voices, a clattering of buckets and an occasional neigh. Mrs Hare shivered as she returned to the waiting car, for another cold Egyptian night was dropping upon them, and its attendant dews had begun to damp everything.

'I hate this hour in the desert,' she said, 'it claims one's soul for its own. Let us get back to the light and brightness of the city.'

'Are you scared of desert afreets [demons]?' asked her husband.

'No, but I feel one's life could slip away very easily into the unknown at this time. Don't laugh at me, I feel the influence of the unknown.'

'I thought one went out easier between darkness and dawn,' said someone.

'The firing line is the best place to test that,' said John.

Over Dahshur Pyramids the evening star hung like a 1000-candle-power lamp, so large was it that it seemed within measurable distance. A car flew by carrying some officers from the Turkish prisoners' camp into Cairo, the staccato note of its open cut-out making the silence of the evening even more pronounced as it vanished. A pariah dog barked near by in the native village and farther off the plaintive call of a Nile boatman drifted in from the river. Quite near a bugle sounded from the Camp and received echo in the other camps which stretched desertwards as far as the eye could see.

The night had come.

'I'm hungry, let us go back to dinner,' remarked Mr Hare, prosaically, and they went.

Broken Idols (1917)

JOAN DUGDALE

(1943–)

Writer. Joan Dugdale was born in the Orkney Islands, but has lived in Australia for many years. She worked as an ABC radio producer and as an information officer for the Australian Council of Churches, before becoming a full-time writer. The two characters we meet in this vivid piece from her first novel, Struggle of Memory *(1991), are Otto Gluck (based upon a Brisbane merchant named Carl Zoeller, who was interned in Australia during the Great War and later deported to Germany), and his wife Miriam. The literary critic Helen Daniel has described* Struggle of Memory *as: 'An intricate and powerful novel, a dark reflection on "the inevitable osmosis of hate" in Australian history and its moral, social and cultural legacy.'*

THE MOUSTACHE

Blood had dripped from the teeth and nails of the frightful, helmeted monster and had fallen in gouts from the dagger upraised in his hand. Blood had fled in rivers, too, from the woman's body sprawled beneath him. She was supposed to represent Europe and her eyes, still open, begged men to avenge her. But she represented nuns and young girls raped, and mothers whose babies had been torn from living wombs. The monstrous face of the Hun was smeared with lust.

Otto had seen the poster first, on the Wilston railway station as he went to work. At every station along the line to Brisbane it had been repeated so that by the end of the journey he could not doubt his eyes. He came home late and in a cab so as not to pass them again that day and he locked himself in his study until the children had gone to bed.

When he told Miriam what had upset him he could only say, 'The vilest recruiting poster, Miriam. I cannot find words to describe it.' Miriam went herself next day, at a time when there would be no-one else on the station, to see what it was he could not say.

Because of its size and vivid colour, the poster was obvious from a distance. Miriam walked briskly on the crushed quartz of the platform and the crunch of her footsteps was reassuring. It was only a picture, after all, and public morality forbade that it should be so very shocking. But when she reached it she was mesmerised by its obscenity. This was the face of the Hun who violated women and speared and ate little children in his rampage through Europe. Unbelieving, she had read such things in the *Brisbane Courier*. Yet now, seeing the poster authorised by the Government to inspire men to enlist, it seemed it must be so. Why else would the Empire be at war? Miriam could not imagine what Germany was like nor what sort of people could commit such hideous crimes. The other side of the world was such a long way away and there things must be different, steeped in a degeneracy she could have no inkling of.

She had heard no warning footsteps but a woman's voice, shaking and deep with emotion, cut through her attempts to make sense of the poster's dreadful message. 'Well might you gaze! Your man and the likes of him is what you're looking at.' Miriam turned. The woman was one she might nod to on the way home from the train, not a person to whom she would speak.

Miriam stared at her with amazement. 'You've got no cause to be hoity-toity!' the woman continued, grasping Miriam's sleeve. 'You ought to be ashamed, married to a thing like that!'

With a violent shudder Miriam shook her off and walked unsteadily away. There was no-one else on the platform because no train was due for hours. The woman had come, as Miriam had done, to look at the poster. As she turned to leave the platform Miriam was compelled to look back. The woman was sitting on the railway bench under the Hun. Elbows resting on spread knees, she was sobbing into her handkerchief.

All the way home the Hun's image loomed in Miriam's vision and his face was Otto's. Otto's face, like the Kaiser's, was dressed in a thick, waxed moustache, but it had never, in her memory, been distorted with hate or lust. Yet these were Otto's people. They were not just the enemy, honourable in war: they were barbaric animals whose cruelty went beyond war's horror to the limits of depravity. It could not be explained by distance or location in the old world: England, too, was at the other end of the earth, yet Englishmen were not barbarous. Some evil must be locked away in a race like that, waiting to spring and rend with the ferocious pleasure of a dog at a wallaby. The same dog would lie by the fire later; would roll, grinning, on to its back and beg to be tickled.

When she got home Isobel and the children were out and there was nothing to distract her mind from the image. She set herself to turn out the linen cupboard, a job she liked and reserved for herself. The cool, starched linen, the appliqué and embroidery, slid pleasurably under her fingers as she smoothed and folded. But now its power to soothe was gone and she was scarcely aware of what she did. Such a picture could not have sprung from nothing. No-one who was not himself depraved could have portrayed it, nor dreamt the awful stories she had read in the paper. They derived their force from truth, she knew; something in her own experience twitched in acknowledgment of it. She stared, unseeing, at the counterpane her hands were smoothing and beside those hands, for an instant only, she saw another, black against the creamy cloth. She flung the bundle back into the cupboard and slammed its door, whimpering against this derangement of mind. She heard Pa's voice then, snarling in contempt. 'Snivelling fool!' he said, and she remembered his face, ugly and frightening. Terrified, she ran out of the house and across the road, calling for Doreen.

'Miriam, whatever is it?'

'It's the poster, Doreen. I must be going mad. I've begun to see things!'

Doreen held her tight, in silence, while Miriam sobbed desperately on her shoulder. Afterwards, when her panic had subsided, Doreen made some tea and Miriam told her about the poster. 'It's so grotesque, Doreen, that if it were not true I'm sure I would have dismissed it, laughed even, or simply been angry at such terrible lies. But I felt it!' She beat with her fist on her breast. 'I felt it was true!' But a profound sense of shame prevented her telling of the black hand beside her own.

Doreen, practical and direct, said, 'I'm sure such things do happen in war, Miriam. We can't imagine what it must be like. And perhaps the Germans are being very brutal. But Otto isn't like that. He's the kindest and best of men and you must keep it all in that perspective, you know, and not let ignorant, foolish people distress you so.'

Miriam knew that Doreen was right but the image of the Hun haunted her, superimposing itself on Otto's every glance and mannerism. She avoided him, ducking from his gaze and busying herself in her own room until at last he took her by the shoulders.

'What is it, Miriam? What have I done?'

'Nothing, Otto. My dear, you have done nothing! But would you ... I would like you to shave off your moustache.'

She had not thought of it until then, as she looked full in his face, and the demand seemed to come of its own accord, shocking her. He did not ask her reason but stared at her, a long resigned look, and then he dropped his hands from her shoulders and went into the bathroom. When he came out the moustache was gone but, as if shamed by his naked face, he did not meet her eyes again all day.

Struggle of Memory (1991)

EMILY DUNBAR

(dates unknown)

Letter-writer or fictional character? In 1973, the Monash University library bought 'an anonymous unpublished typescript novel' from a bookseller. The manuscript, which is in the form of letters between a husband and wife, was published as Arthur and Emily: Letters in Wartime *in 1984. Arthur Dunbar apparently enlists in the Australian Imperial Force in 1915, leaving behind his wife Emily and their two children, Dinky and Ping, somewhere in New South Wales. '...I have no doubt that the letters existed and that the relationship they portray is genuine', writes Warren G. Osmond in the book's introduction. 'This is no ANZAC "Ern Malley" hoax; not even an "Emily Malley" fantasy or fabrication.' The book's editors are rather less confident: 'The correspondence has an air of authenticity and if the manuscript is a work of fiction it is undoubtedly based on fact.' They point out the existence of discrepancies and ambiguities and their inability to establish the identity of the author or authors. I am even less sure that the work is dinky-di than they are. Here is one of the letters attributed, correctly or incorrectly, to Emily Dunbar.*

A LETTER TO ARTHUR

'Mimosa', Tilpa
3rd October 1915

You have been gone three days now, dear, and the waves will be pounding up against the sides, the boat will be leaping forward, the wind will be blowing and making hurried tumbled white caps, and the water will tumble over and over leaving no sign of where you have been. There will be a lazy flapping of things round the boat. I can see and hear it all, and feel the fresh saltiness. When my blinds flap at night, I wake up with a rush of blood to my head, and I sit up confusedly thinking I'm on board too. Then I realise I am quite still, and not moving as I imagined, and that the hot ground is all around me, that the grasshoppers are singing, and the flapping was but a puff of hot wind at my blind. I am so thankful they brought me out here; I am so glad for some one to touch, some one else in the house. I could not have borne to be alone this time.

The children are full of joy here. So many places to play, so many 'cubbies', and when all else fails there are the verandahs to trundle round and round on, till one falls down exhausted. Dinky asked for you two or three times, and seemed to wish for you, and every paper Ping happens to pick up, with pictures of soldiers she says 'Fardie', but they really know and feel nothing. Their unconsciousness makes one love them more, and rests the ache at one's heart. Every one is very kind to the fatherless bairns. They found a knot hole in the front verandah and had a glorious time dropping stones down it; I was minded of the blue jay story. They eat and drink and sleep well, and love everything. They have what they call 'nests' (eggs) for breakfast each morning, and yesterday when a leg of mutton came in for dinner, Ping called out so excitedly. 'Look, look, log of wood'. She really thought it was, they have never seen a joint of meat since you first left home. Dear little Dinky, there are so many biteys to be caught, so many 'bad' ones that he just feels life is nectar. Of course there has been trouble in different ways. Ping picked most of Mrs Englis's best carnations and came in and *gave* them to her! and Dinky hammered all the leaves off the sofrano rose with a little mallet the boys had made for him. Then, while we were sitting over the dinner table one night, they crept into Esther's room, and squeezed out a new tube of lanoline on to the mantelpiece, and powdered a tin of powder completely away on the floor. But the dear kind people do not visit the sins of the children on to the parents, one 'spank' and the matter is done with.

Their little eyes are very round with wonder just now, for to-day the hay-cutting began. We can hear, and also see, the whirring of the binders from the verandah, and row after row of the greeny gold wheat is falling. This afternoon we are all to go out with the lunch, and the children will be playing among the stooks. Oh my dear, if only you were here as you were last year. We never dreamed then, that I would be here alone in the hot harvest sunshine, and you all those miles away and going further from me each day. But I must not think that way; I must not give way again. I had your two little letters, the last one ending when you were up in the early morning getting ready to march to the boat. I know so well the feeling of being called up while it is yet dark to start on a long journey, the confusion and hurry and excitement of it all. I suppose when the reveille sounded, everything would spring into activity at once and you would be marching through the streets at dawn. Good bye Arthur, you seem so far away that it seems this will never reach you.

5th October. Such a find! As we were coming back from the paddock this morning we caught two biteys, a grasshopper (didn't I have to chase him!) and one of those iridescent beetles that can fly, so there is great joy in the family.

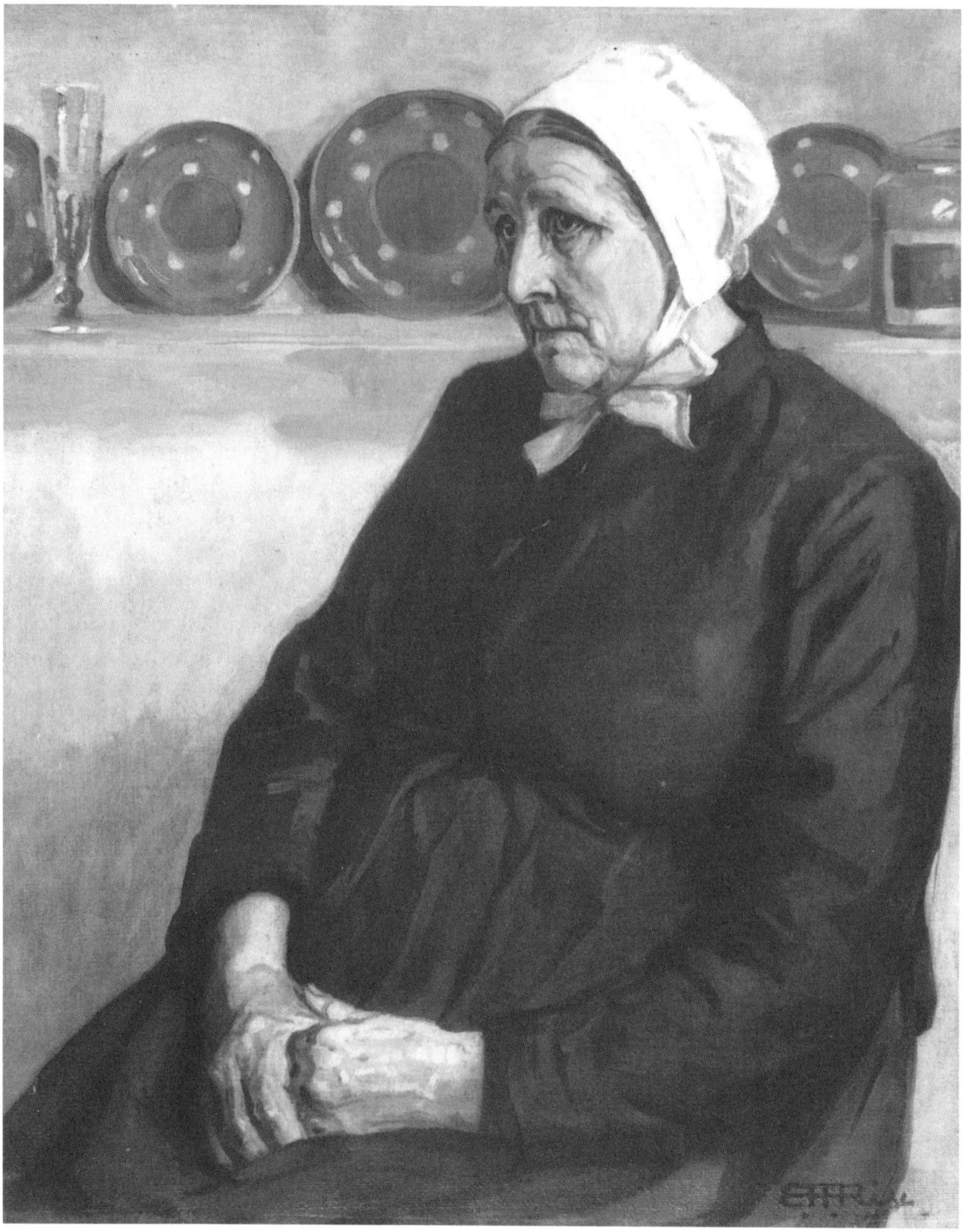

Hilda Rix Nicholas (1884–1961), *A mother of France*, *c.* 1916, oil on canvas, 72.6 x 60.2 cm. Purchased in 1922. (AWM 03281)

7th. The first week has gone. You are a long way out now. The lovely salt wind that will be blowing. Here the days are getting hotter and hotter.

Since I came here Arthur, I am finding out how old I look, my face has thinned so, and there are lines coming in my neck. Miss Carry had kindly told me several times how much I'd aged since you left, and secure in my vanity, I put it down to a little venom. My bedroom at home is so shadowy, and I saw a very different vision in the mirror here, in Esther's bright room. Each time I cross the room I am haunted by a fair faded looking creature, whose most prominent feature is her nose (it's strange how as your cheeks recede, your nose thrusts itself into impertinent notice). I feel wicked to look like that; what would I look like if I were in France or Belgium, if I look like that when I'm here with nothing to fret about.

9th. We went over to Miss Carry's to lunch to-day. The drive through the yellowing wheat was beautiful; the sun was hot but there was a soft south wind, and here and there we came across a few late wattles. Nyangy wore its usual 'touch me not look', but the garden was just a glory, there were beds and beds of scarlet and white verbenas and phlox. Miss Carry knows how to garden, and her love of colour shews to better advantage in the garden than in her dress.

She had dismissed her companion, and has a sister come to stay with her. Miss Mary is like Miss Carry, only hair not dyed, but a soft grey. She is, and also looks, years younger than Miss Carry, but we were told twice, 'how strange it is she looks so much older, although she is really younger that I am'. Before the day was out Esther and I decided that Miss Mary is a dear; and sometimes Miss Carry finds it hard to subdue her. Mention was made at lunch, by Miss Mary, of a brother-in-law who has a dairy farm, but we rushed on so hurriedly to Mr Hughes and his great success that we can only hope it was not noticed. Lunch of course was, as usual, a fairy-like meal. Miss Carry always considered it was vulgar to eat much, and now the call of the newspapers for 'plain fare' is as a trumpet in her ears. Esther and I felt a cold shiver run down our spine when Miss Mary asked for some more chutney to be brought. It put us in an awful hole, we both wanted to have some more to please Miss Mary, and also to make our scanty slices of cold mutton go further, but we dared not go against Miss Carry. Esther said, 'No', and held to it, I thought to show a little more spirit and took some, and between my hurry to eat it, and the looks I got, I nearly choked. Shall I ever forget the day that you, wretched mortal, reached across and speared the roll of butter that was meant for everyone. No wonder you were cut off without a shilling.

After lunch we went into Miss Carry's bedroom to look at her last frock and to wrestle for a long hour as to whether she should have a tête de nègre parasol with it or not. 'Cream voile — such a lot of women are wearing silk, but I think it looks so very out of place in war time! No, mine is just a simply made voile frock, lined with silk, with a lot of tiny tucks coming from the shoulder, no lace. Oh no, not in war time. I said to the dressmaker when I wrote down for it, I want a perfectly simple little frock. I am having a tête de nègre belt, and a tête de nègre hat, with a, — but wait a minute and I will put it on, and show you. There! — does it suit me?' I lied like a gentleman; Esther's face seemed to have got bundled up in the pillows. (The hat itself was beautiful, but when she put it on the dame seemed to have stepped out of the pantomime.) 'They tried all over Sydney to get me a tête de nègre parasol, and they can't. Yes, I *could* have blue to match the buckle in the hat, but then I feel I would have to get a cream buckle for the frock, and I don't want that'. So we went on, till our brains were weary.

Esther came home in the highest spirits, and I enraged as usual, despite the gift of a basket of apricots — wind-falls. However the good solid afternoon tea which waited us at Mimosa restored a little calmness. Who knows, perhaps the poor old thing spunks me up, and makes me take notice! The babies were so glad to have me come back (of course I had not committed the sacrilege of taking them) and gave me extra hugs, and then, while we were not looking, ate most of the apricots.

Emily

Irene MacDonald & Susan Radvansky (eds), *Arthur and Emily* (1984)

MABEL BROOKES

(1890–1975)

Voluntary war worker. The second half of Mabel Brookes's third war novel, Old Desires *(1922), is set in Egypt, where the heroine, Mary Shannon, is engaged in much the same activities as Brookes herself had been. In her* Memoirs *(1974), Mabel Brookes recalled that her duties had included 'taking both British and Australian wounded for outings ... singing in concert parties, visiting hospitals with Red Cross parcels, [and] serving tea and cakes at the Esbekiyeh Gardens canteen'. This scene is from* Old Desires.

CONCERT PARTY

The moon, a thin sickle in the heavens, vied ineffectually with the evening star for supremacy. High above a minaret she hung poised, almost a shadow in the firmament, while the waning light of day transformed tree and shrub into things of mystery. Lamps had begun to glow in Cairo, but on the outskirts of the city the dusk still held undisputed sway, and clothed the road in shadow and uncertainty.

Those who have ever journeyed to Meadi must remember the glimpses of the river, the age-old banyan tree with its myriad roots, the limpet-like villages that cling to the roadside, and the built up eminence that threads a way through cultivated fields of berseem, lupin and sugar cane. Gum trees — modern importations — stand sentinel, here and there, slim-boled saplings, out of the picture, innovations that do not blend with the pattering donkeys, blue robed fellahin and supercilious camels, nor with the Pyramids, that show, rust-coloured, on the horizon. Who can forget those scenes, and the many vignettes of the road, the strolling Arab, chewing a stick of cane, who hesitates and plunges before the car, his draperies blown by the draught as the wheels miss him by a hair's breadth, and the curses that float back to his ears, or the woman with a water-pot balanced on her head, who pauses, statuesque in her black draperies, or the fellahin, Biblical figures at work among the crops.

Mary, huddled in the tonneau between Miss Pinkney and an accompanist, a shaven headed youth from the Camel Corps, did not pay much attention to the surroundings, but tried to keep the keen wind from her throat, for at that hour there lurks the spectre of all laryngial trouble. In the front by the driver, was seated a famous comedian, plucked from the seclusion of a rest camp, and inveigled into rendering some of his best known numbers. As the car flew along he rehearsed his lines in a husky undertone, desisting now and then to supplement the vocabulary of the driver as a laden camel or a donkey blundered across the road.

'To-night we shall have a critical audience,' remarked Mary as well as her enveloping wraps would allow, 'and the piano is tuned to concert pitch.' On her words the comedian continued his rehearsal a key higher.

'Who cares?' enquired the accompanist.

'You will, for one, when I demand my numbers to be transposed a tone,' she retorted.

'Help!' he entreated. 'I'm vilely out of practice: camels tend to cramp one's style, and anyway I never was any good at transposition.'

Digesting the belated admission, Mary cuddled herself still further in the rugs, wishing that Owen Murray were at hand to help her over the difficult passages of her songs. He was the best accompanist she had ever had occasion to sing with. The uncertainty of the Camel Corps representative had shaken her usually equable nerve, for on the ex-manager's behalf she desired to do well. Meadi's lights shone in the distance. A few more minutes and the journey would be at an end. She took a deep breath as a spasm of nervousness shook her.

The hut doors flung wide, revealed a dense pack of humanity in a haze of tobacco smoke, an interior lit by a few hurricane lamps that hung from the roof, and woven matting-walls that were pierced here and there by the fingers of late comers who perched precariously on the cross stays outside and had to be content with peepholes. A cheer, presumably of encouragement, rose as the little party entered in the wake of the Colonel, and deposited their belongings on the side of the stage. Rude footlights had been fitted and the glare caught Mary's face and sharply illuminated it as she unwrapped a scarf from her head.

The Colonel had conducted Miss Pinkney to the front row of benches, where two or three of the Meadi ladies, workers from the nearby canteen were seated, and introducing the newcomer to them, left her in her element, discussing the relative prices charged by the Esbekiyeh canteen and those of Meadi.

Mary, awaiting her turn, seated herself with the rest of the 'company' in the comparative shadow beside the raised platform, while a maiden, hailing from the district, commenced a noisy overture on the piano.

The blue smoke haze thickened over the heads of the audience and the rustle of conversation died into silence as the girl conscientiously rendered, first 'Fruhlingsrauschen' and afterwards a series of noisy variations of a popular tune.

'Fairly put 'er back into it,' commented a grizzled trooper, applauding. 'No soft stuff there.'

A thin tenor, corporal of the Pay Corps and ex-cricketer, followed the pianoforte soloist, and as many of the soldiers present knew him personally or from the distance of the oval, they greeted him with applause and comment. He gave them the evergreen and tuneful 'I hear you calling me,' that somehow fitted into the surroundings. Though none of those listening would have admitted it, their ears had often strained for the callings of far-off voices, often listened in the desert wastes to sounds that came not on the sighing wind, but were of the imagination, born of memory, bred of silence, and nurtured on loneliness and hardship.

'I hear you calling me' sang the sweet tenor voice, and into the stillness the last note sank and vanished, leaving only the packed hut-full of humanity, and myriad glittering stars outside. 'Bravo!' called a woman. Clamour broke out for an encore, while the performer mopped a perspiring countenance in the semi-obscurity beside Mary. ' 'Struth! It's warm above those lights,' he said. 'Me for a drink after this — the piano seems higher than concert!'

'Something with an easy accompaniment for the encore,' prayed the Camel Corps sergeant. 'Mother Machree'll do me nicely.'

A party of newcomers, who had been standing in the doorway, until the song finished, now made their way to the front row. Mrs Pendennis, wrapped in a huge cape-coat of Kolinsky, followed by Owen Murray and the ex-manager, seated herself, supremely content. The dinner had been a success; the episodes of the morning were temporarily forgotten; Yusef Matib was too busily engaged in his own affairs to visit or communicate with her, and a personage from headquarters had personally approached her with words of congratulation.

As 'Mother Machree' held the audience in an orgy of sentiment, she decided that nothing is quite as black as thinking makes it, and prepared to enjoy the evening with a free mind unclouded in its serenity.

The famous comedian next took the stage, and suddenly discovering who sat below him, made extravagant gestures of welcome. He was an old acquaintance in the days when Mrs Pendennis had strolled across the footlit boards of London theatres, a noted beauty sought after and applauded, on whom clothes took an added cachet, and for whom the front rows of the stalls were nightly filled by a throng of adventurous-eyed men.

The soldiers settled themselves for a spell of laughter. It was not often they had such fare handed out to them, for the little squat man seated at the piano was a London idol, whose reputation had filtered to the shores 'down under', even though he himself had never visited there.

It seemed as if the men would never let him leave the platform. Encore after encore was stormed for, until, almost speechless from the effort of making his words carry in an acoustically impossible building, the comedian sought for cover in the dim corner of the 'wings'.

'Give 'em a minute to settle,' he advised, as Mary prepared to take her place on the stage he had just vacated. 'Don't be scared. I am a good foil for you. One can get tired of laughing as easy as anything else, and a straight song comes fine after a rough house.'

His words, kindly meant, were those of a professional, heartening a nervous amateur, and the girl felt a little flare of resentment. Knowing as she did the full value of her gift, and usually unafraid to a degree that had made her the envy of her fellow students, she mentally braced herself to do her best in the numbers she had chosen. His encouragement was the most efficacious fillip that could have been administered, though not in the way that he intended it.

The accompanist, groaning audibly over his part in the 'Chanson Indoue,' followed the girl with an air of martyrdom, as she entered the lighted circle and bowed in response to the applause that the men gave, extra warm because they knew that, like themselves, she was Australian. In alien lands during the war the bond of kind and race became very close, and as the Camel Corps sergeant, muttering imprecations, entered upon his uncertain way (camel tending seeming painfully easy to him at that moment), Mary's eyes went down the rows of bronzed faces, seeking acquaintances, thrilling a little at the unaffected interest she read there.

Her voice held all ears from the first note. The song was a gem, rendered inimitably by a clear, true soprano, in which the joy of living still lingered, albeit blended by a shadow of melancholy. Slim, very self-possessed and unafraid, the girl stood in the dun setting of reed hut and flickering, uncertain light, her white dress moth-like in the footlights' glow, her hands clasped behind her as if she were once again in the gilt French salon of her old teacher, receiving a lesson. She threw a spell over the listeners, taking them with her on the magic carpet of her voice to Indian shores; fluttering forms they saw, heard the swell of the insatiable sea, and the call of the eternal desire harboured in all men. To the last note she held them until the sound had died between her lips in a sigh.

Old Desires (1922)

MARY GRANT BRUCE

(1878–1958)

Writer. Mary Grant Bruce's fame rests upon her Billabong books for children. The fifteen books in the series, published between 1910 and 1942, relate the saga of the Linton family, from a property called 'Billabong', in rural Victoria. Bruce drew upon some of her experiences of travelling to England at the beginning of the war, living in Ireland and England during the war, and returning to Australia on a troop-ship after the armistice in her war or war-related novels, From Billabong to London *(1915),* Jim and Wally *(1916),* Captain Jim *(1919), and* Back to Billabong *(1921). In the following excerpt from* Jim and Wally, *Jim Linton and his friend Wally Meadows are gassed while fighting in France.*

'BLACK, SMOKING DARKNESS'

The breeze came softly over No-Man's Land, fluttering the wings of the cheerful sparrows. Across the scarred strip of grass a low, green cloud wavered upwards. It grew more solid, spreading in a dense wall over the parapet of the German trench.

'What on earth —?' Jim began.

The green cloud seemed to hesitate. Then the wind freshened a little, and it suddenly blew forward across No-Man's Land, growing denser as it came. Before it, the sparrows fled suddenly, darting to the upper air with shrill chirpings of alarm. But one bird, taken unawares, beat his wings wildly for a moment, flying forward. Then he pitched downwards and the cloud rolled over him.

'What is it?' uttered Wally.

Before the parapet of the British trench ahead of them the cloud stood for a moment and then toppled bodily into the trench. It fell as water falls like a heavy thing. From its green depths came hoarse shouts, and rifles suddenly went off in an irregular fusillade. Then the cloud rolled over, leaving the trench full of vapour, and stole towards the second British line.

A great cry came ringing down the trench.

'Gas! It's their filthy gas!'

It was a new thing, and no one was prepared for it. Across the Channel, England was shuddering over the first reports of the asphyxiating gas attacks, and the women of England were working night and day at the first half-million respirators to be sent out to the troops. But to the men in the trenches there had come only vague rumours of what the French and Canadians had suffered: and they had been slow to believe. It was not easy to realize, unseeing, the full horror of that most malignant device with which Science had blackened War. A few of the officers had respirators — dry, and comparatively useless. The men were utterly unprotected. Like sheep waiting for the slaughter they stood rigidly at attention, waiting for the evil green cloud that blew towards them, already poisoning the clean air with its noxious fumes.

'Tie your handkerchiefs round your mouths and nostrils!' Jim Linton shouted. 'Quick, Wally!'

He caught at the younger boy's handkerchief and knotted it swiftly. The corporal shook his head.

'Most of 'em ain't got no 'ankerchers, sir,' he said grimly. 'They *will* clean their rifles with 'em.'

Then came another cry.

'Look out — they're coming!'

Dimly, behind the cloud of gas, they could see shadowy forms clambering over the parapet of the enemy trench; German soldiers, unreal and horrible in their hideous respirators, with great goggle eyes of talc. Ahead, the quick spit of machine-guns broke out spitefully; and, as if in answer, Garrett's Maxims opened fire. Then the gas was upon them: falling from above over the parapet, stealing like a live thing down the communication trench that led from the first line, where already the Germans were swarming. Men were choking, gasping, fighting for air; dropping their rifles as they tore at their collars, losing their heads altogether in the horror of the silent attack. A little way down the trench Anstruther was trying to rally them, his voice only audible for a few yards. Jim echoed him.

'Come on, boys! it's better in the open. Let's get at them!'

He sprang up over the parapet, Wally at his side. There were bullets whistling all round them, but the air was more free — it was Paradise compared to the agony of suffocation in the trench. Some of the men followed. Jim leaped back again, dragging at others; pushing, striking, threatening; anything to get them up above, where at least they might die fighting, not like rats in a hole. He was voiceless, inarticulate; he could only point upwards, and force them over the parapet and into the bullet-swept space. Wally was there — was Wally killed? Then he saw him beside him in the trench, dragging at little Private Wilson, who had fallen senseless. Together they lifted him and flung him out at the rear, turning to fight with other men who had given up and were leaning against the walls, choking. Above them Anstruther was getting the men into some semblance of formation to meet the oncoming rush of Germans. He called to them sharply, authoritatively.

'Linton! — Meadows! Come out at once!'

Jim tried to obey. Then he saw that Wally was staggering, and flung his arm round him; but the arm was suddenly limp and helpless, and Wally pitched forward on his face and lay still, gasping. Jim tried to drag him up, fighting with the powerlessness that was creeping over him. Behind him the roar of artillery grew faint in his ears and died away, though still he seemed to hear the steady spit of Garrett's machine-guns. He sagged downwards. Then black, choking darkness rushed upon him, and he fell across the body of his friend.

Jim and Wally (1981 edition, first published 1916)

MARY EDGEWORTH DAVID

(1888–1987)

War driver. Mary Edgeworth David was born in Maitland, New South Wales, the younger daughter of the geologist and Antarctic explorer Edgeworth David. The Oxford Companion to Australian Literature *(second edition, 1994) is generous, overly so in my view, about her autobiographical* Passages of Time *(1975), claiming that it 'is not unlike Vera Brittain's autobiographies in its representation of the condition of women before and after the First World War'. Mary Edgeworth David also wrote a biography of her father, entitled* Professor David *(1937). From the late 1940s onwards, she lived out an early version of the television program 'The Good Life' in Sydney suburbia. In this passage from her autobiography, she recalls her wartime service in Britain as a driver with the Women's Army Auxiliary Corps and the Women's Legion.*

'SLIPPING CLUTCHES'

I don't remember what Isabel did, but I think she found work in a munition factory. I enlisted in the WAACs — Women's Army Auxiliary Corps. These were enrolled in London at a big hotel commandeered for the purpose, and here I became introduced to army discipline which I loathed. I was barked at by a woman sergeant when I was first being interviewed: 'Stand to attention when you speak to a superior officer!' she snapped.

We, the recruits, were drilled and went for route marches in Hyde Park. As a car driver I was posted, with others, to Plumstead on the outskirts of Woolwich Arsenal. We slept in a hostel, and every morning were called for by a bird cage lorry which conveyed us to the Arsenal. There we breakfasted in a big shed before reporting to our unit, a fleet of Ford vans. These, having the old epicyclic gear, were new to me. However, they were easy to drive—when their clutches weren't slipping. There were ten or twelve of us women drivers, and we were presided over by a lively little he-sergeant who, in civil life, 'travelled' in ladies' underwear.

Every morning the Detail would be posted up in the ASC office. Having perused this, each woman started up her allotted van, and set to work. Our jobs were many and varied—all fetching and carrying, of course—sometimes within the Arsenal itself, and sometimes in the city, and our loads could be anything from periscopes to people. It was quite interesting, and I liked the work, though I hated the Plumstead hostel.

At the ASC garage there were skirmishes between us and the male lorry-drivers, because they were always pinching our only watering can for filling radiators. However, our little sergeant had it painted in camouflage so that it was easily identifiable.

We had air raids, of course. As *Punch* put it:

> Though overhead the Gothas buzz,
> Stands London where it did? It does.

But of course the raids were mild affairs compared with those of World War II. And now this 'rational being', *Homo sapiens*, has devised more effective ways of destroying his fellows in World War III, when it comes.

One of the highlights of my stay at the Plumstead hostel was when I was invited to lunch at the home in Woolwich of Colonel Edmonds, one of my father's friends at GHQ. He had a dry sense of humour and a rather biting tongue, and his comments on current affairs, particularly army ones, were most entertaining. Afterwards, when he was a general, and knighted, he had the unenviable task of compiling an official history of the war.

When I had leave, I would go up to London to visit my actress friend, Una. She was staying with friends—a very charming family, one of whom was Bernard Shaw's secretary—in a flat in Adelphi. Sir James Barrie had a flat in the same building, and they sometimes shared the basement with him during air raids.

I was with Una and her friends for dinner one night, when the 'maroons' went off. These were air raid warnings. Una's friends consisted of a mother, known to her family as 'The Lamb', and two daughters. The Lamb was rather deaf and didn't hear the maroons, so one of her daughters announced in her ear: 'Lamb! Huns!' The Lamb sighed resignedly, put away her embroidery, and we all descended to the basement till the raid was over. One bomb fell very close to Charing Cross that night, very close to where we were.

After a few weeks at Plumstead, I was put in charge of our small fleet of Ford vans. This was a worrying job that I didn't like at all. The little sergeant and I were responsible for keeping the vans on the road, and they always seemed to be suffering from slipping clutches, or some other ailment.

Every morning the day's instructions for our fleet of vans was posted on a board in the garage, and was known as the Detail. One morning the sergeant and I committed a dreadful crime — from a military point of view; we altered the Detail without reference to our commanding officer. A van detailed to go through London we discovered was not behaving well, so we switched it to Arsenal work, and sent out a more reliable one to cope with the city traffic. Our crime was discovered, and we were had up before the ASC officer. I remember the sergeant's cap had to be removed while he was being roared up. I was allowed to retain my hat (the WAACs had hats, not caps) and was treated to a milder reprimand. It was never explained to us in what way we had imperilled the safety of the Empire. The vans, though switched, had done the allotted jobs efficiently. However, ours not to reason why, I suppose.

After some time at Plumstead, I applied for a transfer to the Women's Legion, another army organization employing women drivers. The application was granted, I was fitted out with a new uniform, and posted to Manchester. The Women's Legion I think, though am not sure, consisted entirely of women drivers attached to ASC. It had a much smarter uniform than the WAACs', but this entailed a good deal of polishing — brass buttons, cap badge, and so on.

After some weeks in Manchester I managed to get transferred to Edinburgh. This was heaven, because I was billeted with my sister in Thirlestane Road, and though the garage to which I was attached was on the far side of Princes Street that was only a very minor disadvantage compared with being once more with my family.

Our jobs in Edinburgh were as varied as they had been in Plumstead. Sometimes we drove Ford vans, sometimes staff cars. The job I liked best was taking rations to anti-aircraft gun stations along the Firth. It was summertime, and the country was glorious. I remember singing happily as I drove along.

Once when I was returning from Queensferry, I was hailed by an RAF officer who had missed his train to Edinburgh and was thumbing a lift. We were not allowed to carry passengers, other than ASC, the penalty for this being the loss of a week's pay. However, having explained this to him, I decided to take the risk. He was a very attractive young man. He scrambled aboard, and off we went. Presently we sighted a staff car full of brass-hats which might possibly be ASC ones, approaching. My passenger took off his cap and covered the wings on his chest with it as the car approached. However, it turned out to be a naval staff car, on discovering which my passenger exclaimed 'All's well! It's replete with admirals!', and replaced the cap on his head. I remember this little incident because it was exhilarating to be in the company of a frivolous young man. I did miss my happy-go-lucky Australian friends.

Sometimes we had munitions jobs, such as driving factory inspectors about. We always felt it a come-down to have civilians in our cars — very unreasonable, but there it was! However, civilians were preferable to the loads of smelly fats and bones we sometimes had to pick up at the back doors of hotels. This cargo had to be taken to factories, because glycerine was valuable in making explosives. I used to drive as fast as possible on these occasions, hoping to out-distance the smell.

Once I had to drive a British prisoner up to Edinburgh Castle, and I hated this job. I don't know what crime he had committed (altered the Detail, perhaps?), but he was under escort, and I kept my eyes away from him the whole time, feeling embarrassed and sad.

A really pleasant task was meeting returned prisoners of war at Leith docks, after the armistice was signed, and taking them to trains or wherever they were to go. There were happy reunions with friends or families of the Scottish ones. I had one interesting passenger to pick up there on one occasion. He was an ex POW English officer who was to take the night express from Edinburgh to London. His ship had docked in the afternoon, and as he had several hours to spare before the train left, he wanted to have a bath. He seemed to think it would be quite simple to hire a room-with-bath-attached at a hotel. His problem was complicated by an enormous despatch bag, heavily sealed, with which he had been entrusted and told not to let out of his sight. I drove him round to practically every hotel in Edinburgh, but without success. As usual in wartime, they were all full to overflowing. Then I suddenly had an inspiration. My sister had some very dear friends with a comfortable home in Palmerston Road. They were hospitable, patriotic Scots, and had a commodious bathroom capable of holding at least one officer complete with despatch bag. I telephoned them and explained my predicament. The reply was prompt: 'Bring him here, of course!'

I then told the officer what I had done. He seemed a bit dubious about the arrangement, though I assured him that these people were not enemy agents, but the salt of the earth. By this time he was getting rather tired and hungry, and longing for his bath, I suppose. At any rate, it ended in my depositing him and his despatch bag at my friend's house, after which I thankfully went home to dinner at my sister's flat. Later I returned to Palmerston Road to see how things were going, and found the superconscientious officer, having had his bath, dining happily with his Scottish hosts, the despatch bag by his chair. I forget how we got him to his train, but eventually he was safely deposited there, despatch bag and all. He wrote our hospitable friends a very nice letter of thanks afterwards from one of the stately homes of England.

The ASC officer in charge of our unit was very scathing about this young man and his despatch bag. 'Why couldn't he bung the blasted thing in the cloakroom at the station?' he demanded.

Passages of Time (1975)

MARGERY RUTH BETTS

(dates unknown)

Versifier. Margery Ruth Betts was one of countless Australian women who wrote patriotic and sentimental verse during the Great War. The following is the last poem in her slim volume, Remembering and Other Verses *(1917). Other poems in this gloomy 46-page booklet, which is dedicated 'To their Mothers', include 'The First Australian Casualty List', 'The Maimed', and 'The Day You Went'.*

DIED OF WOUNDS

The time shall come when I shall no more hear—
Not even in my dreams—your voice, my dead;
I shall forget the tones that were so clear,
Never the comfort of the words they said.

So many things I know, so much I prize,
Must fade across the years that are to be,
Even, perhaps, the look of your blue eyes,
But not the hope that lit their depths for me.

Remembering and Other Verses (1917)

LESBIA HARFORD

(1891–1927)

Poet and novelist. Lesbia Keogh began writing poetry in 1910. She graduated in law from the University of Melbourne in December 1916, but chose to work in domestic service and in factories after her graduation. She actively opposed the war and conscription, joined the syndicalist Industrial Workers of the World (also known as the Wobblies) in 1916, and moved to Sydney to help that organisation in early 1918. After the war she returned to Melbourne with her husband, Pat Harford, whom she had married in Sydney. The marriage was, however, short-lived. She wrote a radical novel, set in Australia during the war, but her attempts in the mid-1920s to have it published failed, as did her mother's in the late 1930s, some years after Lesbia's premature death. The manuscript was lost for decades, but was eventually discovered among other papers at the Australian Archives, Canberra, and published in 1987. Helen Garner describes the novel, which is forgettably entitled The Invaluable Mystery, *as 'one of the strangest, clumsiest and yet most striking little novels I know of'. In this chapter soldiers come to the Putman's house (in Sydney), where Mr Putman, a German shopkeeper, his daughter Sally, son Max, and their friend Bob Stepanoff, a Russian, are living. Both Max and Stepanoff are members of the International Socialist Party.*

COOKING THE ROAST

The following day was a Friday. Viv and Max and Stepanoff had planned to go to Gosford, an extraordinarily pretty town on the Hawkesbury River, to spend the weekend. On Friday evening, Stepanoff explained that he would be unable to go. On Sunday, the little news sheet must appear. It was printed on a hand press in the Fellowship rooms on Saturday afternoons. One of the comrades who usually helped with the printing was not at all well. Stepanoff had arranged to take his place.

'But that is only for the afternoon,' complained Max. 'There's another train about six and you would be there soon after eight.'

Bob was obdurate. It was not worth while to go for one day. In any case, he had promised Fanya to bring home some of the Russian type and clean it on Sunday morning. When it wore out it was difficult, almost impossible, to replace.

'You are a nark, Bob,' said Max, 'I don't believe that's why you are not going. You've got something else up your sleeve. Anyway, I'll have to go with Viv and see their bally regatta. As if there weren't enough yacht races on the harbour without going to Gosford for them.'

On Saturday morning it was unusually hot. Sally put on her coolest frock. It was made of blue cotton crêpe, the colour of corn flowers; but in those days all dresses had waists, and long sleeves that buttoned in at the wrists; and the neck, if it were at all low was always adorned by some kind of muslin or cambric collar. So Sally did not feel as cool as the fashions of more recent years would have permitted.

She went about her housework languidly, but with forethought. Her cooking for the weekend must be finished this morning. The heat would be worse than ever early in the afternoon and she did not wish to spend much time on Sunday in the kitchen. At twelve o'clock she basted the joint and put a dish of pears in the oven to bake.

She had just closed the oven door when she heard her father call her from the passage. There was a note of urgency in his voice. He seemed to have people with him. She hurried into the house. Her father was coming through the dining-room door in the company of two or three soldiers.

'Someone has informed against me, Sally,' he said. 'These men have come to search the house.'

One of the soldiers, a pale, loosely-built young man, pulled out the chair at the head of the table and sat down.

'Put a chair there,' he motioned to the others.

When the chair was placed at the table, Mr Putman seated himself.

'Your daughter had better stay here, too,' said the pale young man to Mr Putman.

Sally sat down on the extreme edge of the big chair that Miss Smith had sat in on the night of the party.

'Tell Drake and Collins to begin making a search,' the pale young man commanded. 'Then come back here.'

The soldier to whom the remark had been addressed returned to the front of the house. The third man remained standing behind Mr Putman's chair. There were evidently more soldiers in the shop.

'Close the shop door, Martin, while they are searching,' called the young soldier in charge. He took some papers from his pocket.

'Is there anyone else in the house at present?' he asked.

Mr Putman shook his head.

'Just have a look out the back, Martin,' he ordered the returning soldier, disregarding Mr Putman's head shake. If anyone is there, bring them in here.'

He spread his papers on the table before him and took out a fountain pen.

'I have some questions to ask,' he said.

'Say nothing, Sally,' rapped out her father quickly. 'I will answer him.'

'Come now,' said the youth at the head of the table, 'there should be no need for that, if everything is as it should be.'

Sally felt her blood boil within her. She wished the man at the head of the table were older. It was humiliating for her father to have to submit to such a youth. She acknowledged that his large frame and serious air gave him a certain dignity. She supposed he was an officer of some sort, though he was dressed like the other soldiers.

'What is your full name?' asked the man at the table.

Sally hoped the questions would all be as purely formal. She listened to two or three of them. Then she heard the soldiers come from the shop and enter her father's bedroom. Her attention wandered momentarily from the interrogation. She wondered, with sharpened intelligence, what letters or papers her father might have that would support the charge against him.

'Who is living in the house?' she heard the soldier ask her father.

'My son, my daughter, here, and her husband,' her father answered calmly.

Sally started and stared at him. His back was half-turned towards her. He was gazing intently at the young man at the head of the table.

'Is your daughter's husband German also?' The questioner had not hesitated. Evidently he was not already supplied with information. He was genuinely seeking it.

'No, he is a Russian,' replied Mr Putman.

The answer was written down on the paper.

'Where are these two men this morning?'

Sally turned cold. Her father was not the only one who was threatened. They must be seeking Max as well. Possibly Bob, also, would be taken.

'When do you expect them back?'

'Thank God, thank God,' said Sally's heart. Max was away for the weekend. The danger threatening him was postponed, might be averted altogether. Perhaps they could get a message to him.

Then he could go away.

Her father did not immediately answer.

The two soldiers had finished searching the boys' room. They came to the dining-room door and waited.

'See what they want, Martin,' ordered the young man in command of the party.

Martin went to the door and whispered with the others.

'They've finished in the front, Sergeant,' he said. 'This was all they got.' He placed two or three cardboard boxes, a sheet of folded paper, and an opened letter on the table.

'Send them through to the back, Martin,' came the command.

The two soldiers whom Sally had not yet seen passed through the dining-room doors to the back of the house. One of them, a red-faced, red-haired youth winked broadly at Sally as he went. She heard Carlo yapping at them in the yard. He was still puppyish and friendly and pleased with any company that relieved the tedium of his days.

The sergeant glanced at the boxes and the papers and put them aside.

'They'll go into that with you at headquarters,' he explained to Mr Putman.

A loud knocking was heard at the door of the shop.

'Take her into the shop, Martin,' he commanded. 'Wait with her while she is serving and then bring her back here.'

Sally glanced at Martin. He was thin, tight-lipped, elderly. She hated him. The man behind her father's chair was not young either, but he had an innocent, childish expression that was disarming.

Sally opened the door in answer to the insistent knocks, while Martin remained at the back of the shop.

'By cripes!' said her customer, mopping his face as he stepped into the shop. 'It's hot outside. I was afraid I wasn't going to get in either.'

He was a youth who frequently came to the shop from the Bandsman's Camp at Chinaman's Bend. He wanted milk and bread.

'I had to be away for a minute,' said Sally, 'and when the verandah blind is lowered, we generally shut the door.' At that minute Justine Kerrigan appeared in the doorway.

'Run away, Justine,' ordered Sally, with an appearance of calm. 'There isn't any ice-cream this morning.'

'Now that's a pity! I was just going to have some myself,' said her male customer. 'Give us two or three bottles of stone ginger instead.'

Justine threw a glance in the direction of the soldier.

'I didn't come for any ice-cream,' she said. 'Where's Carlo?'

'You can't have Carlo this morning, Justine,' rejoined Sally. 'Run away now, like a good child.'

'Right!' said Justine, waving her hand. 'I'll be along for him sometime in the afternoon.'

'Well, so long,' said the youthful bandsman.

He too left the shop.

From the back of the shop came the young sergeant.

'When do you expect your brother back?' he asked Sally.

Sally was startled. What had her father been saying? What was it safe to say?

'I don't know,' she lied.

'Sure you don't know?' said the other.

Sally began to cry.

'Here, don't cry about it ...' For a minute the man of military authority was lost sight of in the flustered youth. 'You'll upset your father. There's no need to cry...' He recovered his official manner. 'Is there a telephone anywhere about here?'

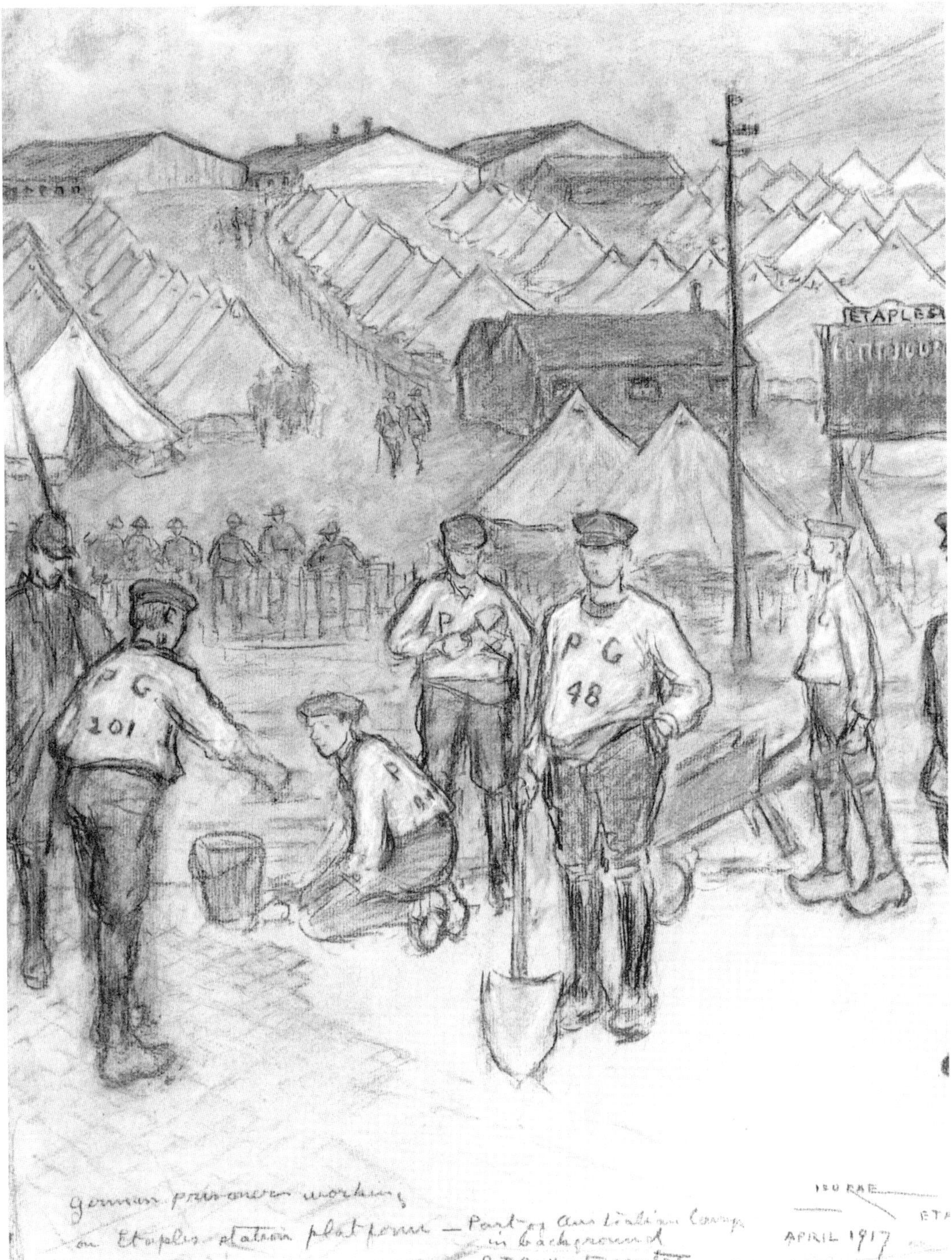

Iso Rae (1860–1940), *German prisoners working*, 1917, pastel, 60 x 47 cm. Purchased in 1990. (AWM 50285)

'There's one for the tramway men,' sniffed Sally. She put her arms before her face. 'I daresay they would let you use it.'

The sergeant stepped out of the shop. Sally wiped her eyes very carefully and gently with her pocket handkerchief, so that her father should not see she had been crying. She took a glass from the shelf and put into it some pieces of ice from the bowl in the ice chest.

'I must give my father something to drink,' she explained to the elderly soldier. 'He feels the heat very much.'

Martin preceded her down the passage, but he did not stay in the room. He went out through the other door. Sally heard him calling to the soldiers in the yard.

Her father was bent over the table. His back was towards her. She could not see his face. The innocent looking soldier had stepped back a pace or two and relaxed his attitude of attention.

Sally came forward beside her father and put her arm round his shoulder. He turned his pale face towards her and pulled her to her knees beside him.

'Get word alone with Bob ... make plan ... save Max,' he said in a low voice.

Sally heard the other three clattering up the yard. She kissed her father hurriedly and retreated to the sideboard where she covered the ice in the tumbler with whiskey. She set the bright glass down on the table beside her father.

The young sergeant came back from his telephoning. At the sight of him Sally felt inclined to weep again. He addressed Mr Putman.

'We'll take you along to headquarters in a minute or two. See what they say there.'

'Dinner ...' faltered Sally, hesitatingly.

'No, no Sally,' said her father. He had swallowed his glass of whiskey. He seemed stronger. He stood up.

'Will he have to be away the night?' Sally asked. 'Will he want pyjamas?'

'No. Nothing at all. He can't wait for dinner here. We must get away. The Military will look after him now.'

He turned to the soldiers.

'Martin and Collins stay here. I've arranged for meals at the hotel opposite. I'll be back some time this evening. Pack up those things on the table, Dale, and bring them with you.'

To the little pile on the table had been added some type, a handbill printed in Russian, a little book printed in German which the soldiers had found in the wash-house, and the electric torch Sally had given Max for his birthday, which the boys occasionally used on moonless nights to light their way to the Camp.

Sally watched the soldier's incompetent attempt to deal with the miscellaneous objects. She would not help him. The sergeant was taking a cursory look round the room in which they had been sitting. Sally went to fetch her father's hat.

'Get some string out of the shop, Dale,' snapped the sergeant in a tone of sharpest irritation.

The party began to move forward.

Sally gave her father his hat in the little passage.

He bent and kissed her.

'Mind now, Max,' he said.

'She'll be able to see you in the Camp,' interposed the sergeant hastily. 'That is, if you are not back here in a day or two.'

Mr Putman walked across the road between the two soldiers and they seated themselves in the back of the tram which was waiting at the terminus. He did not look like a prisoner, Sally thought. No one would know that he was not merely the companion of the two soldiers.

The sergeant took a seat in the front of the car. Passengers from the ferry were already seated. Justine Kerrigan was playing about the tramway shed. Mr Putman did not look round as the tram set off.

Sally went back into the house. The two soldiers who had been left behind, Martin and the red-haired one who had winked at Sally, were talking in low tones in the dining room. They had pulled down the blinds to keep out the glare of the sun.

Sally passed through into the hot kitchen. The gas had been turned high in the oven all the morning. There was a strong smell of burning. She opened the door to find that the pears and the forequarter of lamb she had been preparing were burnt to cinders. She had begun to cry again, but she took the ruined dinner from the oven and set to work to wash up and tidy the cooking utensils around the sink. She tried to think what to do. Bob would not be home till evening. She must get a word with him to explain to him what her father had said, before he could give himself away to the soldiers. The men would think that the room with the big bed in it was her bedroom. Some of her dresses were hanging up in the wardrobe. If she went and sat in there, perhaps they would let Bob come in to her and she could get her first words with him alone. It was the first words that were most important. Afterwards, when they understood each other they could manage somehow.

She finished setting the kitchen in order. One of the soldiers had left the dining room. She supposed he had gone to get his dinner across the road. The other one was rustling the morning paper. She would not speak to him. She felt sure it was Martin. She passed through the room quietly without looking in his direction and, entering her father's room, she hurriedly closed and locked the door.

The Invaluable Mystery (1987)

MOLLIE SKINNER

(1876–1955)

Nurse and writer. Skinner was born in Perth, but educated in Britain. Her novel Letters of a V.A.D. *(1918) appeared between her incongruous first and third books, a textbook entitled* Midwifery Made Easy *(1913) and* The Boy in the Bush *(1924), a novel on which she collaborated with D. H. Lawrence. Published under the pseudonym of 'R. E. Leake',* Letters of a V.A.D. *was inspired, if that is the right word, partly by Skinner's wartime service in Queen Alexandra's Imperial Military Nursing Service in India and Burma, although the book's narrator is a Voluntary Aid Detachment nurse (rather than an actual army nurse), serving on the Western Front. Skinner subsequently wrote another Great War novel,* Tucker Sees India *(1937), and a Second World War novel,* WX–Corporal Smith: A Romance of the A.I.F. in Libya *(1941). In this extract from* Letters of a V.A.D.*, the oddly nicknamed characters 'Criss-Cross' and 'the Bloodless One' are army nurses, members of a group who generally saw themselves as being above the lesser-qualified VADs. 'RX' stands for Red Cross.*

BETWEEN THE LINES

April 10th.

Have I told you that the whole of the Outfit, the Hospital, with all it includes — the Staff and the sick, etc., have been 'planted' on the estate of a local nobleman? We are in the Park, and the house is used by the Staff for quarters and offices. The Bloodless One also lives up there — and the orderlies camp in the stable. I have never been into the house, but I hope to go some day. However, the garden, though it is from necessity now rather neglected, is a great delight to me when I can get away into it. There is a shrubbery where spring flowers abound, and in this is built a dear little shrine to Our Lady, with a tiny roof, a stone back built into a rockery, and a statue of her, with the Child. (You say in your letter that Catholics always separate the Mother and Child — but this I have not noticed so far in my journeyings in these countries which are Catholic.) Mosses, little ferns and creepers are beginning to uncurl themselves after their winter sleep, 'taking no care' of the War within hearing, and at the foot of it all bubbles a little clear brook of the sweetest water.

Here am I at present writing to you with the trees rustling overhead, the bluest of skies shining above them, and the kindest of breezes blowing through my hair and about the paper. It's so warm, too, and nice, although it is April. The birds are very fine in this country — and there are just at present brilliant parakeets chattering in a maze of wild cherry trees in full blossom to my right. The place abounds in cherry trees, and if I interpret aright, the shrine is called 'To Our Lady of the Cherry Blossoms.' That makes me dream — But I want to tell you first of a little incident that happened last week when we had a great storm — who would guess it now in the sunshine and sweetness of this blessed air?

How distinctly people feel 'thought', do they not? It is that which causes intuition, I suppose. Nurses develop the power of intuition so quickly, and patients do it too. I have noticed that the most obtuse patient becomes intuitive when he becomes weak, and even semi-conscious. That is why I like Criss-Cross, her thought is powerful, and good. She can do what she likes behind my back — or to my face for that matter — to lessen my happiness and freedom, for she does it because she honestly disapproves of me, of my outlook on life, my principles, my methods, but she does not *think* evilly. If I do not succeed in my undertakings she grimly says it serves me right, and leaves me alone to recover; — but the Bloodless One —

Poor Criss-Cross — she is stiff and stern, and cold, and very often cross and disagreeable, but the 'thoughts behind' shine forth, and she is really loved by the Tommies. I discovered her true character only the other day; now I am lost in admiration of her, though she still treats me with the utmost scorn.

It was a windy, horrible gruesome night — the sort of night when people die; and you shiver all the time at the draughts, at fluttering lights, and strange noises. Just before I went off duty an enteric had died in my ward, my final duty had been to lay him out, and send him to the mortuary: and there was another with pneumonia as well, whom the Principal Medical Officer said, had not a chance. I had occasion to go back to the ward where Criss-Cross was, just before I turned in. I had no lantern, and the wind and rain beat with such fury that she did not hear me. Daring not to venture into the ward when she was on duty, I hesitated on the doorstep. But her back was half turned to me, and she was wholly occupied with the bad case, and never discovered me at all. I took care that she did not, for she was breaking the rules — Criss-Cross, bless you! sitting on Tommy's bed 'smoothing his troubled brow.'

The ward full of men was apparently unconcerned — each form lay recumbent under neatly folded red blankets, and in the dim light you could just see the smooth heads on the white pillows. Gradually I saw more, however. Each owner of each face was wide awake, they were alert, uncomfortable, waiting for something. It came. The wind had ceased to howl momentarily, the rain to beat, but the sick Tommy had lifted up his voice, and bellowed forth the most awful, the most astonishing, the most vile and malignant abuse it is possible to imagine, straight into the face of poor Criss-Cross. He had 'got 'em bad,' and that is what had upset the ward. It had apparently been going on for some time, and one imagined it would continue for most of the night; perhaps till 2 a.m., when most likely poor Tommy would be carried forth to that other room, where all is still — to lie beside his brother. But meanwhile why was Criss-Cross bearing it? Where were the orderlies?

Gradually it dawned on me. The orderlies had been sent away by the Sister because they had no moral control of the man. They had probably been irritating him into paroxysms of rage. If he got up he would die, that was certain, so Criss-Cross was holding him down by 'thoughts' of moral suasion. Good Criss-Cross, noble woman, breaking rules to try and save another's life; risking her own, in more ways than one; giving herself out with all her moral force, to reach this other soul. It was cold by Tommy's bed, it was stuffy, it was vile. She was very uncomfortable, perhaps she was fighting sleep, which attacks one unawares in the dark and chill. She was certainly at grips with demons, for the light flickered full on Tommy's white face, and it was evil.

'I'll kill you!' he screamed, gibbering. And then the wind howled again, and the rain beat on the roof and deadened sound; and Criss-Cross took both his hands in hers.

The wind died down again.

— 'Help me find my pistol — you ——. Here, it's under the bed. Help me get it — help — help — YOU!! Help me get it. It's for you. A bullet! for you. Oh! you —— Let me get up! Let go my hands! Can't you answer?'…

The wind and the rain then, and a sudden silence, and Tommy—Tommy was silent too, an awful blood-curdling stillness held him. I could see he was tense, ready to spring, and I was ready too to help Criss-Cross, only she did not know this. She sat steadily on, in her white dress, her red cape glowing in the fitful light, her white cap flowing round her shoulders, a steady mighty pillar of a woman, yet so frail—so gentle—so silent.

Another word came from Tommy, like an explosive bullet.

'You——'

He grew tenser, his sharp features more rigid, his eyes more vindictive—'YOU——'

'Oh! you *ruddy GOOSE!*'

Like a wild little clap on a bell Criss-Cross laughed. Her laughter rang out through the whole ward, for the elements still held their peace: and the patients tittered. You know what it is like when a ward laughs.

Tommy took it up. He smiled first; then he gurgled.

Sister relaxed her hold of him and stood on her feet. He was not laughing in dementia now, but with weak little hollow uncontrolled giggles.

'Oh, wipe me eyes!' he whispered. 'I didn't mean to call you that. But your white things, and the red! I thought of 'ome and the ducks, and the pond. I killed a goose for them last year come Michaelmas! ... I won't call you no names again ... Could you put me to sleep ... I'm so tired.'

While Criss-Cross reached for the feeder I crept away.

Yes, it was a crisis. We found Tommy's temperature normal in the morning, though he was, of course, most woefully weak. And he has done well. He is down 'for home' on the next troop train that takes its departure.

And Criss-Cross has not said a word.

Will this letter show you all my thoughts for you behind the words? Yes, I think it will. No need to protest to you how much I love you, and miss you, and want you every day, for the more the others don't want me, so much the more do I want you.

Yours always,
R. X.

'R. E. Leake', *Letters of a V.A.D.* (1918)

OLIVE KING

(1885–1958)

Ambulance driver. Sydney-born Olive King was a daughter of the businessman Kelso King. A great traveller, she was in England when war broke out. She soon went to Belgium with her own vehicle, then worked with the Scottish Women's Hospitals in France and briefly on the Greek–Serbian border, and finally served in Salonika with the Serbian Army from 1916 to 1918, becoming a sergeant in April 1917. Here she tells her father about her work during the terrible fire that swept through Salonika in August 1917, leaving thousands of people homeless. After the war, she instigated the raising of funds for, and opened, numerous Australian–Serbian food and clothing canteens. Olive King was awarded several Serbian medals for her war work. She was later state secretary of the New South Wales Girl Guides Association from 1925 to 1932, assistant state commissioner of that body from 1932 to 1942, and an aircraft examiner for part of the Second World War.

THE GREAT FIRE

I haven't told you anything about the fire, I'm sending you one of the souvenir copies of the Balkan News, the first published after. It gives a very good account so I'll just briefly tell you of my own small part. I was ordered out to Mikra at 4 that Saturday afternoon. On the way back at 6.30 I tried by all possible means to persuade the officers I was driving to let me take them into town, but couldn't get further than the White Tower. Of course I could see there was a thumping big fire on, could see it all afternoon, & was naturally longing to get in & have a look at it. There were some books I was very anxious to buy too. I thought I'd manage it when they said they wanted to go to the White Tower, but just as I was nipping away one wretched old fat fellow clambered back & said he wanted to go to the garage. Cursing internally (I'd have cursed more if I'd known that those precious books would be ashes before midnight!) the unfortunate chauffeur could do nothing but take the old blighter back. We got to the garage just on 7, & I was going over to give Sondi an English lesson when a breathless orderly tore up with an order for three cars to go & evacuate from the Serb Intendance. I don't know what that is in English, unless perhaps it's Ordnance. Bridget & I hopped about breathlessly, hoping to get the order, but three other cars were ordered, & I never would have gone only Lukar ran up to the Narednik [Master-Sergeant] just as they were off & said 'Please Sir, Gospajitza's screaming to go'. So he said 'Want to go?' I said 'Rather!' so he laughed & said 'All right, ide'. You may be sure I 'Ideed' for all I was worth, with 3 passengers, all keen to see the wonderful sight, who crowded in and & hid till we'd got past the Captain. We went down Ignatia St to be as near as possible (the old Via Ignatia built by the Romans, from Rome to Constantinople). From Venizelos Street to the place christened by the ASC & now universally known as Piccadilly Circus, about 2 kms, all the Turkish quarters on the right of Ignatia were one roaring blaze. It's impossible to describe the scenes of pandemonium in the streets, the jammed mass of panic-stricken people getting their goods away in bullock carts, on their own backs, in little open fiacres, or in those long narrow falling-to-pieces little Greek carts that make driving here so difficult. There was a continuous roar of the flames, every moment came a great crash & millions of sparks as some buildings [collapsed], a Vardar hot-wind gale was blowing & showers of sparks & burning fragments poured over us all the time. It was not yet dark, but everything was lit by the weird golden glow, like a wonderfully brilliant sunset. The Intendance was to the left, one block down. I got my load, & was ordered to No. 1

Wireless. As my way was past the garage I called in for my lamps which were on Ella. The Captain said the Slagelishta (our medical HQ stores) were nervous, & I was to go back there and report. I left my load, got a wonderful view from the hill where the Wireless is, & dashed down to the Stores. They had 2 cars waiting, the chauffeurs asleep in them, & didn't want me yet. They only wanted cars in case the fire spread dangerously, & told me to go back to the Intendance. There I met Captain Peshitch (you remember him, we used to give him English lessons) who begged me to go to his house, in the burning Turkish quarter, as all the Intendance was then saved. I got as near as I could, he & his orderly & Major Koppitch rushed off to pack, saying they'd be about 1/2 an hour. The most brilliant journalist couldn't describe the scenes in that little street where I waited, the fire roaring not ten yards away, me dancing all over Bridget beating out the falling sparks. Some tommies came along with the trunks of some American Mission people, & asked me to get them away. When I came back I changed a tyre in the intervals of putting out sparks, & was just pumping when two Serb offices & their families came along & implored me to move their stuff. I said I couldn't till Peshitch came, but they said they were going only ten minutes away, one of the women began to have hysterics because her dress caught from a bit of flying wood, so finally I left one of the officers to wait for Peshitch, & set off, Bridget fairly staggering with the load, the calmest of the women to show me the way. She was so excited she lost her head, & what was worse, lost the way four times, but finally we got there & dumped the stuff. I came back to find the officer mounting guard over P's things. He said P. had come, said I was to finish their job, & P. had gone back for more of his own things. Bridget went off with another load more fit for a camion [truck or lorry] than for her poor little self. When we got back, P. was beating out the sparks on his stuff, waiting for his orderly who had gone for more, & sent me to save a Serb family. We got the last kid into the car, & hadn't gone two yards when the house fell in with a deafening roar. Finally it was poor patient Peshitch's turn. We went out to Zeitenlik to Major Koppitch's hospital. From the hill there the sight was so awful it seemed absolutely incredible. In fact all night I was saying to myself 'This is too dreadful, it *can't* be true, it's too frightful to be really happening.' P. ordered me to wait for him, & disappeared. I waited nearly 1/2 an hour, dancing with impatience and fury, in an agony to get to the poor old Slagelishta. Then he came back, & as none of us had had anything since lunch, they insisted we should have some food. There were only two eggs, & two egg-plant. The eggs were scrambled & the egg-plant cut in very thin slices so we should each get a bite. There were six of us! But two had dined, so weren't allowed anything. You could hardly call it a merry meal, with me moaning continuously 'Oh, please Captain Peshitch, *please* let me go to the Slagelishta'. Luckily it didn't take long as nobody got more than 3 bites. As we came down the hill it seemed as if every building in the town were burning. From Piccadilly to the White Tower was just one leaping flame & the awful hot wind & dust never stopped. They wanted me to go to the rescue of some of their friends, but I insisted on going first to the Stores. Passing the end of Ignatia St, & looking up thru a wall of fire, with the frenzied pushing people & the crash of falling buildings, was something Dante might have described but certainly I couldn't. We got to the Stores at 12.45 a.m., found them working like demons. Captain Millitch said I must stay there, so P. & K. departed. We took the stores to a piece of waste ground not more than 200 yds away but having no buildings near they thought they'd be safe. I'd only done 3 runs when Bridget stopped dead. Winding & grinding only made empty noises, & I realised the awful truth — no petrol. I tore frantically about, & at last struck a lorry with a spare can. They kindly gave me enough to get to a French ambulance station I knew of a mile away, where I knocked them up. They were most kind and charming, & filled me up. It was they who first told me it was burning right down to the sea, & that we were cut off from the garage by four miles of fire. When I got back & reported to Millitch where I'd been he promptly asked me to get 4 more cans, as all the cars were running out, & one had been laid up for 1/2 an hour. As the ambulance had all gone to bed again I didn't like to knock them up twice, so went to a French camion place but couldn't make anyone hear. So then Bridget trundled out to Betch-Shinar, so fast as her little legs could move, to the British garrison. They had none there, but an obliging sergeant escorted me to the Marsh Pier Dump & there after losing ourselves a dozen times, falling over railway lines, & in & out of ditches, we got to the right place, & they gave me six tins. Every moment there was a fresh glare in the sky. They were expecting an air-raid, so at the Dump every man, sleepy and grumbling, was cursing at his post. But Mr Bulgar missed the chance of his life, & no aeroplanes arrived until next morning, when one wandered over to gloat over the damage. I shall never forget that dawn, gradually breaking thru the smoke & glare & flame. And the sun, that even by midday Sunday, shone feebly thru the dirty haze, like a London sun on a foggy day. Every run the fire was nearer, the houses behind the stores went up in a sheet of flame, & for hours the officers & NCOs (we couldn't spare any men) stood on the roofs with fire extinguishers & hand grenades. We had a little hand-pumped hose, used by the wine firm beside us to fill their barrels, & this was playing for hours on the roofs, wherever sparks fell. That big empty court-yard for the wine-barrels was, I think, what saved us, for in the end our precious stores were saved. Always that dreadful hot wind, & for one terrible 1/2 hour the wind changed & the sparks fell all over the stores we had saved. The officer in charge there sent me dashing back for old tents soaked in water which we pulled over those stores. I drove like a fiend that Sunday morning, smoking 'cos I was so hungry, Bridget screaming her siren all the way, thru the mass of people, not caring a cuss if she went over them or not. She began to scream as she left the yard, shrieked all the way, & kept it up all the way back from the dump. By this time the people were in a sort of dumb apathy, but luckily Bridget has very strong lungs, & her piercing yell galvanised them into sufficient life to leap away from her reckless little feet. Soon after dawn the wine-barrels burst, the street beside the stores ran with wine, six or eight inches deep in the gutters, & overflowing in a trickle all over the street, like blood. Dagoes & the soldiers of two of our Allies threw themselves down, & lying full-length in the gutters, drank & drank. A few hours later they could be seen lying everywhere, a horrid mess beside them, sleeping it off. Meanwhile the agonised proprietors, half-demented, were scooping it out of the gutters in petrol tins. On Sunday afternoon I came along the quay at 3 o'clock & saw them doing the same thing in the wine shops, that were ankle-deep in wine. I shall say 'No, thank you,' to wine for years to come! I *was* proud of our men that night and Sunday. They worked like heroes to save the population and their treasures. Large mirrors, by the way, are the chiefest Household God, to judge by the numbers of people who carried them, & next to them brass bedsteads. Looting and shooting were rife, but I'm proud to say not one Tommy looted a thing. The people knew it & trusted them with anything. It gives you a glow sometimes to realize you belong to the only nation that's trusted & respected wherever it goes. Hated and feared by some, but always honored, & never despised, except perhaps for a short time by our latest great ally, when she suffered slightly from swollen head, & some of her people professed to scorn the 'poor old back-number'. But even they have found they didn't see either so deeply or so clearly as they thought they did, & find their feelings for the back-number changed to wondering admiration. It's a responsibility to be British, but by gum! it's worth while. By 1/4 past 12 the danger for the stores was over, the dreadful wind had dropped, & the chauffeurs & men, worn-out, went to sleep. I took a walk round town to see the damage, & the tales I heard and the looting I saw — & other things — wouldn't pass the censor! At 3, being the only chauffeur awake, Millitch asked me if I would try to get thru & make a bolt for home, & send him out four fresh cars, or at any rate four fresh drivers. So I went off, was warned by the guard I went at my own risk, but got along the quay somehow. You never saw such a sight as the quay presented that first day. All the best buildings had been there, everything gutted, the tram wires hanging loose in the middle of the road the remains of a motor-car, the buildings all smouldering, some still blazing (today is fourteen days but everywhere the ruins are smouldering, & late this evening I saw another new line of hose being run out) people, most soldiers, rooting in the ruins for loot, others lying about dead-drunk — you couldn't believe it was real. I stared at the Cinemas, & couldn't believe that when I want to go to a cinema there'll be none to go to, & at the Splendid I couldn't believe that I'll never have another meal in their much-advertised, horrid new restaurant. The two best hotels, with their fine outsides & their bugs inside, the Sister Club, the beautiful new Red Cross rooms, the shops, the bars, the restaurants, the 'Palais de Varieties' — gone, all gone. I saw it happening, & all day long I'm driving among the ruins, & yet I can't realize it, so how in the world can I make you? I was jolly proud of my little Bridget, from 4 o'clock when she started for Mikra, until 1/4 past 12 Sunday she never stopped running, over 20 hours, except the 1/2 hour at Zeitenlik at midnight, & an occasional two or three minutes when there were other lorries loading up ahead. She only had one puncture & up till the last two hours went like a bird. The last two hours she went poisonously, but I wasn't surprised when I filled her up at midday, & found the radiator was less than half full. I got home at 4, to find the floor of my 'salon' (otherwise hall) covered with refugees, a woman & 9 children. I plumped straight down on my bed & went to sleep, got up at 6, had a bath, made tea for the refugees, & went round to Yovi. We were dining with Captain Shapovitch. I was so hungry, so it was rather a blow to be met with 'I hope you're not hungry, I can't get any food anywhere'. It was, alas, only too true. We had a tin of sardines & a very small tinned tongue for dinner. The next day I carted refugees from 7 a.m. till 10 p.m. & the following day started at 5 a.m. I didn't get any loot, at the time I was too busy, & besides it never occurred to me until two days later, when I heard what others had got & then it was too late. This is an enormous letter, poor Daddy, it will take you a week to read it. I meant to write a very brief concise account, but got so excited I couldn't stop. However I promise to now!

One Woman at War, ed. Hazel King (1986)

MAY TILTON

(1884–1964)

Army nurse. May Tilton served overseas with the Australian Army Nursing Service from 1915 to 1918. She later published an account of her war service, entitled The Grey Battalion *(1933), the reference in the title being to the grey of the Australian army nurses' grey and scarlet uniforms. Here she talks about some of her experiences in France in 1917.*

UNDER FIRE

Tuesday, 21 August. Came off duty to watch more thrilling air fights at ten thousand feet. These days were marked by great aeroplane activity over the battlefields. Some days as many as fifty Allied machines were in the air at once, endeavouring, with much success, to maintain their local supremacy.

British superiority in the air during 1916 was reversed in 1917, when Germany brought out their new machines, which were the latest word in aviation. The men said they could out-climb and out-manoeuvre any British plane.

During April 1917, the Germans claimed to have shot down four British planes for each German plane that was lost, so the Germans had all the advantage, until about the middle of May 1917, when the new British models, Bristol and De Havilland two-seater, fighting and bombing planes arrived in France.

In England, we had talked and joked about this Spring Offensive, but I never imagined that anything like it could happen, or that anyone could face such frightfulness. We wondered how far it was possible to go before the limit of human endurance was reached. Tragedy was a commonplace of every hour, every night. We forgot ourselves in the bravery of the boys in their suffering.

Almost dropping with fatigue, my tent companion, Sister Slater, and I went to bed at 9 a.m., and fell asleep at once. At 10.30 a.m. we were wakened by a terrific explosion, and rushed to the tent door to see what happened. A Jock, working in our compound, said:

'They've got us this time; it was a shell. I'll go and find out where it fell.'

Almost at once, a second shell followed and burst much closer, getting our QM stores.

A very agitated MO pushed his head into our tent and said: 'Come on, you girls. Put on your coats and slippers. The CO says you have to get into a dugout at once. They are shelling us.'

We were incensed because he would not allow us to wait long enough to get into our clothes. We wanted to go to the wards, not into a burrow in the ground.

'Good God ! That first shell killed a night sister at 44 in bed asleep. Come on !' he said.

Like Brown's cows, we scuttled across no man's Land, with our plaits flying, to some trenches occupied by Scotch Canadians who were out of the line resting. Before I reached them, another long-drawn-out crescendo followed me closely.

'I'm gone,' flashed through my mind.

The men shouted, 'Run!' Others called, 'Drop quickly!' My slipper tripped me, and I fell, just as the shell fell in the cemetery behind. I looked back to see a huge mass of black smoke and debris flying in all directions; felt myself lifted and dragged into a huge dugout where all the day staff had gathered. Everyone of them was upset at the CO's orders, and distressed to leave the patients.

The DMS and QMG, 5th Army, arrived and ordered all three CCSs to evacuate at once. The MOs and orderlies remained in the wards to get the patients away. It was done without a casualty among them, while the shells continued to fall all over the camp. The Church Army hut, the cemetery and the field ambulance were all badly damaged.

The first shell that broke our slumbers burst in the sisters' quarters at 44 and killed a Canadian night sister who was in bed, asleep. A piece went through her, from back to front, near her heart. She died in twenty minutes. The sister who shared her tent had returned to the Base the day before because she could not stand the noise and conditions there. The sister who should have been asleep in the next tent (which was blown to bits) was out 'lorry hopping,' a form of recreation we took to help us forget the horrors of the wards. It was forbidden us to leave the camp, owing to the shell-fire. The boys, ever ready to accommodate the sisters, would invite us to 'hop up,' and would take us as far as they could before branching away towards the line. Then we would hop down and on to another lorry travelling in the opposite direction, thus working back to the camp. It gave us something besides the wards to think about before trying to induce sleep.

Three of the sisters at 44 were so shell-shocked that they were sent away in ambulances.

After each shell burst, the padre would come from the wards to assure us our patients were all right, and how well the evacuation was being carried out, while we remained in the dugout, listening to the Canadians' gramophone playing 'Pack up Your Troubles.' The Canadians kept bringing us titbits from their home parcels, cake and sweets, and also, as souvenirs, pieces of shrapnel too hot to hold in your hand.

'This is a good opportunity,' said our home sister, K. O'Connor, 'now we are all together, to tell you that dinner to-night will be at 7.15 instead of 7.30 p.m.' Then she wondered why we laughed.

While we were in the dugout, the local mail from the line was delivered. I received only one letter, from my fiancé, asking me to give him our correct map reference, and blaming himself for not teaching me how to read it myself. I was glad he could not see our present predicament. His letter conveyed his anxiety on my behalf.

The news of our hospital being shelled and a sister killed reached our friends in the line, and at 4 p.m., when orders came for us to pack our belongings, ready to leave at once, many of the boys we knew were down, helping us to toss our things together. They rolled up our beds and stacked our luggage.

While this was going on, Matron O'Dwyer, in her calm and collected way, sat on the sandbags with the mess book, calling on us to pay up before she lost sight of us.

'I've no money, matron, I can't pay you now,' I called, in reply.

'Well, find it somewhere,' she said. 'You will probably be scattered all over the country, and I won't see you again, and we must pay our bills.' The boys for once had some money, and paid our debts.

The last of the patients had gone. As we waited beside a brick wall for an ambulance, a shell fell into No. 44 CCS, blowing an orderly's leg and arm off. A second one fell into one of the empty wards. Just as we were seated and ready to leave, a third shell burst right ahead of us on the road. We had only just moved away from the brick wall when it was blown to atoms.

All day, while the shelling was going on, Fritz was overhead, as though he was directing the fire that concentrated on us.

All the sisters, except one (G. McKern), left for St Omer, forty miles back. No one knew how she came to be left behind. She wrote later a humorous account of her experiences, travelling alone all day in a troop train to the Base.

The personnel from all three CCSs, numbering over a hundred, were distributed in hospitals at St Omer.

Fifteen English girls went down shell-shocked. We were happy to know none of our girls went under to it. The behaviour of the sisters under such trying conditions, their fortitude and self-control, surprised, I think, even themselves. The war made me prouder of my sex than ever before.

Sisters Baker, Doherty, Eldridge, Glasson, Slater and I were in one car. We were nearly dropping with weariness, want of sleep and hunger. Some of the girls were vomiting all the way down.

The waste, the devastation and the desolation over the countryside we passed through appalled us. The railway station at Abeele had disappeared. (Fritz succeeded in getting it with a direct hit one day, just after a hospital train had filled up and got safely away. The same night, twice he was over, bombing the CCSs. There were no casualties, but the previous night several nursing orderlies and ten sick German prisoners were killed in a raid on a CCS.)

Hazebrouck was flattened, barely one sound place was left standing. A few poor French folk kept on their tiny shops to eke out a living, hiding mostly in their cellars. Troops swarmed over the place, camping in smashed-up buildings.

It was 10.30 p.m. when we arrived at St Omer, and were accommodated at No. 4 Canadian C.C.S. Just out from home, these great-hearted folk made us very welcome. They could not do enough for us. The girls envied us our experience. Ye gods!

Their camp was situated in the beautiful woods of a chateau at Longuenesse — such a peaceful haven. It was days before we made up arrears of sleep. The CO had orders to put us on duty. He said that officially we were, but he considered we needed complete rest after our experiences. It would do more to restore our nervous systems and fit us for further good work when we were recalled.

During the weeks that followed, we were treated as guests.

After we left Brandhoek, a shell burst on the railway line. It killed 'Snowy' Saunders, the cook, and fatally wounded one of our night orderlies, Harry Thorsen. When the next shell fell shortly afterwards, his mate, 'Woppy' Thomas, protected the wounded boy with his own body. For this act, he was decorated with the Military Medal. This recognition pleased the staff.

We were told 'one' Royal Red Cross was being awarded each CCS after our shelling. Sister Kelly (WA), received the decoration at No. 3. The decision was a popular one. When the first shell fell, she rushed for the enamel wash basins and covered the patients' heads to protect them from bits of flying shrapnel, then stood in the middle of the ward, encouraging and cheering her helpless patients.

The Huns shelled our camp for days after we left, damaging nineteen wards. It was a week before our luggage was restored to us again.

The Grey Battalion (1933)

MARY MARLOWE

(1884–1962)

Actor, writer, and broadcaster. Margaret Mary Shanahan was born and educated in Melbourne. Known as Mary Marlowe, she acted in Australia, England, Canada, and the United States. 'Her dimple was adorable', according to the poet Zora Cross. 'She had hazel-green eyes, sleek black hair and exquisite teeth.' Marlowe served as a Voluntary Aid Detachment nurse at the Quex Park Territorial Red Cross Hospital, Kent, England, for two years from 1916. She also published a novel called Kangaroos in King's Land *(1917) and a war novel,* The Women Who Wait *(1918), in which she exhorted British women to have babies. After returning to Australia in 1920, she worked as a journalist (her duties included writing Dorothy Dix answers between the 1930s and 1950s), wrote more novels, and took up radio broadcasting in the 1930s. One of the men she nursed in England remained firmly imprinted in her memory.*

'MY GHOST IN NOVEMBER'

Some days later I joined Kent Auxiliary 178 and became afternoon nurse in C Ward at Quex Park Territorial Hospital, nervous in my blue print uniform down to the ankles. Quex had accommodation for forty-six patients. I had only a fragmentary knowledge of Red Cross lectures to help me.

The hospital occupied a stately mansion, Georgian in style, and it had all the traditions. There was a White Lady who walked in the moonlight, two other ghosts and a cricket pitch bounded by fields yellow with buttercups in the spring.

Major Powell Cotton, the owner (I can't be sure if he was the rightful heir or a wealthy interloper), had spent his early life shooting big game and his middle age writing books about it. The victims were stuffed and displayed in a private museum attached to the mansion. There were two large rooms with glass ceilings and walls and trick lights. They were set up to represent an African jungle with a watering pool in the foreground. Around this the stuffed creatures were grouped. On wet days the Major removed the scrim screens which shut off the jungle and gave lectures on his adventures. The beds were turned round to face the jungle.

'Straighten the beds in here first and then the other twelve on the long verandah,' said the nurse I was relieving. 'Then empty the cigarette trays and scald the sputum cups. Fetch two large cans of water from the kitchen at the other end of the house. Don't spill it. The men might slip.'

'What do I do with the water?'

'Wash the bandages. They are in soak now in the surgery sink. They will be boiled afterwards but you must get the pus off first in cold water. You'll find clean bandages drying in the conservatory. Roll them ... Oh, by the way, there's an appendicitis in the far bed. I didn't have time to change his dressing. You do it. Just a dry dressing. He's wearing a many-tailed bandage so you won't need to move him. Goodbye, good luck.'

I washed the dirty bandages and felt sick. The appendicitis was an Australian boy from Forbes, New South Wales. He had kind eyes and the helpful spirit of a man from the outback. I am never likely to forget him. His name was Paddison.

He opened his pyjama jacket and took the pins out of the many-tailed. The dressing underneath had slipped. I had not seen a man's naked body before. I picked up the dressing with the forceps and gently dropped it on the patient's navel. That looked like the scar I was seeking. Paddison moved the dressing to the right spot and held it in position while I did up the many-tailed.

My cheeks were flaming. I was ready to run out of the hospital. But when the last safety pin was in Paddison said: 'Very comfortable, sister. My word, isn't it grand to have an Aussie nursing you!'

We voluntary nurses received no pay and we provided our own uniforms. The afternoon nurses were given tea and bread and jam at four o'clock but we took our night meal in our own homes. We bought our own thermometers, our own surgical scissors and we were invited to contribute small prizes for the bridge tournaments. We worked Sundays the same as weekdays.

Towards the end of my first day a Canadian walking patient called me behind a screen. There was a young man on the bed. His dressings were off. The whole of his hip had been blown away by a German shell. Where the hip should have been there was a mass of raw, bleeding flesh like uncooked steak. He was lying on his right buttock so the wound would not be touched by the bedclothes.

'There's a dandy hole for you,' said the Canadian. 'Fritz did that job well, didn't he?'

My bread and jam turned over inside and started to rise. Could I stand it? The men were not aware that this was my first day in hospital and that I had never seen raw flesh before. To them this was just a wound that a man could have and still be alive. They found the young man's tenacity a fine thing, and wanted me to share their admiration.

Matron appeared around the screen to finish the dressing and looked surprised to find me there. 'Help me, now you're here,' she said. 'Soak that pad in the saline. Use the forceps, please.'

When we had finished, when all the men had settled down for the night, the Matron called after me as I was leaving. 'Tomorrow, nurse, when you come on duty and have done the bandages and made the wards neat, take the methylated spirits out to Corporal Dow on the verandah. He is in the third bed from the far end. I want you to give his head a thorough doing. He's got nits in it.'

'Yes, Matron.'

I lost the bread and jam as soon as I reached the park gates on the way home. This, indeed, was war.

The other nurses had homes in the village and bicycles to ride there and back. I had neither and made my lonely way a mile across the fields at the end of the day to my rooms at Copeland House — high-sounding but humble — where Mrs Sharpey 'did for' me above the village china shop. My sitting-room windows looked over the cornfields which still — courageously — breasted up to Birchington's main street. Beyond the fields you saw the hills of Canterbury.

There was a good-sized bedroom at the back but the bathroom was filled with Mr Sharpey's tools. Every morning Mrs Sharpey brought a large jug of hot water to the bedroom. There was an oilcloth mat. There was a wash basin. There was a pail. Wash the upper part of the torso first, empty the water into the pail, wash the lower part of the body, and there you were ... clean.

In eighteen months I had four baths. Two were stolen at Quex on days when I was on a twelve-hour shift. Matron sent me to lie down on her bed for an hour and the bathroom was next door. It was worth taking a chance. The other two were taken at the house on the cliffs where our quartermaster lived after we had been swimming from the thirty-nine steps which feature in John Buchan's novel.

At five o'clock in the morning at Copeland House, Mr Sharpey, a house painter, would climb the stairs with a cup of tea for Mrs S. He would then get his own breakfast, mount his bicycle, and ride five miles to Margate to commence work at seven. When he reached home at night he would be so tired and irritable that his children would not be allowed to talk above a whisper. Eventually he went mad.

At eight Mrs Sharpey would bring me an egg on a tray to my bedside, and a good pot of tea. When I was not on morning duty I breakfasted in bed. Mrs S. would relate the village news while I ate the egg, giving me a vivid description of the air-raid of the previous midnight. We spent our first few air-raids together but I soon got tired of that. It went like this: when the 'Take cover' alarm boomed out, Mrs Sharpey would rush into my room and

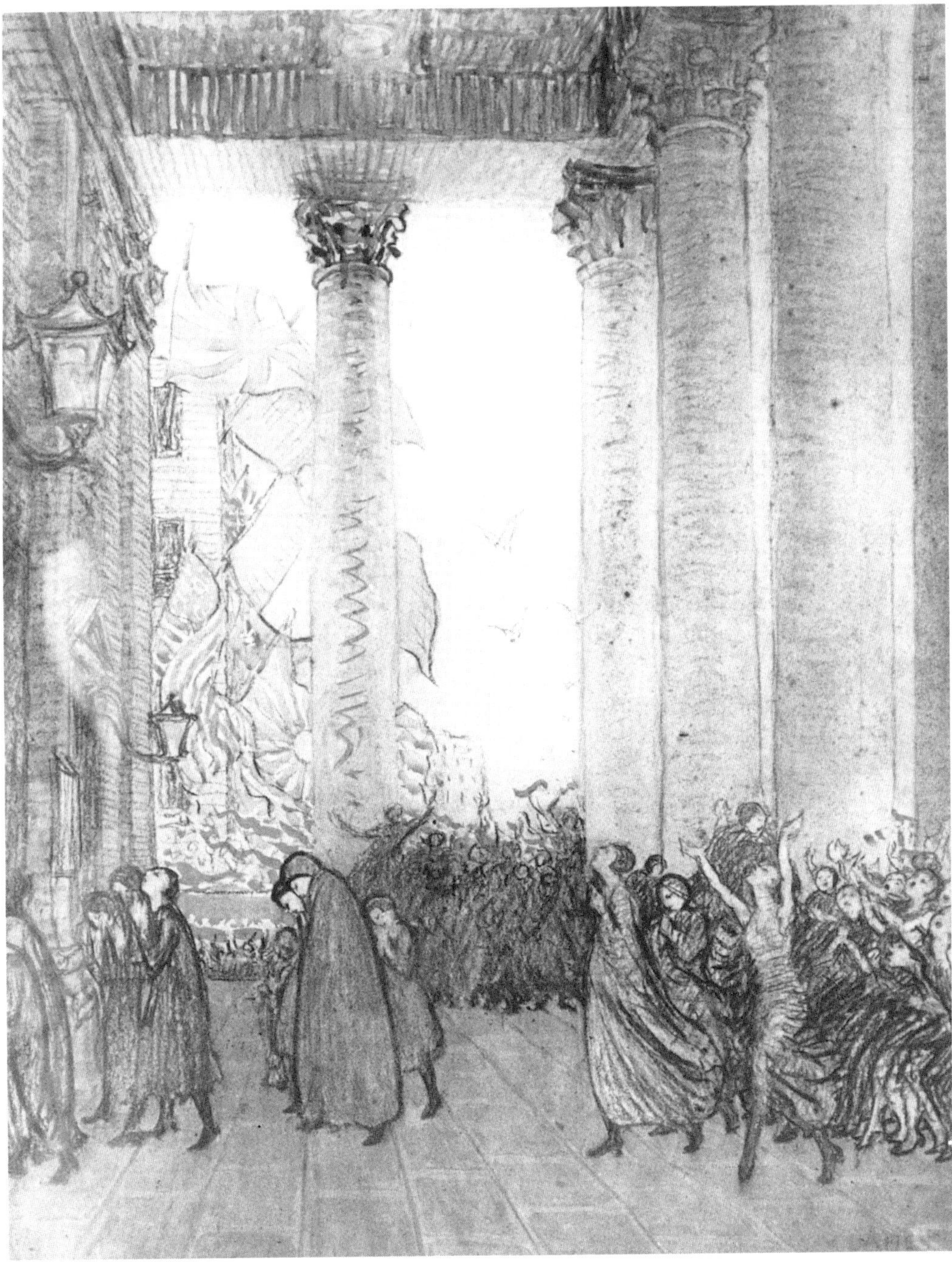

Vida Lahey (1882–1968), *Rejoicing and remembrance, Armistice Day, London*, 1918, charcoal and watercolour, 74.5 x 56 cm. Purchased in 1978. (AWM 19592)

wake me up. She would sit, trembling on the side of the bed, with me holding her hands, telling her that you could only die once and that now was as good a time as any. She would sit on until the silvery siren of the 'All clear' rang out and then return to her own bed. By then we would both be thoroughly exhausted. At length I had to be ruthless and tell her that I could not do my work at the hospital properly the next day if I had to spend the night waiting to be killed.

Breakfast over, the penny section bath, a think-walk on the chalk cliffs with the skylarks overhead and by ten o'clock each morning I and my little Corona were at work in the window that overlooked the cornfields. We never stopped until Mrs Sharpey came in to set the table for the midday meal.

At 1.30 p.m. I set out for the hospital, walking a mile across the fields. After a few weeks they trusted me to do the real things at Quex. Nurse Hilda handed over the trench feet case in B Ward. She had had the stench of them in her nostrils for weeks and she was glad of the relief. Black stumps, suppurating freely; bandages to be soaked off for every dressing. You need enthusiasm for trench feet.

The chronic lung case in C Ward was in my care from the beginning. He was a seventeen-year-old lad from Liverpool, a thread of a boy who had lied about his age to get to the war. It was touch and go with him for six months. He was not a spectacular hero, poor little, cross-eyed, demi-man. He grumbled a lot, but I grew fond of him, for all that. We made him well enough to go back to his humble home in Liverpool. With so little left to fight for life, we knew he must leave it early. But we got him home.

The night nurse who patrolled the wards with a storm lantern every hour was a Cockney widow. She was a capable nurse, jocular with the patients. She sat on their beds and predicted their futures. She was engaged to a jockey who had been at Quex. He had a piece of shrapnel in his heart. When her annual holiday came she went north to meet him and he came south to meet her. When he ran for his train, the shrapnel moved a fraction and he died on the spot.

Of course, we mended many soldiers who went back to be killed by the guns in France. Mostly they would write when they went back. Then there would be no letter. Eventually we would hear what had happened to them.

I had applied for duty in France. Twice my call came and both times the commandant asked that it might be postponed. It was Mozart to my ears to hear her say I could not be spared from Quex.

Fomentations were my strength. One day I heard a patient say—when I was out of sight but not of hearing—'She drops a bloody red coal on yer bloody wound and looks up, so flamin' innercent, and sez she, "Is that comfortable, laddie?" I 'aven't the 'eart to tell her it 'urts like 'ell.'

There was Bradley who had a wound in his side the size of a saucer. So deep was it and he so weak that sometimes the functions of his body operated through it. He was not my case but he liked to talk to me. Bradley was a Lancashire lad of medium mentality who resented the war which had sent him back to England a bit of human flotsam. Latterly he was transferred to Herne Bay. I sat beside him in those last few minutes at Quex—he knew no other home now and seemed to have no people—and in those final moments he said to me:

'When I'm better, sister, I'm going to have a full bottle of wine all to myself. I'm going to drink the whole bottle.'

The ambulance came to the hall door. We waved until it was out of sight, lost down the long winding drive. Two days later Bradley died. Sheer inability to face the future? Homesickness for the only home he had known for nearly two years—Quex?

In the two minutes silence every November it is Bradley who comes to me and stays until the noise of the world breaks through. I hear him say: 'When I get better, sister, I'm going to have a full bottle of wine all to myself. I'm going to drink the whole bottle.'

Of all of them, why should it be Bradley? A lonely man without a family. Is it that? He was a ghost in life. He is my ghost in November.

That Fragile Hour (1990)

MARY GILMORE

(1865–1962)

Poet. Mary Gilmore née Cameron was born and educated in New South Wales, where she became a teacher. She took part in William Lane's New Australia movement, living at the Cosme settlement in Paraguay from 1896 to 1899. After periods in Patagonia and England, she returned to Australia in 1902, where she lived for the rest of her life. Her first volume of poetry, Marri'd and Other Verses, *was published in 1910. The following beautiful poem is taken from* The Passionate Heart *(1918), the royalties from which she gave to blinded soldiers.*

'THE SATIN OF THE BEE'

Thundering of hoofs
In the fields of France,
Thunder of the cannon
Where the troops advance;
Dust out of hell
Spurts with every gun,
But the satin of the bee
Flashes in the sun.

Very still the dead;
Thick as fallen leaves
From the shattered tree
Where no shadow weaves;

Stark tree and stark dead
Tell of what is done;
But the satin of the bee
Flashes in the sun.

Deep among the dead
Grows the tranquil flower;
Early wakes the ploughman
Answering the hour;
Trade calls her markets
At each day begun;
And the satin of the bee
Flashes in the sun.

Life, that laughs at dying,
Lifts her other forms
Where the tempest rages
And the battle storms;
Turns the shuttle over,
Shifting sands that run—
And the satin of the bee
Flashes in the sun.

The Passionate Heart (1918)

GLADYS HAIN

(1887–1962)

Lawyer and journalist. Educated at the University of Melbourne, Gladys Taylor began practising as a solicitor in 1912. On 25 April 1915, she married a barrister, Rex Hain, who served on Gallipoli and in France, before he was sent to 'Blighty'. Gladys Hain sailed to England in 1916, to be close to her husband. There she did voluntary war work and worked as a journalist. She also anonymously published a collection of short stories, The Coo-ee Contingent *(1917), the cover of which bears the description 'BILL JIM as Fighter, good Chum and Lover'. The following moralistic little tale reflects the book's overall tone. Hain, who had two daughters, continued with journalism in Melbourne in the 1920s, gave legal advice to many women's organisations over the years, was president of both the Victorian and federal housewives' associations, and eventually resumed her legal practice after her husband's death.*

'AN UNRECORDED WAR WEDDING'

We were smoking in the lounge — our second Henry Clay — and all around us the war-fevered girls of England were making love to the subaltern on leave. Between the puffs of his cigar Jim became prosy — and the stark materialism of his point of view worried me. We talked of the girls — he rather fancied the fair one with slant eyes. But there's no such thing as love, you know. I've spent a year at each of five hospitals and had the love affair of my life in each. I'd have married any one of them, even the fat nurse in the German hospital at Frankfurt; but love — no!

He was twenty-six, but, with the maturity of the Colonial, no boy, a man in years and experience. The face of the girl I left behind me was clear in the cigar-blurred atmosphere, and I laboured to convince him of the efficacy of *la grande passion*.

He only laughed. 'Drop it, H——; indeed, you're not as clever as you think you are — there's nothing in it.'

I dropped it, and we continued our conversation in medical terms — he was a Regimental Medical Officer on leave, I dabble in the sciences, so we could keep each other company without the wholly distracting subject of Love.

It was the night before our leave was up, and we were celebrating it as should warriors — quietly, deeply.

'If I ever marry,' he said, 'I want to see her with her hair down, and I want to meet the boys who made love to her when she was at school and hear what they say of her. I'm not letting my heart run away with me.'

He went off to bed, and next day we parted at Boulogne — he to go to the Somme lines, I to Ypres.

We didn't write to one another, but we pledged to meet on our next leave if we could. We did. It came in July. We used to string out the days in desolate London, and only God knows how desolate London can be to a Colonial. In the evenings we dined and went to the theatre and wandered mournfully from supper-house to supper-house looking for Heaven knows what. Sometimes we strolled round Piccadilly and Leicester Square. He was still young enough to be curious, and liked to talk to the flapper on her beat. The girls used to rush us as soon as they spotted the uniform, and they'd have eaten us if we hadn't been pretty spry in getting past them after a few minutes' conversation.

'Let's go to the Coal Hole,' one would say pleadingly.

'Nothing doing, Maria,' Jim would say. 'Got to meet my mother-in-law.' And then we'd go on to the next. When one is a medico there's a certain peculiar fascination about the kerb amazon. She's a type worth studying. But one night we got a bit of a shock.

'Come on, boys, I've got a mate; let's have supper at Romano's,' said a fair girl, with thin, anæmic cheeks and hysterical eyes.

'Nothing doing, Maria,' said Jim, plunging into his formula, 'got to meet —— Gee whiz! what the dickens is this?'

I turned; he was supporting with one arm a fainting girl and trying to push her arm away from his neck. He shook her roughly.

'Look sharp,' he said brusquely. 'None of these tricks.' He tried to put her on her feet, but her head tumbled helplessly, and I struck a match and looked at her. He cursed me fiercely. 'Blow out the blasted match!' he said, and prepared to sit the girl on the kerbing. 'Here, get a policeman.' But I had seen the girl's face.

'She's fainted, Jim.'

A timid touch on my elbow startled me, and I turned hurriedly to see another girl at my side.

'We don't live far,' she said. 'Can't you carry her? She — she hasn't had anything to eat today; we're broke.'

The cheap little face with its halo of peroxide curls was pitiful, and I hailed a taxi and Jim put the girl inside.

'Come on,' I said, 'we can't leave them like this — the girl's ill.'

Jim looked at me cynically. 'You're a fool,' he said shortly, 'but in you go. I don't suppose they'll get the better of me.'

The dolly-face gave the taxi driver directions, and in two or three minutes we were outside one of the miserable buildings given over to flats that this ghastly city produces in such wearying numbers.

By this time Jim had made up his mind to see it through. He picked up the girl who had fainted and carried her in and up the stairs to their dingy flat.

Once there we told the dolly-face to put her to bed, and then he examined her. She was half starved. Her body was a skeleton. Jim wrote out a list of things she needed, and handed the other girl a five-pound note. Then we made to leave. But the girl on the bed opened her eyes and looked at Jim. They weren't bad eyes; the mouth was hard and sensuous, but the eyes had some girlishness in them.

'Thank you,' she said very faintly. 'Will you come again?' Then she flushed. 'I don't mean as I asked you to to-night, but to — well, just to see me.'

We promised, though I don't think either of us had any intention of honouring our promises.

We walked back to our hotel and went to bed, and neither mentioned the matter to the other.

In the morning Jim was surly — he seemed worried; finally I missed him. When he turned up to a late lunch I explained with some show of moroseness that I'd been looking for him everywhere. He offered no explanation of his absence. Then I suggested that perhaps we might as well look in and see the girl who had fainted. By this time my newly-raised conscience was getting to work. He didn't take up my suggestion, but when I said that if he couldn't I would go alone he remarked dryly that I'd better join the Christian Endeavourers, and that if it was any use to the blanky donkey he might inform me that he had been already. I was relieved. I didn't want to be bothered going, but the girl's face had been pretty ghastly, and, after all — well, we had promised.

'What's the matter with her?'

'All right this morning; just anæmia, I suppose — these silly girls are all the same. Everything on their backs, and nothing in their stomachs. It's a child,' he said briefly, and turned on the steak savagely.

I was surprised. I questioned him.

'Oh, shut up, can't you?' he said irritably. 'It's not my fault, and I daresay it's not yours. Why should we worry?'

'What will become of her?' I asked in righteous indignation.

'Well, same as all the rest, I suppose — first charring and then selling flowers in the squares. Drop it, we aren't an orphan asylum, are we?'

It's no use arguing with a thoroughgoing materialist, so I dropped the matter and we pursued our weary round of gaiety. Just a day or so before we left Jim got a telegram to say his mother was dead, and I went along to Headquarters with him to get an extension of leave. He seemed to think he wanted a day or two more.

I had to go, of course, and he saw me off. We had argued a bit, but I liked him and he liked me, so far as I could tell. He shook hands and he made some remark about seeing me later, and he took my address. But he never wrote, not for weeks. Then his regiment went down to Sailly and was pretty well bled, and Jim was reported missing. The German lists didn't include him when they came out, so we guessed it was a shell that must have got him.

About a month later I got a letter from his Colonel enclosing some papers from Jim, which the Colonel said he had wanted sent on to me in case 'anything happened.' I glanced at the will and saw that he left everything to his child. I thought that pretty close of him — he's never mentioned a wife, but the chap you chum up with on Service doesn't necessarily tell you all his soul's secrets. It's no schoolgirl friendship at the Front. Then came a letter addressed to me, and the shock of it is still present to my mind as I recall the writing:

> Dear old Chap, — I'm in a rather slushy mood to-night, so I think I might as well unload on you. I've gone and been and done it — made a God damned idiot of myself over that anæmic tart who floated into my arms in Leicester Square. Now don't you go and think I've fallen in love, or that she's got me under the cardiac orifice. The thing that did it was the kid.
>
> It seemed pretty rotten to know that it might be a boy and be brought up in that dirty flat, so I married her when she promised me to give me the child as soon as it was born. She's no damn good — I knew that within twenty-four hours of marrying her, but the kid belongs to an old friend of mine in the Rifles, and I'd like it to get a start.
>
> When my mother died I had no one who would throw fits over my mesalliance, so I made the interesting experiment.
>
> If I had lived I'd have brought up the kid and divorced her as soon as I had enough evidence to go on. I never lived with her, of course — she sickened me when I looked at her — but she found plenty of consolation elsewhere.
>
> Please make all arrangements to have the kid brought up as I have instructed in papers herewith — and don't let her pull your leg about money.

Do you remember the kind of girl I was going to marry the time we talked of *la grande passion*? It's rather a joke, isn't it? But I'll forgive you for having the laugh over me provided you make it clear to anyone who ever hears of it that it was no damned sentiment on my part. — Yours,

J. BLACK.

P.S. — I'd rather like the kid to know me as his father. It's rather rough to be orphaned on the father's side and owned by that kind of woman on the distaff side, and so I became an orphan asylum after all!

The Coo-ee Contingent (1917)

VIDA GOLDSTEIN

(1869–1949)

Feminist and pacifist. Victorian-born Vida Goldstein campaigned very actively for female suffrage in Australia, the United States, and Britain. She stood unsuccessfully for the Australian federal parliament five times between 1903 and 1917. Goldstein was the only president of the Women's Political Association (1903–19), and of the Women's Peace Army (1915–19), both of which she had founded. This glimpse of her thoughts comes from an article in the Woman Voter, *a weekly journal that she edited from 1909 to 1919. This particular article was published several months after Billy Hughes's first attempt to introduce conscription (for overseas service) by referendum failed, and several days after Hughes's Nationalists won the 1917 federal election on a 'Win-the-War' platform.*

FROM 'WORKERS OF THE WORLD, UNITE! WOMEN OF THE WORLD, UNITE!'

Immediately on the declaration of war many of the foremost women in the woman movement in every country set to work to bind together the forces that stood true to peace and internationalism in war-time as in peace-time. In far-away Australia the Women's Political Association took the lead, and when news came through it was found we had taken exactly the same line of action as our fellow-women in other countries. In spite of every difficulty placed in their way by Governments and by the Press, the women held an International Congress at the Hague in April, 1915, for the purpose of formulating terms for a constructive and permanent peace. Quietly, steadily, surely the gospel of internationalism has spread, and nowhere has it spread more rapidly than in Russia and in Germany amongst the women, the workers, and the soldiers themselves. It is good indeed to think that the men who have borne the brunt of the actual fighting and have survived it will return from the battlefields to swell the forces of anti-militarism and internationalism. **And the people must not fail them**. It will be said that the small number of votes cast for me as a straight-out peace and anti-militarist candidate proves that the people of Australia do not want peace. Nothing of the kind. It only proves that party allegiance is stronger than allegiance to principle. The Labour vote in each State, except, perhaps, West Australia, represents in the main a peace vote, but the domination of the 'ticket' was stronger than fidelity to peace. The seeming triumph of the National Party is not a war vote so much as a Press, anti-Labour, and fear vote, backed up by a few thousand men and women of the working classes with capitalist minds. An election does not decide principles as a referendum does; prejudice, personalities and side issues overshadow the real issues. Bendigo, for instance, does not mean a victory for Mr Hughes' policy. It means that thousands voted for Mr Hughes merely because they are flattered by the idea of their constituency being represented by the Prime Minister. My vote represents the number of people in Victoria who put principle before everything else, the small number who could be reached by an organisation which is absolutely ignored by the powerful daily papers; but I would rather have my 7000 votes than the 200 000 recorded for the Labour Party, which betrayed the working people of Australia. It is a fact that cannot be gainsaid that any party that does not stand resolutely opposed to militarism is the enemy of the working people, even though it professes to represent them.

The vote against conscription was a magnificent **triumph for principle by the people**, but unfortunately the Labour Party could not follow up the victory to its logical conclusion — peace and anti-militarism, because the Labour Party in Australia is a Militarist Party. It stands for a worse phase of militarism than any other country — conscription of boys of 13. After October, 1916, the oppressed people of the world looked to Australia to save them from militarism. **Australia has failed them**. The honour and the privilege of giving the lead in this direction has fallen to the working people of Russia, and the working people of Germany are the first to respond to their Russian brothers. The Russian workers demand **PEACE WITHOUT ANNEXATIONS**. The German workers, as one would naturally expect Germans to be, are more direct and logical, and demand in addition the **ABOLITION OF COMPULSORY MILITARY SERVICE**.

We of the WPA have demanded this reform since the election of 1913, and it must now be our task to urge the workers and the women of Australia to unite in working for this great ideal. But we cannot work against compulsory military service, militarism and navalism, without working against the whole capitalistic system which militarism and navalism are instituted to defend. And that brings us to the root of the whole matter — the material foundation of individual and national life. The capitalistic system means a competitive struggle for existence, which is opposed to every law of justice and love. Until mankind is governed consciously by this law, existence will continue to be materialistic and competitive, instead of inspirational and co-operative.

Woman Voter (11 May 1917)

GWEN KELLY

(1922–)

Novelist, short story writer, and poet. Gwen Kelly née Smith was born and educated in Sydney. Variously a public servant, teacher, and lecturer, she began publishing stories and articles in the 1950s. One of her novels, Always Afternoon *(1981), set between 1915 and 1918, tells the story of a love affair between Freda Kennon, a young Australian woman, and Franz Müller, a German interned at Trial Bay, on the New South Wales coast, the site of an actual internment camp during the Great War. The book was made into a television mini-series in 1988.*

'COSMIC VENGEANCE'

Freda knew from the beginning they would capture him. He could not possibly get all the way from Trial Bay to Liverpool. Europeans and islanders lived in such tiny worlds. Those miles of distance which made up Australia deluded them. Yet she feared and hoped. He was clever, he was resourceful.

The soldiers called at the house, the evening following his escape. They had spent a futile day dragging the bay and searching the coastline. They were now searching the nearby homes. They had reason to believe, they told Nancy Kennon, that one of the prisoners had stolen food and clothing in the local area. They had found his camp suit washed up on the breakwater, but they did not think he had drowned. He could not wander through the scrub naked.

Freda recognized Sergeant Walker and the young guard, Frederic, whom Flora had married. She looked at him with such hostility that he was puzzled. This girl had been his wife's bridesmaid. 'It is unfortunate,' he said. 'Very,' said Freda.

Walker said to her mother, 'As a matter of fact you knew the chap. He stayed here last year. Herr Müller. We do not think he is dangerous.'

Freda saw clearly the deepening lines which now marked her mother's smooth skin. 'Oh dear,' said Nancy, 'not Franz. He played so beautifully. It's such a foolish thing to do.'

'This isolation can be killing,' said Walker almost bitterly. 'Actually, we suspect he swam the bay to avoid the sentries. Don't worry Mrs Kennon. We've combed the bush within the sentry lines. We don't really think he's still in this area.'

Nancy smiled. 'I shouldn't worry if he were,' she said. 'Franz would not harm us. He's not a violent young man. We became very fond of both him and Dr Stein.'

Freda felt a desire to hug her, but knew it would be unwise. She stood silently by the door watching the conversation.

Her mother pushed her hair back behind her ears, a sign of disturbance. 'But it is so foolish and Franz was not foolish. No one could get away from Laggers Point.'

'Exactly,' said Walker. 'That's why we're sure to get him. One prisoner did manage to make the break from Liverpool successfully but all the others, who tried it, have been either recaptured or killed. Laggers Point is worse.'

'What does Dr Stein say?' said Nancy.

'He says he knows nothing and I believe him, but all the prisoners have been confined within the walls for the moment. The Major is furious. He grilled Stein. Apparently the doc tried to get a transfer to Holdsworthy for Müller, and Berry turned it down. He thinks Stein encouraged him to escape.'

Freda said sharply, 'Why should he want to escape? If Dr Stein intervened, he must have had a legitimate reason.'

'His mother died and apparently his old man went a bit off his rocker as a consequence. He probably thought his father would end up like old man Schrieber.'

'I knew about his mother,' said Nancy. 'Poor boy. We should have tried to help. Surely the Major could have let him go.'

Walker cut in sharply, 'This war isn't a game, Mrs Kennon. The Major has had quite a few problems at the camp. I don't blame him for putting his foot down. It is unfortunate it had to be a pleasant chap like Müller. I'd rather get that arrogant swine, Edel, but Franz Müller has not been exactly co-operative. For that matter, none of the prisoners are Jesus Christ.'

Freda saw her mother stiffen. 'I am well aware of the problems of war, Sergeant Walker. We have not been immune in this house. Nor do we take the Lord's name in vain.'

The soldier muttered, 'I'm sorry, Mrs Kennon.'

Freda looked at him with distaste. She wanted to shout aloud, 'He's been walking out under your silly noses for almost a year.'

Walker said, 'I even liked Müller, but this is war and I am a soldier.'

'That's all right,' said Nancy gently. 'Do not feel distressed about doing your duty, Sergeant. My son, John, feels just the same way and I'm sure Greg would too. Make yourselves a cup of tea while we look through the rooms. Freda, you can search upstairs.' Suddenly the woman stopped. She looked straight into Freda's eyes. It was a strange look. 'No,' she said, 'you and Ella search downstairs. I'll go through the bedrooms myself.'

Freda felt distress, but she tried not to move even a muscle in her face. What was her mother implying? She could not ask.

'If you don't mind,' Walker said, 'Private Wollonski and I will come with you. Frederic, you go with Miss Kennon.'

'Very well,' said Nancy stiffly.

In John's wardrobe, Nancy looked at the empty hanger. John's best uniform. She knew exactly where it should be hanging, for she had recleaned it herself only last week, polishing the badges to keep everything bright and shiny for the Victory March. Suddenly she remembered Bill grizzling that morning about his missing work boots, and she had been sure she had sufficient fruit for the week, even though Freda had disagreed. For a second, she hesitated, then her eyes met those of Sergeant Walker. 'What is missing, Mrs Kennon?' he asked. She was an honest woman. 'My son's uniform,' she said, at last.

Bill was furious when he heard that Müller had probably escaped in his son's uniform. 'His rage,' thought Freda, 'is almost comic. He has turned the war into a religion since the conscription campaign and the Anzacs are the saints. He has even begun to collect the holy relics; badges, ribbons, uniforms. As if they matter.'

'My God,' he said, 'I hope they shoot the fellow. None of our women will be safe, if those Huns start climbing the walls.'

Nancy understood him better than Freda. He felt his hospitality to Müller had been abused. He had never been happy about Stein's visit that year.

'Calm down, my dear,' she said, her hand on his arm, 'look at it from his viewpoint. The perfect disguise. You'd be proud, if John or Greg escaped in an enemy uniform.'

'It's an insult,' said Bill. 'The fellow isn't even a soldier, but you have a lot of commonsense, Nancy, and no doubt you're right. Even so, I'm going to have a few words with Berry. That whole ruddy camp is too slack. I'm sick and tired of being treated like one of their tradesmen who forgot to go to the back door. I won't have them round this house at night stealing our possessions.'

'They think he climbed the verandah,' said Ella. 'The bushes on that side have broken twigs.'

Bill turned paler. 'He might have attacked Freda,' he said. 'I'll get a new bolt for her verandah door.'

'If you wish,' Nancy sighed. 'But you're wrong you know. There's no danger to Freda.'

'What do you mean?'

Nancy looked at her fingers, worn with housework and bleached with washing. 'Nothing,' she said, 'I was merely thinking a bolt would be superfluous.'

The little man was bewildered. She walked behind him, and took his head gently in her hands. 'We can rely on you to keep us safe,' she said.

Ailsa arrived home on leave the following weekend. The fear within Freda was stifling. Surely Ailsa would notice it. She felt a constriction in her throat, which made it physically difficult to talk, yet Ailsa wanted to talk, about her job, about Sydney, about John's chances in a land ballot, about Mary. When she heard the news of the escaped prisoner, she was as indignant as her father. The escapee might have killed them. If only, thought Freda, she could forget the subject, but Ailsa loved excitement. Every walk, she watched the bushes for the almost imperceptible movement; on the sand she scanned the sea for floating bodies, dead or alive. 'Every road is the road to Bapaume,' thought Freda. 'John is my brother. Erich was my boy friend. I will repay. Vengeful Ailsa.'

Ailsa lay on the rock in the centre of Little Bay. Her long, black hair hung loosely and uncharacteristically over her shoulders, the intense dark eyes and fierce brows gazed into the sky. Freda, standing knee-deep in the water below her, saw the ghosts of Franz and herself. She felt a premonition of disaster. Ailsa belonged to the fates. Not Andromeda but Atropos waiting patiently with her shears.

'You must understand, Freddie,' Ailsa was saying for the hundredth time, 'those men are dangerous. No German would hesitate to kill in the circumstances.'

Freda suddenly grabbed the water in her hands and threw it high into the air, a cascading mountain of water. 'Shut up, shut up,' she screamed, 'Franz Müller would kill no one. You know nothing about him. He was worried about his father. He's human, just like the Schriebers.'

Ailsa was white with anger. 'How dare you compare him with Kurt; what were his sufferings compared with Tom's and Erich's?'

Freda shook the descending water from her hair and looked up directly at her sister. The eyes of the sea maiden met the brown eyes of the earth maiden.

'Why not?' she demanded. 'That woman who died in Shantung was Franz's mother and the man shut up in Liverpool is his father. How does that differ from Marta and Kurt? They're people. Do you think our flesh is super-refined, simply because we were born in Australia?'

'Don't talk to me,' said Ailsa, 'don't ever talk to me again.'

She slid from the rock into the water and shook her sister by the shoulders. 'What do you know, stuck up here at Arakoon? John said you were crazy. He's right. You ought to see the men come off the ships, blinded, maimed, coughing out lungs destroyed by gas, minus legs or arms or hands. Personally, I hope they shoot the bastard. I'd like to do it myself.'

'And do you hope the Germans do the same when our boys escape? That some swine like you, will shoot them?'

Freda was shaking. Her whole body trembled, then stiffened like a child with convulsions. She forced herself to dive under the water where she lay limply face down in the sea to hide the spasms that ran over her.

'Freddie,' said Ailsa, 'darling Freddie, are you all right?' She put her arms beneath her body to support her sister. 'I shouldn't have said that. I know it's not easy to be cooped up here with Mum and Dad. I know one of us had to stay to help Mother.' The girl pushed the arm away and began to swim towards the ocean entrance. Ailsa noticed, as their bodies parted, how thin she was. What had happened to Freda in this backwater?

Freda swam to the sandbank, where the first breaker crashed into the bay, then she turned and looked back, her hair white against the blue of sea and sky. Ailsa swam to join her. A wave broke over their shoulders. Freda's eyes were fire below the fine silk of her brows, creased into two tiny lines above her nose.

'Don't be silly,' said Ailsa. 'The sea is too high for surfing. We'll drown.'

The girl simply said, 'Don't ever say things like that to me again, Ailsa. You're so full of slogans, religious and patriotic, that I sometimes wonder if you love at all; if you know what love means.' She turned to meet the sea and a wave carried her across the bar into the bay.

Ailsa swam back to the rock. There she lay face down and wept where no one could see her. What would Freda have done, if she had fallen in love with a devout Catholic in their tight little Protestant world? She raised her head and watched the back of her sister walking into the scrub, and knew within herself the answer. Freda would have gone with him. It was the unforgivable thing about her. She moved by instinct. Ailsa pushed the thought away. What right had Freda to talk about love? A kid's affair with Bob! And then, it was Erich who died, not Bob.

Back at the house she asked her mother, 'What's wrong with Freddie? She looks as if she's dying of TB.'

Her mother said, 'The wattle is lovely this year.'

She looked at the tree in the middle of the lawn. A new-born sun. Christians awake, but not a happy morn! 'Freda is quite well,' she added. 'The doctor says nervous strain combined with too much growth.'

'Nervous strain? Here?' There was scorn in Ailsa's voice. Nancy looked at her daughter, felt the hard core of resentment. 'There are great strains in Miltonic virtues,' she said. 'Standing and waiting day after day. Wondering about Greg and Bob, knowing that Erich and Kurt are dead. So much death, while we crouch at the still centre.'

Ailsa put her arms around her. They were firm and muscular. The practical girl. 'I'm sorry, Mother, and blind. I was caught up in my own nightmare, as if no one else suffered. It's hard not to resent, when you smell the decayed flesh, watch hands groping without vision. I find it hard to forgive those responsible for the war.'

Nancy looked calmly at her. 'I doubt if anyone deserves the present wrath,' she said, 'British or German. It's a cosmic vengeance.'

Ailsa shrugged. 'Well, it's my lot to see the broken individuals. It lessens the cosmic impact.'

Nancy merely nodded.

Always Afternoon (1981)

ADELA PANKHURST

(1885–1961)

Political activist. English-born Adela Pankhurst worked in Britain for the Women's Social and Political Union, which her mother Emmeline and sister Christabel founded, and was repeatedly jailed for suffragette activities. After falling out with her mother and Christabel, Adela arrived in Melbourne in 1914, where she became an organiser for Vida Goldstein. The latter's Women's Peace Army published Pankhurst's anti-war book Put Up the Sword *in 1915. Pankhurst subsequently went to work for the Victorian Socialist Party, which published her pamphlet* After the War — What? *(1917), from which these words are taken. Soon after her marriage to trade unionist Tom Walsh in September 1917, she was jailed for four months for having led a demonstration in Melbourne against the high cost of food during the war. Adela Pankhurst Walsh, as she became known, and her husband were founding members of the Communist Party of Australia, but later rejected communism and became right-wing in their views.*

'WARS AND THEIR AFTERMATH'

But if we are to look for the bright side of war, to the effect upon the personal character of the soldiers, judging by past experience, we shall find but a fitful gleam, and then return again to unrelieved darkness.

Never was our country more cruelly oppressed than after the Napoleonic wars, in which so many young men learned the higher virtues at the cannon's mouth. Every form of greed was practised by the rich upon the poor, until parents were driven by sheer starvation to sell their young children into the slavery of the factories and the mines, where many were beaten or worked to death, or became, both boys and girls, the victims of the unnatural lusts of their brutal overseers, while on their labor men grew rich and rose to positions of honor in the State.

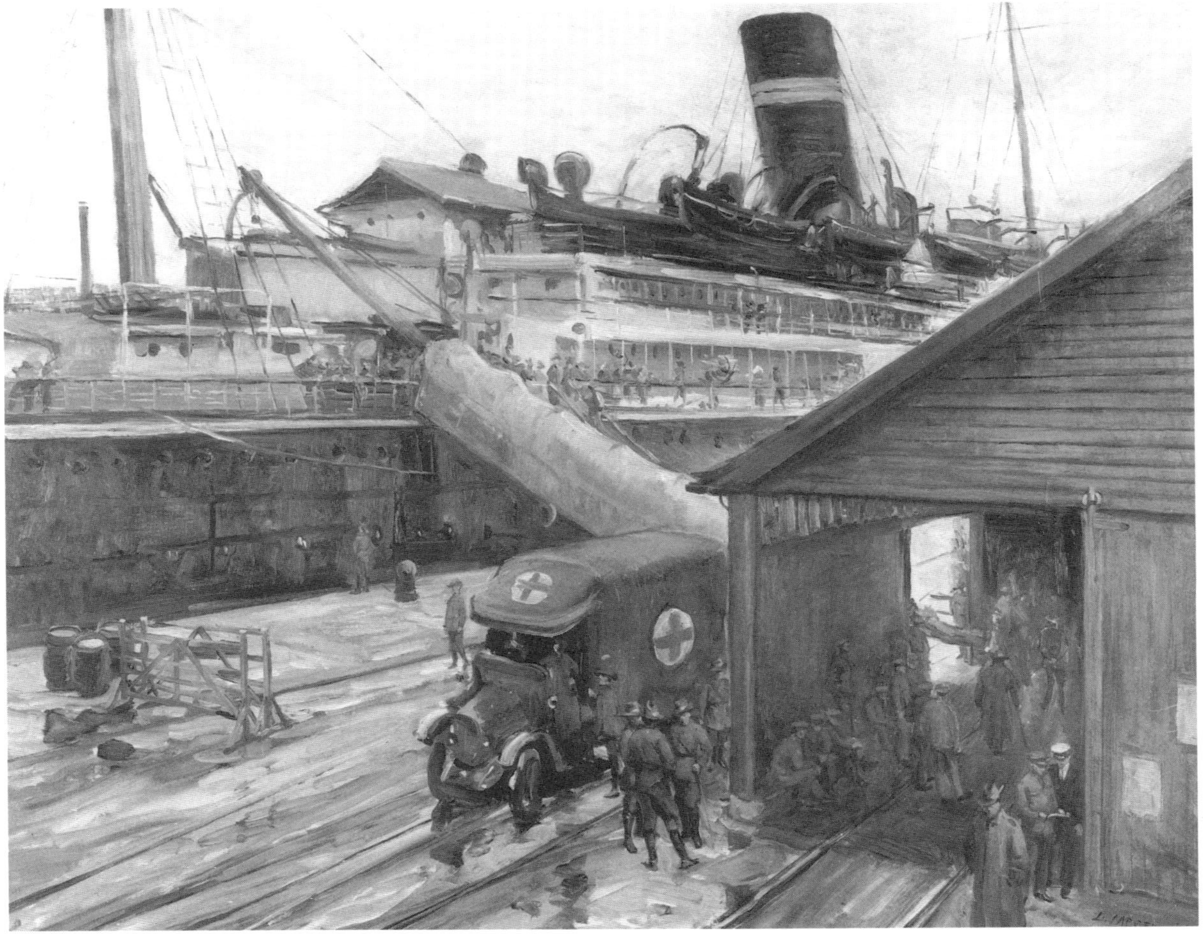

Dora Meeson (1869–1955), *Departure of the last Australian hospital ship from Southampton, England*, 1919, oil on canvas, 71.2 x 91.2 cm. Purchased in 1921. (AWM 3190)

Wherever hunger and misery drove men and women to revolt, they were violently repressed by the soldiers, who charged the wretched, unarmed crowds, and sabred women and children as readily as they faced the French in Europe. Pressed by hireling gangs, half-starved, beaten and tortured themselves, led by officers to whom the common people seemed scarcely human, the soldiers had ceased to be men with hearts and brains, and were but hired cut-throats, to whom bloodshed was a natural business.

Sooner or later this war, too, will end, and when it does the full effects will gradually make themselves felt. Materially they will be terrible.

Thousands of men will flock back from the battlefields to find their places in industry filled by women or children at lower wages. Scarcity of production will make prices high, ruined territories will destroy export trade and cause unemployment, the interest on the war loans will necessitate heavy taxes. These are but cold words; in human terms they mean homeless families driven to the workhouse, where even the holy tie between a mother and her children is broken; they mean the herding of boys and girls into cheap factories and sweat shops, where every form of vice is rampant; they mean the slow murder of mothers and babes by cold and hunger and diseases which privation and foetid slums must breed; they mean the sale of young girls into prostitution and the luring of young men into careers of violence and crime; they mean the watering with blood and tears of the seeds of racial decay which have choked and destroyed every nation which lives by the sword. Most terrible of all is the moral effect which hostilities on such a scale will inflict upon all whom the war touches. Immorality of the basest kind flourishes on the soil of poverty, and when millions are plunged into destitution, to whom are added hundreds of thousands of refugees from the invaded districts, the virtue of women, on which depends the sanctity of the home and the family, cannot fail to break down to a deplorable extent.

These facts do not find their way into our history books, but they are as potent to the nations which war with one another as defeats or victories, and their effects are deeper and more lasting. Where masses of people are herded together, where young girls and children are wandering without guardians in a strange country, the white slave traders find their best opportunity — especially when millions of troops, quartered in foreign countries and far from the civilising influences of their homes and families, provide an unparalleled market for their human wares.

After the War — What? (1917)

KATHARINE SUSANNAH PRICHARD

(1883–1969)

Writer. Katharine Susannah Prichard was born in Fiji, but grew up in Tasmania and Victoria. She was educated at South Melbourne College before becoming a journalist, writing for Australian and

English newspapers. The first of her numerous novels, The Pioneers, *was published in 1915. Her Western Australian goldfields trilogy,* The Roaring Nineties *(1946),* Golden Miles *(1948), and* Winged Seeds *(1950), is described in* The Oxford Companion to Australian Literature *(second edition, 1994) as her 'most contentious work'. The weight of historical and political detail in the trilogy, both a strength and a weakness, is evident in this extract from* Golden Miles, *in which Prichard focuses on the period around the two conscription referendums (October 1916 and December 1917) and the 'Win-the-War' federal election (May 1917).*

POLITICS

After the first referendum Sally hoped that Morris and Tom would forget their differences and settle down to a normal tolerant attitude towards each other. She hated to hear them bickering, and to see the antagonism that flared so easily when this subject was mentioned. Home had become merely a place in which they flung the most vicious hostilities of the campaign at each other.

Morris still could not forgive Tom for the part he had taken in defeating the referendum—though he thanked God, the West had voted solidly for conscription.

The Prime Minister said he would accept the verdict of the people, but Tom was sure the last had not been heard of the matter. Already voices were raised declaring that the referendum had been a mistake. A bill should have been introduced to enforce military service for overseas, or regulations promulgated under the War Precautions Act which would have had the same effect.

It was generally admitted that Mr Hughes might have tried either measure, had he been able to muster a majority of Labour members in support of such proposals. But this he could not do and was loath to precipitate an election. His expulsion from the Labour Party for persisting in a policy to which a majority of the members was opposed, created a situation that split the party and before long made an election inevitable.

The election campaign took a more or less normal course, with a few stormy meetings: but little doubt—in the minds of most people, that the elections would reflect decisions of the referendum. When it did not many Labour members lost their seats, and the Opposition 'swept the polls'. Even Morris was disturbed, although conscriptionists everywhere whooped jubilantly. The elections were regarded as a personal triumph for Hughes and the 'win-the-war' policy. Had the people regretted their verdict on conscription? Or was the election merely proof that the people of Australia would go any lengths to win the war, short of conscription. It was obvious after Hughes' policy speech that another referendum was on the cards.

The first referendum had stirred a lot of muddy water. Facts in relation to it were well known before the second referendum was taken.

On the goldfields, revelations in connection with the Maltese affair were a decisive factor in making many people vote against conscription. Everybody knew that before the first referendum there were hundreds of unemployed tramping the country in search of work. Mr

Hughes was accused of bringing a shipload of Maltese to work on the transcontinental railway. He denied that he was doing so. But after the referendum the facts leaked out. The French steamer *Gangé* was approaching the West Australian coast with two hundred and forty Maltese on board, when the French consul in Sydney was authorised to instruct the captain of the ship not to touch any West Australian port. He was directed to coal at Adelaide, and put the ship in quarantine: give out he was bound for Noumea and reduce speed so as not to reach Melbourne until two days after the poll. Tom had copies of the telegrams which were sent.

In relation to the soldiers' vote, there had been suppression of the results for a long time, and then a widespread impression gained ground that they had been 'doctored' to give a 'yes' majority.

All the prosecution, censorships and vilification levelled against men and women opposed to conscription, were continued with renewed violence during the months before the second referendum.

Most people smiled, but did not attach any importance to a poster which read: 'To arms, capitalists, parsons, politicians, newspaper editors, and other stay-at-home patriots! Your Country needs you in the trenches! Workers, follow your masters!'

It was hard to believe that the man responsible for that poster had been arrested and sentenced to fifteen months' imprisonment.

Soon afterwards twelve men of the IWW were arrested in Sydney and sentenced to ten and fifteen years' imprisonment and the IWW was declared an illegal organisation. Then mine men in the West were charged that, together with these members of the IWW, they had conspired 'to raise discontent and dissatisfaction amongst the subjects of our lord, the King'.

Among the accused men were Monty Miller and Mick Sawtell. Sally knew them both. Monty was eighty-four: a white-haired champion of the rights of working men, as courtly and dignified in his manner as a foreign aristocrat. Dinny and he were old mates. Monty had often sat on the verandah, expounding his views on socialism and industrial unionism, or reciting in a powerful, sonorous voice whole essays from Emerson, and speeches from the plays of Shakespeare. As a lad of eighteen he had fought in the Eureka stockade, and Sally had often heard him reminiscing about the historic struggle of the miners at Ballarat. Mick was a few years older than Tom, but they were good friends. A red-headed young man, full of fiery ideals and pacifist zeal for 'the emancipation of the working class', Mick was a bit confused in his ideas about practical organisation, Tom said. But Sally liked to listen when Mick talked to Tom about the books he had been reading. He was fond of poetry, and had given Tom a poem in a plain folder by Furnley Maurice, a young Australian writer. 'To God from the Weary Nations' it was called. Sally could remember Mick's voice, intoning passionately in the dark:

> The dreamers wait. What can the spirit urge
> Against the madness of this sorry day?
> How can the timid form of Peace emerge
> Unless the marshals let the dreamers say?
> And they are few and most forsaken, Lord,

Who slaved and suffered for their human hope,
Though Thou shalt give the martyrs to the sword,
Preserve the future from the hangman's rope.

Sally had learnt the verses. They haunted her, their lines recurring and running through her head as she went about her work, worried about Dick, the war and the referendum.

The trial of Monty and Mick on that seditious conspiracy charge disturbed her a good deal, although it gave Tom and Dinny a lot of ironic amusement.

Monty had defended himself and cross-examined Mick in order to make their point of view clear to the court.

Monty asked Mick whether he agreed with Emerson: 'That every government was one of force. A government of love had never been known, but if one ever was it would bring to their knees in contrition and tears those members of the community, previously looked upon as useless and criminals.'

Mick quoted Emerson back at him, to the effect that a government was a conservative force. If there was no one to come forward and risk jail, or at least prosecution, the world would never progress.

'Do you consider that Socrates was a good citizen?' asked Monty.

'Yes, and he died because of his good citizenship,' said Mick.

Between them, Monty and Mick traced the history of the struggle for progress from the time of Plato to the present prosecution, quoting from memory Shelley, Godwin, Tolstoy, Kropotkin and Marx: outlining revolutions in architecture, music and aesthetics, and defending 'the sacred right of members of the IWW to work in the interests of the working class to make the world a better place to live in'.

Even the daily press referred to 'the dramatic force and flow of language with which the two accused had held the attention of those in court'. Mr Justice Burnside, sentencing the men, said they had been found guilty, and he had to accept the verdict as being correct. But he was entitled to form his own opinions as to the circumstances in which these men had found themselves. 'Against not one of them had he heard anything stated to show that they were other than men of good character … The gravamen of the charge was the distribution of literature for which he did not think they were really responsible, and which he thought, in their calmer moments, they would themselves strongly denounce.'

There was a good deal of truth in all this, Dinny admitted. The accused were released on a bond to be of good behaviour, keep the peace and to obey the laws of the land.

Before the second referendum was taken, Sally was satisfied that Tom and Dinny were right. Their reasons for opposing conscription had been justified by the course of events.

She had read a book, exposing manipulation of the war loans in the interests of financial combines, the *Nation*, and other illegal publications which Eily and Tom were distributing. Why were those papers and books illegal, Sally asked. She resented being told she must not read something of vital interest to her. If information was false and unreliable, it could be disproved: if not, people were entitled to it. Women like herself felt the lives of their sons and husbands were at stake: the future of their children. It was outrageous that any government should tell grown men and women they must not read criticism of the way the war was being conducted, or hear what anybody had to say about the causes of war.

Sally felt as if she had been buffeted about in the suffocating heat of a goldfields dust storm. First of all, prepared to accept all the Prime Minister said as gospel, and agreeing with Morris that reinforcements for the men on active service must be kept up at all costs. Then wearing herself out in endless arguments with Tom and Dinny: shattered by the conflict between Morris and Tom. But now she had seen how the rights of the people were ignored by censorship and prosecutions: how unnecessary violence had been used against anti-conscriptionists, and that there had been a cynical abuse of law to incriminate them for putting the facts of their case before the people.

Dick had been wounded and was in hospital: she could think more clearly. He wrote that he had voted against conscription, and that most of the men in his platoon, in France, had done likewise. None of the boys were so favourably impressed with life in the army that they believed every single man in Australia ought to be run in to it.

'Happiest day of our lives,' Dick had written, 'will be coming home, and getting out of the army. We've had a bellyful of it, Sal-o-my! All very well for Billy Hughes to say "Allied generals have learnt much" since the Somme offensive and Pozières (20 000 casualties a month!). But most of us reckon we'd have to have a lot more confidence in army methods before we'd give the military a free hand with our young brothers. It sticks in the men's gizzards that in England it's against regulations for a common soldier to eat or drink in a pub frequented by officers. You wouldn't believe what a big effect this, and the everlasting saluting, has had on the attitude of Australian troops towards the military having any more rights over them. Tell dad I'll put on the gloves and give him a go round the yard if he votes for conscription.'

Morris was shaken by Dick's letter, but said Dick was influenced chiefly by concern for Tom and Din. Both of them were in reserved occupations, and Morris asserted conscription would not affect them. But in any case the wider issues had to be considered. There was a falling-off in recruiting, and the war had to be won.

'No, Morris,' she said firmly. 'I don't any longer believe conscription is in the best interests of the Australian people. Reinforcements have been kept up, and I wouldn't trust this government any further than I can see it.'

Golden Miles (1948)

GRACE ETHEL MARTYR

(dates unknown)

Writer of patriotic verse. Some of the poems in Martyr's very slim volume, Afterwards and Other Verses *(1918), originally appeared in the Melbourne* Argus *and elsewhere. The second edition is padded out with two pages of extracts from reviews of the first edition, which are, to say the least, mixed. The* Sydney Morning Herald *reviewer, for example, says, 'Miss Martyr's work is unequal, but is always characterised by sincerity, depth of feeling, and a burning patriotism, which redeems many short-comings. Her technique is usually correct, and at best she can reach a high level of dignified expression.' What more can one say?*

'AFTERWARDS'

When all this long-drawn agony is past
And he returns, he will have memories
That cling about his heart, and hold him fast,
It will be hard to take up life again,
And he will often long and long in vain,

For that high purpose of those dangerous days,
And for beloved and splendid comrades gone.
And he alone, amid our narrow ways,
With poignant thoughts he never can forget
Will stand apart, amid the toil and fret

Of life. And sometimes on a sultry day,
When sudden thunder speaks among the hills,
And summer lightning flames its yellow way
Across the sky, then he will see once more
The flash, and hear the thundering cannon's roar.

Or 'neath the still white wonder of the moon,
Or in the sunshine of a summer day,
Or in the deep blue glory of the noon,
Some bygone scene will stab his heart as he
Stands sudden face to face with memory.

He watched so long the doors of Death beside
While many passed him by and entered in
Between its portals, flung so welcoming wide,
And there he learnt how grave is Life, how great;
Learnt its solemnity beside the gate.

And light regard of any sacred thing
For which he suffered so — the thoughtless word,
The careless laugh, will wound his heart and sting.

Heart sore, he'll stand among forgetful men;
With you it lies to be beside him then,

With faithful friendship, quick to understand,
To watch and cheer, to comfort him and shield,
The one thing steadfast in the shifting sand—
A rock unshaken in a restless sea—
The motive power to lift him, so that he

Will look with courage to the heights afar,
And climb the path of life that lies before,
And fix his eyes in hope upon the star
That shines above that distant goal and dim,
Where many a watching comrade waits for him.

Afterwards and Other Verses (second edition, 1918)

ALICE DAVIES

(dates unknown)

Farmer. Alice Davies was the mother of Evelyn 'Tevie' Davies, who appears earlier in this anthology. During the war, Alice and her son Rupe were running the family's fruit farm, called 'Fron', which was situated on the road between Healesville, then a popular holiday destination, and the Blacks' Spur. Alice Davies was a woman with very strong opinions, some of which she expresses in this letter to her daughter.

LIFE AT FRON

Fron,
Healesville
20.3.1918

My dear Tevie,

Just a short chat.

They never tell us when the mail is going until the day before. I wrote last week perhaps the two will go together. We have had storms and hot weather alternately, but the hail has not been as bad as the storm I wrote about. Rupe had to send most of the apples to the jam factory, as the hail cut holes in them. We have been ever since picking up falls. I wrote for you to get it for your birthday. I hope you got it although there was nothing but good wishes in it. I was thinking about you all that day, wondering what you were doing and did anyone know it was your birthday. 'Jimmy' Downey and wife have left and the Footscray brother & family are up. He looks smaller and uglier than ever but they are none of them handsome. Easter will soon be here, a big crowd is expected. Mannix has been trying to rouse the RCs to a riot. Hughes is as weak as water and takes all his time hanging on to his billet as Prime Minister. He was and is a great disappointment to all Loyalists. One of the Lalors came back lately, he was gassed another is coming back next week paralysed. There was a boy 17, rushing up and down the roads with a lot of loud women in a Motor. The women were about 30 years of age but the singing and shrieking could be heard a mile off. It seems the wretched boy stole £175 of his grandfathers and the harpies got hold of him and helped to spend it. Miss Stephens has gone and I am so sorry, it was nice to have an educated friend to chat to. The Healesville Band have been having ructions but a meeting was held last Monday and things were smoothed over. One of Lawyer Reg Kelly's sons has returned from Active Service with a blind eye. We are always hearing rumours of Mails sank and some time ago several said they saw aeroplanes of the enemy flying over the coast. Now we learn there was the seaplane belonging to the German 'Wolf' flying over. So it is getting near home. Perhaps it will waken people up. There was a record crowd at the races last week and some of the papers described the women's dresses. It disgusts me! The little boy is growing fast but is very slow in talking. I have been writing a lot of labels. I still use the stamp you made years ago. It is alright yet and does good work. Rupe has to go into camp with the Civilian forces next month. He was to have gone this month but got leave because of the fruit. Major Downey told me how monotonous the food was in England. I feel sorry for you and wish I could help. I hope at least some of the parcels turned up. A Captain Mitchell came to see me Sunday. I knew him forty years ago. His son is in the Flying Corps, England. Good bye dearest little Tevie. We are all keeping well and I do not have to wear glasses yet.

From your ever loving Mum

Evelyn Davies Papers

GERTRUDE MOBERLY

(dates unknown)

Army nurse. Queensland-born Gertrude Moberly nursed in England, on hospital ships, and in India, with the Australian Army Nursing Service, from 1915 to 1919. According to Lieutenant-Colonel E. Hilmer Smith, who wrote the foreword to Moberly's horribly titled book, Experiences of a 'Dinki Di' R.R.C. Nurse *(1933), 'The experiences related herein are not those drawn from the imagination, but are really a collection of letters written at the time when impressions and incidents were fresh in the mind.' That is not quite the case. Gertrude Moberly* was *an army nurse who was awarded a Royal Red Cross. But she had not actually met the fiancé to whom the letters are addressed in the book at the time of the war. However she decided to rewrite her war diary in the form of love letters. Her fiancé (later husband), Jim Hogan, is called Peter in the book, she is Babs. In this extract from one of the 'letters', she writes about the Hislop War Hospital, near Secunderabad, where she was matron from February 1918.*

LIFE IN INDIA

Now about this Hislop War Hospital. First of all I must tell you I have had to purchase a bicycle, for the distances are so great—quite two miles from the far-away barrack building, where some of our infectious patients are—then we have all the sick Sisters to nurse from the other hospitals as well as our own. Colonel Way is splendid, and upholds me in everything. It is a pleasure to work with an OC one has such respect for. You would smile could you take a peep at the scene enacted daily. Generally at 11 sharp the OC's boy, or rather orderly, appears at the door of my office, salutes, and informs the 'burra memsahib' (for that is my official name), meaning 'great lady' or 'head serang,' that Colonel sahib awaits to go on our daily round of the hospital. On to my bike I am like the shot out of a gun, and join the OC, who is also on an iron horse; behind comes the senior MO, the Adjutant and Quartermaster. Quite a procession of us. But, my dear, this is nothing to when we have a visit from the numerous Generals who come periodically to inspect Hislop. I have counted as many as ten of us in a line, and I have to introduce the nursing staff, who all stand at attention. By the time I have come to the thirty-seventh a prayer of thanksgiving goes up above for being helped to remember all those Sisters' names, for really, it is addling to the brain, so many names one after the other. My dear little bungalow, called 'Bleak House,' I have to myself. My boy is splendid—keeps it like a new pin. Indians make splendid servants; he not only attends to my wants in my bungalow, but waits upon me at table, sees to all my wearing apparel, keeps my shoes as white as snow, and at mid-day, after tiffin, brushes my yards of hair, and when I drop to sleep, awake to find a peculiar bun of hair tightly coiled on top of my head. Really, Peter, I never have to glance at my mending or darning, he gets the derzee (tailor) for that, the dhobee for my laundry, the mo-chee for making and mending my shoes, and the marli to keep the garden in order. I am sending you two snaps of my bungalow and one of me just off to meet the OC for our daily round. I sleep out under the trees, and God's Heaven is full of bright stars this time of the year. June, July and August are the monsoonal months. Shall I ever forget the Indian Ocean? She was for all the world like one would be on the horns of a mad bull, tossed in the air till one's inside was like curdled milk. Do you know, Pete, once I dragged my youngest sister off the horns of an angry cow? but, 'Deo gratias,' she had not reached the stage of curdled milk. But now, dear, to return to the beauties of the 7th Hussars' Bungalow. By the way, do you know how this crack regiment derived its name? because I have only come by the knowledge since being an inmate of their 'mess.' (Orig.): A soldier of the national cavalry of Hungary. (Hun huszar-husz, twenty, because at one time in Hungary one cavalry soldier used to be levied from every twenty families.)

Peter, I had to run away in the middle of writing to you, and now we are in March, and I am still smiling over a letter from my sister Ethel, in which she tells me 'rain teeming down, all the clothes on lines sopping; painters in the house. Poor old daddy turned out of his study, and I in the very devil of a temper.' Peter, in answer, am telling her 'to every cloud there is a silver lining.' I (her sister Babs) am roasting hot, one million letters to be answered, the d—— mosquitoes drawing my life-blood, but still smiling, and thinking of all the dear ones in Aussie. Am sitting in my bungalow sitting-room, from the window of which I see first the large stone verandah, with stone steps; on each step, both sides, are lovely pot plants; then, immediately in front of bungalow a huge old tree stands in the centre of drive, at the bottom of which is a white gate; then the road to Secunderabad, and just beyond, the polo ground, with a background of undulating hills. As I write the sweeper (a woman marli) is sweeping up the leaves; such a queer-looking soul: bedecked with bangles, anklets, rings, ear-rings and necklace, with only a scant covering over her poor, thin old body. They sweep with a broom made of fine sticks, and keep going from daylight till dark. The marli keeps her going; she has no other occupation. I had to go at this juncture, for another sick Sister was admitted from the Station Hospital. The Matron returned my call yesterday. We only have four beds. This Sister will have to sleep on the verandah. We have such a very pretty church at Bolarum, where we cycle on Sunday evenings. The service is at 6.30, so that gives us good time to get back to our mess for dinner, which is at 8.30 p.m. We have the old-fashioned punkahs in this church. The punkah-wallahs pull them from outside, ropes being attached. I like the preacher, C of E, with a very cultured voice and good delivery. We are dreadfully busy, and although thirty-seven nurses is a fair staff, the 1000 beds being scattered makes it much harder to arrange, and at present, two are away on annual Leave, two have malaria, with temperatures often reaching 105 and 106 deg.

The Colonel is quite pleased with me for taking chota pegs (whisky and soda). He says it is a preventive of malaria, and really, Peter, it will be jolly ripping if I escape the diseases of India. At present we have in isolation four officers, each in a separate room, one with smallpox, another measles, another diphtheria, and the fourth mumps — quite a variety. I am most interested in the smallpox patient, not having had much experience with that horrid disease. The OC orderlies and I are his nurses, for we are most anxious not to have it spread any further. Fancy, Pete, the railways are very particular over here. Today I was amused to receive twelve annas (1s.), refunded to me, as they had over-charged on my fare that huge sum, though how, when or where, I know not.

Experiences of a 'Dinki Di' R.R.C. Nurse (1933)

RUTH PARK

(1923–)

Writer. Ruth Park was born and raised in New Zealand, where she became a journalist. After their marriage in 1942, she and her Australian husband, D'Arcy Niland, travelled in the outback, then settled in the Sydney suburb of Surry Hills where they became full-time writers. From 1973 to 1985, Park lived on Norfolk Island (Niland had died in 1967). Her novels include Swords and Crowns and Rings *(1977), which won the Miles Franklin Award for 1977. The book's main characters are*

Jackie Hanna and Cushie Moy, who grow up in the fictitious New South Wales town of Kingsland. Here they take part in some of the celebrations that occur after news of the armistice spreads. Jerry MacNunn ('The Nun') is Jackie's stepfather, Peggy MacNunn his mother.

PEACE

As he left the house he noticed how bright everything was. People had left all their lights turned on. The Salvation Army marched past, all six of them. Their one lassie was a stout old duck who'd been a naughty barmaid in Sydney in her youth and had repented it ever since.

Jerry was astonished that his little town had so large a population. The main street was so crowded that no one could move. They fought, wriggled, fainted, screamed, cursed, amongst growing clouds of dust. A hysteric sentimentality prevailed. The mayor, sunset-faced on the hastily assembled official platform outside the town hall, inaudibly prayed, condemned, thanked, and was cheered to the echo. The half a band played 'Boys of the Dardanelles', 'Rule Britannia', 'The Old Hundredth'.

There was liquor everywhere. The publicans of three of the hotels had rolled out barrels of free beer. Quickly emptied whisky bottles passed amongst the crowd. The Nun, even as he drank, hoped that his old woman wasn't getting stuck into too much of it.

In the park, closely watched by the Fire Brigade, the flames licked up the post where the effigy of the Kaiser hung, his withered arm pinned across a chest heavy with jam-tin-lid medals. People threw things, clods, potatoes, dried horse manure, at the smouldering figure. Jerry, though he felt foolish and shaky with goodwill, thought it was an ugly scene, and he was glad when some moron hit the dangling dummy fair and square with a bottle of kerosene and the whole thing exploded in a pillar of fire. Some were burned, some knocked off their feet by the hoses being dragged here and there. Jerry was glad to see his wife's blue hat, now askew above a flushed face, well back in the crowd, and Jackie and Cushie on the very edges of it, dancing with excitement.

He pushed his way to them. 'Keep away from these boneheads,' he advised. 'You're likely to get wet to the skin.'

But of course the Fire Brigade didn't dare put the bonfire out, in spite of the captain's bellowed threats. They would have been mobbed if they had.

'You mind you look after Cushie, now,' Jerry said to his son.

Father Link went past, looking friendless, though there were many of his parishioners amongst the crowd. He had soft ginger hair like wool, a mouth pulled down into a strange shape as though it had been paralysed in the very act of saying 'Pip'.

'Poor lonely bugger,' thought Jerry. He wrung the priest's hand, said, 'Great night, eh? All over.'

Then he gave him a nerve nut. It must have done Father Link good, for some time later Jerry saw him moving self-consciously around in a circle, hand in hand with the blacksmith on one side and Mrs MacNunn on the other, singing:

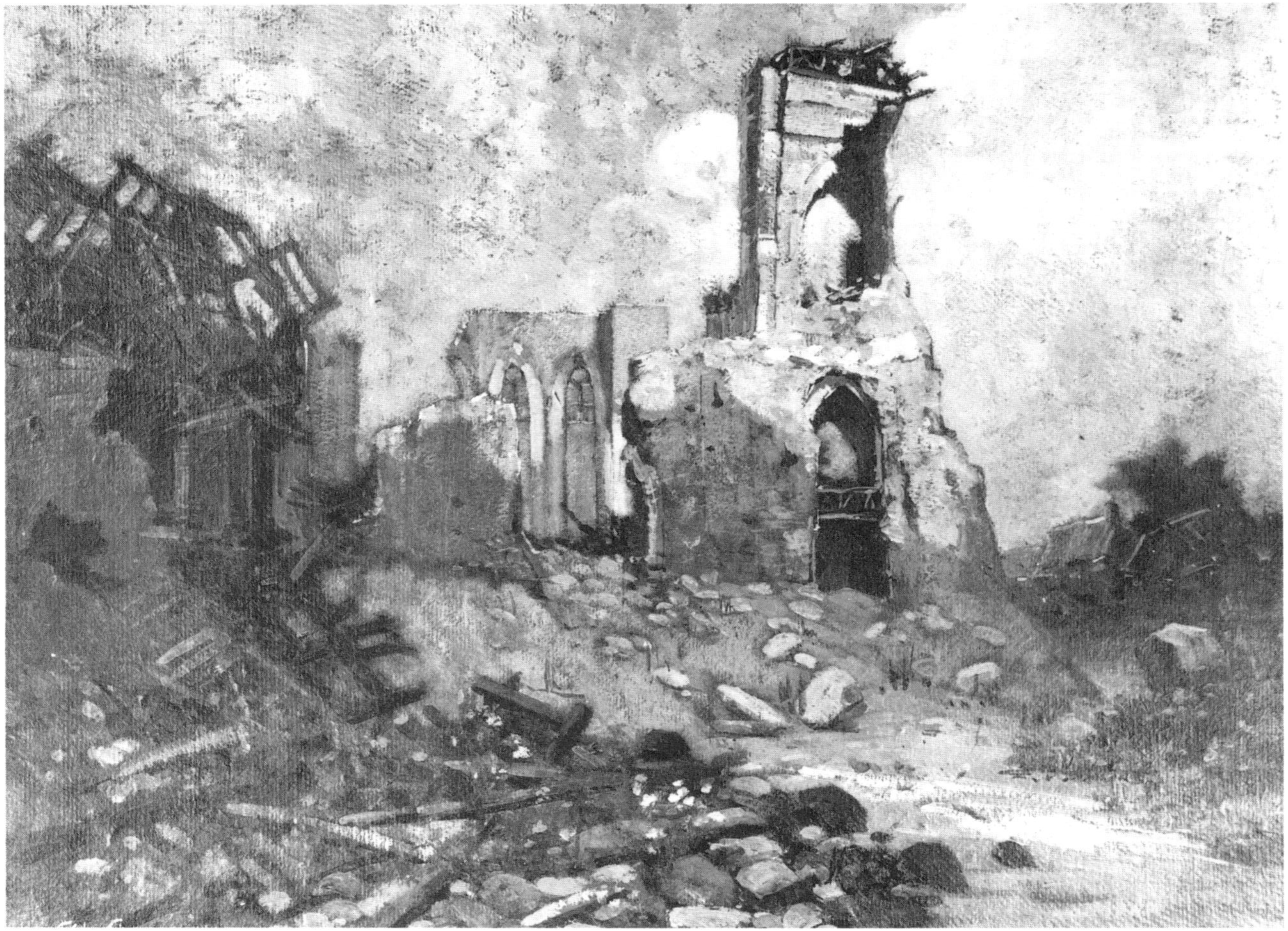

Evelyn Chapman (1888–1961), *Ruins of the church of Villers-Bretonneux*, 1919, tempera on cardboard, 55.6 x 74.6 cm. Purchased in 1977. (AWM 19585)

In the sweet by and by
We shall meet on that beautiful shore,
In the sweet, in the sweet, in the sweet by and by.

The Nun thought he had better sit down somewhere. The combination of whisky and Hean's Tonic Nerve Nuts had sent him into a curious languor. His fingertips were numb, and his bad leg in limbo, the pain having changed to a long-distance kind of pins and needles. Half-sprawled in the plushy dust near the Gallipoli memorial, he enjoyed a blissful melancholy.

The figures that staggered and jerked about the bonfire were all known to him. A few were friends, many were customers; but they were more than that. They were members of the Kingsland tribe, split up into septs and families, his tribe now, their involved folklore part of his own life and history. They were all part of the poor silly bloody human race, pitiable, mindlessly stomping around in the dust, off their heads because some other silly bloody humans had been killed, pauperised, bereaved, humiliated, beaten.

In his god-like drunken remoteness, Jerry felt nothing for them but impersonal affection.

'The Huns, too,' he thought. His wife found him. A beatific smile was fixed on her face as though tacked there. It stayed there even when tears began to trickle down her cheeks.

'God, you're a sloppy old bint,' he said. 'What's up now?'

'I was thinking,' she babbled. 'I was thinking of Piper Nicolson. His boy and all. Gawd, I been hard.' She burst out, 'I want to go and see him, Jerry. Tell him I'm sorry about Baillie.'

'Better not,' said Jerry. 'Come on now, you sit down here and forget it. You've taken too much aboard, not being used to it.'

She appealed to Jackie and Cushie, standing interestedly by.

'That's the decent thing, isn't it, kids? Make it up, comfort poor old Piper, the Christian thing to do. Holding grudges all this time, it's wicked.' She broke down and sobbed copiously.

'All right, all right, I'll take you,' said her husband.

Slowly and uncertainly they moved towards Edward Street. The main street was so carpeted with confetti that in places it was as soft underfoot as a lawn. Outside the post office the Salvation Army band continued to play between two carbide lamps.

'Wait, got to give them something,' mumbled Mrs MacNunn. She pressed a shilling into the elderly captain's hand. 'Goo' man,' she sobbed. 'Peace now. All brothers, goo' will to men. Play "Faith of Our Fathers" for me now.'

Swords and Crowns and Rings (1977)

DOROTHY HEWETT

(1923–)

Playwright, poet and novelist. Dorothy Hewett was born and raised in Western Australia, the daughter of a Wickepin wheat farmer. She wrote The Man from Mukinupin, *a two-act musical play, in response to a commission to write a play to mark the sesquicentenary of European settlement in Western Australia in 1979. It is, in the words of the blurb of the 1980 edition, 'a musical celebration of country life in Australia, set in a Western Australian wheat belt town at the time of the Great War'. The following lines about poor Harry Tuesday, 'a shearer who becomes a shell-shocked war hero', are from the second act. The war is over. The other characters whom we meet here are Clarry Hummer, the town dressmaker, her sister Clemmy, Eek Perkins, the local storekeeper, his wife Edie, and their beautiful daughter Polly.*

HARRY TUESDAY

(The light begins to fade as HARRY TUESDAY enters in ragged moleskins, a black singlet, a slouch hat, bare feet and drinking a bottle of beer. He is already very drunk. He sits at the foot of the war memorial.)

CLARRY: (*whispering*) There's Harry Tuesday.

HARRY: I was awarded a VC an' two bars for givin' a corp. a kick in the arse.

(He chuckles wildly.)

CLEMMY: Harry's back home.

CLARRY: It's a wonder he's saved his neck this long.

(HARRY *begins to sing drunkenly.*)

HARRY: (*singing*)

I wanta go home, I wanta go home,
I don't wanta go to the trenches no more,
where hand-grenades an' whizzbangs they roar.

(*Speaking*) I'm shickered, an' may the best man win.

EDIE: I never speak, I cannot speak of these matters, without I ... choke with emotion.

EEK: The Albany doctor'll [a southerly breeze] be blowing up soon.

HARRY: (*singing*)

So send me over the sea
where the Heinies can't get at me,
O my, I'm too young ter die
I wanta go home.

EDIE: Lowest creatures on God's earth. They're all only animals ... animals ...

HARRY: And there was nobody left in the whole bloody platoon.

(*He collapses, laughing again.*)

EDIE: Well, I hope she's gone for good, that's all. I hope she's gone for good. (*Firmly*) Because I tell you, Eek Perkins, I've never been so humiliated—serving your bastard.

(EEK *drops his paper and stares at her. There is a long pause. He picks it up again.*)

EEK: Wheat's up seven and fourpence ha'penny a bushell.

(*Long pause.* EDIE *stares hiccuping into the night;* EEK *reads his paper.*)

The only way you can teach a nigger is with a big stick.

(CLARRY *sews,* CLEMMY *fans herself, as* HARRY *continues to sing into the darkness.)*

HARRY:

Where whizzbangs are flyin' and brave men are dyin'
for bastards like you, dinky-di, dinky-bloody-die,
dinky-die, dinky-di, dinky-di.
dinky-bloody-di ...

(HARRY moves off, singing and taking a swig from his bottle, as the lights come up on POLLY entering with bolts of material. POLLY, CLARRY and CLEMMY make a semi-circle sewing bee; EEK changes his paper for the earphones of a crystal set [radio]. POLLY begins sewing.)

The Man from Mukinupin (1980 edition, first published 1979)

AILEEN YOUNG

(dates unknown)

Army masseuse. Thirty or forty members of the Australian Army Massage Service, mostly female, served overseas during the Great War, one of the originals being Aileen Young. In June 1919 she wrote this account of her war work, which now would be called physiotherapy, for the official Australian medical historian, A. G. Butler. The No. 1 Australian Auxiliary Hospital, where she spent most of her time while abroad, occupied a large house and grounds at Harefield, about forty kilometres north of London.

MASSAGE

I joined No. 1 AAH as masseuse on 10th of Aug. 1915.

There were 3 of us there at that time and the work was fairly strenuous the majority of the patients had not had any massage treatment before coming to us and as it was sometimes months before we got them the results were pretty bad. However about November 1915 we were reinforced, and our staff gradually increased to 11. By this time the Hospital had grown to 1000 beds, and we still had plenty to do. At the beginning all our work was done in the wards, but when Colonel Dennis took charge of the department we were given wards of our own for massage and electric treatment.

We did some medical work but owing to the fact that we were nearly always short-staffed most of our attention had to be turned to the surgical cases. A great percentage of the fracture cases also had nerve lesions, I was fortunate enough to have a good deal of this work to do. We did not keep the patients long enough to see any absolute recoveries of course, but the improvement in many cases was more than satisfactory. Radiant Heat and Electricity were a large factor in our treatment of stiff joints and Rheumatism especially.

Our wards were splendidly equipped which gave us every chance of getting the best results from our work, and I think the men for the most part were satisfied and happy.

I was in this hospital for $3^1/_2$ years when I was sent to No. 1 AGH at Sutton Veny, to make another start, with another of the original No. 1 AAH Masseuses. The AIF had just taken over the Hospital, and we had nothing to work with at all.

Captain Brown was in charge of our department here and he very soon had a ward fitted up for Electric treatment & Radiant heat.

As there were only four of us working we again had a busy time, doing about 9 hours duty a day. Each having about 24 or 25 patients. There were a great many fractured Femur cases. I had 17 on my own list out of 24 cases. Many of these had not had any massage treatment although they were very old wounds some of them ununited. Most of them responded well. We also found that massage helped in the healing of old wounds.

I have been out for 4 years. We have had some very good times amongst the bad ones. And I have been fortunate enough to be in Hospitals where our work has been made as pleasant as possible.

Butler Papers

NETTIE PALMER

(1885–1964)

Writer and critic. Nettie Higgins studied at the University of Melbourne and overseas, before a brief period of teaching at her old school, Presbyterian Ladies College, Melbourne. She married fellow Australian Vance Palmer in London in May 1914. In France when war broke out, they soon returned to England, where their first daughter was born. They came back to Australia in 1915, where their second daughter was born in 1917. Both Nettie and Vance (who served abroad with the AIF in 1918 and 1919) opposed censorship and conscription. Nettie had already had two slim volumes of poetry published before this moving poem appeared in the War Memorial Number of the Melbourne University Magazine *in July 1920. Nettie Palmer was to become one of the most influential literary critics in Australia in the 1930s and 1940s.*

'THEIR PEACE'

Now peace has come, but they that fell
Know only that they sought it well.
They cannot know that peace has come!

How did it come? Like dawn, like night?
Like one bird singing for the light?
Surely they knew that peace would come!

How did it come? On silent feet,
Across the grass that dew made sweet?
They could not hear the stillness come.

O, still joy after changing years!
Fathers and sons bring home their spears
(But *they* know not that peace has come).

'Peace!' we have said, yet held our breath.
'A moment free from lowering death!'
They know not such faint peace has come.

Joy in our hearts, yet bitter dread,
Lest vainly, vainly life was shed.
For *they* must know that peace has come.

Let us make haste and let us build
Great worlds with strength and wonder filled,
Then shall they know their peace has come.

Melbourne University Magazine (July 1920)

MARY GRANT BRUCE

(1878–1958)

Writer. The main characters in Mary Grant Bruce's series of Billabong novels, David, Jim, and Norah Linton, and Wally Meadows, are still in England at the end of the war. They return home in Back to Billabong *(1921), which Bruce wrote in 1920, in Traralgon, after she and her family had returned to Australia on the troop-ship* Nestor*, the same ship on which she and her husband had sailed to England early in the war. Mary Grant Bruce's biographer, Alison Alexander, comments that 'Mary described what she knew, and her characters return to Australia in just the same sort of ship as the Bruces had done (although in the Lintons' case it is not exactly the same ship, as that would have been too much of a coincidence, though it had happened in real life).'*

'FAMILIAR LANDMARKS'

They watched the light pass slowly from the dim region that meant the Heads, until, as the pilot boat swung out through the Rip to where the *Nauru* lay, her other lights grew clear, and presently her whole outline loomed indistinctly, suddenly close to them. She lay to

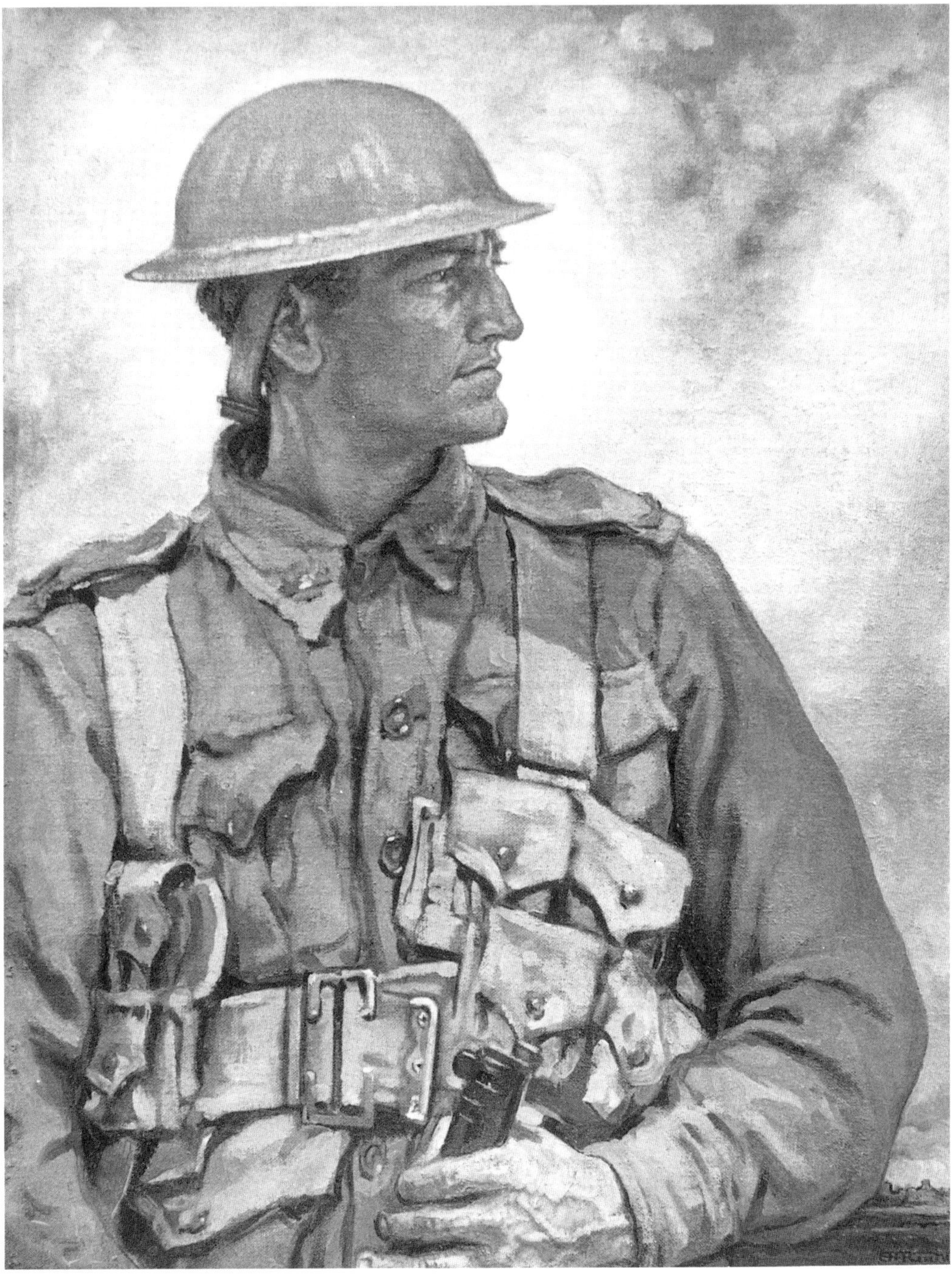

Hilda Rix Nicholas (1884–1961), *A Man*, 1921, oil on canvas, 92 x 75 cm. Purchased in 1979. (AWM 19613)

across a little heaving strip of sea, and presently the pilot was being pulled across to them by a couple of men and was coming nimbly up the *Nauru*'s ladder, hand over hand. He nodded cheerily at his welcome — a fusillade of greetings from every 'digger' who could find a place at the railings, and a larger number who could not, but contented themselves with shouting sweet nothings from behind their comrades. A lean youngster near Jim Linton looked down enviously at the retreating boat.

'If I could only slide down into her, an' nick off to the old Alvina over there, I'd be home before breakfast,' he said. 'Me people live at Queenscliff — don't it seem a fair cow to have to go past 'em, right up to Melbourne?'

The pilot's head appeared above on the bridge, beside the captain's, and presently the *Nauru* gathered way, and, slowly turning, forged through the tossing waters of the Rip. Before her the twin lights of the Heads opened out; soon she was gliding between them, and under the silent guns of the Queenscliff forts, and past the twinkling house lights of the little seaside town. There were long coo-ees from the diggers, with shrill, piercing whistles of greeting for Victoria; from ashore came faint answering echoes. But the four people from Billabong stood silently, glad of each other's nearness, but with no words, and in David Linton's heart and Norah's was a great surge of thankfulness that, out of many perils, they were bringing their boys safely home.

The *Nauru* turned across Port Phillip Bay, and presently they felt the engines cease, and there came the rattle of the chain as the anchor shot into the sea.

'As the captain thought,' said Jim. 'He fancied they'd anchor us off Portsea for the night and bring us up to Port Melbourne in the morning, after we'd been inspected. Wouldn't it be the limit if some one developed measles now, and they quarantined us!'

'You deserve quarantining, if ever anyone did,' said Norah, indignantly. 'Why do you have such horrible ideas?'

'I don't know — they just seem to waft themselves to me,' said Jim modestly. 'Anyhow, the quarantine station is a jolly little place for a holiday, and the sea view is delightful.' He broke off, laughing, and suddenly flung his arm round her shoulders in the dusk of the deck. 'I think I'm just about insane at getting home,' he said. 'Don't mind me, old kiddie — and you'd better go to bed, or you'll be a ghost in the morning.'

They weighed anchor after breakfast, following a perfunctory medical inspection — so perfunctory that one youth who, having been a medical student, and knowing well that he had a finely-developed feverish cold, with a high temperature, and not wishing to embarrass his fellow-passengers, placed in his mouth the wrong end of the clinical thermometer handed him by the visiting nurse. He sucked this gravely for the prescribed time, reversing it just as she reappeared; and, being marked normal and given a clean bill of health, returned to his berth to shiver and perspire between huge doses of quinine. More than one such hero evaded the searching eye of regulations; until finally the *Nauru*, free to land her passengers, steamed slowly up the Bay.

One by one the old, familiar landmarks opened out — Mornington, Frankston, Mordialloc, while Melbourne itself lay hidden in a mist cloud ahead. Then, as the sun grew stronger the mist lifted, and domes and spires pierced the dun sky, towering above the jumbled mass of the grey city. They drew closer to Port Melbourne, and lo! St Kilda and all the foreshore were gay with flags, and all the ships in the harbour were dressed to welcome them; and beyond the pier were long lines of motors, each beflagged, waiting for the fighting men whom the *Nauru* was bringing home.

Back to Billabong (1921)

ANGELA THIRKELL

(1890–1961)

Writer. Angela Mackail was born and educated in London. A great beauty, she married a bisexual, alcoholic professional singer, James Campbell McInnes, in 1911, but divorced him in 1917. On the rebound, she married a Tasmanian engineer, George Allnutt Thirkell, in London in December 1918. 'Thirk', who had served with the AIF in Egypt, Gallipoli, and France, was a thoroughly decent chap, but no match culturally for Angela. They and her two sons by McInnes sailed to Australia on the troop-ship Friedrichsruh *in 1920. The nine-week voyage was a nightmare. One of Angela's sons, Graham McInnes, later wrote that 'The* Friedrichsruh *deserves a special word as possibly the most exasperating ship that ever put to sea.' The Thirkells had a son, but Angela was unhappy and returned to England minus her husband, temporarily in 1927–28, and permanently in 1929. Her novel* Trooper to the Southern Cross, *based upon the 1920 voyage, was published in 1934 under the pseudonym 'Leslie Parker'. Unaware of its author's real identity, the literary critic H. M. Green, in his* A History of Australian Literature, *vol. II (1961), described it as 'an entertaining as well as informative account, coloured strongly by the simple, practical, and consciously and unconsciously amusing personality of the narrator, a medical major, of what may well have happened more than once on a repatriation voyage'. In fact, it is a witty, biting satire. Angela Thirkell went on to make a name for herself as the author of numerous novels about English county society. This is the final chapter of* Trooper to the Southern Cross.

'GOOD OLD AUSSIE ONCE MORE'

I am now coming near the end of my story. We had had a rotten deal, but we got some fun out of it too. When we sighted Fremantle the worst was over, for we were in touch with Defence then and the diggers couldn't play up the way they had been doing. It only remains to tell how we got home.

Next morning Fremantle was actually in sight. It was late summer, or very early autumn, and there must have been bush fires up in the hills, for we could smell the gums right out at sea. More than one of us felt quite sentimental at seeing the good old bush again. It was after twelve, midday, that we tied up, having made pretty good going since Schultz got the machinery going. Of course everyone was wild to go ashore, but there was a lot to be done first. Old Colonel Bird got busy with the medical authorities, and before anyone left the ship a stretcher came on board and poor old Higgins was taken away to hospital. I had carried him to the first-class surgery while everyone was on deck, hanging over the rail and pointing out things to each other, and the stretcher-bearers fetched him from there, so no one knew where he had been for the last thirty-six hours. His pals were much upset about it, and they scrounged round and collected his kit, borrowing anything they needed to make it up, so that he left the ship with more property than he brought on board. The digger is wonderfully decent to a sick cobber, and there is nothing he won't do for him.

Presently we heard that there would be twenty-four hours leave for most of us, except for those on duty. Old Doc Bird was very keen to get up to Perth and see his sister, whom he hadn't seen for forty years, so I said I'd stay on board. The Fairchilds were going up to Perth with the kiddies, so Celia was to go along with them and I was to join them at the hotel the next day if I could get away. I was a bit disappointed not to show Celia her first sight of Aussie, but reflecting that I'd have the rest of my life to do it in, I soon recovered. Doc Bird said he daresaid he'd have had enough of his sister by breakfast time, and if so he'd come back and relieve me.

Several of our passengers were leaving us to go home by the Transcontinental, among them Captain Smith, the Browns and their kiddies, and the Peels, the ones that had had the measles. We had no business to let them leave the boat really, but the kiddies had had it so lightly that the spots didn't show, and it seemed a shame to keep them on board, especially as their mother was a real wowser, never happy unless she had a grouse against someone. Besides, if the health officers at Fremantle didn't notice, I felt there was no reason for me to interfere. No use keeping a dog and barking yourself.

I saw Smith before he went, but I don't think he knew a thing about what had happened. Whether he pulled himself straight or not I can't say, as that was the last I saw of him. I never lost any sleep about him.

There was a big mail waiting for us, but only two letters for me. My family had lost interest in me during the War. If the Mater had been alive, she would have written. She was a great little hand at writing letters. I could have wished I had a larger mail when I saw everyone else with stacks of letters, but then I hate writing letters myself, so why blame others? I had a letter from Sis, giving me a lot of news about a crowd of people I'd never heard of, and a cheery letter from little Moses Colquhoun, the one that got his pants peppered at Gaba Tepe. How he had kept track of me, or found out I was on this ship, I don't know. Anyway this was to wish me the best, congratulate me on my marriage and tell me to look him up as soon as I came to Sydney. This I did, and as I told you earlier, he proved himself a real good pal.

The diggers were all ready to take what is called French leave but it wasn't so easy for them here, with quarantine, and sentries from shore at all the gangways. However, finally they got off, and such of us as were left on board were well and truly pleased to be rid of them for a few hours.

Just as it was getting dark, Colonel Picking sent for me. Why he didn't send for Major Barrett I don't know, as he was his second in command, but somehow the Major, though mind you he was a nice old chap, didn't seem to cut any ice and we would have done just as well without him. You may have noticed that I have not mentioned him much. That is because he never did anything. He would come to the meetings and just sit there till they were over. If he hadn't been senior Major he would never have been heard of. What Picking wanted to tell me was that the crew had walked off the ship and said they wouldn't come back till the prisoners had been trans-shipped.

'I don't blame them,' I said.

But all Picking could say was what should we do? I was about fed up with that remark of his, so I said there was an officer in charge of disembarkation at Fremantle and why didn't he ask him. It wasn't a doctor's business anyway. So presently they got hold of Captain Lewis, the officer in charge ashore, and I left them to it. I shall not go into details, especially as I do not know all that occurred, but what happened in the end was that we were held up for three days at Fremantle while telegrams passed between Picking and Lewis on the one hand and Defence at Melbourne on the other, the result being a nice long holiday ashore for most of us. There was also the best free fight I've ever seen between the diggers and the crew. It took place on the wharf, the onlookers joining in according to fancy. The big arc lights were on, and Hobson and I leant over the railing and saw everything comfortably, and the casualties were taken to hospital, so we had no trouble.

Next day Doc Bird turned up bright and early. He said his sister had been like a small belly-ache when she was a kid, and she was a larger one now, and I could take all the leave I liked. So Hobson and I got a taxi and drove up to Perth. In those days it was a taxi, or a slow dirty little train, but now I believe they have motor buses running every half hour.

Well, we had a bonzer time in Perth. The lot of us hired two cars and we went right up into the hills for the day, as far as the big new dam at Mundaring, taking the kids and their nurse. It was great to be out in the bush again. There were a few fires here and there. You'd see some little flames through the trees, looking for all the world like a bush of those azaleas. The air was as clean as creation and the smell of the gums was good-oh. We had lunch at Mundaring and a good sleep on the hot grass, while the kiddies paddled. I must say though that the ring-barked trees all around had not a very pleasant effect. It was the same at Mount Lyell, where looking down south from the entrance to the mine you saw nothing but dead white gums as far as you could see. What they do is they ring-bark the trees which gradually kills them. Then they run a fire through, and after that the young growth makes splendid food for cattle. But it always seems a waste of good timber to me, besides spoiling the natural look of the place.

I had always promised Celia a good drink when we got ashore, so we had Minchinbury's sparkling hock that night at the hotel. Coming straight off a dry ship it went to the kid's head and she made us all laugh. So then we left Dick and Mary with their nurse, and all wandered out to one of those little open-air theatres they have in Perth in the hot weather, and saw quite a good variety show.

Next day we kept ringing up the ship, but there was no news of her leaving. At last Doc Bird rang me up to say we were due to leave at noon next day, so the following morning we all went down early, as I didn't want to take advantage of the Doc's kindness. He told me the guard was to be composed entirely of officers till we got to Melbourne, and we were not to stop at Adelaide because of possible further trouble there with the crew. Mrs Jerry was as savage as a meat axe, because she didn't know whether she would try to make a dash for the Transcontinental which left the next day, or go on to Melbourne and take the train back. Finally she decided to leave the ship, so she raised hell to get permission and to get her luggage. Somehow she got all her trunks brought out and packed. I never thought she would have time, but she said she had lived long enough on the 'Rudolstadt' to know that if it was scheduled to leave at noon it would be lucky to get away before midnight, and so it was. There wasn't another woman who could have got around the baggage master and had all her trunks got up out of the luggage room, but when Mrs Jerry had made up her mind you had to get out or get under. We all said goodbye with many regrets and I gave the kiddies each an English sovereign that I had managed to get hold of early in the War. We often have the kids over to us in the holidays, and Celia sometimes goes over to the Fairchilds for a trip. I can't get away much at present, but I am taking a partner, and then I'll get a spell from time to time.

I missed Jerry greatly for the rest of the voyage, also Mrs Dicky, who was a nice bright little soul. We had no further troubles except an unpleasant feeling among everyone. The officers had revolvers issued to them at Fremantle, so we had no difficulty in keeping a proper guard going. Old Picking made the officers hold a court-martial on the ringleaders and they pronounced all sorts of sentences, but they knew it was all eyewash. I kept out of it and stuck to the surgery. We had plenty more patent food in, and I spent my time trying to fatten up those poor little kiddies, who certainly did me credit after a week in the Bight. Apart from an appendicitis case which old Doc Bird cut up on the third day out, we had little else to do but weigh the babies and check the stores.

Some hopeful chaps thought there would be an armed guard at Melbourne, and the prisoners would be taken off in irons, but they were expecting a shipping strike, or a train strike or something in Victoria and hadn't any time for us. No, the diggers who lived in Victoria or Tasmania just went ashore quite peacefully or otherwise, and that was all.

The night before we got to Sydney I was down in the lower deck surgery, shutting up shop, when Father Glennie came in with Cavanagh.

'Here's a friend of ours who owes you an apology, Major,' he said.

'That's all right, Padre,' I said, 'I'm big enough to look after myself.'

'See here, Mr Bowen,' said Cavanagh, 'if I'd known that bastard Higgins was a pal of yours, I wouldn't have stoushed him, see?'

'Right-oh, Cavanagh,' I said, 'and I'm glad I stoushed your pal Heenan, and I only wish I'd hit him a bit harder.'

Cavanagh grinned, and we shook hands and he went away.

'I'm sorry we'll be saying good-bye, Padre,' I said. 'Perhaps we'll meet again. I haven't thanked you decently for looking after poor old Higgins. It makes me feel pretty small, I can tell you.'

'If I did God's work as you do, Major, I'd be a better man,' he said.

This made me feel my name was mud, so I looked out of the window.

'All right, Padre,' I said, 'you're one of the best.'

'I shall pray for you my son,' he said.

Well, I don't know that I wanted to be prayed for, but he was doing the decent thing as he saw it, so I thanked him and said I was sorry I couldn't reciprocate.

'Think of me sometimes when you've been up all night with a patient, or a woman having a kid,' he said, 'and that will do as well.'

We shook hands like old friends and I've never seen or heard of Father Glennie again. If ever he reads this book and remembers the way he kept the sergeant in his cabin, he will know he isn't forgotten.

One last occurrence happened which I must not omit to mention, having said earlier that I would do so. You may remember that Celia had a picture with the medieval name of 'Melencolia' by some Boche artist, which she was wonderfully fond of. Well, the customs weren't bothering the returned diggers, but one of their men who came aboard in Sydney Harbour wanted to know what the picture was. Celia had it done up carefully and carried it in her hand so that the glass wouldn't get broken, and I suppose he thought it was something very valuable. Anyway he made a bit of a fuss about it, and wanted to know what it was worth, and whether she meant to sell it and so forth, till Celia got a bit fed up, especially having to untie it and tie it up again. So she said:

'It's a family portrait, and that's my auntie and her flying fox that she makes a pet of.'

So he went away quite pleased.

I wanted to call this book 'My Life on the Ocean Wave', or 'How I nearly didn't survive to write it', but a friend of mine who is very literary, having several times contributed to the 'Sydney Bulletin', says that wouldn't do. So he gave me the title you see on the outside. It may be literary, but I still think mine is better.

Trooper to the Southern Cross (1966 edition, first published 1934)

ZORA CROSS

(1890–1964)

Writer and poet. Zora Cross, whose unconventional personal life shocked contemporaries who saw making war as more acceptable than making love, published several books of love poetry, namely A Song of Mother Love *(1916),* Songs of Love and Life *(1917), and* The Lilt of Life *(1919). Her* Elegy on an Australian Schoolboy *(1921), written in memory of her brother John Skyring Cross, a nineteen-year-old soldier killed in the war, is one of the finest Australian Great War poems. The following lines comprise the poem's fourth section. Cross also published several novels, children's verse, and a literary pamphlet.*

FROM 'ELEGY ON AN AUSTRALIAN SCHOOLBOY'

There is a football match this sunsweet day
In the park close at hand;

And in their jerseys blue the young lads play,
A careless, merry band.
The scores are mounting. Hear the whistle blow
And see the ball fly by ! The boy spectators watch the contest grow—
I know the old school cry.

Brown ball, you should be black. Play is no more;
The fields are desolate.
The ghostly goal is kicked; and on Death's shore
The awful umpires wait.
The skies grow heavy with their blood and tears;
The loud, exultant cheer
Leaps like a curse along the crying years
Of agony and fear.

Let there be war! I heard it in a land
Where fields were green with corn
Down to the curves of brown child-haunted sand
Where mirth was ocean born.
I sang to men a moving martial song
And asked for grace of gold—
Gold for God's soldiers! Ah, dear God, how long
Shall the red murder hold?

Children were hungry in the city streets
And many poor went by;
Children were lying in their winding-sheets,
Dead from their first weak cry.
Not for such need could I have gathered gold
By any song I made,
But for Death's armies steadily it rolled—
A tribute blindly paid.

❧ ❧ ❧

I thought I sang a soldier-song last night
To a great throng and sad;
They smiled at me through eyes of still affright—
Drear ghosts that nought made glad.
They sang each ringing chorus eerily—
Sounds as from distant lands—
And some were bloody and waved back to me
With dreadful, ghastly hands.

I thought I danced with many a step and whirl
Of wild abandoned speed.
I loosened from its pins each flowing curl
To match my maddened need.
'Bravo! Bravo!' I caught a mingled cheer
And flung my kisses far,
When over me fell, like a sudden fear,
A single blood-red star.

My flimsy draperies were red with fire.
They burned and blazed around
As part of that fierce dance of mad desire—
Flame, fury, rapture, sound.
And then the hosts gave me their manly tears …
Ah, anguished dream and thought!
Mad to the death, the women of the years
Thus with their bodies wrought.

Should I not dread to breed a living man
And give him to the world?
Should I not start and my white bosom scan
Lest strange beasts lie there curled?
We sing. We dance. We urge our bodies on
To fight through our strong sons;
We slay and in that murder life has gone
Ere one mate-season runs.

But who considers woman day by day,
Who pangs to make the race,
Starving her soul to give a child its play
In some green, healthful place?
War? It is war for ever all about
Her and her tender brood—
Heartache and fever, death and fear and doubt
Of each to-morrow's food.

Ah, England! Breeder of the noblest race!
Shall your false pride forget
Your base-born mother in some cruel place
Where claw and talon yet
Foster fierce war within her and deceit?
The savage lingers late.

Left, right! New soldiers tramp within her feet
To join the ranks of hate.

Elegy on an Australian Schoolboy (1921)

JESSIE TRAILL

(1881–1967)

Painter and etcher. Victorian-born Jessie Traill, a banker's daughter, was educated privately and in Switzerland. She studied art in Melbourne, London, and Paris. Traill exhibited at the Royal Academy in 1909 and at the Old Salon, Paris, in 1909 and 1926, and was awarded gold and bronze medals at the Panama Exhibition in 1914. She worked for more than three years as a member of a Voluntary Aid Detachment in military hospitals near Rouen in France during the war. Later she helped to raise funds to rebuild French villages destroyed in the fighting. Her papers, held in the State Library of Victoria, include this poignant piece.

'A VISIT TO THE DEVASTATED AREAS IN 1925'

New towns, new villages, red bricks and slates, red bricks and tiles, and little cottages of wood, fine new Railway Stations, big new factories, young trees planted where still are stumps of the old forests, and young saplings clothing the wastes, with rosie shoots where the battered trunks of the parent trees still stand. The country is pale with dry grass and stubble, and covered in patches with a light mantle of snow which lies white and pure in the little even squares where are the gardens of crosses, still. Old dugouts and ruined pill boxes are still visible, and old abandoned poltoons lie in marshy fields. This is the North of France. This is where our boys agonised Winter after Winter. Six years in spite of prodigious energy, have left the country bleeding, bleeding still. Ruins still stand among all the new. New churches raise up their spires showing that in the new France the faith of their fathers is not forgotten.

The new houses are simple, plain, robust, but among them still are old nissen huts, now but rusty heaps of corrugated iron, surely outgrown their utility. Yet there are people still living in miserable temporary shelters, and still fighting the cold and wet that must still penetrate the old rotting walls, and roofs.

Great stacks stand in groups — the year's store from these fertile fields.

What memories the names of the stations recall as I flash past in the luxurious express — Albert, Achiet, Arras, etc. Then the country changes. The forests are of old trees, the houses are old but unruined, — this is the once occupied areas. The train glides into the great station of Lille.

The great city of Lille — busy, industrial, doesn't now outwardly show many marks of the war, — a statue in a square headless by a shell — German words written in the doors of the Bourse only half defaced.

The great Musée recently reopened, has one small treasure among all its beautiful things. They were stored in the cellars for safety, during the occupation, the 'Tête de Cire' above all; that was well hidden. But this small treasure is a beautiful little old frame about 9 x 6, enclosing a bare canvas and on it is written 'Tableau volé par un militaire allemand durant occupation ennemi de cette ville' [Painting stolen by a German soldier during enemy occupation of this town]. Below is the artist's name — Verelst, Pierre 1614–? (Ecole Hollandaise [Dutch School]). This is the only one that was taken I am told. How significantly and with what dignity the Lillois have recorded for all time their agony of 1914–1918.

Jessie C. A. Traill Collection

KATHARINE SUSANNAH PRICHARD

(1883–1969)

Writer. Katharine Susannah Prichard's novel Intimate Strangers *(1937) is described in* The Oxford Companion to Australian Literature *(second edition, 1994) as a 'psychological study of the marital breakdown of Greg and Elodie Blackwood, with a not very credible reconciliation, through their joint work for a new social order'. There is a ghastly reason for the book's ending in this way. When she went overseas in 1933, Prichard left behind an earlier version ending with Greg's suicide. In her absence, Prichard's own husband, Hugo Throssell, an Australian Victoria Cross winner from the Great War, killed himself, metaphorically, some might say, with a bullet from that war. Many years later Katharine Susannah Prichard confided to their son her fear that Throssell had committed suicide after reading the draft and believing that he was the model for Greg. After Throssell's death, Prichard rewrote the ending, before the book's eventual publication in 1937.*

GREG AND ELODIE

He had plagued Elodie to marry him, Greg remembered. Of course he had. Given her no peace. She was in love with him too: it was not easy for her to hold out against him. He had argued ... how he had argued ... that marriage need not interfere with her career. Persuaded her, and promised Mrs Marzic that after the honeymoon Elodie might go on with her music. He would even send her to Europe himself. He could manage it: had some money saved. Perhaps they would both go. He would study art while Elodie was working with Leschetisky or some other master of whom Mrs Marzic approved. It was a beguiling dream. Elodie had only to marry him for it all to come true: go on with the life she had planned. Only he would be there to protect and care for her.

Had he ever believed it, Greg wondered. He thought that he must have. Elodie did; and Mrs Marzic, after discussing contraceptives with him to her heart's content, had fallen for it. Elodie practised on her mother's Bechstein grand, happily, industriously, for the first few months of their married life.

And then ... why had he refused to keep his part of the bargain? Been so demented when Mrs Marzic told him she had arranged for Elodie to live with relations in Austria while she studied under Leschetisky. Greg believed that his mother-in-law died of chagrin when she knew Elodie was going to have a child: flatly accused him of having broken faith with her. A great old girl! Greg wished he had not let her down like that. Elodie sold her mother's diamond earrings when they got out of their depths in debt, a year or two later; she still had the grand piano. He had heard her confiding in it with a rage and misery there was no fathoming, after Billy was born. A career was never mentioned between them again. It was as if he had set a trap for her. She was caught for life and knew it, Greg told himself. Had she ever forgiven him for having stolen her from herself?

Elodie. How she had obsessed him! The sound of her name still stirred and filled him with a fury of desire to absorb and dominate her. Elodie! Elodie! He had to have her. It seemed as if he could not let her have a life away from him. Every instinct fought and clamoured for her. It was absurd ... extraordinary ... how a man could get like that, so mussed-up and gone-to-pot over a woman, one woman more than another, not just any woman, and then ...

His gaze covered Elodie steadily. He was conscious how steadily, without any of the old tremulous adoration and beatitude. There were no illusions between them, it seemed. Could he prevail on her, now, to throw up a life of her own for drudgery in a home beside him? Not likely. There were the children. Perhaps they were a consolation. He did not think so. Something died in Elodie when she lost her way in music. She had devoted herself to the children, faded, become prosaic for them; given them her health, her grace and charm. After her second baby died, for years she did not touch the piano. Elodie! He lamented over her. The fury and horror of those times when with one child toddling, they had known another was coming. The years through which they had struggled, quarrelling, tearing each other to pieces, worn to shreds by wakeful nights, fractious youngsters: the effort to provide food and clothing, a house for them to live in.

God, how awful it had been! Greg writhed; remembering. And Elodie, looking seaward and talking of mirages, was she remembering too?

There had been no mirage on their lives then. How they had lived, loathing, despising each other, something of pity, tenderness, surviving: some incalculable bond, if it was only responsibility for what they had done to each other. But the bitterness, the disillusionment!

Greg could see Elodie as she had been, ugly, weary, bad tempered; unable to cook or sew well, careless with money, ridiculously worried about any little ailing of the children; without help, doing all and any sort of dirty and laborious work about a house, sweeping, cleaning fire-places, scrubbing the kitchen floor, washing and ironing. He had not existed for her except as the means of providing a little money for the family to pay its way. He had left the Lands Department for a rise in wages and better prospects at Morrow-Pigott's.

He had given up something, too, when he married. Or had he? Wasn't that talk of painting just a bait to catch Elodie? He had said so often that he wanted to paint, he had almost come to believe it: liked loafing out of doors, sketching, of course, experimenting with the processes of colour printing. Was there more than that in it? A romantic kick about being thought an artist, of course. Intended, some day, to work out the sort of life he would have preferred for himself: making things, pictures, furniture, using his skill in design to establish himself in some profitable industry.

Then had come the war with its frenzy of patriotic idealism, grim awakening. Nowadays, he rarely spoke of the war, tried not to think of it. Strange, here in the sunshine, by the sea, to be plunged into that inferno again. He sweated, haunted still by the horror and nausea of his first day in the trenches in France.

Could see the platoon going up to the line, at dusk, in the rain. There had been a heavy bombardment a few days before. A section of the trench was blown in. Greg saw himself among other heavy, stooping figures, digging out the trench. He had dug out decomposing bodies, arms, legs and faces, flung down his shovel to vomit. Retching, had crouched against the earth: been ordered back to the trench, refused to obey. Two men volunteered to do this work. The stench and sight of those rotting, blasted limbs and faces had driven him almost insane. He would have faced a firing squad rather than go near them again.

All the months of fighting, bombardment, floundering through mud and slush on the Somme, had not been so bad. He went through them, as though dead, after that first night: could see himself a mouldering corpse, like those others ...

Wounded at Passchendaele, he had spent a few weeks in hospital, returned to the line, been mentioned in dispatches, gone down with trench fever, put in some time at an officers' training school.

Then, incredibly, the war was over. He had come home: not permanently incapacitated the repatriation doctors said: only suffering from nervous strain, hardships of the campaign and so on. Astounded to find himself alive, when he had seen so many men blown to pieces about him, Greg felt it was indecent, somehow, to survive them. It had taken him a long time to live among people who knew nothing of dug-outs and countrysides blackened by shell fire, men lying smashed and dying in unutterable confusion: to live among people who talked of 'honour and glory' in connection with the colossal atrocity beside which all other atrocities were a flea-bite: to hear fools talk of 'paying for the war'. As if it could ever be paid for. Such damnable suffering and loss of life. He loathed the whole civilian population which had driven men like sheep to this shambles: the farce of a civilization which maintained itself by war: was cheerful, pious, and made money out of the beastly business.

He had brooded over it: brooded almost to madness. But to live, a man had to have work and wages. He had contrived to secure them. At last he had reached the stage when he would play the grasshopper again. 'Enough unto the day — ' But he was caught in a rut; couldn't see beyond it, or any chance, now, of having the sort of life he had promised himself. Any more than Elodie.

Intimate Strangers (1981 edition, first published 1937)

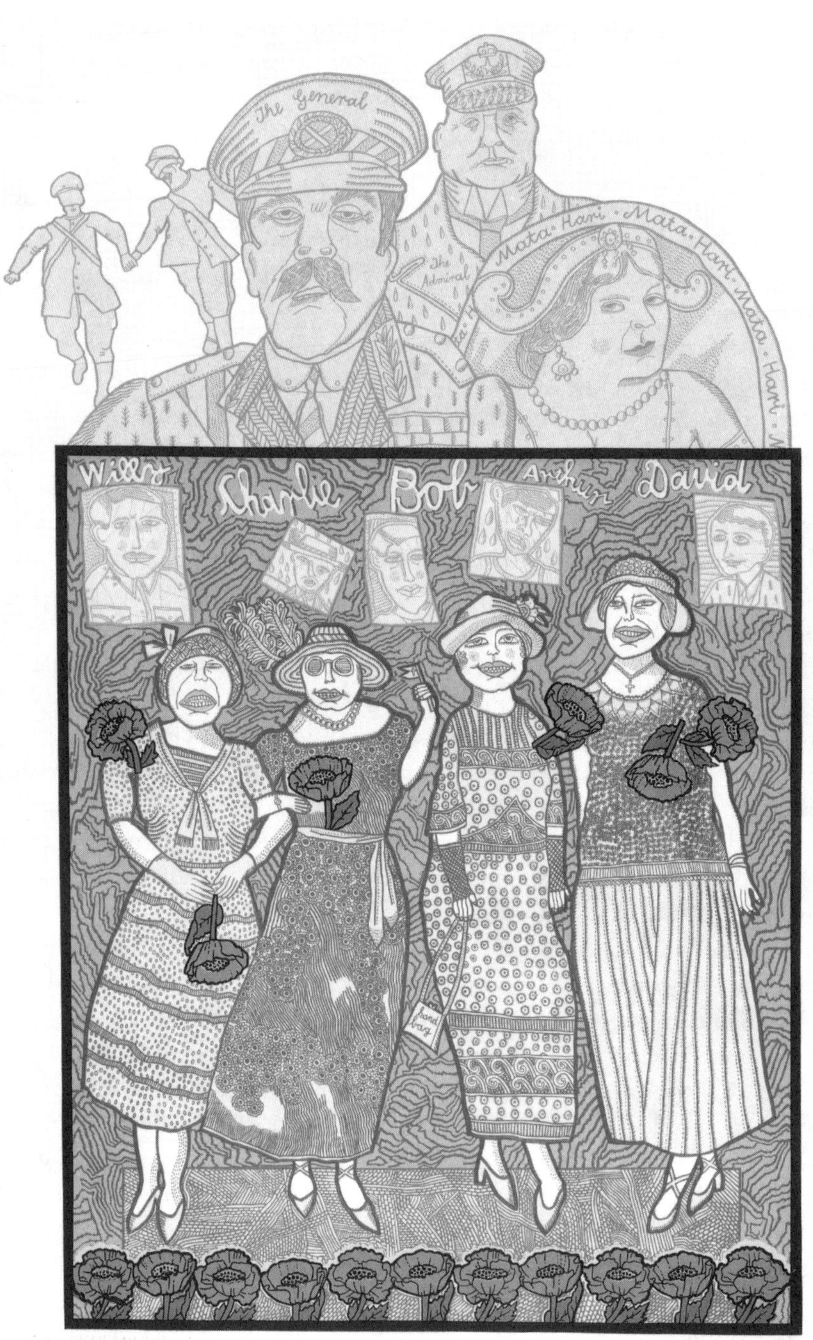

Barbara Hanrahan (1939–91), *Poppy Day*, 1982, screenprint, 76 x 57.4 cm. Purchased in 1992. (AWM 29757)

SHIRLEY HAZZARD

(1931–)

Writer. Shirley Hazzard was born and educated in Sydney, but left Australia with her parents in 1947, subsequently living in Hong Kong and New Zealand. In one of her non-fiction works, she has written about the United Nations, for which she worked from 1952 to 1962 in New York. Some of her numerous short stories are collected in Cliffs of Fall *(1963). The best known of her several novels is* The Transit of Venus *(1980), a very fine book, which won the National Book Critics Circle Award for Fiction, in the United States. Its two main characters are sisters Caro and Grace Bell, seen here in a haunting scene set in Sydney, where they grow up before becoming expatriates. Now an American citizen, Hazzard has divided much of her life between New York and Italy.*

DREADED SPECTRES

When they got down from the tram there were windows brilliant with coloured gloves and handbags and silk shoes, and shopping arcades lit like rainbows. The women passing along Pitt Street or Castlereagh had cooler faces and wore hats of violets or rosebuds, with little veils. Kegs of ale were nonetheless drawn on drays right past the best shops by pairs or teams of Clydesdales: chestnut necks straining in collars of sweated leather, great hooves under ruffs of streaked horsehair. And the driver collarless, frayed waistcoat open, no jacket, with his leather face and stained mop of horsehair moustache. Manure underfoot, and a bruised smell of dropped cabbage trodden by blinkered ponies harnessed to vegetable carts. Along the curb, barrows of Jaffas and Navels, or Tasmanian apples. All this, raffish and rural, at the fashionable conjunction of Market and Castlereagh streets.

At the same corner they would come upon the spectres dreaded by Caro and by Grace; and, from the looking and the looking away, by all who passed there. Apparitions of the terrible kind were dispersed throughout the city and might be expected at any shopping centre of the suburbs. For a dead and atrocious certainty they awaited you at this particular and affluent corner, which for that reason seemed not to be a street at all, but a pit or arena.

Some of them stood, including those with only the one leg. The legless would be on the ground, against shop-windows. The blinded would have a sign, to that effect, around the neck — perhaps adding SUVLA or GALLIPOLI. Similarly, on the placard GASSED that hung beside pinned medals, might appear the further information, YPRES or ARRAS. Or the sign might say MESOPOTAMIA, quite simply, as you might write HELL.

They took up separate places, perhaps having a dog with them or a child, or a gaunt woman silently holding out the cap. More usually, each alone. Who or what they had singly been, however, was sunk in the delved sameness of the eyes. Nothing more could be done to them, but their unsurpassable worst would be sustained forever and ever. Stillness was on the eyes even of the blind, closed on God knew what last sighting.

What music they made, and how they sang, that ghastly orchestra in lopped and shiny serge, with unstrung fiddles and wheezing concertinas and the rusted mouth-organ grasped in the remaining and inexpert hand; the voices out of tune with everything but pitched extremity. How cruelly they wracked, for Depression pennies, an unwilling audience with their excruciating songs — 'The Rose of No Man's Land,' and 'The Roses of Picardy,' and 'The Rose of Tralee,' and 'Oh My, I don't want to die, I want to go home.' The war of the roses, roses, and smile, smile, smile.

Ighty-tiddly-ighty,
Carry me back to Blighty
Blighty is the place for me!

Even children — children who had not yet experienced virtue and might be ruthless in tormenting playfellows — were struck adult in pity: the Great War being deeply known to them, learned before memory, as infants know the macabre from dreams. Nothing would have truly surprised them, not if they had been explicitly told of the exploded horses, exploded men, the decomposing gestures of the dead, the trench-foot, trench-mouth, the starshells, the terror. The bully of a sergeant-major howling about clay piping to those as good as dead, the visiting statesman jocose behind the lines. They knew about Wipers and Plug Street and the Line. They had found it all out somehow from the speechless instruction at street corners and the songs of the roses and 'Inky Pinky Parlay-Voo.' Uncovered it in defiance of the brittle brown wreaths at cenotaphs, two minutes' silence, and the pools of remembrance where beer bottles lolled, and the monuments to war's sweetest symbols — the soldier, bronze rifle rested, supporting his decorously felled comrade, the marshal cleanly victorious on his flawless mare.

How long they were, how immensely long: the four years that would go on forever.

On Anzac or Armistice Day, Grace and Caroline Bell had been let through the crowd to watch thin-faced men walk in rows, in the decent suit if they had one, pin-stripe, with scraps of braid aligned in small rainbows on the breast, the poppy of red paper in the lapel, the sprig of rosemary. Being little children, Caroline and Grace Bell had been brought to the front of the crowd to see this, as having the greater need.

In the wringing of their hearts, knowledge had entered. Knowledge stood formidable and helpless in their small rib-cages as, glancing aside, they dropped tuppence in the extended cap, or ground the rosemary to death between their fingers for the smell.

The Transit of Venus (1980)

Part Three

Second World War

HELEN LIGHT

(?–)

Migrant. Recently arrived in Australia at the time, Helen Light was a schoolgirl when the Second World War began in September 1939. Many years later, she told her story to Betty Goldsmith and Beryl Sandford for their collection of accounts given by civilian women and girls about the war years, The Girls They Left Behind *(1990).*

SCHOOLDAYS

When I was thirteen my mother, brother and I arrived from Poland. It was three months before war was declared, and we had come to join my father, who had arrived one year before.

It is interesting the way my father came here. He used to be a chess player, quite a good one I imagine, because he was sent from our town to different places to play chess nationally, and at that time they did not have many Jews participating. He became very close friends with a non-Jewish policeman, and one day this man told him, 'Look, try and get away from here and take your family with you, it's not going to be much fun for you here being Jewish'. The police had already been told not to move on the pickets who stood in front of Jewish shops to prevent customers entering, and we had a shop. I was still a young child but I heard what was going on, and the policeman saying, 'I can't help you unless I stand near your shop and let people go in'; then my father replying, 'If it's good enough for the rest, well I'm Jewish too. I don't want preferential treatment'. This was some years before the war, but my father made up his mind that we would all leave Poland.

My father wanted us to arrive here with some basic knowledge of English, so I had a teacher for a couple of lessons before we left. He was an English poet, and instead of teaching me 'good morning', 'thank you', etc. he taught me poetry, English poetry, like 'the sun comes through the window'. My tongue just wouldn't get round the words, though, it was so funny, and when my father came to meet us on the boat when we arrived, he asked if I could speak any English. I said 'Oh yes, the sun comes through the window', and he said 'Oh, no'.

My brother and I started school at Lee Street State School in Carlton, Victoria, and if it hadn't been for a wonderful teacher there life would have been so much more difficult. Miss Moroney helped me so much, I can't tell you how much it meant to me at the time, and still does for that matter. I'll never forget her; she just understood how difficult it was for me. I mean, here was this thirteen-year-old kid, wearing an outfit which must have looked ridiculous to the other kids, with a European haircut and hardly a word of English. Miss Moroney gave a lot of her own time, even taking me out on weekends. In the beginning I don't think I liked it one bit when she loaded me with all this extra spelling, but after a couple of weeks I could see what she was trying to do. I think I shut up at school for about six months, as whatever I said made the children laugh. I didn't have anything against them; it was my problem, not theirs. One day in class, they were talking about arithmetic and I knew the answer. I'd been put into a lower class so that I could concentrate on the language. I automatically put my hand up and Miss Moroney said, 'Yes Helen, get up'. I did, but I just couldn't come out with the answer, and the children started to laugh. I don't blame them, but it was a bad experience for me. Miss Moroney told them they should be ashamed of themselves and said, 'Look, Helen can speak Polish, and Yiddish, but you don't understand those, and neither do I'. She tried so hard to build up my self-esteem. At that time our family was living in a crummy little place in Carlton. The war had started and we were feeling pretty low anyway.

Before the war there was a tremendous amount of anti-Semitism in Poland; that was a fact, so much so that on the ship on the way to Australia I didn't expect non-Jewish kids to make friends with me. One girl came over to me and asked me to join in the play, but I found it hard to understand her and went to look up a dictionary so I could tell her not to play with me because I was Jewish. I went up to her and said, 'Audrey, I am Jewish', and she said 'How do you do, I am Church of England', and I thought, she doesn't know, she doesn't know she's not allowed to play with me. After that we became the best of friends — she used to come to our place on weekends. Now she's in England, and we used to correspond. Sometimes she recollected, 'Do you remember when we first met and I could see you couldn't speak English, so I said how do you do?'.

It is hard for me to describe what it was like for us during the war. My mother worked full time; she didn't have a trade, so she worked in an underwear factory and would also bring home work to do at night. She was always working, cooking, going to the market, cleaning; the Jewish style of cooking is very time consuming so it was very hard for her.

At the very beginning we didn't know how horrific it would be for Jews in Europe. There was a war going on and we knew the Jews were in the middle of it. We also knew that whenever there was some terror there would always be extra killing of Jews, as being Jewish meant persecution. Well, after the war we found out that all our relatives had perished in the Holocaust, but even during the war at certain stages, like everybody else, we knew there were concentration camps and gas chambers.

My parents were the only members of their families out here, the rest were back in Poland. I knew that they would all be together, as they were all very close. When we were there we lived in a block of flats with many relatives; grandparents on the first floor, and others on different floors; we were one big family. When I had friends in to play it wouldn't matter which flat we played in, aunties' or grandparents'. It's different here in Australia because it's so huge, and families live in different suburbs to one another. So you can see how anxious the wartime was for us and the way we fretted over our loved ones back home.

It was worse lying in bed at night and thinking about the family, not knowing what was happening to them. My poor mother — I can't begin to describe about my mother. She used to shake; she would say she was shaking inside when I took her to the doctor. She had high blood pressure. Sometimes in the middle of the night I would hear her screaming; it was a nightmare. She just suffered so much during the war and she was never ever the same again. Nor was my father; it just broke their hearts.

When we came out on the boat we came with twenty Jewish boys without their parents; they were just kids. The Jewish Welfare Society had worked to get them out of Poland.

Some of the parents came to see them off, and some asked my mother to 'look after my boy'. At the time I didn't take it to heart so much, but those boys had nobody here, absolutely nobody. Sometimes my parents would invite one or two of them for a meal and they would just sit there, very quiet and shy. I don't know how they coped. I mean I had my parents and my brother here; they had no one, but for a short time they had 'foster parents'.

Those boys were so patriotic; they all wanted to fight and most of them joined up. Some of them were killed. Life then had an unreal feeling about it. Being Jewish here, you see, was like fighting a double war, the war in Europe, and the extra war against Hitler. By then we knew he wanted every Jew killed, only because he or she was Jewish.

I had a special girlfriend in Poland — I've still got her picture and it still haunts me as to what became of her. She was very special to me; I used to visit her home. Her parents were very poor and at meal times they used to eat just herring. In Australia herring is expensive, but in Poland it was the cheapest food possible. They would ask me to have some and I would have loved some, but I felt I would take it away from their mouths. It was an instinct, one had an instinct for that sort of thing.

During the war we used to meet friends at Monash House in Carlton. Many of the boys we knew were in uniform. We'd meet there and talk and dance. Sometimes I would be at a party dancing, enjoying myself. Suddenly, quite out of the blue, the memory of my girlfriend would come flooding back to me.

After the war ended and we knew for sure what had happened, well, it is not possible to describe in words the effect this had on my life and the lives of all Jewish people. A few years ago when I was compiling a list of our family, and filling in forms for each of them to send to Jerusalem for the archives — well I must have filled in fifty forms for my relatives and friends. I would sit in my workroom, writing; I did it because I felt it was my duty but I nearly had a nervous breakdown after it.

I have told you of my life during the war to perhaps give people an understanding of something of the way we lived out the war years here — and also as a tribute to the special person in my early life here, who helped me over so many hurdles, and always has a special place in my heart. My teacher at Lee Street State School, Miss Moroney, she saw me through. It would have been much harder without her.

Betty Goldsmith & Beryl Sandford, *The Girls They Left Behind* (1990)

MARY KENT HUGHES

(dates unknown)

Doctor. After Australian military authorities rejected her offer of service because she was a woman, Mary Kent Hughes sailed to England, where she joined the Royal Army Medical Corps in April 1940. During the next two years, she served in England and the Middle East. In his foreword to her book, Matilda Waltzes with the Tommies *(1943), her former lecturer Professor William Osborne writes,*

'I believe Mrs Kent Hughes could have written an attractive record of travel in the hum-drum days of peace, but as a spectator of, and as far as she was able, a participant in the mighty events of global war, she now offers something likely to have permanent historical interest.'

'THAT BLOODY WOMAN'

A week later, trussed up in a uniform that made me feel like a small bottle of beer in a large crate of straw, I reported for duty at the appointed hospital in Southern England, rather nervously. A faux pas just outside the entrance was not helpful to one's confidence. A group of Tommies was being drilled on the road: as I passed they all clicked their heels and stood at attention, and their sergeant actually stopped in the middle of a bellow and saluted me! I nearly fell in my tracks with fright, for I just did not know the answer. All I could do was to manage a feeble smile and 'Good-morning,' with the uncomfortable realisation that I was not living up to the occasion. The ATS officers were soon to change all that! They were extraordinarily good soldiers. They took to regimentation as a boy to mischief.

My Commanding Officer, unfortunately, did not run true to the form set by the War Office. In his eye was the look of one who is thinking: 'That bloody woman!'—a look with which I was to become only too familiar during the ensuing two and a half years.

'I don't know how you will get on, I'm sure,' he groaned. 'Women in the Corps—the men won't like it. But you must do the best you can. You will live in the ATS Officers' Mess. Good-morning.'

Perhaps the patients were not too pleased at being attended by a woman doctor but they could take it. The Tommy can take anything that calls for dogged endurance and good humour. So long as I kept my maternal instincts in check, all was well with the Tommies. But on one occasion, when I caught sight of one of my staff weighed down by 'full web equipment,' I involuntarily exclaimed—

'Oh, you poor boy, do you really have to carry all that?'

His friends never let him hear the end of it. His face, when he knew me well enough to tell me how I had humiliated him, reminded me of that of my five-year-old son, years before at a school speech night, who had cut me dead when I smiled at him.

'You see, Mum,' he had explained later, 'I was afraid, if I gave you any encouragement at all, that you might call me "darling" in front of the boys!'

Work at the hospital was intensely interesting, and one felt it a privilege to be associated with men whose names were, not household words, say, clinical words, throughout the medical world. Once I kindly tried to show a new arrival how to do something in the way of investigating a patient's heart. He took it so kindly. Later I found to my dismay that he was one of Harley Street's leading heart specialists! Now I laugh at myself every time my eye lights on the binding of his famous text-book.

Matilda Waltzes with the Tommies (1943)

META MACLEAN

(?–)

Ship escort. A Queenslander living in Britain, Meta Maclean was asked by the Children's Overseas Reception Board (Corb) to act as an escort on the Batory, *a Polish ship carrying almost four hundred and eighty British evacuee children to Australia, early in the Second World War. A 'specialist in the psychology of child education', she also served as the ship's pianist. This is a chapter from the book that she wrote about the ten-week voyage from Liverpool to Sydney,* The Singing Ship: An Odyssey of Evacuee Children *(1941).*

'DEMOCRACIES IN SONG'

Wherever I had found a piano standing in a temporarily quiet spot on my journeys through the ship, I had found minutes of respite and happiness during the first strenuous days on board. I was unaware that any one had noticed me or that, if any one had, he or she would recognize the player again in such a big shipload of adults and children, especially as I was not as tall as many of the older girls of Corb and was sometimes mistaken for one of the children — from a back view, of course!

But, short as had been the snatches of enjoyment and muted as had been the playing, I found myself waylaid round corners by children and soldiers. The latter wanted community singing as soon as I could give it to them, and the children wanted to know simultaneously could I play 'Roll Out the Barrel', 'Abide with Me', 'Boomps-a-Daisy' and 'Jesu, Lover of My Soul'. When I nodded back at the eager young faces a soldier passing said:

'Lor luv a duck, miss, what will you do? Serve 'em mixed? Well, don't forget the aft deck later on.'

'Yes. "We are but little children weak" ', sang a tall Tommy, and the children laughed.

So, I thought, there's a piano where the troops are, up on the aft deck. I'd found one in the children's dining saloon and another in the adults', usually referred to as the 'first saloon'. With three pianos, what couldn't we do for the children — and apparently for those other 'children', the English and Scotch troops? Within four days of embarking the promises began to be fulfilled. The love of singing was so marked in the boys and girls and their requests for favourite songs so numerous (they included, after popular numbers of the day had been sung, such characteristic songs as 'On Ilkla Moor' from Yorkshire children, and many Welsh and Scotch numbers of olden days) that Mr Kilby, removing his friendly-looking pipe, made his way to the piano to say:

'We can't give them too much of this. Carry on.' And Bill Oats held up his notebook to wave it at me over the crowded young heads, indicating that we'd get down to plans and time-tables. This was essential with such a large body of children, even in their singing, because no one place anywhere on the ship where a piano stood or could be put could accommodate all of them at the same time.

In the meantime we both made daily notes of the children's requested songs, getting additional information from other escorts. Some of us would meet at the first saloon piano in the comparatively quiet territory forbidden to Corb juveniles and find out what we could from one another of traditional music and folk songs. The setbacks of war had robbed Mr Oats of some of his valued manuscripts collected on his travels through Europe, and they lay at the bottom of the English Channel. But he sang and played melodies so that I could write them down and set accompaniments to them. English, Scotch and Welsh escorts helped us with others. And Mrs Fox, the escort in uniform denoting her work with the wolf cubs, brought some of her sturdy cubs and scouts to complete our acquaintance with the verses of 'Ilkla Moor' begun by the AFS men in the night watches, down in the Liverpool shelters.

We got a highly satisfactory amount of material together, and I think the children felt that the music set before them on the ship had sprung from their own requests when they had gathered round pianos during the first days of the voyage; it was they who guided the piano in expressing themselves. I remember long periods, at the end of the first week in the Atlantic, when I sat at pianos and said nothing except:

'Who asked next? Let's keep it fair, shall we?'

' "Loch Lomond!" ' yelled the Scotties.

' "Men of Harlech!" ' cried the Welsh.

By that time two escorts in charge of Scotch sections, Miss Moncrieff from Sydney and Miss Gray from Edinburgh, had their songbooks of Scottish songs out and were ready to take special periods with their own children, while a young Welsh escort who had sung much on the wireless, Miss Herbert-Jones, though she showed no book, sang beautiful traditional songs of Wales that brought a new charm into our music.

The Church of England clergyman escort, Mr Martin, smiling broadly, 'dug up', as he said, a collection of verses of campfire songs published in a centre in the Australian bush. The boys hailed this volume with interest, finding some old favourites of rollicking rhythm in it.

Father Kelly sought a quiet spot where he could write out the verses of a Celtic song from Ireland of which I knew only the melody and which the boys wanted to learn.

'Will you sing the words of any verse we give you in the songs you ask for, instead of whistling the tunes?' said Mr Oats, trying to look stern.

They grinned back at him happily, still whistling in spurts.

'*Will you?*' demanded the Rev. Mr Phillips in the foghorn voice he kept in reserve for special occasions.

Sudden silence. Companionable grins. Some guilty faces. A very small Welsh girl put up her hand.

'Okay!' she squeaked.

'Answer properly, Gwennie', said her escort, referring to the use of slang when addressing authority.

Gwennie tried again.

'Okay, *sir*!' she amended.

'Oui, oui!' hazarded an English girl, laughing.

So, in languages of other democracies than our own, the children sealed their happy vows to be contributors to and partners in the harmony of the musical life of the ship.

The Singing Ship (1941)

FAITH RICHMOND

(1935–)

Artist and writer. New Zealand-born Faith Richmond grew up in Brisbane, Canberra, and Melbourne. She draws upon her childhood memories for her book Remembrance *(1988), which is subtitled* A Daughter's Story. *She does note, however, that 'Some of the characters in this book are real, some are imaginary and others are composites.'*

WAR GAMES

I think my sister's anguish at the hand of my mother turned early from fear to terrible fury. Through the prism of her rage she watches the world go by with angry eyes. She screams, bites and scratches and lies kicking on the ground over minor issues. She perceives monstrous injustices toward her in the way our mother treats us all. She scrutinises the amount of food that is given to us at meal times to make sure that no one gets one pea more than she does. Her blue eyes are like precision instruments. On Christmas Day of 1940 we receive identical dolls. But my mother hasn't been sufficiently scrupulous in her observation of their tiny voile dresses. Mine has pink, blue and green smocking and my sister's, only pink and blue. She is distraught and hysterical at this seeming favouritism.

Her sensitivity extends into every area of her life, and before she's even started school she has become her own tyrant. She learns to read at three and straddles my father's sawing horse in the sun with a pile of children's books from the library. She is able to hold sophisticated conversations with our parents at an early age, especially with our father. They sit together blue-eyed and fair-haired and share secrets in words I'll never understand.

At eight she parades her many talents with panache. She climbs the tallest trees. Reads the longest books. And uses the most complicated words with unfailing accuracy. Her vocabulary is both her stock-in-trade and often her undoing. The local children taunt her. They call over our front fence as they pass by:

'You think you're the Queen of Auchenflower.'

My sister looks up from her game of fiddlesticks on the verandah. Her reply is both simple and alienating:

'I don't merely think — I *know*.'

One Sunday evening while we wait for dinner. my sister and I discuss who we'll marry when we're grown up — or rather, our options in case our big brother can't wait for us:

'Well, I'm going to marry the Government.'

I hope to impress my sister with my grasp of current events. My father reads the paper to my mother sometimes while she stirs the groats for breakfast and the Government is frequently mentioned. My sister aged eight replies:

'That's stupid—you can only marry someone *in* the Government.'

And adds unhesitatingly:

'I shall marry the reigning King—that is—if he's suitable.'

Our games with the children in the street are often about the war. Our little brother, aged three, staggers about with a homemade wooden rifle over his shoulder. My sister listens to 'First Light Fraser, a Drama of War-torn Europe', on the radio at five o'clock. It's the story of a spy who is forever being captured by the Nazis and escaping. When neighbouring children come to play she and her friend Rilla Reid organise us into Germans and prisoners. As internees we are lined up with our backs against the custard apple trees. Blindfolds made from tea-towels prevent us from seeing our captors. but we can hear with almost real terror their guttural tones:

'Ze next to die are Fraulein Reid, Fraulein Clark and Herr Richmond.'

A report from our big brother's Daisy air-rifle gives the signal that the firing squad has done its duty and we slump to the ground. An executioner rushes over in her pinafore to push our bewildered little brother so that he too lies groaning and writhing and is finally still. One of the girls pulls a photo of her family from her pocket as she falls and it flutters to the ground beside her. Then it's our turn to be the SS. We decide among ourselves that it's an opportune time for my sister to be sent on a spying mission. She is briefed accordingly and warned that she may be captured by the other side and tortured. The words she utters in spontaneous response make her the heroine of the hour:

'Ze torture, it may be unendurable but it is *nozzing* compared with death.'

Remembrance (1988)

NEILMA GANTNER

(1922–)

Writer. One of the children of Sidney and Merlyn Myer, Neilma Gantner née Myer was born in San Francisco. She grew up in Melbourne and Sorrento, but later lived in California. Educated at the University of Melbourne and Stanford University, she has published a number of books under the pseudonym 'Neilma Sidney'. These include an autobiographical novel, Beyond the Bay *(1966), from which this piece about the beginning of the Pacific War is taken.*

'THIS WAS WAR'

It was Sunday, December 7th, 1941, a grey cool morning. Sandra, at 9.30 a.m., was preparing breakfast. Werner still slept. Sandra switched on the news while she squeezed the oranges.

She didn't listen for a moment, but the sombre male voice penetrated. The Japanese had attacked Pearl Harbour. This was war.

She stood stunned. It could not be true … the Japanese Peace Envoy was in Washington. There had been much publicity. Yet the voice was real. She flew to Werner, not caring how abruptly she'd awaken him.

'War, Werner … here, here!' She clung to him. 'It can't be, after all this time, but it is.' Yes, she knew it was. They were all in it now — Britain and America, David and Pedro and … oh, heavens no … not Werner! He couldn't. But …

He sprang up, thrust her aside, and wrapping his kimono around him, hurried to the radio. He had to hear it for himself, the story of the lone plane flying in Hawaii, the Sunday flip of the Honolulu lawyer and his son up there above Waikiki when they saw this drove of planes, three waves of them, coming out of the clouds. They got down just in time.

War! They sat at the kitchen table, Sandra shivery and shocked, Werner with his hand stretched over his eyes, his face as grey as the grey light of the morning. Finally he aroused himself with a shudder. They dressed quickly, took the car and joined the thousands of other San Franciscans who for some reason all gravitated towards the ocean beach. From the Cliff House all the way south to the winding coast highway the roads were packed with cars. Anxious people peered uselessly at the sullen wintry ocean as if they were going to be the ones to spot a Japanese submarine arising or a plane lurking off the coast. Rumours were rampant as the news of casualties in Hawaii came over the air.

In Washington at noon on the Monday, Roosevelt asked Congress to declare war. In San Francisco the Civil Defence Authorities went to work immediately. There would be a black-out that night. On the previous evening — the night of Pearl Harbour — two unidentified planes had been detected flying over Marin County. Would the citizens please take note of the air raid siren that would sound at noon. If that same siren, with its three short blasts, was to sound again at night, all lights were to be out or the property owner or tenant would be prosecuted.

Sandra went downtown to purchase enough black cloth to cover their kitchen window. That was the simplest and most economical. She sent one long letter home, full of platitudes … how they were all in it now and she'd understand a lot of things better. The American Navy was on the job and the Japanese couldn't get too far, they just couldn't.

Strange though it seemed, life still went on. Werner practised spasmodically, she attended to the house, clouds scudded over the Golden Gate, and gaily painted neutral ships still entered the harbour. But there were more men on the street in uniform, draft boards were working overtime. Soon gasoline would be rationed and meat and sugar. One wished it were not December. It seemed wrong that Christmas should come, in wartime, along with such news from the Philippines. But the downtown stores were decorated, carols poured out their doorways, and the Salvation Army women rattled their little tins to attract the generosity of the passers-by.

'Did you know that all the Japanese are going to be sent away from the West Coast,' someone asked.

'And the Japanese Tea Garden taken over by Chinese.'

Werner was silent. He loved the Tea Garden with its arched bridges, dwarf cypresses and statue of Quon Yuen. He loved a Japanese dinner cooked at the table in front of them on an individual brass stove. How could he be expected to ignore people they had smiled at yesterday, and many Japanese in San Francisco were more American than Japanese. Werner looked haggard, as if he was fighting a deep internal battle.

It must have been Wednesday, December 10th, when the phone rang. It was Mrs Jorgen. Could they come over for a simple dinner? Werner was practising at Paul's, and when she phoned him he asked her if she'd mind going on her own ahead of him so that he could keep working awhile. She went, and unthinkingly left two small lights on, as was their custom.

She reached the family house before seven and Werner walked in around 7.15 p.m. just as the air raid signal rang. They extinguished all lights, Mr Jorgen putting down the evening paper with a growl. Mrs Jorgen went into the kitchen to arrange something for Wong.

Sandra and Werner went up to the roof garden, unconscious of the cold air. There was something beautiful and sad about the dimming lights. They watched Sausalito disappear, Alcatraz plunged into darkness, and the East Bay slowly fade out. Below them they could hear police cars and loud-speakers driving around urging the populace to hasten and get off those last lights, while on their block an angry householder was walking along with a torch shouting up at someone.

'You didn't by any chance leave anything on at home?' Werner turned suddenly to Sandra.

'Oh, my God,' her heart turned to stone. 'Of course I did … reflex action. Same lights we always leave on. Oh, let's get in the car and rush over quickly.'

'For gosh sakes use your head! We can't drive over in a blackout.'

'Why couldn't you have reminded me when I phoned?'

'Oh, you're hopeless.' Werner ran down to the telephone just as Mrs Jorgen called to them to come to dinner.

Sandra went down disconsolately. They were to eat with a torch wrapped in blue paper laid on the table. Wong had managed to dish things up with the light of a candle in a cupboard. Werner joined them, growling at Sandra. He had tried to telephone the janitor, but there was no answer, nor was there with Paul. The Fire Department said it was not their concern, the Police Department was jammed with calls. Werner gave a big sigh as if the world made him utterly weary, and a thoughtless wife was intolerable, but Mrs Jorgen rose to Sandra's defence and asked him to keep silent.

Wong provided the only diversion.

'Me go work in factlee now. Elleebody work. No more Chinaboy in house.'

'That's enough, Wong. We'll take each day as it comes,' Mrs Jorgen replied gravely.

At 10.15 p.m. the 'All Clear' sounded and Werner and Sandra drove home to find the light smashed on the landing outside their flat, their welcome vase broken and glass and flowers all over the floor.

'You see,' said Werner accusingly.

They entered the living-room and there was Paul. He had poured himself a whisky. The fact that Werner had again given him a key without consulting her made Sandra fume.

'I knew your habit of leaving on a light, so I thought I'd run over,' he said nonchalantly. 'I was too late for the hall, but I got here in time to stop your door being beaten in. Old Rat-bag downstairs panicked. I'm sorry I was late.'

Sandra might have said, 'I'm sorry I left it on,' but Paul's casualness and the way he sprawled infuriated her.

'Stupid lot of fuss,' she said angrily. 'There wasn't even a plane overhead. They don't know what war is. This time last year was the Battle of Britain and here shops are groaning, everybody's stocking up for Christmas and they think they can scare people with a few sirens. The whole thing makes me sick.' She flung herself down angrily, glaring at Paul.

'You just don't know,' Werner said quietly. 'Terrible things are already happening. People are learning to hate. From now on everything will change. Many Americans are being killed, and people will have only one thing on their minds ... to kill Japanese. Then it will be the Germans, then the Italians. Just think of this hill. Maria will come running in here one day and say someone has thrown something at their window. You'll call someone and her husband will have left for the war; you'll call another and her son will be dead. I can see it all, and you Sandra sitting here mumbling about how right must out. There is no right in wartime. There is nothing ... nothing but the exaggeration of everything dreadful. The arts will be dead. I will feel dead.' He stood looking gaunt and lifeless, drained of anger. Suddenly he opened the door and was gone.

'Werner,' Sandra called, racing after him out into the hall. But he was already down one flight of stairs.

'Let him be,' said Paul. 'He'll just go off walking. Let him be.'

Soon Paul left. Sandra swept up the scattered glass and poured herself a whisky before she went to bed, though she hated whisky. She felt defeated. The world was heading for destruction and her husband was utterly remote. She lay with whirling head a long time, and though she heard Werner come in and noticed it was 3.05 a.m., she did not speak to him. They were too far apart.

Beyond the Bay (1966)

JESSIE STREET

(1899–1970)

Feminist. Jessie Street née Lillingston was born in India, but grew up on a family property in northern New South Wales. She was educated privately, at Wycombe Abbey in England, and at the University of Sydney. Street helped to found the United Associations of Women, which fought for legal, political and civil rights for women, and was its president for some twenty years from its foundation in 1929. She was Australia's only female delegate at the founding conference of the United Nations in San Francisco in 1945. In this section from her rather disorganised autobiography, she recalls some of her wartime activities.

MILITARY DRILL

With the outbreak of the war in the Pacific and the rapid advance of the Japanese everyone was preparing to defend Australia. We were very encouraged by President Roosevelt's 'on the way' cable, but we knew the United States of America was almost as unprepared for waging war as was Australia and that we could not expect their forces to arrive overnight. The main difference was that most of our men were overseas fighting the Nazis, while those in the United States, with the exception of the regular army and navy stationed at Pearl Harbour and the Pacific bases, were still working in the factories and on the farms, so were available for recruits for the armed forces.

In Australia a 'dim out' was imposed in Sydney and other towns in case of Japanese air-raids or coastal attacks. Area wardens were appointed who were allotted certain duties in case of emergency. It was reported in the paper that it had been decided that a Women's Voluntary Services should be established.

Soon after this announcement Miss Ruby Board telephoned me and said she had an important matter to discuss with me. I had worked with her for various causes and had a high regard for her. She was a senior member of the National Council of Women. She lived near my home, so I invited her to come over straight away. We discussed the situation in the Pacific and of course we shared the general concern of everyone in Australia about the whole situation. She then told me the reason for her visit. She had been invited to accept the position of head of the Women's Voluntary Services, and to organize these services throughout New South Wales. She came to ask me whether I would accept the position of deputy head. I was rather taken aback by her offer, at the same time I was very pleased. We discussed the whole situation at length. I told her about the formation in England of the Women's Army Auxiliary Corps in the first world war and some of the problems they had come up against. Among these was that men members of the military and naval establishments had taken it for granted that they could give orders to the Women Auxiliaries whatever their rank, and had seemed to expect them to do many tasks they did not want to do themselves. The Women's Auxiliaries eventually decided that they should have their own officers and that orders should be transmitted to the Corps through their own officers. I suggested that a similar situation would inevitably develop here and that a similar procedure should be adopted in the WVS to prevent confusion and to give direction and effective control of their work to the officers of the WVS. I said that if this was agreed upon I would be very happy indeed to accept the position of deputy head. We talked over the position at some length. Ruby Board said she would discuss the matter with those concerned and would let me know. However, my proposal was not adopted. It would have avoided many disputes and incidents had they been far sighted enough to see the inevitable consequences of subjecting this fine body of women to the foibles arising from the vanity and desire to dominate of a number of inexperienced young men who just because of their sex believed they had a God-given right to control and direct women, even though many of the women were old enough to be their mothers and had forgotten more than the same young men had yet learned.

However, there was plenty to do and everyone was busy, and we were all doing something to help in the defence of Australia should it be necessary. There were a number of rifle-clubs in and around Sydney, and since all the eligible men were in the army and the others working overtime in various industries the facilities of these clubs were not being used. The Committee of the United Associations proposed to its members that they should form groups of women to learn to shoot, so that in the event of a Japanese landing they could assist in putting up some sort of defence. We saw some of the rifle-club members and they were quite agreeable to allow us to use their facilities, if we could get a permit to obtain ammunition. This permission was granted and women members of the rifle-clubs were quickly enrolled. Without any difficulty we found retired army men to instruct the members and we also decided that the women should be taught the basic elements of military drill so that in the event of an emergency they could assist in moving the civilian population about in an orderly fashion. More and more women were joining the rifle-clubs and learning to drill when suddenly an order was issued by the Defence Department that no more ammunition was to be issued for the use of the women rifle-club members. No one would take the responsibility of saying who had issued this order so we decided to ask for an interview with Mr Forde, the Minister for Defence. [Forde was actually Minister for the Army at this stage.] He was a friend of mine and he fixed a day and time to receive our deputation. We notified all the rifle-clubs and asked them to appoint their delegates for this discussion and suggested we meet at Mr Forde's office. The day arrived. As I was leading the deputation I arrived a little early to meet the other members. When I got to the building I found the street outside was a seething mass of women and they told me there were many inside the building as well. I could not see any members of the deputation so I made my way through the crowd into the building and found the passages almost as densely packed as the street outside. I was very happy to find such determination among the women to take their part in preparing to defend our country. I got up to the Minister's anteroom and knocked on the door, a crack of which was opened. When the Secretary saw me he let me in. The Minister had heard about the crowds outside and put a limit on the number he would receive — it was quite a generous limit. I had the list of women appointed on the deputation and went to the door and called their names and the Secretary let them in as they came forward. They were all there and we let in some others to make up the number the Minister had said he would receive. We all crowded into his room and told him about the reasons for forming the rifle-clubs and the tremendous support they had evoked, and the co-operation we were getting from ex-servicemen in teaching the women to shoot and drill. Then Mr Forde spoke. He told us of the admiration he and the Cabinet had for all that the women were doing to help the war effort. He spoke of their work in the Red Cross, in the hospitals, in looking after the children, how they had taken on much of the work of men in the factories and in other fields and then he went on to say, 'but ladies, you don't want to learn to shoot — to kill people.' He got no further — practically everyone in the room protested. When order was restored I said to him, 'Well Mr Forde we came here to put our case and to tell you that we were learning to shoot to help defend Australia and to

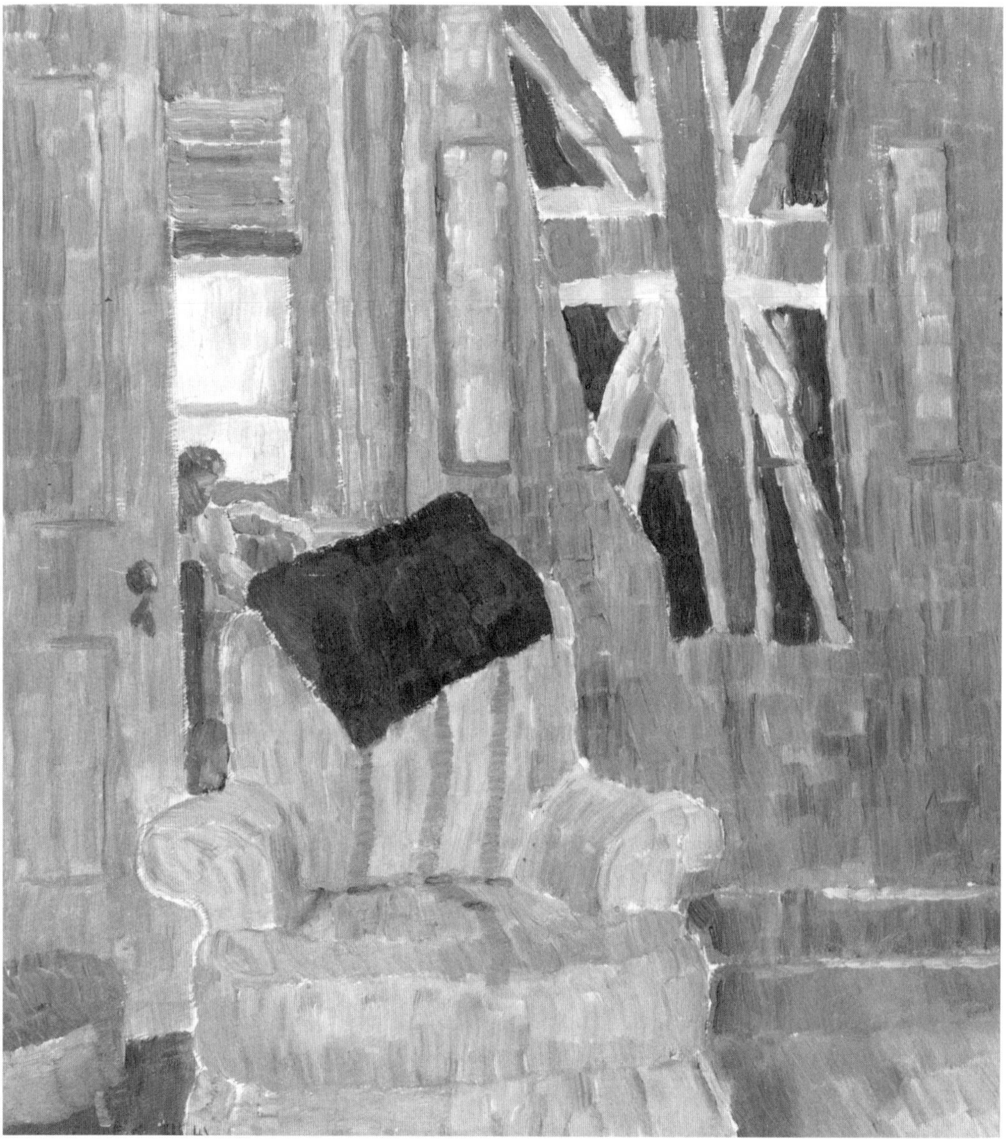

Grace Cossington Smith (1892–1984), [*Interior with flag*], 1941, oil over pencil on cardboard, 33.2 x 29 cm. Purchased in 1997. (AWM 90721)

protect ourselves as the last resort if the Japanese landed. But if you would prefer us to be defenceless and to be raped by the Japanese, well, we know where we stand. The matter is in your hands.' Poor Mr Forde was quite speechless with embarrassment. He was a very kindly and proper person and I doubt if he had ever before heard women talk of being raped. The picture it conjured up was evidently too horrible for him to contemplate because the embargo on ammunition for the rifle clubs was lifted and we continued our activities.

Truth or Repose (1966)

DOROTHY ELMES

(1914–42)

Army nurse. Sister Dorothy Elmes was a member of the 2/10th Australian General Hospital during the Second World War. She sailed from Sydney in February 1941, with troops of the Eighth Division, who were being sent to garrison Malaya, in the face of the anticipated Japanese threat. She lived a pleasant life in Malacca until her unit was evacuated from there to Singapore Island in January 1942. Elmes and her nursing colleagues were then seconded to other Australian units in the general vicinity, before rejoining their own unit. During this period of upheaval, Buddy, as she called herself, wrote this letter, the last in a series, to her friend 'Dear Old Smithy' in Australia. The tragic reason for the abrupt ending of the correspondence will become apparent when readers look at the biographical notes about, and the piece written by, Betty Jeffrey, which appears next in this anthology.

LETTER FROM BUDDY

NX 70526. S/N. D. G. Elmes
10 AGH
AIF
Malaya
20.1.1942

Dear Old Smithy,

Haven't heard from you this week but the mail isn't quite so regular as it was. Or perhaps it is because we have been moving. Anyway we have at last settled hope this time for the duration. Had a very nice holiday in the rubber; did two days work at the CCS which was very interesting wished we could have stayed there: but we are now in quite a nice place. Old & very dirty but have had a good bit of cleaning scrubbing & scouring etc. Externally it is most picturesque built early in the eighteenth century (or looks like it) situated in beautiful grounds nice trees & lawns etc. Also some nice air raid shelters (we hope) as am getting quite partial to getting there first to avoid the crush. As often get bits of shrapnel lying about from Ack-Ack's & have no desire to stop a bit unnecessarily.

Our quarters are in a way most comfortable although a bit crowded as its only a flat but have a wireless & fridgadaire. Amahs to do our washing & cleaning etc which makes a lot of difference to our personal comfort.

Sorry there isn't a great deal to tell you Smithy. We were just saying what an interesting letter we could write if there wasn't a censor who might open it but will try & remember to tell you the tit-bits when we get back.

Suppose you have more or less guessed where we are now by this time as don't think you will need to stretch your imagination much.

Cheerio
Love
BUDDY.

D. G. Elmes Records

BETTY JEFFREY

(1908–)

Army nurse. The Vyner Brooke *was carrying members of the Australian Army Nursing Service, including Betty Jeffrey, among its passengers, when it sailed from Singapore on 12 February 1942. Two days later it was sunk off Sumatra by Japanese bombs. Some of the army nurses were killed when the ship went down or drowned afterwards, others were massacred on a beach on Banka Island. Jeffrey and the rest were interned, some of them also dying before the end of war brought release. In this extract from Betty Jeffrey's memoirs, she tells the story of the massacre, of which Vivian Bullwinkel was the sole surviving woman. One of those machine-gunned on the beach was Dorothy Elmes, whose bright, chatty letters to 'Dear Old Smithy' now form her memorial at the Australian War Memorial in Canberra.*

FORBIDDEN SUBJECT

Vivian is a tall, slim girl, with very fair straight hair, cut short, and blue eyes. She is not an excitable person at any time, and she quietly walked in through the door of the jail, clasping an army-type water bottle, which was slung over her shoulder, to her side. We immediately saw why she did this. It was hiding a bullet hole in her uniform.

We took her into our dormitory, and as we all gathered round her she told us what had happened.

Vivian was with a group of servicemen, civilian women, and twenty-two Australian Army Nursing Service sisters. They had all gathered at this one spot on the sandy beach about two or three miles from Muntok, and had come ashore in lifeboats or had swum in. They spent the first night sitting round the fire we had all seen from the sea. There were quite a few wounded people with them, so they decided that when morning came they would search for some Japanese and see if the wounded could be cared for properly.

They waited all day, but nothing happened, and when night fell they were still there.

Next morning it was decided that a naval officer should walk into Muntok and bring back some Japanese with stretchers for the wounded, also informing them of the presence of the party on the beach.

After an hour or two of waiting the civilian women decided to walk on to Muntok themselves and so meet the Jap party on the way along. Our sisters, with Matron Drummond of the 13th AGH in charge, stayed behind to look after the wounded members of the group.

A little later the naval officer returned, bringing a party of Japanese with him. To everybody's amazement, the men were then separated from the nurses and then taken along the beach round a bluff and out of sight.

Later the Japs returned, wiping their bayonets, and everyone realized what had happened to the men.

The nurses were told to form a line, including the wounded, and walk into the sea. They were then machine-gunned from behind. All were killed outright but Vivian. A bullet passed through her left side just above her hip and sent her headlong into the water. She floated there for some minutes, then, when the Japanese had gone away, was able to struggle ashore. She realized she was the only person to survive. She wandered into the jungle, lay down by a tree, and went to sleep.

As soon as Vivian was able to walk she went back to the beach, thinking it was the same day and she had been asleep only a few hours. On the way she found an English serviceman, who told her he had been lying there for two days. His arm was badly wounded and he had been bayoneted. She helped him to move into the shade of the jungle, then went off to look for some food and water. She found a stream and was able to bring back water in her bottle.

For about ten days Vivian looked after this sick man, going each day to a small native settlement and getting food from them and water from the stream. The natives told her to give herself and her companion up to the Japanese; they had seen white women wearing Red Cross arm-bands in Muntok. They did not want to help them. As both were feeling a little better they decided to do this and so they set off for Muntok.

On the road they heard a car coming and it tooted at them. Quite unconsciously they moved to the side of the road to allow it to pass, then it dawned on them that the car must have Japanese in it, so they waited. It pulled up and a Japanese naval officer motioned them to get in. They did so, and he gave them a banana to eat.

This officer took them to Naval Headquarters and questioned them, then later brought them to the jail to join the rest of us.

What a wonderful relief it must have been for that poor girl, only in her twenties, to see familiar faces after going through a hell like that!

Vivian's companion was desperately ill and was put into the crude hospital here. He died a few days later.

After we heard this story we decided then and there never to mention it again; it would not do for it to go back to Japanese ears. The subject was strictly forbidden.

White Coolies (1954)

JESSIE SIMONS

(1911–)

Army nurse. Like Betty Jeffrey, Jessie Simons was interned by the Japanese during the Second World War, after the sinking of the Vyner Brooke. *In her account of those years, she recalls a particularly stressful incident that occurred in March 1942, when the women were at Palembang, on the island of Sumatra.*

THE CLUB

The next day was just another day until about 3 p.m. when we were hurriedly assembled and marched across Palembang, about two miles, to more permanent quarters in some abandoned Dutch houses. Our route lay along the main road to the aerodrome, and the trip was made both unpleasant and dangerous by erratically driven lorries and cars with their legacy of fumes and dust. We were, of course, a centre of unashamed curiosity to the civil population, Indonesian, Dutch and Eurasian. The Dutch were very distressed and would have come to our aid, but the presence of the Japs made them wary. We were vastly amused at the Jap photographers who stalked us constantly. Some took their pictures openly, but others hid in hedges and behind buildings, hoping to catch us off guard. Presumably the photos were for propaganda purposes, though we could not imagine what a polyglot crowd of incongruously clad prisoners, decorated with looted rubbish, would illustrate.

Two houses, close together, were allocated as quarters to the party of thirty-two nurses. Probably the houses had been built to accommodate less than a dozen between them, but the sight of normal cooking facilities and electric light, together with the prospect of a little more privacy, sent us eagerly touring our new quarters. In the yard behind the houses we eagerly snapped up half-empty bottles of pickles and sauce, and quickly shared the contents with little thought of either their quality or their previous owners. So starvation makes gluttons of us all!

The yard of the second house was occupied by a goat with a young kid, a discovery which summoned us all into consultation as to the best means of capitalizing the find. We were not yet hardened to duping our captors, which later on became the established practice, so we enjoyed the suggestion that the kid should be killed and eaten. In the light of later experience we now know that the Japs had only crude records even of prisoners, and certainly were unaware of the goat's existence. However, no-one had any qualms about starving the kid if necessary, so we went a-milking. One nurse held the goat's head and another the forefeet. A third clung grimly to the hindfeet while a fourth tried to coax milk from the indignant nanny. The stern determination of the milkmaids was equalled by the helpless laughter into which the spectators dissolved. What a Nip candid cameraman would have given for *that* photo!

Malayan women who had worked as servants for the dispossessed Dutch were very kind to us. One of them provided rice, native fruit and a kettle of beautifully hot coffee as a welcome to our new home. From the same source our wardrobes were expanded with clothes no doubt looted from abandoned Dutch houses. We settled down for the night better fed and more comfortable than we had been since Singapore.

Both our spirits and our comfort continued to improve for the next week. Some Dutch people, who had not yet been interned, more or less adopted us and, at some risk to themselves, provided bread, packs of cards, sets of chess and the luxury of cushions. The Japs showed little interest in us, and this week was a happy one, marked by relief and thankfulness. Our food was much better, thanks to the Dutch and Malays, and, shut off from strangers, we were together again under conditions which reminded us remotely of our bungalows at Singapore.

The interlude was a short one. During the second week the Nips showed much more interest in us and would wander into the house at any time, even into the bathrooms. On one occasion a Jap visitor found one girl in the nude doing her best to have a wash. After a brief inspection he laughed noisily and went out again, much to the victim's annoyance and relief. We scented trouble when the Nips informed us late in the week that the houses we had been occupying were required for entertainment purposes and that we would, therefore, be required to move to new quarters. Unanimously in favour of moving as far as possible from the proposed houses of entertainment, we planned to take over a couple of houses on the far side of the suburb, but the Nips frustrated this plan by ordering us into two vacant houses within a stone's throw.

You have never seen such a shift as that was. We took everything movable, and I mean *everything*. The fly-wire was stripped from the windows, the furniture was dragged down the road, and even an electric stove was persuaded from its place and laboriously hauled across to be installed in our new home. I remember that it was a Sunday and Iole Harper's birthday—she had no party and we no day of rest. The new houses were not so good as the old, but we were determined to make good the deficiencies, if possible, at the expense of the 'houses of entertainment'. We asked a Malay whether he could secure any electric globes for us as those in the new houses had all been looted or broken. He assured us that he could, and returned not merely with globes but with the whole fittings ripped from their places in our old houses.

The next week saw us back in the old houses as charwomen under Jap orders, cleaning and furnishing the rooms as a club for Jap officers. We had a fair idea of the type of entertainment which would be dispensed, so we named the houses 'Lavender Street' after an unsavoury thoroughfare in Singapore.

It is hard to express our feeling of horror and helplessness under these most trying conditions. Certainly we did not want even to arrange furniture for the club, but we knew what had happened to the other girls on the beach, and we wanted to get home some day.

A British collaborator was put in charge of the club and our disgust knew no bounds when she began to canvass throughout the camp for *geisha girls* to 'entertain' the Nips. To make it worse, she and her two young children had been with us on the *Vyner Brooke*. We did not feel that either her long residence in the cosmopolitan East nor her own obvious overdose of sex excused this latest exploit.

Despite the persuasion of how her own freedom resulted from her being in good favour with the Japanese, this lass found no-one pining for the delights of freedom or favour as a *geisha girl*. The club authorities were forced to recruit their entertainers by compulsion, so the AANS were ordered to attend on the club's opening night to assist in the entertainment of the camp's six Jap officers.

On the day of our assignment the thirty-two nurses met at four o'clock to lay out a plan of campaign. As a result we left at home those who were sick and chose the most glamorous of the remainder to stay with them as nurses. The rest of us set out to make ourselves as hideous as possible, putting into reverse all the beauty tricks we had picked up through the years. A few of the girls had come ashore with lipstick in their pockets, but for this night we discarded all make-up. With hair plastered down in the most unbecoming style, or dragged back in imitation of a nineteenth century school ma'am, we looked as unglamorous as Zazu Pitts at her best. Most of us went barefoot, but some added the ludicrous touch of heavy men's boots worn with bare legs. Altogether we achieved our uncomplimentary objective before we set out for 'Lavender Street'.

The six Japs were startled by the invasion of twenty-seven gaunt harpies. They had not expected that we should all obey orders, and were no less surprised by the thoroughness of our discouraging make-up. It was soon fairly clear that many advantages lay with us. Our numbers made the Japs' romantic ideas a little difficult to put into practice, and we densely refused to comprehend their poor English. Rapid comments between ourselves, which they could not follow, helped the campaign along.

On a table in the room was a hypodermic syringe and drugs. We had not the nerve to steal them, but often regretted it later when the drugs would have come in very useful.

Two Englishmen were acting as waiters, together with a British boy, a good scout whose service to the Japs was anything but voluntary. In accordance with a previous agreement, we all refused the liquor which was served with biscuits by the waiters. One of the Japs queried in astonishment, 'But what do Australian girls drink?' The girl addressed had often drunk too much of what was not good for her, but she answered off-handedly, 'Oh, we never drink anything but milk.' Despite the gravity of our plight I nearly burst out laughing as I caught her eye.

At that moment nothing would have delighted us more than the nourishment and vitamins of milk, of which we had had none in Sumatra if the goat's few unwilling drops are omitted, but the Nips compromised by serving soft drinks. We sipped these and nibbled the biscuits for a couple of hours. When the Japs were not looking, we pocketed biscuits, sugar and cakes for the home larder. We sparred with the Japs until they were bored into sending us home about 11 p.m. with the instruction that on our next visit we must add a little colour and attractiveness to our appearance.

Though the experience of the half of our party which had gone to the second house was much the same, they were not so fortunate in their dismissal. Four of the girls were detained when the rest went home. The girls who stayed were chosen by us all in advance as those most likely to outwit the Japs. We sweated with anxiety, imagining the worst, until the four returned weary but unharmed at 1 a.m. These girls put up a great show, outplaying the officers at every turn. The Nips could not understand spoken English, but could write and read it with some difficulty. They made no secret of what they wanted from the girls, whose refusal was no less emphatic. The Nips then wrote, 'We'll starve you,' and received the reply, 'That won't make any difference.' Apparently amazed, they wrote back, 'But you will die,' to which the reply was a laconic 'OK'. So the argument swayed until the exasperated Japs angrily sent the girls home to think things over. We kept the notes as a grim souvenir for two years, and then only destroyed them in fear of secret police who insisted on searching us. I think all the girls would agree that this club experience was the most repulsive and unpleasant in our whole imprisonment. I know it stands out grimly in our memories.

For two weeks after this we were under enormous tension, and became mentally worn with expectation. Any sound, at night especially, set our hearts pounding. Then we were able to make our plight known (through our MO Dr McDowell) to a Dutch Red Cross official who reported to the Jap headquarters and, to our great relief, the whole club project was abandoned.

In Japanese Hands (1985, first published as *While History Passed,* 1954)

JUDITH WRIGHT

(1915–)

Poet and writer. The daughter of a grazier, Judith Wright was born near Armidale, New South Wales, and educated at New England Girls School and the University of Sydney. For decades she has been acknowledged as one of Australia's finest poets. The following beautiful poem was published in her first book, The Moving Image *(1946). In a brief foreword to her* Collected Poems, 1942–1985 *(1994), she provides a context for it, talking of 'the great displacements of people during World War II, their snatching into armies and other defence forces, the desperation of lovers faced with the prospect of a separation which might last forever, and the urgency of need which drove the young into each others' arms'.*

'THE COMPANY OF LOVERS'

We meet and part now over all the world.
We, the lost company,
take hands together in the night, forget
the night in our brief happiness, silently.
We who sought many things, throw all away
for this one thing, one only,
remembering that in the narrow grave
we shall be lonely.

Death marshals up his armies round us now.
Their footsteps crowd too near.
Lock your warm hand above the chilling heart
and for a time I live without my fear.
Grope in the night to find me and embrace,
for the dark preludes of the drums begin,
and round us, round the company of lovers,
Death draws his cordons in.

The Moving Image (1946)

KATHARINE SUSANNAH PRICHARD

(1883–1969)

Writer. This extract is taken from Winged Seeds *(1950), the final volume of Prichard's Western Australian goldfields trilogy. One of the main characters, Sally Gough, is thinking of her communist grandson Bill, when she sees Pat, a stepdaughter of the capitalist Paddy Cavan. Like many other writers, Prichard has comments to make about the presence of 'the Yanks' in Australia during the Second World War.*

'CARRYING ON'

'Missus Sally — what luck! I was hoping there'd be time to dash out to see you. But the Trans is late, and we've got to go straight through to Perth.'

Sally looked up from the trestle table she was swabbing down at a canteen on the railway station. A girl in the uniform of the WAAAF, with an officer of the United States Air Force beside her, had stopped suddenly as she was passing.

For the fraction of a second Sally did not recognize Pat in the smart dark blue uniform and peaked cap. Her mind was still busy with men from the troop train which had pulled out an hour before, hundreds of them swarming over the platform, in their shoddy khaki, unwashed and hungry. They were travelling in open cattle trucks to the coast; lads, most of them, with big guns loaded into their trucks, about which they were as proud and protective as young mothers. So like Bill they were with their sun-brown faces, cheery grins and rowdy chiacking, as they shoved and wrestled for a place at the table near her. She felt as if she had been handing out cups of tea and bulky corned-beef sandwiches to innumerable Bills — although a gunner's shabby beret was pushed back on their heads, not the felt hat with its turned-up flap Lal had worn so jauntily, then Dick, and Bill. That hat was more the distinguishing mark of an Australian soldier than the badge he wore on his sleeve. Sally was thinking of Bill as she cleaned up after the gunners had gone. Where was he? What had happened to him? It was so long since she had had a letter, or any news. She was worrying about that when the transcontinental train pulled in, and civilian passengers, officers of the army and air force, sailors going to rejoin their ships at Fremantle, streamed past to board the western express at the far end of the station.

Pat dropped her suitcase, and turned to the man beside her.

'This is Mrs Gough,' she explained blithely. 'Meet Mrs Gough, Major Anthony Jefferson Dekker of the United States Air Force. I've been posted to Geraldton, Missus Sally, and he's going further north. We met on the train. What's the news of Bill? I haven't heard from him for months.'

'Neither have we,' Sally said, acknowledging the major's salute mechanically with a nod and smile.

'I won't believe anything could happen to him,' Pat cried. 'I just won't. These days,' she added, her face crumpling in vague distress, 'you've got to do your job and not think of anything else. I've just been given a responsible position. Look at my pips — ' she turned to show the stripes on her sleeve and its air force wings. 'Three hundred girls under me, and our training's stiff. At first I thought I could never stand it. But, now, I'm as hard as nails: can walk miles, eat like a horse and be as shrewd and stern as a sergeant-major, maintaining discipline in the WAAAF.'

'If you want that drink, lootenant,' Major Dekker remarked, glancing at his wrist-watch, 'we'll have to hustle.'

Pat saluted briskly and picked up her suitcase.

'Marching orders,' she laughed back at Sally. 'We've got about ten minutes to catch the express and I'm dying for a glass of Hannan's. Give my love to Dinny. And Daph! How is she?' Already she was moving away with the major's arm under hers. 'Let me know if — when you hear from Bill,' she called. 'I'll write from Geraldton. Hop over to see you when I get leave.'

Sally lost sight of her in the crowd surging towards the bar and restaurant further along the platform. Most of the men were frantic for a drink after two days of crossing the sun-blasted desert of the Nullarbor plains, and with the prospect of a hot night before them, sitting up in the rackety western express. As Sally stood watching Pat and the American, pain and uneasiness stirred her bemused weariness.

So that's what Bill's love affair had come to: something to be mentioned casually and thrust aside. There was no place for it evidently in Pat's mind at present. She was very pleased with herself, and her importance as an officer of the WAAAF, Sally thought. She had cut her bright hair and tucked it away under that smart cap with the gold embroidered badge in front; she looked robust and handsome in her trim uniform. Military training had improved her physique, and Pat was more concerned, it was evident, to be correctly military in her bearing, than to exercise any feminine charm on either Major Jefferson Dekker or Bill's grandmother. But she had not abjured feminine charm altogether, Sally perceived. She still reddened her lips, and the siren lurked in her grey-green eyes as she smiled at the American. Major Jefferson Dekker had caught a glimpse of the siren, Sally guessed, and wondered whether Pat had become 'Yank happy' like so many other girls who were fluttering gaily with American soldiers.

It was a shame the way the girls were 'carrying on', Sally considered. Of course, Australian soldiers in their ill-fitting, shoddy, khaki uniforms were not so well turned-out as the Americans. They did not have as much money to spend. They did not address a girl friend as 'Beautiful!' and make her feel she was as alluring as Dorothy Lamour. But it was galling for Australian soldiers to see how girls fell for the Americans. At the picture theatres, every Yank had a girl beside him, and men on leave from distant training camps glared at them, sore and disgruntled. The perfidy of the girls and the swanky superior airs the Yanks gave themselves had caused many a brawl.

It was to be expected, people were saying, that thousands of young and vigorous men, separated from their own women folk, on the eve of battle, as it were, should make the most of any time left to them for gay living. Drink and women gave most of them all they required: the pub lounges were full: queues lined up outside the brothels. But so many Australian women and girls, deprived of their husbands, lovers and sweethearts for over two years, were forgetting them for the newcomers that ill-will between men of the AIF on active service and the United States forces was smouldering.

The Yanks had charming manners, plenty of money and were generous and amusing, the women said. The young girls, particularly, thrilled to the happy-go-lucky Yanks who looked like film stars, picked them up in shops and milk bars, presented them with orchids, took them about in taxis, and made whoopee every night of the week when they were on leave. There were letters in the newspapers about drunken girls in their teens going round with soldiers, being sick in the streets of the big cities, and lying about with them in the parks. Public outcry had demanded the passing of regulations to make it an offence to serve girls in their teens with alcohol in a hotel, or to take them to an apartment for immoral purposes.

The spate of sordid sexuality, scandals, brawls, domestic tragedies, divorces, crimes of passion and perversion, continued. It was recognized that all this was part of the cost of war. And, of course, there were romantic love affairs, engagements and weddings, as well. But the reaction of Australian men to the Yanks who were ousting them from the favour of their women had become bitter and resentful. Men on active service, or men coming home on leave from training camps, who found themselves jilted lovers or deserted husbands with broken homes, neglected children and gossiping neighbours to contend with, nursed a sombre grouch against the Americans.

Now the battered 6th and 7th Divisions who had been fighting in Libya and Greece were returning, it was rumoured. They had threatened to settle scores with the Yanks.

It was a bad business, Sally knew, this hostility which had cropped up between men of the AIF and the United States forces.

'What the flibbertigibbets do doesn't matter,' Dinny said. 'Or the women who make a living by the game. But I feel as mad as the boys when a man coming home from Libya and Greece finds his wife's cleared out with a Yank.'

'You can't help being sorry for the Americans, too,' Sally demurred. 'Their wives and sweethearts. Some quite decent lads've been caught by real trollops.'

'More fools they,' Dinny had growled.

Sally hoped Bill would be coming home with the 6th Division. Thinking of Pat and Major Jefferson Dekker, she wondered whether Bill, too, might have a score to settle with the Yanks.

Late one afternoon when she had been collecting for the Red Cross, Sally turned down the end of Brookman Street, where most of the houses were brothels, barricaded round with barbed wire. Troops had been swarming through the town that day, and a racket of gramophones, radios, raucous voices laughing and singing uproariously, came from the drab, weather-beaten houses. Brazen sunshine beat down on the wide, dusty street, and Sally was hurrying along, shamed and hurt by the sight of those high fences and barbed-wire barricades, as she always had been, when the eerie wail of a familiar air caught her ear — 'ma chandelle est morte … je n'ai pas de feu …'

Sprawled on the door step of a house more dilapidated than the rest, she saw a drunken old woman in a pink chemise. Her shrunken limbs were exposed: her withered face had been carelessly rouged, her lank, disordered grey hair hung about her, yellowed by peroxide. She was a tragic and pitiful spectacle. Sally fled from it.

'Poor Lili,' Dinny said when Sally asked him what had happened to Lili that she should have sunk so low, 'she's been havin' a rough spin, lately. She and Belle were livin' in comfort, like ladies; but when Belle died a man, name of Guarez, took over the house Belle was running and put Lili to work for him. He had to hold her down, screamin', at first, the local boys say. Now she's rotten with disease. None of them would go near her. But women are scarce. The bludger who owns the place picks up drunken soldiers and sailors and tells them Lili's a high-class French piece. He's made a lot of money out of her, Tassy says.'

'God!' Sally exclaimed, outraged and furious. 'It's unbelievable. We must do something to stop it, Dinny. For the soldiers' sake — as well as Lili's.'

'That's right,' Dinny agreed. But he did not want Missus Sally to take Lili under her wing. 'The military can stop a diseased prostitute bein' used like that. I'll have a word with Tassy and some of the old-timers. P'raps we can pass round the hat and have Lili moved into a room of her own, somewhere.'

Dinny got busy. When action was threatened against the brothel keeper if Lili remained on his premises, Dinny and his mates took charge of her. They arranged for her to live with two old friends of hers, Mrs Rosy Ann Plush and Mrs Amelia Green. Rosy Ann and Mrs Amelia prided themselves on being respectable, although when they had had a glass too many they were often in trouble with the police. They were good sorts, and not so respectable that they would look down their noses at Lili, Dinny pointed out. As a matter of fact she had wept and kissed Dinny and all the old men, when they left her with Rosy Ann and Mrs Amelia.

''E was a wicked man, *ce cochon de Guarez*,' she said tearfully, 'and verry cruel to poor Lili. It will be so good to be togezzer with friends, now.'

Sally had been to see her soon afterwards and found Lili very frail but with something of her old sprightliness, living contentedly with Mrs Plush and Mrs Green. Rosy Ann had had a win on the races that day, so they went off to the Reward to celebrate. Sally had never been there except with Marie, and the 'Ladies Room' in which they used to take their pot of beer with other old-timers, after a shopping excursion, looked dingier and shabbier than ever. God-Save-Us-Sarah had disappeared from her dark corner. Lili would be missing Belle, too, Sally thought.

As Rosy Ann and Mrs Green gabbled hilariously to the barmaid, who had served their drinks, about their luck on an outsider, Lili raised her heavy schooner and whispered: '*Aux amies parties*'. Sally did not understand those words; but she drank with Lili, knowing they were both thinking of Belle and Marie.

Winged Seeds (1950)

ELYNE MITCHELL

(1913–)

Writer and grazier. Elyne Chauvel, whose father was a Great War commander, married a grazier named Tom Mitchell in 1935. During the Second World War, which saw her husband become a prisoner of war of the Japanese, Elyne Mitchell ran the family's cattle property, Towong Hill, at the foot of the Victorian Alps. In these words from her autobiography, she describes a wartime winter. Her other publications include the well-known Silver Brumby series for children.

THE WINTER OF '42

That winter of 1942, it rained and a lot of snow fell in the mountains. Then in July torrential rain fell on the snow, and we had a huge flood, the Indi River coming right out as well as the Swampy Plains, so our Top Plain paddock was inundated. We spent one day rabbiting there, riding through the icy flood waters, armed with plum sticks, and with several rabbit dogs. The next day we rode down into the Big Paddock, having to start the day by swimming the runner — anabranch — in that fierce cold, so we were wet from the waist down. The wind blew, the wet clothes clung to frozen bodies, red hands slipped on the wet reins.

The horses were wading through water almost all day, cantering, splashing up freezing water even on to face and hands. The grey clouds made the water dark. Swirling current gave it an ominous look. There were deep holes in the paddock here and there, I knew, and to fall into one would be nasty to say the least, but it would be disastrous if my horse, wading on and on through water, suddenly stepped over the invisible bank of the river and floundered into the current.

The small fox terriers and whippets shivered with cold when they were not galloping through the water after rabbits. Jack Reiners, who owned them, would give them a ride in front of his saddle, in turn — little foxies with their cold, pink skin showing through sparse white hair. We, too, galloped after rabbits, killing those on tussocks or tree trunks, really with barely any sympathy for these animals who ruined the good earth, ate all the grass and caused massive erosion.

We ate our lunch, standing shivering on high ground between lagoons that were filled with flood water, and not far from the surging river. The clouds dropped lower, grew darker. Presently, up in the mountains, snow would fall again and quieten the waters streaming off every ridge and down every gully.

I enjoyed the fearful power of the floods, the raging snow waters, the sound of it at night, roaring round the hill on which the house is built. It was not till I had young children that I realized the truly dreadful strength of these floods, and visualized a small child caught in the swift, freezing torrent. Then afterwards, when there were no longer young children who might get out of the garden and run down to the flood water, I could once again hear that roar of the melting snow and feel strange excitement in its primeval power. I could see with pleasure the quiet filling of every lagoon in the paddocks so that they were glittering crescents, and think of ski tracks I have made on the western face that had melted and washed away, and became part of the water sweeping round the foot of the hill.

The water is now controlled to a degree by dams and tunnels in the mountains, and if the Snowy Mountains Hydro-electric Scheme is letting a lot of water through the tunnels from Eucumbene dam, and opening the gate of the Khancoban Pondage, they usually warn us that they are 'pulling out the plug'. A hot wind on the snow, followed by rain, will bring an immense amount of snow off the western face, more than the dams on this side can hold, and we will have a flood without any warning except our own years of experience.

1942 was a heavy snow year, though I know now that it was not as heavy as the winters of the nineteenth century and earlier this century.

After our July flood, and after a great deal of snow had fallen again, we had some bright frosty weather and could see the great white horizon rimming the valley in an arc from the Dargals on to the Grey Mare and the wall of the western face, right through to Pinnabar.

That was when Jill Macdonald and I rode into Geehi, camped there, at the time of the full moon, and went on up the Hannel Spur to the snowline, and skied from there to the Chalet, with the black shadow of Roley padding along, silent-footed in the snow, behind

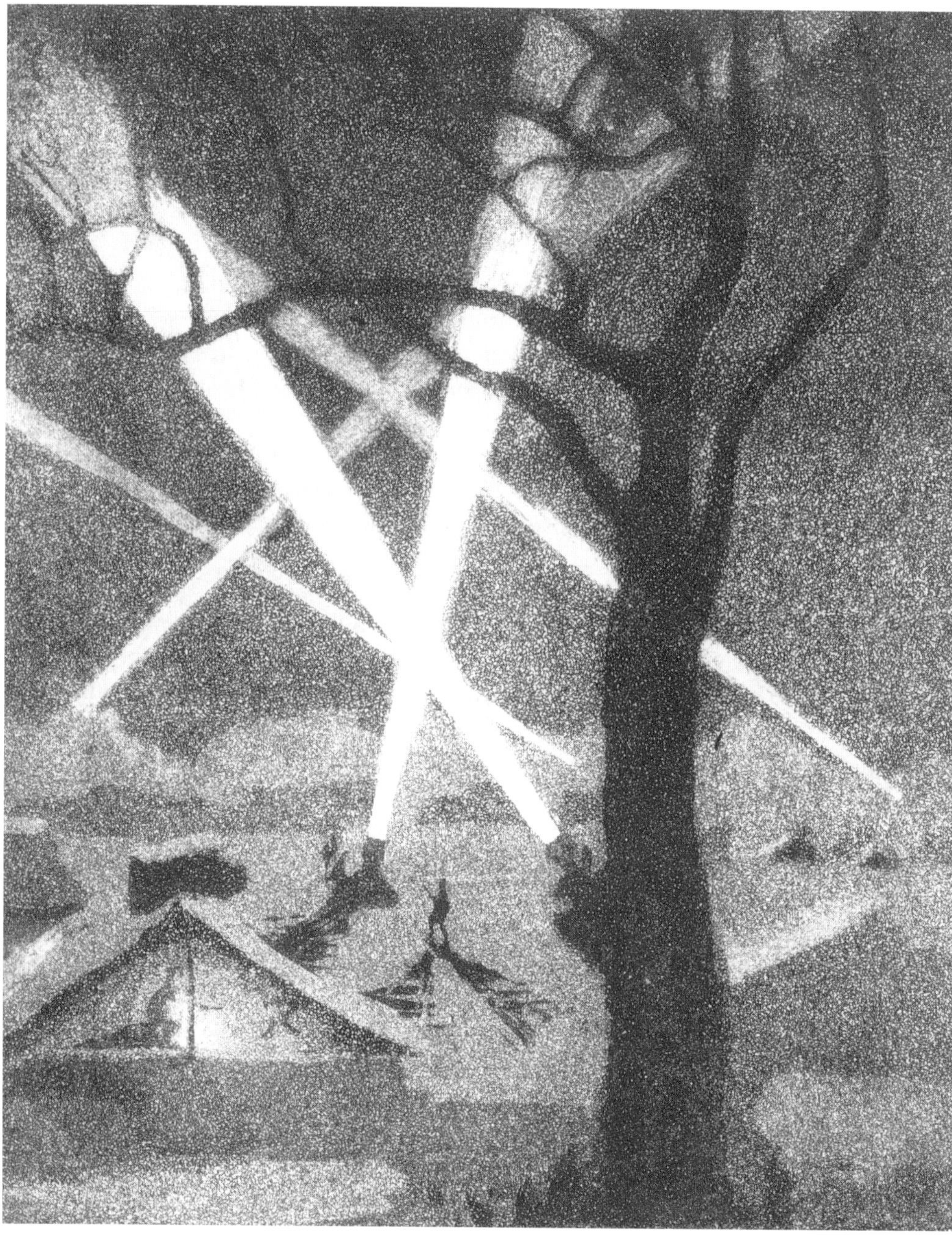

Christine Miller (Aldor) (1913–70), *Searchlights*, 1942, aquatint, 24.4 x 19.2 cm. Purchased in 1987. (AWM 29348)

us. That was when, in the winter of 1942, we spent one miraculous day of frosted powder snow, skiing the steep face of Mount Northcote, climbing up and skiing it again. I remember standing on the top of Northcote with Roley beside me, looking along the cascading cliffs and gullies of the western face, where I had made some of the first ski tracks ever made, with such excitement, only the year before, and looking out over the Murray Valley, weighing out my loyalties.

There, on the glittering snow, I knew that the trust borne on the south wind each night as I went out on to the terrace at Towong Hill would be demanding my allegiance on and on into the desperately uncertain future, but knew, too, that these mountains would hold my love for ever. On their slopes I had expended strength and passion with the touch of my skis on their snow, and they seemed part of my home, part of what I saw each day — an enduring anchor against the unimaginable thunder and storms to come.

We skied: and I returned to my sheep vigil.

I had another, fruitless, effort to get a day's skiing on all that untouched snow of 1942. In September I loaded my skis and boots, sleeping bag and rucksack of camera gear, spare clothes and tucker for myself and Roley, and he and I drove as far as we could, to the 1900-foot mark on the Unemployed Relief road that still exists up a spur of the Dargals Range. From there I walked, having great difficulty crossing flooded creeks, boots slung round my neck, ski pants rolled up, wading on slippery stones with a ridiculously lame foot. By the time I reached the foot of the Long Spur it was becoming obvious that the weather might turn bad; however, I had an oiled japarra cover for my sleeping bag, and I got a good fire going. I made Roley a bed of ferns under a big log.

'The comfort of the red blaze of my fire began to see right into me — red blaze, bodily weariness being soothed by food, tall white gums, mountain "cattle road", just the bush around me … ,' I wrote in my diary.

I heard the drone of an aeroplane high overhead, the sound coming and going through the cloud ceiling that had gathered. There was no civil aviation then, and the sound of a plane always set one wondering.

Roley was jumpy, barking at everything, every soughing strip of bark, every crack of a stick. I thought I heard claws scratching as something climbed up a ribbon gum, and I looked up and saw something black outlined for one moment. Roley's barking stopped just as there was a staccato 'quark, quark, quark, quark' from up at the top of the tall white ribbon gum … and the black shape took off, zooming from the tree, gliding on outspread 'wings', a long gentle glide, and it landed in the darkness of the bush.

A giant glider. It was a gift from the night that was indeed going to turn wet by two o'clock. Rain drops woke me then, pattering on to my oiled japarra cover. Roley snuggled in under the little tent-like flap tied to a stake behind my head. He tried to keep dry beside me, but he might have saved himself the trouble, because the rain kept on. By morning we had to walk back to the car, through dripping wattle fronds and hop scrub, and wade through rising creeks. So the skis on my shoulder had not had the chance to skim over spring snow, and there would be no more camping for months because the hard work of springtime was already starting, and I had to return to it, to the cattle mustering, the dagging, footrotting and shearing of the sheep, the thistle-cutting, rabbiting, haymaking, and the long, lonely waiting.

Towong Hill (1990 edition, first published 1989)

KYLIE TENNANT

(1912–88)

Writer and editor. Kylie Tennant, who was born and educated in Sydney, worked in many jobs, ranging from those of barmaid to lecturer. Such experiences helped in the writing of her many novels, which include The Battlers *(1941). The following extract is taken from* Ride On Stranger *(1943). The book's main character, Shannon Hicks, has married a farmer called John Terrill. This scene follows his unexpected enlistment.* Ride on Stranger *was made into an ABC television mini-series in 1979.*

'WOMEN LYING AWAKE'

The bustle of their return; the responsibility of Aunt Edith; the luggage; the long journey; and, when she arrived, the preoccupations of the house; even the flood of news from Minnie Sandleberry, helped to set a surface over the grave indignation which seethed like lava through Shannon's thoughts. Aunt Edith approved of the farm. She was more interested and cheerful than Shannon had known her since the old boarding-house days.

'I wonder if you would mind,' she asked at tea-time, glancing around the bare room, 'if I asked them to send some of my furniture down here? It is no use whatever stored away.'

This furniture of Aunt Edith's, particularly a mahogany sideboard, had been a bone of contention when she was selling up the Clayton House. Where Aunt Edith went, there she was followed by a trail of huge crates containing her household goods. Shannon's lack of such impedimenta seemed to Aunt Edith as shocking as nakedness.

John cast an uneasy glance at his wife's set face. 'Shannon told you I'd enlisted, Aunt Edith?'

'Why yes, John.' Aunt Edith called him John quite naturally. 'But she will be keeping the farm?'

Shannon nodded. 'I'll be keeping on this place, John, if that suits you?' Her voice was mild, almost expressionless. She might have been asking if she would give him another cup of tea. 'We might even take in a few boarders over the holidays.'

It was not until Aunt Edith had retired to the stretcher-bed which John had borrowed, that he felt free to open up the very sore subject of his enlistment. He had got leave to settle his affairs, and if she persisted in her determination to remain on the place, it would complicate all his plans.

'What I thought,' he suggested, almost humbly 'was that you might go back to Sydney or Melbourne?'

'I could always get some kind of a job, couldn't I?' Shannon agreed, still in that dangerously mild voice. 'I'm so capable?'

'Yes, I'd thought of that.'

'But you weren't willing to talk it over with me first ?'

He was silent.

'You just disposed of me quite easily with your other chattels?'

'Now, Shannon, what's the use of being savage?'

'You don't expect me to sing: "We don't want to lose you but we think you ought to go?" That's a little too much.' She cupped her chin in her hand and watched him intently.

'Shannon, I never wanted you to become a drudge, a farmer's wife. I hate seeing you worked to death, milking and cleaning and washing, always eternally busy about something, a sort of domestic Martha. Don't hate me so, darling.'

'I don't hate you, John. You were always so sane and honest, the only sane person I'd ever known, I thought. And now the insane streak is coming out. Why of all people do you need to fling yourself into this? Your work is so important. There are thousands of men who aren't doing anything half as important.'

'Shannon, no man is more important than another. You can't weigh and judge and measure men. I just felt I had to do it. And I was afraid,' he admitted, 'of what you'd say. Yes, I was cowardly enough to wait until you were out of the road.'

'And it wasn't just an impulse?' she asked, her voice still mild and reasonable. 'You had it planned all the time?'

'You see I knew your views. You'd told me so often that this war was just another kind of madness. But, damn it!' he burst out, 'if the rest of the human race is mad, then I'm mad too, and I'd sooner share with other people than sit aside and judge.' He began to wander about the room, fingering a book on a shelf, dropping it, taking up one small article after another. 'You're an anarchist, Shannon. You simply refuse to accept people as they are, things as they are. But you can't alter them.'

'Then why did you join the army if you don't think you can alter things as they are?'

He would have been happier if she had stormed at him, wept, done anything except preserve that steely self-control. 'I joined up because it was the only thing any one could do.'

'You joined up to escape, to escape life. Half the world is committing suicide and you join that half. It isn't I who's running away, now, John. It's you.'

'Have it your own way,' he said sullenly. 'You might try to understand me, Shannon, instead of judging.'

'Weren't you happy with me?'

'You know I was happy. Damnably happy.'

'And you had to leave me, leave this place … Oh! I know there's no sense in talking, but do sit down and stop prowling around like a trapped cat. Tell me this,' her voice was suddenly fierce, 'if we had had any children … would that have made a difference?'

'Yes, no, I don't think so. I felt I just had to go.' He was profoundly miserable, and indignant that she should make him feel guilty. 'You turn everything upside down. I'm not deserting you or skulking away. I'm just doing what any man would do.'

'Yes,' she sighed. 'That's what I'm complaining about.' Then, with a swift, impulsive movement, she caught at his hand. 'Let's not waste time arguing. There's so little time left. Let's not say any more. Just kiss and forget it.'

'But, Shannon, we've got to settle what you're going to do.'

'I've told you. I'm staying here. Aunt Edith will look after the house. I'll have to do what I can with the Jerseys. Why, if it comes to that, Dad would sooner give up his job at the butter factory than see a neat little herd of milkers go out of the family.'

'But I tell you I didn't want you to drudge,' he argued wearily.

'Well, if I must drudge at something,' she said more cheerfully, 'I prefer drudging at what I like. This is my place. I'm sticking to it. And if you come back with a few arms and legs blown off,' her eyes filled with tears, but she brushed them hurriedly away, 'there'll be somewhere for you to come. See?'

He was moved by her attempt to stifle those tears. 'I haven't treated you well, Shannon. I'm sorry I …' She came over and curled up beside him, her arms about his neck.

'When do you go into camp?'

'In a few days.' His face was averted.

'Well, let's make the most of them. Let's go and look at the sea and neglect the place and be late with the milking and use up all the petrol we can, and then when you get leave and come home, Auntie will have the house all civilized and full of silver forks and cake plates. She's really a grand old stick.' When he looked lost and miserable like a little boy, Shannon could do nothing but console. 'And I'll have Minnie Sandleberry and George, and George's two boys are big enough to help. You'll see. We'll manage somehow.'

He began to be soothed, but the lost look was still about him. 'You always were a demon for responsibility, Shannon.'

'Then when you come back, it will all still be here. You can go on sorting soil and testing it for amino-acids and you'll be surprised at all the new chicken-runs and the pigs … I think I'll have some pigs and turkeys. And, by golly!' she was talking on and on just to smooth over the hurt. 'I'll have Auntie write to old Briscoe, you remember, Briscoe and the Wyandottes, prize show-birds, every one. Briscoe is living on the old-age pension and he'd love to come and bring his hens.'

'Don't complicate things too much,' he warned her. 'I know you, Shannon. One of these days you'll want to up and quit. You'll just walk out and leave the lot.'

She laughed. 'But, darling, how could I? I'll be waiting here, you see, a good, faithful wife …'

'You make me feel like a skunk.'

'Well, stop feeling a skunk.' She kissed him soundly. 'There! Now, let's go out for a walk to clear our heads, and you can tell me all about the sergeant and the camp. Think of the beautiful parcels I'll be sending you.'

She went on talking brightly, carefully, while her hungry eyes watched him, storing up the way his hair fell over his forehead, the clean profile, the little wrinkles around his mouth, the few grey hairs above his ear. In a few days' time she would not have anything of him except letters and the waiting for him to get leave. She would have to fill in the days, work very hard, so that at night she might be able to sleep instead of lying awake thinking of him. There were so many women lying awake all over the world. Into her head came the words that South Quilter had uttered on that night, when they had looked over the dark water toward the glow of the city. 'I think of women lying awake at night.'

Ride On Stranger (1988 edition, first published 1943)

PATSY ADAM-SMITH

(1926–)

Writer. Patsy Adam-Smith grew up in country Victoria, moving around with her parents, who were railways workers. During the Second World War, she served with the Voluntary Aid Detachments and their successor, the Australian Army Medical Women's Service. Her many publications include The Anzacs *(1978),* Australian Women at War *(1984), and* Prisoners of War *(1992). She makes the following criticism of the changeover from VADs to AAMWS, which occurred in December 1942, in her autobiography,* Goodbye Girlie *(1994).*

'KHAKI!'

Thinking back, I believe we young women in this quite humble and laborious VAD service could never, then or now, have gathered together a greater group of women than we had in those years.

The system of using VADs worked smoothly and well. Our Commandant in each State cared for us and saw us as *her* girls. From this distance in time it could be seen as an exclusive group, and it was in one sense: all had volunteered to work under any circumstances and hours under the discipline of army orders. There never was any need for discipline—mostly because we had all enlisted in our home town areas where everyone knew one another, or in the case of city girls, were known to the group they had enlisted with. We were proud of our distinctive uniform and shoulder flashes and Red Cross on the upper arm.

And then, in 1942, an announcement: we were to discard all VAD uniforms and the bits and pieces that went with them and don khaki. You could almost imagine you heard the cry go up from Hobart to Port Douglas and across to Darwin. No! We most certainly wouldn't change our uniforms. Khaki! Even the men of our hospitals were against it. We were adamant. We would stay with our time-honoured uniform. We were still outraged when the next blow hit: we were to go into Darley training camp in Victoria, as did the soldiers and the service-women, and we were to learn to march and, God help us, salute.

I honestly tried. To salute you had to take a swing of the arm and elbow that could decapitate a stander-by; and worse, you could almost tear out an eye with the nail of your middle finger with no difficulty at all — I bore witness to this. For the whole of the three weeks we tottered up and down the parade ground my bloodshot eye was bloody, hideous and embarrassing. Everyone, including the poor First-World-War sergeant-major whose charges we were, did a poor job of sympathising. There was more, worse, and everyone said 'But how did you manage to do that?' How would I know how I did it? I thought I'd executed a perfect about-turn. I didn't do it on purpose, as many accused me. None recognised that I had believed I would surprise them all — including the sergeant-major — with my dexterity. When four or five girls fell to the ground I had assumed it was their doing, not mine.

Goodbye Girlie (1994)

ELEANOR DARK

(1901–86)

Writer. Eleanor Dark, daughter of the poet Dowell O'Reilly, was born and educated in Sydney. She is best known for her trilogy of historical novels, The Timeless Land *(1941),* Storm of Time *(1948), and* No Barrier *(1954). In these pages from* The Little Company *(1945), a novel of ideas set in wartime Sydney, we meet Gilbert Massey, a left-wing bookseller and author, during his extra-marital affair with Elsa Kay.*

'AN HONEST ANIMAL'

For the first time in years he fell asleep with his mind blank. Sleep was not a slow-rising tide, submerging a brain exhausted but still helplessly active — it was a tidal wave of obliteration. The war did not go with him into this blessed nothingness, but snatched him from it by way of a split-second dream that was all climax. It rolled into a tight, hard ball, it grew fiery red, and then, at its core, white, as if fire were consuming itself. This central vacuum contracted, sucking flame inward like a whirlpool, spinning and absorbing with such intensity that he knew it must explode. Then he was awake; it had exploded, and he was looking into a darkness that still seemed to shake with sound. He felt Elsa stir beside him.

'What was that?'

'I don't know ...'

He was listening, his heart thumping from the shock of a dream colliding with reality. There was gunfire now, but it was not gunfire which had burst his dream and set the floor vibrating. His brain, returning slowly from the confusion of sleep, reminded him that he had heard the window rattle in its frame.

'They're practising,' Elsa said sleepily.

'Yes.'

He heard her sigh, felt her huddle down beneath the blankets, and lay down again himself. She fell asleep quickly; he heard her light breathing. He listened to the distant sound of heavy guns, and then to the sharp clatter of nearer firing. A shaft of vivid light swept across the window blind. He got out of bed, felt his way cautiously into the dark living room and across to the window; as he reached it the air split with noise again, and the floor shivered under his feet. He pulled the curtains back and lifted the window, feeling a rush of sharp wintry cold on his face. The sky was reeling drunkenly on long stilts of light, the trees were black and silver under the moon, the glimpse of harbour between them was flat and polished like a steel plate; the air was full of the roaring of 'planes.

Elsa, wrapped in a thick dressing-gown, came to stand beside him.

'What is it?'

'There's something up.'

'An — air raid?'

'There wasn't any siren — was there?'

'I didn't hear it. Those guns sound close.'

'Yes.'

The next explosion seemed to hit them like a blow, but by now his mind had seized on its muffled quality, and he said quickly:

'Depth charges. There must be a sub. about.'

'In the harbour?'

'Sounds like it.'

She shivered, and he put his arm round her. She said with a faint note of annoyance, pulling away from him:

'I'm cold.'

He watched the searchlights sweeping low over the water. Something in her tone and her withdrawal had disturbed him, but he could not think about it now. There was an urgency of sound which anchored all his attention to listening. The crescendo and diminuendo of the 'planes, the agitated noise of patrol vessels and the vicious challenge of the guns were all grotesque against the still serenity of the moonlight; his eyes denied the possibility of what his ears were hearing. Another detonation shook the house; they heard the glass in the window of the next flat crack: He realised that he was cold too. Someone knocked at the door.

'For goodness' sake,' Elsa whispered sharply, 'go back into the bedroom!'

He felt a sudden irritation at having this small furtiveness imposed on him, but he obeyed, closing the door behind him, and stood in the dark listening with only half his attention to her voice and another woman's, while the other half still concentrated on the noise from the harbour. Elsa came back.

'It's no good standing about and getting cold, Gilbert. It was Mrs Slade from the next door flat. She's a motherly old dear who's always telling me I should drink more milk because I'm too thin. She was afraid I might be scared and like some company. She thought it must be an air raid. I had quite a job convincing her it wasn't.'

He stretched out in the grateful warmth of the bed, felt her hand groping for his, and held it.

She said:

'There's less noise now.'

'Yes.'

'Do you think they've — got it?'

'If they haven't they will.'

'Gilbert.'

'Yes?'

'I'm glad you're here.'

'There's no danger — to us.'

Her hand moved impatiently in his.

'I know. I wasn't thinking of that. I'm just glad you're here.'

He supposed that he should have responded to that in some loverlike way, but the most he could do was to tighten his grip on her hand, and refrain from asking 'Why?' He could not refrain, however, from wondering rather dejectedly why he should want to ask such a question. The war and the world had crowded back into his life while he slept, and the noises of their devastation had wakened him to a dreary sanity. He knew now that no physical union, no shared emotional tumult between himself and Elsa could bring them together while they stood apart on the issues raised by those searchlights and explosions. Unless you were together there, you were together nowhere. Stretched beside him in the dark she was a thousand miles away; his thought was as solitary as ever, brooding over men — perhaps not half a mile from where he lay — dead or dying, trapped under the moon-cold water in a steel prison. There was a sort of imperviousness about Elsa, he thought, barricaded behind her armour of egotism she paid for her inaccessibility to the world by being inaccessible to everyone. She had said that she was not afraid. Is fear only for oneself? He was afraid; not only cold was making his body rigid, and stretching his nerves to a tense wakefulness. Though you are not yourself a military objective at the moment, can you not fear the destructive mechanisms of war merely because they exist? Can you not fear for a world that makes and uses them? And as the room shook suddenly to another explosion his memory brought him a picture of two men whom he had seen die in France in 1917. Though he had not thought of them for many years, their faces were vivid to him now, literally blasted to the surface of his mind by the association of the sound of high explosive. They, he thought, had been military objectives, but they had not looked afraid. They had looked angry — and astonished. And why not? For drill people as you like, discipline their minds, condition their reactions, regiment their thoughts — they still keep an obstinate conviction that there is a certain bit of time — round about threescore years and ten — which is *theirs*.

Old people, dying in bed, don't look angry or astonished. Why should they? They are not being cheated. Yet in that last second when a man knows that his half-spent life is being snatched from him in an explosion and a red flame — then, surely, there is enough righteous anger in him to have reformed the world single-handed. It's when our bodies are not in danger, he thought, that our minds can leave them unattended, go out and have a look at the world — and be afraid.

Yet from her stillness beside him, and from his own sense of isolation from her, there did come a gleam of illumination. Did not at least some of his own fear have its roots in a deep, but now brutally baffled protective instinct? Her withdrawal from his arm, the impatient tone which had answered his reassurance, became significant, and he asked himself whether there might not lie at the back of every man's fear the knowledge of himself as no longer a protector. Some disembodied voice of composite womanhood said to him dryly: In the past we have been grateful for the shelter of your strong right arm against tigers, spears, swords. But can you shield us from the weapons of your scientific warfare — this precious, ultimate bloom of your masculine inventiveness? Forgive us, gentlemen, if we are no longer greatly impressed by your protective instinct. Forgive us if we feel that our children now need a more reliable guardianship — our own ... The thought was his, but the tone was the tone of Marty. The monstrous unnaturalness of modern warfare oppressed him like suffocation. You could not any longer respond with jungle-action to jungle-law. You could not leap up to join a battle outside your windows, for science had removed it from your reach, into the sky and under the sea. You could not strike the attitudes of courage to sustain your cowering woman; she did not cower — she slept. She slept, knowing you as helpless as herself. She slept, stronger than yourself, now, because unburdened by the tradition of belligerence, and therefore free of your unnatural frustrations ...

He was watching the blind, shining and fading as the search-lights swept across it; listening to noises which, though they meant death to other men, touched him only as a disturbance of his night's sleep. That was a thought so outrageous that it was almost unendurable. That he should so sharply feel his identification with that chaos outside, and yet be forced to lie here with a raging, denunciatory spirit imprisoned in an inactive body, gave him a feeling of forcible banishment from his world, of solitude which amounted to torture. And suddenly he was bored, bored, bored with the whole business. He was sick to death of going about his daily affairs, waking every morning to the grinding labour of thought and the omnipresent burden of anxiety. Suddenly he felt the true danger of war assail him in a flood of longing to stop thinking and act instead. He wanted to go and find a Jap and kill him — not for any logical reason, but merely in an explosion of resentment against a world which denied him peace. He felt an insane desire to be rid of the self which the long years of life had built — to throw his faiths overboard, to abandon his convictions, to repudiate life because it had become an intolerable nuisance. Nothing had ever frightened him so much before. For he knew now, not only intellectually, but from actual experience, what moral collapse meant. He had felt the temptation of self-sabotage. In the roar of another explosion, louder than all the others, instinct turned him to Elsa — not because she was Elsa, but because she was a woman with the power to black-out his temporarily not-to-be-trusted mind. He knew as he took her in his arms that it was better to be, for a little while, an honest animal than a renegade human being.

The Little Company (1945)

KATHARINE GALLAGHER

(1935–)

Poet and short story writer. Victorian-born Gallagher was educated at the University of Melbourne. She taught in Melbourne high schools, at a secondary school in the United Kingdom, and in Paris, before settling in England in 1979.

'1942'

They'd hoped he'd be home for Christmas—
the lights shining down on him, the tree
somehow shielding off the horror. A break.
The family hadn't seen him as a soldier
—in his uniform, among sun-browned paddocks,
the dried stubble that pricked your legs.

When he came, he joined in and said Merry Xmas,
hugged people and slapped them on the back.
Wandered about the place, his eyes crinkled
with strain, lines etching his forehead. So young,
he seemed to be either laughing or very sad
as though there was nothing in between.

Times Literary Supplement (20 December 1996)

GWEN HARWOOD

(1920–95)

Poet and librettist. Gwen Harwood née Foster was born and educated in Brisbane. At the time that she wrote this letter to Thomas (or Tony) Riddell, who was serving in the armed forces in Darwin, she was living with her family in the Brisbane suburb of Auchenflower, working at the bureaucracy-bound War Damage Commission, and playing the organ at All Saints' Church. Joe, who flies through these lines as a Sopwith Camel, is her brother. After her marriage to one of Riddell's friends at the end of the war, Gwen Harwood and her husband moved to Tasmania. She was to have four children, become one of Australia's best-known poets, and write libretti for Larry Sitsky and other composers.

LETTER TO THOMAS RIDDELL

Examining Officer's Dept.,
Tuesday [4 May] 1943.

My dear Tony,

Mafeking has departed for Sydney. I am sitting in his chair, writing to you. I am only hoping that a few phone calls will be put on to me by mistake, but none have so far. Being at Mafeking's desk gives me a feeling of intense pleasure. I must be careful that the seeds of ambition are not sown in my soul. It would be dreadful to have a secret desire to become an Examining Officer — I could never face you again. Mafeking has two cushions on his chair — one of leather, nicely padded, with a dip in the middle (caused evidently by many months of examining), and another that fits into the dip — a pleasant affair with springs. I have distributed my belongings over his desk, and my clothes hang on his coat and hat rack (some of them, that is). So far I have had only one visitor — Mr Battersby, who came to ask if I had plenty to do. Several people have looked over the sheep-pen at me, and seem to be surprised to see me occupying Mafeking's chair. Nobody has said anything.

… Mafeking has on his desk — I mean, I have on my desk, a bunch of dates with little notices on the page for each day … There is also a note saying 'Dowling's birthday'. I don't know who Dowling is, or I'd ring him up and wish him a happy birthday from Mafeking.

… When we heard that Darwin had been raided I felt rather worried about you. Joe, who is bloodthirsty, said he was glad, and gave a convincing imitation of various planes taking part in an air engagement. Of course his heart doesn't lie with present day aviation — his heroes are Richthofen, Boelcke, Immelmann, and the fliers of Neuport 28's and Fokker D7's. But when he remembered you were there, he expressed concern, and flew up the hall as a Sopwith Camel. You will not be surprised to hear that he is still wearing the same clothes. The green shirt has several more holes over the stomach. Joe says that after the war he is going to buy a model of a 1914 plane and have it shipped out here. He is going to perform those feats with ease which Richthofen and Immelmann performed, and is going to 'check up' on literature concerned with 1914–1918 flying. He built yesterday a little solid model of a 'Zerstörer' and painted it grey and blue. He takes infinite trouble with his models, and if they are only slightly imperfect when finished he smashes them up.

Last night All Saints had its 'Annual Parish Meeting' — a gathering which never fails to amuse me. I appeared in my capacity as organist. Several votes of thanks were passed to me for the 'fine work' I was doing. I enjoyed this immensely …

After the meeting was over pious ladies fed us with stale cakes and dry scones. The material arrangements of our Holy Mother the Catholic and Apostolic church must amaze the heathen!

I called in at the Gramophone Society after that and was introduced to one of the 'promising' poets of Brisbane, a youth of the most appalling type, with thick lips and a wonderful accent. Most of his words were produced from the back of his nose. I said 'Good morning. You look like Dylan Thomas.' He was quite overcome, and said 'Oh, I say, thank you.' He asked me if I had read somebody's commentary on *Finnegans Wake*, if I thought *Ulysses* was 'permanent' and if Wales could possibly produce any good poets. I was glad to abandon him for a cheerful Irishman who had just read *Mr Justice Cocklecarrot* and we spent our time praising Royal Gertrude, to the disgust of the poet. In parting I recommended Eliza Cook to the poet. I said 'She repays close and careful study.' He had never heard of her!

Well, Tony, even examining officers must have lunch. I am beginning to feel like an examining officer already; soon my letters will be full of—'as to whethers' and 'yrs of 17th ult.'. What a pity you're not here! We could bring in some beer and have a little party among the expanding files.

With my love,
GWEN

Blessed City (1990)

ETHEL TURNER

(1872–1958)

Writer. Ethel Turner's many children's books include three Great War novels, one of them being The Cub *(1915), an extract from which appears earlier in this anthology. During the Second World War her son, Adrian Curlewis, became a prisoner of war of the Japanese. The letter reproduced here is taken from a collection of Adrian Curlewis and his family's wartime letters and diaries, published by his daughter, Philippa Poole, in the 1980s.*

LETTER TO ADRIAN

'Avenel'
Mosman, Sydney
18 August 1943
(*received 8 Feb 1944*)

My darling Adrian,

Again I walked on air for in a broadcast of prisoners' messages three nights ago an AIF in Singapore, Bill Barnes, is reported to have said among other things, 'Curlewis is here and well and says treatment is good'. So that is that!

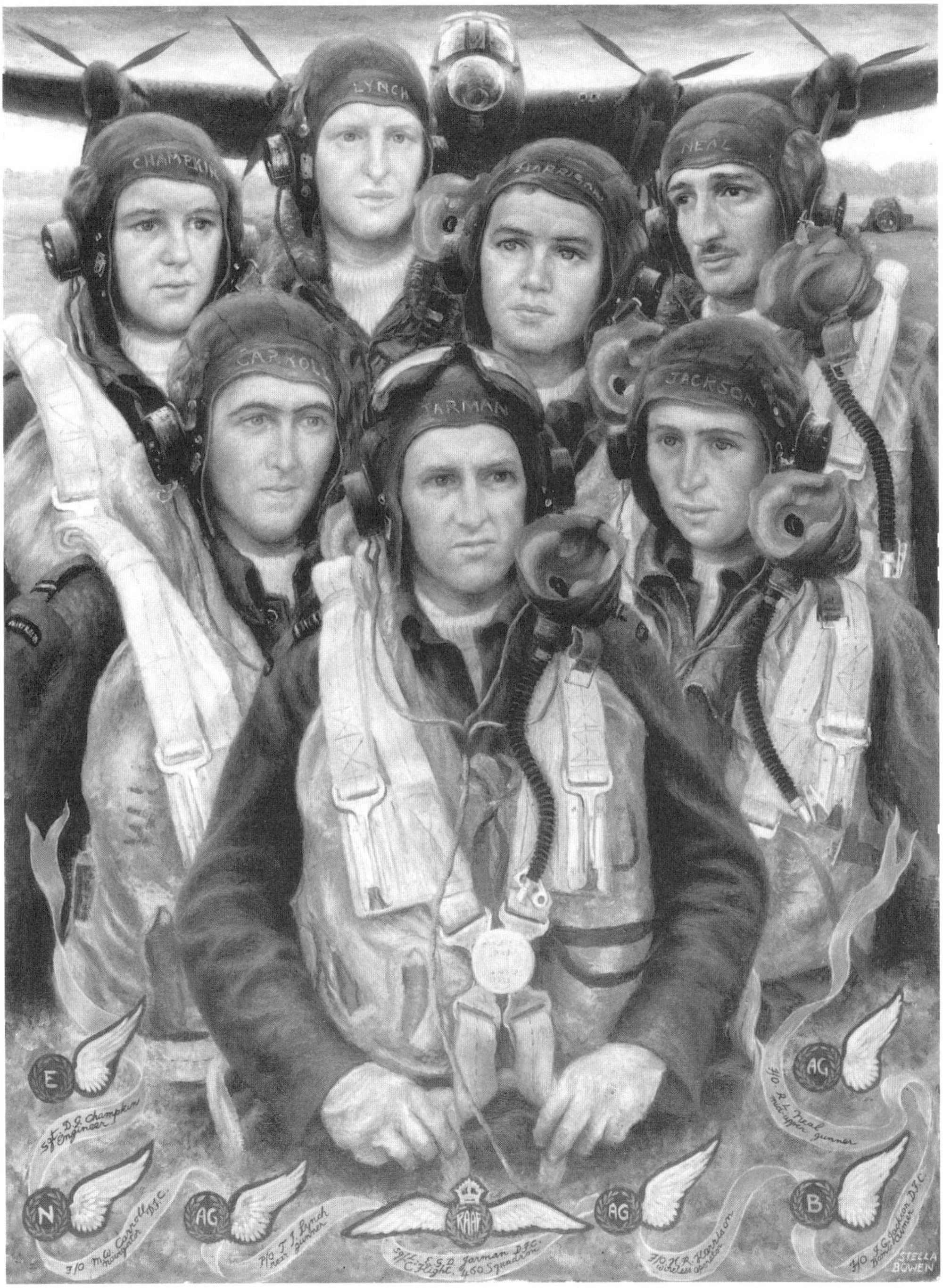

Stella Bowen (1893–1947), *Bomber crew*, 1944, oil on canvas, 86.1 x 63.3 cm. Acquired under official war art scheme in 1944. (AWM 26265)

A wet, very cold fortnight has passed; coldest weather I remember in this house, and dreariest. But then the weather now entirely depends upon whether I can vision plainly enough my bright-faced big boy moving about the rooms or gardens as he did two years ago.

I went to town yesterday despite the rain; lots of things to be seen to. I got a new book by Aldous Huxley about the miracle of his sight healing by certain eye exercises without glasses after having been three parts blind since he was 16. He says that within two months he was reading without glasses and without strain or fatigue. The book is only just out — 1943. I shall have a shot at the things though they sound troublesome.

I am writing this at my study window — typing it I should say to fulfil regulations. You don't need to be told I am a rotten typist. Philippa is catching me up. Ian rarely does any.

They hope to go to the mountains by 1 September for the term holiday. Philippa broke up a week earlier as the epidemics — chickenpox, mumps, etc were so bad.

Just my love and love and love. And then some, my darling.

Ever and ever
MOTHER

Philippa Poole, *Of Love and War* (n.d.)

OLA CALDERALA

(?–)

War bride. Daughter of a Sydney horse-trainer, Ola Byrnes met her Italian–American husband, Frank Calderala, at the Sydney Trocadero in 1943. She became one of up to 15 000 Australian women who married American servicemen stationed here during the Second World War. Unwilling to face lengthy separations from their husbands, she and another war bride sailed to the United States in 1944, as stowaways on a merchant ship. Ola and her husband made their life in America.

MARRIAGE

He had just got out of the hospital and was going by, heard the music, walked in, and asked me to dance. Frankly, he asked my sister to dance — she liked him — but then he asked me to dance, and that's how I met him. After that he took me home and I went out with him for the next ten days.

It was not love at first sight. I don't think I even liked him at that first time. The second day when I met him he was there, obviously drunk to the world, and I felt so sorry for him that I started giving him coffee. Talking to him I found out it was his birthday the following day, invited him home, and he met my mother. It was wintertime, so we sat in front of the fireplace and talked.

Frank proposed to me on the third day, at Prince's night club. It took me about two hours to say yes. I knew him ten days. He went back to New Guinea. He wrote. He got permission to get married and we were married in October [1943].

I was out on a date at a movie the night he came back down to Sydney. I was out seeing James Cagney and George M. Cohen. I got home about midnight—my mother was standing at the door and she informed me that Frank was in the house. I was not expecting him. I didn't expect to see him till November. He just said we were going to get married now or were not getting married at all. So Friday we got a licence and Saturday we got married.

I got a white dress and got the Justice of the Peace. The only time we could marry was at twelve o'clock. My mother and father were witnesses. It was sort of a hurry because my father had a horse running in the first race and he had to be there to saddle the horse up. He kept pushing the wedding up real quick. We were having a party for my brother who was just back from New Guinea—his twenty-first birthday—so it turned into a combined party, twenty-first/wedding party.

For our honeymoon you could not get a hotel room at the time. It was just impossible. Especially on that short notice. I had a cousin whose husband had enlisted so she moved in with her mother-in-law. She lived in Maroubra and she gave us her house. We had the house for the week that Frank was there. Unfortunately, on the third day I fell down the steps and I couldn't walk for the [next] three days. I hit my knee and the knee was completely gone, so that was our honeymoon. And Frank went back after that.

The Americans were lonely. Frank had been away from home for two and a half years when I met him. He had been in the jungles most of that time, flying combat. He told everybody that after being in the jungles that long practically everything looked good to you.

Annette Potts & Lucinda Strauss, *For the Love of a Soldier* (1987)

GERALDINE HALLS

(1919–96)

Novelist. Born Geraldine Melville, she was the daughter of an Adelaide nose and throat specialist. During the war, she and a friend moved from Adelaide to Sydney to live, an experience that she used as the basis for her book The Last Summer of the Men Shortage *(1976), one of the novels that she published under her own name. She also published a number of thrillers, under the pseudonyms 'Charlotte Jay' and 'G. M. Jay', the best-known of these being* Beat Not the Bones *(1952). Set in New Guinea, where she worked for some years as a court stenographer, the book won the inaugural Edgar Allan Poe prize, awarded by American mystery writers. After living in various other countries, she and her husband, John Halls, an Oriental specialist, settled in Adelaide in the early 1970s.*

THE SUMMER OF '44

At the tram stop waited three old men of fifty or so and half a dozen girls who, coming from moderately wealthy families, would not have had to work if it had not been for the War. The girls, as they waited, complained of their lot to one another, for it seemed a crime to them that they should have to leave the beaches on such a day and bury themselves in stuffy offices. The sunshine, the blue sky with its decoration of frothy white clouds, made work seem like an injustice, tyrannically imposed upon them. Something had gone wrong. Value had become distorted and turned upside down. But what was to be done? And who was to blame? Hitler and the Japanese, obviously. But the situation they had created was remote, and beyond the understanding of those six girls who, though they submitted to the duties that were expected of them, did so rebelliously, with the sense of being captives, and felt under no obligation to arrive on time or give their best.

Dinah bought a paper and, when the tram pulled up, rushed for a window seat. Claudia managed to snatch the seat beside her from a sullen man who thought her young enough to stand.

'Did you see that? After all, he hasn't lost a leg or anything.'

Dinah wasn't angry any more but it was difficult to ease yourself out of being disapproving once you had got so far. She opened the paper, glanced at the headlines announcing how many planes had been shot down, and turned to the back pages to see if any of the old Bing Crosby films might be showing in the suburbs.

The tram, packed with young women and old or ugly men (the young and handsome were fighting the War), rattled past a gap in tall buildings and Dinah, having abandoned her paper, caught a glimpse of the water, shifting its colours and sparkling like a fold of blue lamé on a luxurious dress. And she was wrung with sorrow. Why did I say those things to Claudia? Why? But for the people in the tram, she could have wept.

Then suddenly, carried away by a rush of delight, she exclaimed, 'Claudia! Look at those flame trees!' No leaves as yet, but each branch tipped by a scarlet flower. Birds, about to take flight, spreading their wings. Half closing your eyes you could see them. All those scarlet birds lifting into the air and flying away.

'Aren't they divine!' answered Claudia.

The tram began its descent into Double Bay, passing high walls where purple creepers streamed down almost to the pavement or hung in flowery loops, and came to a halt at that interesting stop by the fruit shop opposite the hotel. This was the area favoured by American officers, that fascinating new species who in no time at all had alerted Australian girls that it wasn't absolutely necessary to put up with rudeness and indifference from men for ever more, and that a man who was courteous, smelt of bottled lotions and wore well-cut clothes need not necessarily be a pansy. The fact that you couldn't believe a word they said to you was a disadvantage, but of little significance when weighed against the compensations.

In they came, glittering with buttons and insignia, their olive green jackets fitting them like skins. Some hung on straps with the graceful elasticity of gibbons, while those who found seats arranged the creases in their dove pink trousers and opened American magazines. All had impeccable, unblemished skins, lightly tanned, as if they were wearing make-up. And almost all had beautiful teeth, so perfect they could have been false, but weren't, just carefully tended and straightened into faultless rows, giving their smiles the look of being cast into the public world, rather than at anyone in particular.

Dinah and Claudia discussed the Americans' diet in whispers. Only a special sort of diet could account for the look they had of being made of wax. Lots of milk, they agreed. They knew about that from Spike, who had always required a glass of milk when he came to dinner. But he had also plaintively asked for 'canned beans', which didn't sound very healthy. So could it be mixed blood? Bits of Europe blended together with a touch of Cuba, and even Africa hidden away but never mentioned.

The tram became restless and noisy with the influx of the Americans, the girls talking together with great animation, their eyes darting about like butterflies faced with a profusion of flowers. The Australian men, who had been dragged out of comfortable retirement and were all that the city had to offer of its native manhood, huddled over their pipes and papers, resentful of being placed in the position of representing a nation twenty years too late.

In Rushcutter's Bay the ugly buildings looked grimy and the dogs had been mongrel for generations. Kings Cross wasn't even awake. Its population spent the day sleeping off their hangovers and reappeared in the evening to get new ones.

The Last Summer of the Men Shortage (1995 edition, first published 1976)

JEAN SIMS

(1922–)

Land girl. Jean Sims was a photographic assistant before serving with the New South Wales Women's Australian National Services Land Army, then the Australian Women's Land Army, between 1942 and 1945. Her placements took her to various places in New South Wales and to Renmark, South Australia. As Jean Scott, she later wrote a book about the Australian Women's Land Army, entitled Girls with Grit *(1986). This letter to her parents was reproduced in Sue Hardisty's collection of letters by, and interviews with, members of the Land Army,* Thanks Girls and Goodbye! *(1990), a book with a title that neatly sums up the post-war treatment of the land girls by governments and other organisations.*

LETTER TO JEAN'S PARENTS

'In the Dumps at Hanwood',
23.4.1944

Dear Mum and Dad,

How's everyone? OK, I hope. Yes our job is continuing at present getting the prunes up. When this is done will open the furrows for irrigating, then Mr Langly will probably finish us up, I think he's running out of dough, poor old guy! It must be very hard on some of the farmers who've relied on the family and he's lost both sons. First time I've met anyone who has so much sorrow and yet when he speaks about the first world war, it's usually with funny things that happened.

Actually when I think of the life some of the farmers live it really makes me curious why they stay—roast in the summer, freeze in winter, rain at the wrong time, winds bashing the trees, birds, bugs, beetles, moth, soil deficiencies, glut, poor crops, and then you have to try and market it before it drops in price or goes bad—even the animals live in better quarters than the families at times. NO THANKS, NOT FOR ME!

The other night after mess Matron said that we all had to attend a Nitting Bee in the Rec. Room and some of the kids asked to be excused, because they are unable to knit. Mrs Bethel said, 'No. All to attend' so along we all go and have a head examination for 'nits'—what a laugh Gay and I were free, but two had their hair cropped and given a kero treatment, one has to go home.

Well, on that note I'll close and give my hair another going over I'm all itchy now.

Love and Kisses and Scratches.

JEAN

Sue Hardisty (ed.), *Thanks Girls and Goodbye!* (1990)

NANCY WAKE

(1912–)

Guerrilla. Nancy Wake was born in New Zealand, but grew up in Australia. Educated in Sydney and London, she was a freelance journalist in Europe before the Second World War began. A member of the Allied escape route organisation in occupied France between 1940 and 1943, she then joined the Special Operations Executive in London in 1943, parachuted back into France, and worked with the French Resistance for the remainder of the war, under the guise of being a captain in the First Aid Nursing Yeomanry. Called 'the White Mouse' by the Germans, she is said to have become the most highly decorated Allied servicewoman, receiving medals from Britain, France, and the United States. After the war she worked with the British Foreign Office and the Women's Royal Air Force, before marrying a British fighter pilot, John Forward, in 1957. Her first husband, whom she had married in 1939, had been killed by the Gestapo in 1943. She recalls the following memorable event in her autobiography.

'THE BIKE RIDE'

For several days groups of men kept arriving with exciting tales of their long cross-country hike. Denden turned up, footsore and weary, without his transmitter, which he had buried, or his codes, which he had destroyed. We were back to square one, out of contact with London and useless to everyone. From that day on until the end of the Occupation I don't think I ever stopped for more than two or three hours. If I wasn't walking or riding a bicycle, or fighting, or being chased by the Germans, or the Vichyites, it just wasn't a normal day.

Fortunately, through contacts I learnt of the whereabouts of a Free French radio operator living just over the adjacent mountain. It was hoped that he would co-operate if I mentioned the name of our mutual acquaintance. Someone lent me a man's bicycle which I half pushed and carried up the mountain but literally flew down the other side. The bike was getting up such speed that the brakes were useless, and I fell off several times. I pedalled about twenty kilometres only to find that because of all the German activity in the region, the Frenchman had left the day before. The mountain lying between me and Saint-Santin did little to lift the disappointment I felt.

Denden knew there was an SOE radio operator in Châteauroux because that is where he had spent his idyllic week while we were waiting for him in the Auvergne. He gave me as much information as he could remember and it was decided I would leave as soon as I could make myself presentable, even though it was 200 kilometres away.

We had been given the name of a friendly tailor in Aurillac but I had to wash and mend my slacks and blouse before I could appear anywhere without arousing suspicion. Just then Laurent drove up in a car of all things; he had driven right around the Germans without any trouble. We were so happy to see him but livid when we thought of his comfortable trip, whereas we were all exhausted.

Laurent wouldn't give me a car to drive to Châteauroux as he said that since our battle the Germans had tightened up all regulations, and road-blocks had been installed all over the entire region. Furthermore any identity cards issued in the Cantal were suspect and by law had to be exchanged at the local police stations under the supervision of the Germans. As my identity card was from the Cantal I would have to travel without any papers. Added to which he doubted that I would get to Châteauroux on a bicycle, let alone return, and he strongly counselled Hubert to prevent me from continuing with my plan. Laurent thought that quite apart from the problems with identity cards, papers and tighter regulations, 200 kilometres was just too far to cycle. But, as I pointed out, we were useless without our radio, and this was our only immediate hope.

Once Laurent accepted the fact that I would make the trip irrespective of all the obstacles he put in my way, he lost no time in doing everything he could to make my journey less dangerous. Men were sent in all directions to collect local information about German movements and then when he had studied all the details he mapped out the route he advised me to take. I would have to cycle about 200 kilometres of the roundabout route, without an identity card or a licence for the beautiful new ladies' bicycle a Maquisard had been able to purchase for me 'under the counter'. If I reached Châteauroux safely I would have to return by the best way I could.

While all these preparations were going on I was busy trying to get my wardrobe together. I needed an entire new outfit plus some walking shoes. I cycled into Aurillac where the tailor agreed to make me a costume in twenty-four hours, with one fitting in two hours' time. He also gave me the name and address of a cobbler who could supply me with shoes without a coupon. When I arrived at the cobbler's shop I was dismayed to hear the tailor had phoned to warn me not to return for the fitting as the Milice who were next door to his shop already been enquiring about the woman in slacks.

The Germans had, meantime, placed road-blocks on all the main roads leading into town. I escaped by crossing several fields and heading north between two main roads until I could cross one of them and regain Saint-Santin, which lay to the west. All the way back I had been trying to think of a way to go back for my fitting. I had to find a disguise. But what? Then I had an idea.

The parents of the handsome young man in whose house we were hiding lived in the village. I went to see them and asked if they had any old clothes I could borrow. His grandmother had an old trunk with an amazing array. I borrowed a long white piqué dress which must have been fashionable before World War I. They introduced me to a farmer who was taking his horse and cart to the market in Aurillac early the next morning. I became secretive about my plans as I knew Hubert, and Denden in particular, would rag me if they saw me in my disguise. I crept out of the house early and waited for the farmer. Unfortunately, just as I had installed myself in the front of the cart beside the farmer with a pair of his trousers on my lap, which was my reason for the visit to the tailor, Denden appeared and alerted everyone else. Of course they had a good hearty laugh at my expense. Who wouldn't? There I was sitting up in the cart surrounded by fruit and vegetables looking like a real country bumpkin, wet hair pulled back tight, no make-up, an old-fashioned dress, and wearing a pair of the farmer's old boots.

Our cart and the produce were inspected several times by the Germans as we entered Aurillac: they did not give me a second look, even their first glance was rather disdainful. I did not blame them. I did not look very fetching. The only thing that boosted my morale that day was when the tailor failed to recognise me as I entered his shop. My costume was delivered the following day, and I set off for Châteauroux the day after.

On the eve of my departure Laurent sent several men on ahead to warn as many villages as they could in the Cantal and the Puy-de-Dôme to look out for me and to warn me if trouble lay ahead. In the Allier he had not been able to make any contacts so I just had to trust to luck. I had company as far as Montluçon. A Maquisard was going to visit his wife, who was ill. When we had to take the National Route we pushed our bikes instead of riding them in case any Germans approached, in which event we would have time to dive into the culverts by the side of the road until they passed.

I by-passed Montluçon and was heading for Saint-Amand. It was getting dark and I wanted to make a few enquiries. I went into a bistro and had a simple meal and a glass of wine. Listening to the conversation of the other customers, I gathered that the Germans in the area were quiet for the time being. I found a barn not far away, removed my costume and slept until the sound of an air raid awakened me.

At Saint-Amand I stopped for a coffee and overheard that Bourges had been raided the day before. When I arrived there I thought the place was quiet — not a soul in the streets and all the shutters were closed. It was only afterwards I found out that the Germans had shot some hostages that morning. I passed two groups of Germans but they made no attempt to stop me.

At Issoudon I stopped for a black-market meal, cleaned myself up and entered into conversation with the owner of the restaurant, who shared some of my wine and brandy. The dangerous part was yet to come and I needed all the local information I could obtain. There is nothing like brandy to loosen the tongue! I cycled to the local markets and filled my string bag with all the fruit and vegetables I could buy without food coupons, hoping that I would pass for a housewife out shopping. I was still making good time although my legs were beginning to ache because of the mountainous terrain I had crossed. I had cycled 200 kilometres.

There were continuous streams of German vehicles leaving Issoudon for Châteauroux so I cycled west to Brion then south-west to Villedieu-sur-Indre, and entered the city without any trouble. One German patrol was checking on the opposite side of the road but they waved me on when they saw me hesitate. I pedalled round and round the town and was just about to give in, with much despair, when I came across the bistro I was looking for. It was exactly as Denden had described it. But when I called at the SOE house they refused to help me; they refused to send a message to London. Actually their performance was completely stupid because if I had been a German or one of their agents, they would have been arrested on the spot. I left the house in disgust and returned to the bistro.

They must have been saying prayers for me back in the Auvergne because as I was pedalling around Châteauroux I had run into a Maquisard I had met several weeks before in the Corrèze. He was looking for a Free French radio operator as their operator had been killed in action. We had both agreed to help each other if one of us found our contacts and I had left him at the bistro where he was waiting when I returned with the bad news.

Off we pedalled to find his contact, who was also a patron of a bistro which was situated opposite the home of the radio operator. He warned us that the Germans had not caught the radio operator but they were in the house waiting to trap any callers.

The town was literally swarming with Germans. They were completely surrounding areas and checking the houses systematically, so we decided to leave immediately. We separated and arranged to meet outside the town. Both of us were able to by-pass the road-blocks and, wasting no time, we headed for a Maquis group my companion knew in the Creuse. The leader belonged to the Free French and had come from Algiers, where his headquarters were. He was understanding when I told him the trouble I was in and said that if his radio operator did not object to sending my message, neither would he. The operator agreed to my request to send a message to Colonel Buckmaster in London via the Free French in Algiers. I wished my travelling companion good luck and was on my way.

By now I was so tired I resolved to take the quickest route home. Every kilometre I pedalled was sheer agony. I knew that if I ever got off the bike, I could never get on it again, so I kept pedalling. Halfway across the Allier the companion I had left in Montluçon was looking out for me. He had guessed the road I would take if all went well. His wife had presented him with a baby son and they were both well, so he was happy. I arrived back in Saint-Santin twenty-four hours before the time they had anticipated I would, even though they were well aware I might never return. I had pedalled 500 kilometres in seventy-two hours.

They greeted me with open arms and shouts of joy. All I could do was cry. When I got off that damned bike I felt as if I had a fire between my legs and the inside of my thighs were raw. I couldn't stand up, I couldn't sit down, I couldn't walk and I didn't sleep for days. But thanks to all the help I had been given by one and all, I had succeeded and all we had to do now was to wait and see if Algiers sent our signal on to Colonel Buckmaster. They did. As I said to Hubert, Denden and Bazooka, I never wanted to be told any more that the Free French agents in the field would not help the British ones, because I knew better. I never heard of that group in the Creuse after that so I have never been able to say 'thank you' in peacetime.

It took me a few days to recover. The doctor from the village had dressed my thighs which were in a horrible state but there was little else anyone could do. My three close colleagues looked in frequently to see how I was faring, but I just wanted to be left alone. When I'm asked what I'm most proud of doing during the war, I say 'the bike ride'.

The Autobiography of the Woman the Gestapo Called the White Mouse (1985)

JEAN DEVANNY

(1894–1962)

Writer. Born in New Zealand, Jane (known as Jean) Crook married radical miner Hal Devanny in 1911. She had already published four novels and a collection of short stories before coming to Australia with her family in 1929. Jean Devanny joined the Communist Party of Australia in 1930 or 1931, was expelled from it in 1940, rejoined in 1944, but eventually left in 1949. She spent much of her life in Queensland, dividing her time between writing and politics. She includes this interview with a stoutish munitions worker in one of her non-fiction books.

'SHE WORKED IN MUNITIONS'

'I wasn't in love with work in munitions. I took it on simply with the idea of helping my husband and brother in the Forces. We are a war-minded family. My father is in essential industry, my sister is in the WAAAFS. But, of course, tons of girls I worked with would tell you the same thing.

'Well. — *The Sydney Morning Herald* advertised for girls to work a certain line of explosive and I decided to have a go at it. The only thing that worried me was a "girls not too stout" provision tacked on to the ad.' She laughed and indicated her buxom body.

'But I went along to Mr Harrod, the section manager of the Fuse Division at the works and let him give me the once-over. He studied me for some time and then told me: "You might be all right, Mrs Enoch. On the other hand you might be bloody awful." He gave me a slip for a medical, X ray and blood count.

'On November 11th I was directed to proceed to Victoria with a number of other girls and report at the National Service Station. There I met up with two girls, one a dressmaker and the other a barmaid, who agreed to share a flat with me. I myself in my pre-marriage days had been a photographer and waitress in turn, with a running ambition to make good in the theatre. In my time I have appeared in twenty-seven amateur musical comedy shows.

'I won't say that everything ran smoothly in the flat at all times. We were different types. Gladys was a short, dainty brownette; very sensitive, sweet and charming. Edith was the typical barmaid, generous and good-natured. I, of course, was impossible.' A light chuckle.

'Want the routine of our first day's work? Here it is. Reported at the Commissary's office at 7.30 a.m. and from there proceeded to the clothing store to receive our issue of the ghastly apparel designed for the girls on the job. Heavy wool navy slacks — wool for protection against fire and explosions — belted jacket and navy cap, heavy welted brogue shoes furnished with wooden sprigs. The only metal allowed on the job was wedding rings, and those only because some of the older married women refused to part with them.

'From there to the change room where we sat on a bench, removed our street shoes, threw our legs over the bench to a clean section of the floor and there put on our brogues. It was like a ballet movement, the almost simultaneous throwing of the legs over the bench. Above us our street clothing was suspended in mid-air by pulleys.

'Outside the change room we contacted our section foreman, Mr Ralph Yates. A charming little man, quite young and handsome, with an unusual tinkling affected laugh. Everybody liked him. I am five feet seven, he was barely five feet five and when we teamed up, as we often did, the girls were highly amused. He took us on tour of the fuse division and gave us the idea of our future work.

'My feelings were of absolute horror! Part of the work shown in process was a fuse being assembled with detonator and striking pin; to me it looked as though a slip meant kingdom come.

'I was introduced to the work per medium of a most tedious task, removing minute screws from the fuses with a very fine screw-driver. It soon put my nerves on edge. The monotony of the jobs called for a change of operations every three or four hours.

'My next assignment was flattening and combing detonators. I mucked quite a lot in sheer terror, but after a month or so I felt as though I had been doing it all my life.

'After three months all the Sydney girls became terribly homesick. Day after day we stormed the manager's office for information as to when we might return home. On the 1st February we were notified that our transfer home had come through and on Feb. 5th we reported for work at Sydney.

'A dreadful disappointment awaited us. The works were nowhere near completion. We had no job to do. We filled in our days trucking, cleaning, sweeping, painting, hosing and growling. Mostly growling. About a month went by before we got a real job.

'This time the clothes routine differed in my case in one particular. I take a size six in shoes but since the sixes were held up I had to make do with a pair of nines. I became so attached to them that I continued to wear them after the sixes had turned up.

'Our next excitement was the allotting of charge-woman and senior charge-woman positions. When the list came through it revealed that Gladys had been appointed senior charge and I and two others were charge-women. That meant we were instructors to the girls who came on the job.

'Entering that great building never ceased to impress me. The place was drab, though new. One rose tree bloomed outside a change room door. Mountains of piled-up earth surrounded the place and going into it out of the daylight, into the wide corridors so long that their perspective was like a railway track, with the strange clothing of the girls beneath the blaze of the heavy lighting, — well, it was like another world. — H. G. Wells, you know.

'There were some great characters among the girls. A French Jewess, still homesick and unhappy after seventeen years in Australia, would hold the girls entranced with her tales of Parisian life. The way she contrasted it with the dead flat of living in a tiny Sydney suburb, used to hold them like a play.

'Yes, in those war factories, where all types and classes of women have been gathered together, you get a line on all sorts of problems and troubles. A few women were of the mercenary type; thought more of the big money than of the war. And some of the younger girls were only concerned with having a good time. Some, mostly the older women, put the war before everything.

'The most striking thing about the job, to me, was the loss of class feeling in the girls. Class backgrounds were lost in the general huddle. For instance, one day a girl told us she had smashed up a racing car, had injured a man and would have to pay heavy damages. No one commented on the fact that she must be rich. There was only interest in the story. A poor woman's tale about her home troubles would rouse the same interest and sympathy. I can't help thinking that that sort of thing must have a bearing on the post-war period.

'Having the trade union outlook on the collective principle, I was interested in finding out the attitude of the men on the job towards the women workers, in connection with post-war conditions. In some cases it was anything but satisfactory. I think myself, judging by the way the women worried over their children, children left in the care of neighbours, running the streets after school and so on, that those with home obligations will be only too glad to hand over their jobs to men after the war. Those women were filled with worry. I am sure that only great economic pressure or patriotism can account for their presence on the job.

'After our social committee was organised each section competed in raising funds for pianos. My area, the fuse section, headed the list with eighty-three pounds. Quite a lot of talent had been recruited into the works and so we were able to put on some fine lunch-hour concerts. We also ran successful dances and socials in outside halls.

'The interest some of the women took in the cultural classes organised by our Welfare Department was amazing. We had lectures, play readings — from Shakespeare to light comedies — all read by the workers. Some unusual discoveries were made in unexpected places. For instance, a farmer's wife from Grong Grong, a very rough and ready type, was filled with enthusiasm and pride at finding herself very good at reading.

'You know, anyone with half a mind must draw conclusions from that kind of thing. It made me wonder what could happen to the world if all the talent in women on farms and in the factories was given scope for development.

'When our absentee committee was set up, composed of representatives of the management, the workers and the unions, the idea being to handle complaints and make readjustments, — quite a lot of the women opposed it. They didn't like the idea of their fellow workers passing judgments on their private affairs. But the majority were in favour of it.

'After some time I was promoted to the rank of senior charge, in company with all the girls who had started down in Victoria. Then the Arms and Munitions Union got busy on the job and started to organise shop stewards and union delegates. I was elected as steward and delegate for my area, which led to my becoming very active on behalf of improvements in our conditions. No, no major troubles. Just little things that cropped up during the daily routine.

'Presently I found it impossible to cope with the responsibility of my charge work and the union activities. The management pointed out that I would have to choose between them, but before the matter was resolved I was elected to this job, State organiser for the Union.

'I can't help thinking that from the point of view of the war effort far too much money was expended on those works. Lots of the time there was just simply nothing for many women to do. For days they did nothing but sit and talk. Rates and conditions were excellent, but patriotic women anxious to help their menfolk at the front, women who would bring their letters from their men for me to read, put production before everything else. When they were compelled to idle they grizzled unceasingly. That was the chief cause of trouble out there. Even now I can't get onto the cause of the hold-up. Recently, on the way out to the works, I met up with a woman from the country, on her way out to start on the job. Three days later I met her again and she told me that for those three days she had done nothing for her money but sit in the change room and read.

'Another thing, many of the girls have to travel too far to work. Some of them leave home at 4.30 a.m. and return home at 8 p.m. Yes, they do their war job all right!

'For the post-war era? I hope that the women who have won emancipation from an inferior sex position during the war will hang onto it. I'm all in favour of mothers having the right and the means to look after their own children should they desire to do so, but childless women are in a different position.'

I rose from my seat at the office desk. 'Mrs Enoch, one last question. Why did that initial advertisement refer to the stoutness of women?'

She laughed. 'That is something I have never found out. As a matter of fact, numbers of very stout women work on the job. But we shall find out. I will ring up Mr Harrod.'

She got onto the telephone and after a few minutes' talk and laughter over it, put down the receiver and again turned to me. 'He says that at the outbreak of war everything was being speeded up and it was thought that stout women would not be active enough on their feet.'

Bird of Paradise (1945)

DYMPHNA CUSACK

(1902–81)

and

FLORENCE JAMES

(1904–93)

Writers. Australian-born Dymphna Cusack and New Zealand-born Florence James met while undergraduates at the University of Sydney. Cusack had been invalided out of teaching and James was a former journalist, married with two children, when they temporarily shared a cottage in the Blue Mountains during the last year of the Second World War. There they collaborated on a children's book and an adult novel, Come In Spinner *(1951). The manuscript of the latter won the 1948* Daily Telegraph *competition, but the authors were forced to make big cuts before its publication. The unexpurgated version was not published until 1988. A clear-eyed look at Sydney during the war, the book focuses on the lives of several women working in a hotel beauty salon. These are some of the reflections of a character named Val Blaski, whose husband had been listed as missing in action soon after their marriage earlier in the war.* Come In Spinner *was made into a television mini-series in 1989.*

'MONDAY V'

The oppressive heat still lingered and the air was stifling with the powdery dust brought down by a two-day westerly from the drought-parched plains. The full moon swung so low and close in the heavy air that it seemed tethered to the black tracery of the trees beside the old mint. Val looked up at the gilded hands of the clock on the old barracks. Half past seven ... No use calling for Betty yet, she wouldn't be off duty till nine. Between the rattle of the trams, faint gusts of music came to her from the band playing in Hyde Park. She and Ven had listened to the band on his last evening. 'Oh, darling,' she whispered, ' "come back and wake my winter heart"... Come back, come back,' and he was with her again.

She made her way across the broad intersection above St James's Church where five roads meet and the holiday traffic shuttled swiftly to and from the city. Three Indonesians loitered by disconsolately, their voices a low, liquid gabble. Two young English sailors watched her with heartsick eyes. So pitifully young, she thought. All these people so lonely, so far from home. The city is full of them, adrift on the tide of war, talking of home in alien tongues ... servicemen and women, refugees, evacuees who have lost all the dear, familiar things — all those to whom this city is a refuge without sanctuary.

'I am lucky,' she told herself, 'for here, at least, I am at home. This is *your* city, Val Blaski, every point of light, whichever way you look, means something to you. Down there where the lights end and there is a pool of darkness, your eye knows even in the dark that the waters of the Harbour are moving as the tide runs out to sea. If you were to come back from Ven's northern mountains or the South Pole, these city towers against the sky would knock on your heart. This is *your* country ... even the hot smell of the western dust, borne by winds across the earth your great-grandparents ploughed to make a home out of a wilderness, is yours. You are at home.'

A young GI and his girl sauntered hand in hand up the steps to the park and stood a moment by a blossoming peach tree, their lips joined in a long kiss. It was as though a hand squeezed her heart and she stumbled past them along the concrete path between the lawns, her face so lost and withdrawn that the solitary serviceman who stepped out to accost her hesitated and drew back.

In front of her an avenue of frosted light globes stretched through the park, leading her eye to the towering bulk of the War Memorial, now silver-grey under the moon. 'It's not shrines to the dead we should build,' Ven had said once when they stood together watching its reflection in the Pool of Memory. 'The dead are safe, they've gone out with their illusions still upon them and we can't hurt them any more. It's shrines to the living we should be building, to remind them of what they fought for, so they can't be fobbed off when they don't get it, and to remind the others back home that a block of marble and a wreath on Remembrance Day won't pay their debt.'

She walked through the lighted park, where each shining globe was a magnet for the blundering bogong moths that the hot wind had blown in a cloud over the city. Dance music and laughter floated out from the Anzac Buffet and she stood a while watching the dancers as they moved across the lighted windows.

Surely ... no, it couldn't be. But that girl looked like someone she knew. She racked her brains, but the girl had passed the window. Val moved forward a few steps and waited for her to come into view again. Yes, there she was, and as she passed her partner swung her round so that Val saw her full face.

The girl was extraordinarily like Helen McFarland ... but she must be mistaken. The McFarland girl was so shy and quiet, she could not imagine her looking like that, gay and ... Val searched for the right word. It was not 'abandoned' in the free-and-easy sense; but as though she had left her old self behind. There was a shining look about her as though there was nothing else in the world but this moment of happiness.

When the couple came round for the third time, Val knew it was Helen. They were not so near the window, but had moved into the floor a little and were dancing slower and

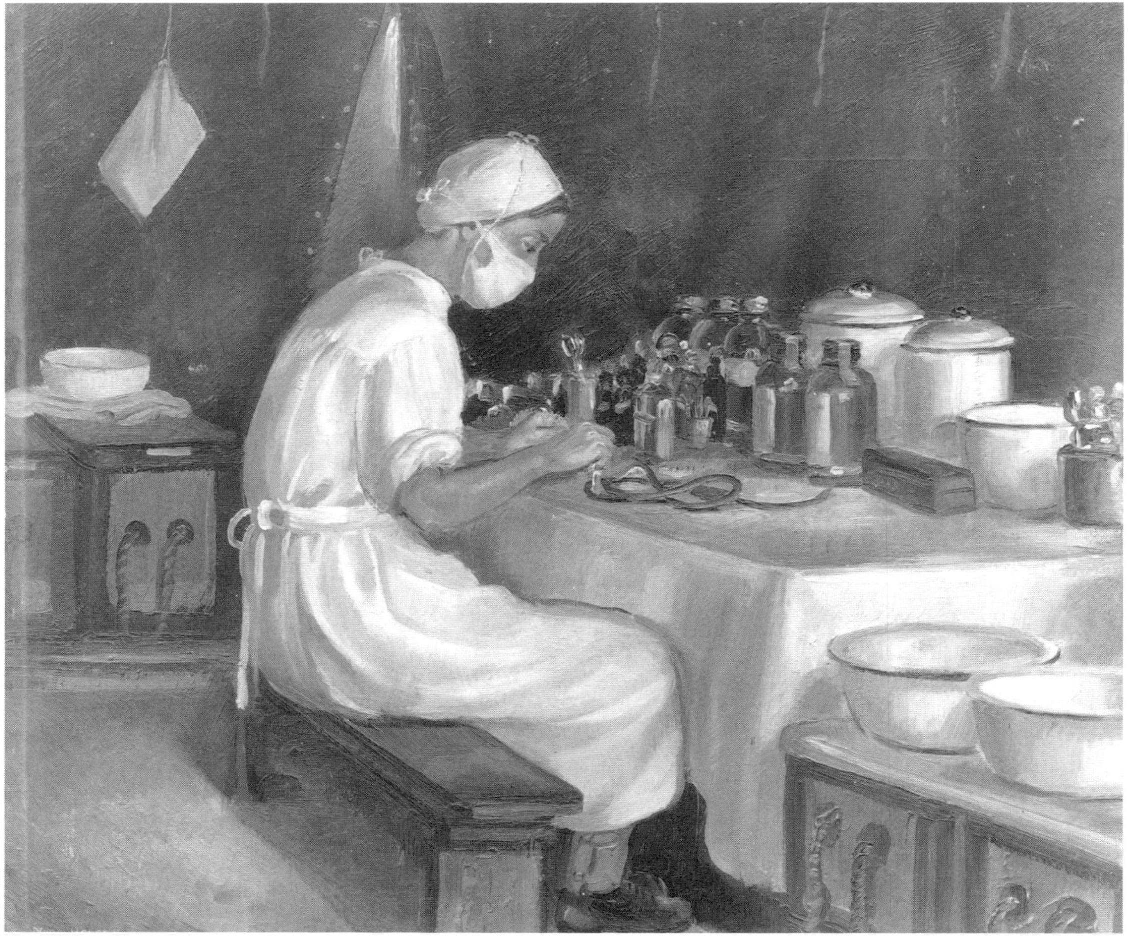

Nora Heysen (1911–), *Sister Minnie Goldstein working in the blood bank, Alexishafen*, 1944, oil on canvas, 40 x 45.6 cm. Acquired under official war art scheme in 1944. (AWM 23921)

talking. Val caught a glimpse of the man's face, rapt and happy. 'It's Helen McFarland, and she's in love,' Val said softly under her breath. 'And he's in love too ... like Ven and me.'

She turned away from the lighted window and walked slowly back into the shadows. Night and the heavy trees softened the sound of the band to a windy sigh and touched familiar melodies with unbearable poignancy.

I've seen Ven look at me like that when we've danced together ... and perhaps I looked like her, because that was how I felt—as though nothing else in the world mattered but Ven and our love. But it was Ven who taught me that love isn't enough for happiness; you have to understand other people too. Here, in the park, where Ven and I walked so often as other lovers are walking tonight, here where every path, every shadowy retreat, the garden seats, the tramped lawns, are like old and known things to me, here he taught me to understand.

Her lips moved. 'Darling, I understand it all now, you made me see it. It isn't ugly any more. This endless procession walking aimlessly up and down, these girls and men, their arms around each other's waists, these couples sprawling on the grass, embracing in the shadows, lost in a world of their own.'

'Oh you poor lovers!' she cried soundlessly. 'Ven knew. The old and the wise, all those whose lives and houses are safe and solid around them and whose future stretches like a broad high road out of their past, they may say you're tawdry and vulgar because you lie unmoving cheek to cheek, lost to the old shame. It's easy for them to condemn you meeting casually, loving briefly; laughter and lust a shield against the black shadow that hangs over us all. He made poetry of you, sailor clasping your girl in the shadow of a tree, abandoned and lost. For you there is no yesterday and no tomorrow; the only reality a girl's lips soft against yours, her breast round under your hand, body cleaving to body as though all the passion in the world must be gathered and used before the moon goes down.'

'This is happening back at home too,' Ven had said, 'it's happening all over the world wherever people are uprooted. And the old and the safe will never understand.'

She stood a while under the big tree overhanging the footpath near the underground station; above her in the thick foliage a colony of sparrows still chattered like men in a bar at closing time. Across the street she could see the lighted windows of the American Centre and the stream of khaki figures drifting in and out, pausing on the edge of the footpath, laughing and talking with the shoeshine boys, moving on again, crossing in twos and threes the broad street to the park.

In all the restless crowd, only she was alone. There was nothing so terrible and terrifying as being alone. All these people were trying to push loneliness away for an hour, for a night...

That was why the girls stood in pairs on the steps near the station entrance, their young faces hard, their voices raucous, brazen and enticing, waiting for hungry men, some man, any man, so long as his need matched their own. Live while there is yet time, before the young men's bodies are broken and the young girl's flesh stale from too much lusting without time for love.

We were lucky, Ven and I. 'We are invulnerable,' he had exulted, holding her close that last night ...

We are invulnerable, you and I.
Twin worlds spun to a star
Between dark and dark ...

'For these others,' he had said, 'there is no time for love, no time for the shy flowering from glance to speech, from speech to touch, and from touch to ecstasy. Why should they wait,' he asked, 'when tomorrow their ship may be among the missing, their plane go down in the mad spiral to death? These bodies steeled to perfection, these minds trained to watch, to observe and to kill, maybe to slow and die instead. The enemy is mortal. Yes, but we are mortal, too. And when the old rules were made, the old customs set, the old patterns designed, mortality had a biblical span before it. Three score years and ten. But today, the life of a flier in the air is twenty-four hours ... Shut it out, shut it out—the past and future. There's only tonight.'

Somewhere a clock was striking eight.

Come In Spinner (1994 edition, expurgated edition published in 1951)

ANONYMOUS

More than 24 000 women served in the Australian Women's Army Service between 1941 and 1945, working as signallers, mechanics, drivers, storekeepers, stenographers, and in a host of other occupations. The official policy was that they did not bear arms. An anonymous former member offered this story to Ann Howard for her collection of first-hand accounts and documents about the AWAS.

'SURRENDER'

When I was at Tamworth, I had an afternoon off and being a city slicker thought being alone in the bush a big deal. I set off armed with an apple, big stick, biscuits, an old hat and stout Army boots. I wandered for miles and lo! there were two burgundy clad figures waving in the distance. One was hobbling with a sprained ankle and in broken English they explained that they had escaped from Brisbane and were bound for Uncle Giuseppe's farm in Leeton, pronounced Leeeeeton.

They offered surrender as the farm was too far for three ankles. The injured one moaned and nodded emphatically. When I pointed to the camp, they became frantic, convinced that they would be shot on sight. I reassured them and we escorted each other to the camp, getting on to the subject of opera. One was a set mover from Milan. He proceeded to entertain us with glorious excerpts from his favourite operas. I was faintly sorry to reach the camp and tried to set in operation a plan to take them straight to the CO, instinctively feeling that taking them to the Military Police might not be a good idea. How right I was! The sergeant spotted us limping in and shouted to his trusty band, who assembled with fixed bayonets.

This all took about eight minutes. The CO arrived and remarked mildly to the sergeant that he did not think all this was necessary and to put the bayonets away before someone got hurt! My recognition from the incident was the nickname of 'Frank Buck', who brought them back alive. It was my only contact with the enemy.

Ann Howard, *You'll Be Sorry!* (1990)

MARJORIE BARNARD

(1897–1987)

and

FLORA ELDERSHAW

(1897–1956)

Writers. Marjorie Barnard and Flora Eldershaw, both of whom were born in Sydney, collaborated on various novels, histories, and essays, using the pseudonym 'M. Barnard Eldershaw'. The last of their joint works was a futuristic novel entitled Tomorrow and Tomorrow *(1947), which switches between the twenty-fourth and twentieth centuries. Originally censored, it was published in full and with its proper title,* Tomorrow and Tomorrow and Tomorrow, *in 1983. This is the account by 'M. Barnard Eldershaw' of celebrations in Sydney at the end of the war in the Pacific in 1945.*

'MASS HYSTERIA'

But love, sacred nor profane, could not hold the sweep of event. After a long and costly indecision in Europe, while thousands upon thousands died on both sides and famine took its stealthier toll, Germany had broken under assault from East and West, the aerial hammering of her cities, war exhaustion, and internal turmoil.

The victory was celebrated but with reserve. It was not the end. There was still food for the vast war machine whose stopping would pile chaos among the victorious upon the chaos of the defeated. For a little longer the scientists would work upon the problems that had become their life, the army of state servants would exercise their extraordinary powers, the munition workers would draw their large cheques, the excitement of war would inflate the headlines. The world was weary of war, but war had become its norm. The return to peace was likely to be as painful as the thawing of a frozen limb. It was not yet. The might of the nations swung against Japan. Her war had been launched behind the barricade of the European war. Now that that shelter had been torn away she was exposed to a weight of armament far beyond her strength to withstand. The structure of her conquered empire buckled and collapsed. Russia declared war, the long-maturing atomic bomb ripened and fell. Japan was surrounded by a ring of mathematically precise destruction. Within the circle were the prisoners of war, the armies of Malaya and Singapore.

The end of the war brought sudden violent release of long-pent emotion, a mass hysteria. For days, rumour, advancing, retreating, had kneaded the popular imagination. When the authentic news came through soon after nine on a working day, Sydney turned with a sort of slow abandonment to celebration. Everyone had the same impulse, to go into the street. Factories, shops, offices emptied. As the streets filled the traffic stopped, the crowd became a procession, all the scattered particles fused. As naturally as leaves before the wind, the procession converged upon the heart of the city. Martin Place became a vortex, a cauldron. A vast crowd filled it, never still, turning on its own axis, continuing in the restricted space to be a procession, dancing, singing, sending up its miasma of jungle noise. When they danced, the steps were chosen for them; when they sang it was not of any individual's volition. The song that dominated the crowd was *Waltzing Matilda*. Those who were left in the buildings tore up any paper that was to hand and sent it drifting down on the crowd beneath — like a stage snow storm. The streets were drifted with paper.

Hour after hour the celebrations went on, they became demonaic. All night the crowd did not diminish. The dancers could scarcely stand but they continued to dance. Boys and girls lay down on the tram lines and went to sleep; they woke again and again to dance. No one ate, no one smoked. Some stood aside, watching and recording it all, took photographs, broadcast descriptions, some could not sink themselves, some could only remember and grieve. They went home to the blank suburbs and stayed there. The city turned like a great record throwing off sound, or it was like a brazier piled high its own fuel.

Good will was born again. Wireless announcers wept at the microphones. The starving poet of King's Cross passionately embraced his wife from whom he had been long estranged. And many other curious and unlikely phenomena occurred. King's Cross excelled itself. Young and old came forth to dance in the streets. Such motor cars as had braved the streets were overturned in sheer exuberance. Shops were broken into and their contents distributed as largesse to the crowd. In its freakishness the mob chose as its mascot Elsie Todd, the ageing prostitute who had won the lottery and graduated as an identity of the Cross by her fantastic and fickle generosity, carrying her about the streets shoulder high, plying her with strange drinks. In the flaring lights, bedizened in her finery, she did look like some barbaric idol being carried in procession. It was her apotheosis. She screamed with laughter and delight, and as she became drunk, sang bawdy songs and responded in kind to obscene witticisms. When she became quarrelsome, yelled abuse, and wanted to fight, the mob thought her funnier than ever and plied her with more drink. At last she became inarticulate and purple in the face and collapsed into a helpless mass. Her captors, tired of her by then and in no very good shape themselves, for it was about four in the morning, dumped her in a doorway and left her. There she lay and there she died at an undetermined moment before the street cleaners came in the dismal soberness of a new day.

The next day Sydney was filthy and dishevelled, and looked not unlike a city that had been sacked. The respite was over, the celebrations were dead. A world debauched by six years of war, by defeat and victory, by restriction and licence, had to take up the most difficult and urgent task that had ever confronted the nations. The conquerors suffered a mass disillusionment. Behind the splendid curtain of victory they found their own unsatisfied revenge, suspicion of ally as well as of the enemy, all the ugly problems, the irremediable tragedies of war, the wastage, the consequences. War had not ended, it would not end in the lifetime of any man who had known it, it could not end. The victors could not rest. An even greater effort was required of them, only the vanquished could rest, for by losing the war responsibility had passed from them.

'M. Barnard Eldershaw', *Tomorrow and Tomorrow* (1947)

ELIZABETH KATA

(?–)

Writer. Sydney-born Elizabeth Kata married a Japanese concert pianist in 1937, and lived in Japan for the next ten or so years. Several weeks before the atomic bomb was dropped on Hiroshima, her son was born in a Japanese village. Her first novel, Be Ready with Bells and Drums *(1961), was later made into an award-winning American film, under the title* A Patch of Blue *(1965). Another of her novels,* Child of the Holocaust *(1979), which opens with this chapter, was made into a television series. As the latter book's blurb says of Kata, 'She is no stranger to the tragedy of orphaned children left behind in a war-torn country.'*

'A TRAVEL-WEARY, BEWILDERED CHILD'

It must have come as a great shock to my great aunt, when, in 1947, an Allied Forces organisation operating in Europe had contacted and informed her that she was the sole surviving relative of one Hans Herman Baum, the orphaned son of her nephew and his wife.

I, Hans Herman, was said to be four, going on five. I had been born to become just one atom of a mass of children orphaned during the holocaust that was the Second World War. Children tamed into instant obedience and accustomed to being shifted from one group to another, from one location to another. *Children who never asked questions — too young to understand.* Children who wore name and number tags, who never laughed or heard other children laugh, ever.

Whatever my aunt's emotions had been on learning of my existence, she had no doubts about her duty. Her attorney, Mr Everett, had made the complicated arrangements to have me flown across the Atlantic Ocean from Germany, and thence taken to her apartment.

It had been a blustery, snow-falling night and I had been a travel-weary, bewildered child when old Mr Everett had led me up the stairs and into the apartment to meet Aunt Trudy for the first time. She had been born way back in history, in 1862, in Germany, and my arrival must have disrupted her way of life and presented her with many perplexities and problems, but at least she had Miss Sly, who came every day to do chores.

Thin, whispery-voiced Miss Sly, idolized her mistress. My intrusion into the household displeased her intensely. There were times when she managed to ignore me so adroitly, I was certain that she was unable to see or to hear me, even when she tubbed me, towelled me dry, or stood by while I attended to Nature's calls. My aunt, however, cosseted and kept me close to her side. Daytimes, Aunt Trudy and I sat together in the over-furnished, over-heated parlour; the windows were kept closed, and because Aunt Trudy disliked glare, the heavy drapes were drawn. A red-shaded lamp lit the dimness and no sounds from the outside world penetrated into the room where she spent most of her time settled in the huge basket-weave chair she favoured, because it yielded to her billowy figure. I spent most of my time perched on a low, leather-covered stool close by her side and I did not favour it, because the stool was hard and slippery.

She utilized the hours dreaming of the past, re-reading old letters, eating snacks and napping. Occasionally, she gave tremulous sighs. I spent long periods of time staring into space, gazing blankly at illustrations in heavy to hold, damp-smelling books; always on the *qui vive*, scared, waiting to be moved on to yet another 'location'. No one had thought to tell me that I was no longer classed as a displaced child.

I felt scared and guilty about the disappearance of my identification tag. Occasionally, I too gave tremulous, though more tentative, sighs. Life was not yet divided into past, present and future. I had no sense of time. Aunt Trudy's sighs were nostalgic, with many memories to think back on. Some brought smiles to her lips, some, tears to her eyes.

When a young woman, she had married against her family's wishes, married a foreigner, a Mr Angus MacPherson, leaving her family and the land of her birth forever, and even though her husband had died some thirty years before my eruption into her life, she was still mourning and lamenting his passing. She unfailingly wore black and often gazed at a silver-framed photograph, murmuring, 'Oh, you dear, *dear* man!' Then she would turn her gaze upon me, tears would glisten in her eyes as she whispered, 'Lost! So many dear ones lost and gone forever. No matter, no matter! See! Look, Hans Herman, Aunt Trudy is *smiling*.'

The only language I heard spoken was English. Other words in another language that I had once heard and understood began to fade from my mind. I paid strict attention to my aunt's every word and gesture, understanding very little, usually completely at a loss. Aunt Trudy would sometimes hold my limp hand in hers, pat my cheek, smile and feed me treats of peppermint candy, which I bracketed along with the bitter-tasting medicine spooned out thrice daily under instructions from old Dr Deacon, who had been called in to examine my spindly body from head to toe.

Miss Sly was never impatient with me, only and always disinterested. Her manner intensified my clumsiness but aroused no resentment in me. I accepted her unwilling care of my person incuriously, lethargically, obeyed her gestured instructions to the best of my ability, but there were times when my heart pounded with fear, such as the first time she had approached me, waving a pair of clicking scissors. Maybe at some time during my life my finger nails had been trimmed but I had no memory of such an event. I had been convinced that Miss Sly was out to do me bodily harm, perhaps cut my hand off!

Meal times were difficult and filled with puzzlements. I had never used a knife, a fork. I had never seen an egg in its natural state and the hot, hard-shelled object that Miss Sly placed before me, gesturing — eat it up — presented me with a terrible problem. It was solved by Miss Sly, who, probably believing that I disliked eggs, prepared the mysterious object, readying it for eating and then ate it herself with some relish.

I knew that I was alive but life had no rhythm, no purpose. I had no idea why the rouge glow of the lamp caressed my puzzled heart, but it did. I would stare and stare at it, then go back to stare emptily at my empty hands. Night and day was as one. Week followed week, month followed month, hushed, meaningless and monotonous.

Then one morning Miss Sly crept into the room. She pulled the drapes aside and opened the windows. A gust of clean, fresh air flowed into the musty room and sounds came up from the street below, causing my body to tense, overwhelming me with a strange mingling of awe, curiosity and excitement.

I heard voices! High-pitched, strident voices, yelling, laughing. I wanted to jump from my stool, run, wildly, to the open window and look out, but habit was too strong. I remained sitting on the stool, quivering, and with both hands pressed against my mouth.

Miss Sly had continued on with her chores, and Aunt Trudy had napped on, peacefully, until a sudden, extra loud barrage of noise from the street below startled her into wakefulness. Slowly, she became aware of the world about her. She listened, intently, then turning her gaze upon me, she smiled, saying, 'Spring! Spring has come! Go downstairs, Hans Herman. Go and play with the children. It will be nice for you. Go down to the street. Miss Sly, show him the way.'

With my heart pounding and my legs as stiff as sticks I stood on the sidewalk, surrounded by a suddenly silent group of children who curiously and cautiously looked me over. Abruptly, one small boy threw the ball he was holding directly towards me. Clumsily I caught it, and after a momentary hesitation threw the ball to one of the little girls. The five children continued on with their game. They let me play along and I caught on to the rules with ease, but with the seriousness of an aged man and making not one sound; the game continued until Aunt Trudy interrupted it by calling to me from the window. Because of her slurred pronunciation the other children heard my name not as, Hans Herman, but as harmsamarm, and they began to chorus gaily, 'Harmsamarm. What's a harmsamarm?'

All at once, I felt wildly happy. Jumping up and down, pointing at myself, I yelled above the din, 'Me! Me! *I'm* Harmsamarm. Me!'

As though on cue we began to roll about together on the sidewalk, all six of us, laughing hilariously.

My life of suffocating loneliness was over! Just like that! Like magic! The past lay submerged in the background of my mind. Without being told, I was confident that I had found my niche in the world.

Gradually, I ceased thinking of my playmates as a group, they became separate entities, and I would whisper their names over and over, like a song of names — Mick, Tom, Molly,

Ingy and Peggy ... Peggy and Ingy, Molly, Tom, and Mick. Gradually also I came to understand that my playmates had parents and permanent homes.

For a while the children continued to call me, Harmsamarm, then, miraculously, I became Harm. 'This is Harm! Ma, this is Harm.'

'Hullo, Harm! My, what a nice, neat boy.'

The mothers in the street were pleased that their children had a new friend and they welcomed me into their homes, but the street remained our playground, our chief meeting place, our battleground, and during that spring, that long hot summer and that glorious energetic fall, I was in a perpetual state of ecstatic intoxication. I yelled the loudest, laughed the loudest, I ran everywhere. I bumped into things, into people. I often fell down. I repeated 'new' words over and over under my breath, mad with desire to understand, to be understood. I was seldom hungry but drank everything that came my way, milk, water, coffee, anything.

Although Aunt Trudy allowed me great freedom she insisted on my following a code of ethics that she laid down. She impressed into my mind the fact that 'manners maketh man' and when I behaved in an unmannerly fashion, her softly intoned, 'That was not nice, Hans Herman,' hurt more than a hard slap. It was not mannerly to run into my playmates' homes when their parents had company. 'Please, dear Hans Herman, please, *bubelah*, you will remember to be always polite and good and kind.'

I would promise to try, always, to be polite, good and kind. Everything that my aunt requested of me seemed sensible and reasonable, except for one edict. Aunt Trudy insisted that I remain indoors on Sundays; all day long and on every Sunday. On those days I would feel forlorn, set apart from my friends, feeling that perhaps I was being punished for a misdemeanour I was ignorant of having committed, but I never questioned her edict. Grown up men and women set the rules. Children obeyed them.

At night, every night, when in bed in my neat bedroom, I would begin to cry. I cried quietly, softly, always and only because I was so happy. Then, as time went by I accepted happiness as my due. I went to bed, tired out after wonderful, rollicking days, to fall asleep instantly.

Child of the Holocaust (1979)

LILY BRETT

(1946–)

Poet and fiction writer. Lily Brett was born in a displaced persons' camp in Germany in September 1946, to Jewish parents. The family migrated to Australia in 1948 and Lily grew up in Melbourne. Much of her work is haunted by her parents' wartime experiences, especially those of her mother in the Nazi concentration camp at Auschwitz in Poland. This poem is from her collection The Auschwitz Poems *(1986), which won the Victorian Premier's Literary Award in 1987. Like some of her other books, it is illustrated by her husband, Australian artist David Rankin. Brett moved to New York in 1990.*

LILY BRETT

'POSSESSIONS'

A bowl
was a life-saving
piece of equipment

any bit of bent metal
rusted tin
worn enamel

without
a
bowl

you
couldn't
eat soup

had
to
make do

with
sawdust-soaked
mud board

that
passed
for bread

a spoon
meant
good fortune

dignity
and
humanity.

The Auschwitz Poems (1986)

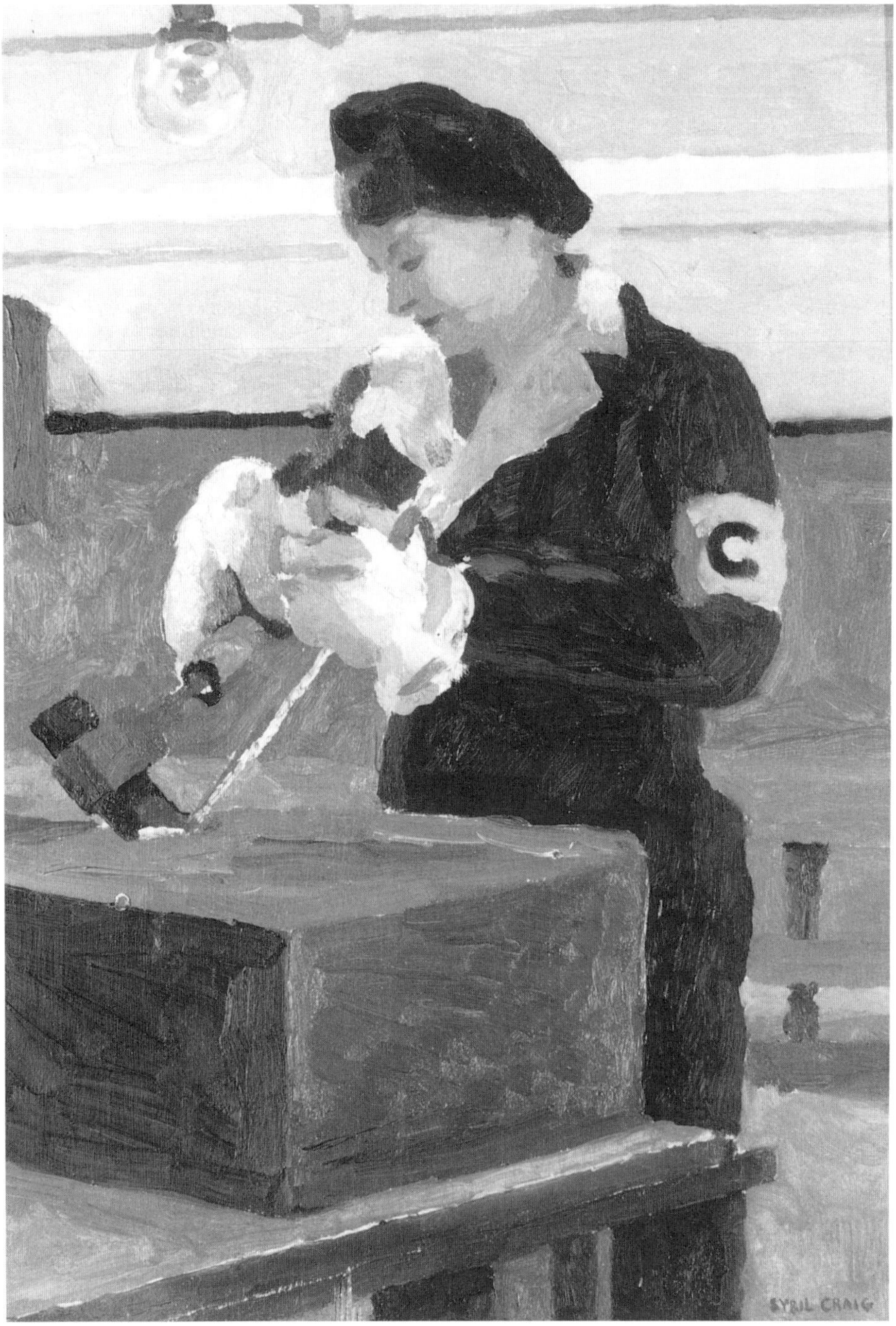

Sybil Craig (1901–89), *Chargewoman Stasia McGillivray*, 1945, oil on canvas on plywood, 36.6 cm x 26 cm. Acquired under official war art scheme in 1945. (AWM 22605)

SUSAN VARGA

(1943–)

Writer. Susan Varga was born in Hungary. Five years later, she, her mother, sister, and stepfather came to Australia. In a moving non-fiction book entitled Heddy and Me *(1994), she explores her relationship with her mother. In doing so she highlights some of the long-term legacies of war.*

'HEDDY'S BABY'

No one had news of my father. Nothing was heard from besieged Budapest. Pubi had one card from him six months before. No news of Pali either, for more than eighteen months. About those who had disappeared, there was a silence, broken by rumours, terrible snippets of revelation.

I have no evidence of my father's movements after he parted from my mother on that June morning in Budapest. All I have from that time is a small photograph, probably taken at a labour camp and sent to my mother. He has on a ludicrous army-style cap, making his full face even fuller. His neck is crammed into an ill-fitting uniform collar. He looks straight at the camera, solemn. His eyes are not so much frightened as baffled. They make me feel sorry for him, but angry too. Bafflement might have been the human, the intelligent response, but not the right one. Fear would have been better, a better weapon.

I went looking in the library for accounts of Fertörákos labour camp. I found the testimony of some men who had survived, first Fertörákos, then Mauthausen and Gunskirchen. In July 1945 one Sándor Hermann, clerk, gave his account of the camp to the National Committee for the Care of Deportees; in August an I. Ban, electrician, gave his testimony. They are distressingly similar, and from them I can get a picture of my father's last days.

On the way to Fertörákos, the men were deprived of any good winter clothing they still had. They were beaten by their Arrow Cross guards and put on starvation rations. On arrival they were housed in open barns. They would wake to find themselves covered in thick layers of snow; frozen limbs were commonplace. Young SA and SS guards beat them and played target practice with any Jew they disliked particularly.

At least 400 men died of cold and exhaustion. The dead were not recorded and their bodies were thrown into a common pit dug by other Jews. The survivors were taken on foot to Mauthausen; many were shot along the route.

There is no surprise in such accounts, but instead of vague and terrible imaginings I now have concrete images. I see why my father turned his face to the wall and died. I begin to sense him, to flesh him out. At the hour of his death he is coming alive for me.

It occurs to me, too, that maybe I am not just searching for him, but also for a small child who didn't die. I am beginning to wonder about her, that child who drank in anxiety and terror with her mother's milk and who hovered apathetic between life and death for months. Until now she has been no more than an object. Heddy's baby, not me.

I inch a little closer to her. She may be nearer than I know, deep within me, still alive. Waiting.

In January 1945 the baby — I — was beginning to put on weight. In February, when I was sixteen months old, I sat up for the first time.

Heddy and Me (1994)

RAMONA KOVAL

(1954–)

Broadcaster. Melbourne-born Ramona Koval was a microbiologist and academic before becoming a radio broadcaster and journalist. These are the opening pages of her first novel, Samovar *(1996). The book is described as 'a story of unquiet souls, both ghostly and real, wrestling with the silence and pain of their own history'. Koval has also published several non-fiction books.*

MOTHERS AND DAUGHTERS

Mother, you are sitting by the desk as I write. Your hair is twisted into a chignon that you learned from the hairdresser in Paris. He told you that you must suffer to be beautiful. You used to tell me this while you brushed the knots from my hair, pulling the curly fringe from my face.

I told you not to hide your strong forehead, with all the brains in it. And I said to sit up straight, to be proud of your breasts. To be proud you were a woman.

Were you proud to be a woman, Mother?

I had you, didn't I? And your sister. My diamonds, I used to call you. A golden diamond and one fiery red. And now your sister has two babies, and your own two are nearly women. Do you tell them to sit up straight?

They used to listen. Now they don't. I'm waiting for a lull in the proceedings, when they realise I have something to say.

You have? What have you learned, my daughter, in these years we have been apart? I'm ready, I'm here listening. The dead, you know, have time for listening and musing ... I'll put my feet up and we will begin. See?

I can see. How long has it been — nearly fifteen years since we buried you that miserable October day? I was pregnant with the younger girl, and I wore your grey wool dress to the graveside. It was muddy and there were only a few people there — not my father, of course, but a few close friends and your cousin who had been absent over the years since you fell out with him, I don't know why. But he helped carry your coffin ... A rabbi who didn't know you, and your first granddaughter who was just over two. Many years have passed since I was accountable to you, Mother. I am nearly forty.

Ten years younger than I was when I died. Tell me, if you had only ten years to go, my dear, how would you spend this last decade? After all, you have had so many opportunities — an education, jobs and husbands — why so many husbands?

You had one long miserable marriage, is that better? And I remember you saying that you didn't take anyone else's husband, but you borrowed a few. Remember in the hospital when you were getting another blood transfusion — the last one before you decided you couldn't stand it any more — you said that you had borrowed a few husbands. I borrowed a few and married two.

But I had an excuse. Where was your war?
There is no conversation once you play that card, Mother. You know that and I know that. Now. It's a show stopper, a grand finale, with all the elephants and the tigers and the acrobats parading around.

Why are you talking about circuses? It was no entertainment. It was something to live through. To survive.

Yes, all right. I know. I understand.

Nobody knows. How can you understand? Ah ...

You sigh. It upsets me. You used to sigh like that when you lit the Friday night candles, and covered your face in prayer. Or when you lay on the couch reading *Time* magazine during the afternoons when we came home from school.

It was many things. The candles always reminded me of home, of my mother, my brother. Time *magazine was filled with other cruelties, insanities. Vietnam, Cambodia ... What we went through our war for I do not know. What was the purpose? What did we learn?*

You had us, didn't you? That's what I used to say when I saw you sad. Here we are — your two shining diamonds. We were the reward. You were pained, even when you were silent. I remember you'd say a few sentences, something from a memory, and you would lapse into a terrible silence; your eyes would mist up and I felt I had to fill the silence. With a kiss or a joke or something, anything. I tried to understand. That's all we can do as human beings, surely? To imagine others' pain, their ordeals. I can't live your experience for you. Just as you can't live mine.

Naturally, because I'm dead, stupid.

But you're not at rest yet, are you? I thought perhaps the dead would be ... serene. You used to say, It will be quiet in the grave — and yet you're struggling with the flesh and blood, with the marrow of your life. Are you still tired?

I'm struggling with you, my darling. Not with death, not with life.

Why struggle with me then?

Because you need it. You want it. You called me up.

I called you up to talk, I hope. We are nearly the same age now — we can be frank, we can be friends. See how I'm sitting up straight here — proudly, as a woman. We can meet, woman to woman. Why don't I make us a cup of tea?
A long vermouth and dry with a slice of orange at the top would be better. But cut the orange thinly please, not like a peasant.

I'll do my best. But listen, Mother, let me tell you what happened this morning. Your granddaughter, my fourteen year old, came to me at four in the morning. She came to my bed because she was worried about her school camp. She couldn't sleep. She's going for two months and she didn't know if she'd like the kids sharing her house. Do you know what I said? I said, your grandmother was fourteen in the war, totally alone. She walked to Warsaw and survived as a Christian. And you're simply going to a school camp for eight weeks! I actually said that — I can hardly believe my harshness. I mirrored you. Your words out of my mouth. Can the dead speak for the living, what do you think, Mother?

Samovar (1996)

Part Four

KOREAN WAR

OLWYN GREEN

(1923–)

War widow. Olwyn Warner grew up in Ulmarra, New South Wales, where she married a soldier, Charles Green, in 1943. After the war, Charlie found settling down difficult, so he rejoined the army in January 1949. As commander of the first Australian troops sent to the Korean War (Third Battalion, Royal Australian Regiment), he arrived in South Korea in September 1950, was severely wounded by a North Korean shell on 30 October, and died the following day. Olwyn and their daughter moved from Grafton, where they had been living, to Sydney, where Olwyn later studied. She subsequently taught for twenty years. In 1980, she began to search for 'the real Charlie', eventually writing a book entitled The Name's Still Charlie *(1993), which she says is 'a true story as far as memory permits'. Olwyn had had a premonition about Charlie's death before it occurred.*

'THE COW'

He was gone.

Returning to the empty house and the empty bed, I wondered if I could survive if he never came home. There's no blurring in my mind of those black days. Nightmarishly they live on. So does the cow incident that now seems pathetically theatrical. But it happened. Its bizarreness a measure of my distress.

With Charlie gone, I fell victim to my premonition. I became possessed by the idea that Charlie would die and that would be my fit punishment. All that he wanted was a normal life with the woman of his dreams, and a nice farm. He'd be the happiest man alive. His dreams didn't come true. Because I was snobbish and fastidious I hadn't wanted Charlie in a flannel shirt and Wellington boots, squelching around in the cow yard, tied to cows day in, day out, for ever. I'd wanted tall, handsome Charlie the commander in an elegant home leading a sophisticated life. Only some convincing sign that I repented could assuage an angry God or restore Charlie's belief that I was the wife he'd dreamed about, the wife who loved him.

I seized on the idea of the cow, though I have no recollection of how it came about. I'd show God and Charlie. I'd learn to milk. Before Charlie left we must have planned the cow and talked about the farm we'd get this time when he came home. It must have been Charlie who organised the cow with Herc. It arrived after Charlie left. Herc sent it in a truck. It was a little, cream, gentle-eyed thing with a pedigree, whose nickname I can't recall. Herc, with his sharp eye and razor perception, named cows after people. He'd say, 'That's Mary,' and you'd know there would be some uncanny resemblance to its namesake. One cow was named after me, someone let fall one day.

The cow went into Charlie's paddock, the one at the back of the house where he'd once planted potatoes. Probably it was Charlie who threw up an improvised bail, before he left. Or it might have been Harry Smith. Harry and Elvie were brought into the scheme. They could have seen through the drama and joined in to help, out of love for Charlie. By this time Harry and Elvie had two more babies, twins, to provide for. They kept fowls and grew vegetables, and after the cow had to be taken away they got two goats. One goat would have been lonely. It astounded me to see those butting creatures with their strange, yellow, slit eyes overwhelming their backyard. Until I learned to milk, Harry and Elvie would come night and morning with a milk bucket, going through my place to reach the paddock.

From Korea Charlie was to write, curious and amused, wishing he were a fly on the wall. With a little smile he would have mused on Harry and Elvie sterilising everything. God knows how he pictured me! 'Your farm,' as he called it, didn't go to plan. I didn't learn to milk. After Charlie left, I was desolate. I could not function. It was as though all the blood and all my life had been drained out of me. Try as I might, I couldn't drag myself around. If I'd cried, it might have been easier. It was the end; it was too late, said my burdensome pessimism. I did not learn to milk. I couldn't.

Then it started to rain, as though nature itself was disturbed. It rained and rained. Confined in the paddock that became a quagmire, the little cow had to be hand-fed and milked, night and morning. In dripping oilskins and gum boots Harry and Elvie would struggle past as I looked on dumbly.

Recalling all this, I had one of my typical nightmares last night:

> Charlie and I went to Finland, apparently on a holiday. There, we set out to find a particular house. When we found it we realised it was different from all those around it, and we were pleased. It was old and basic, and appealing, compared with the other modern ones. Expectantly we set out across the street to enter the house. That's when Charlie slipped in the mud. At first he gestured amusedly how deep the mud was. But then he started sinking; he kept on sinking till he was up to his neck. Then he indicated he was trapped and was going under! As he sank out of sight he called, 'I can't see.' I tried to scream for help but no sound would come — this was the frightening part of the dream. Then I panicked and wildly sought help, desperately trying to make a sound. I noted though that instead of going to his aid, I ran around frantically. Someone appeared and said, 'That's very bad (or evil) mud.'

That's all I recall. After such a dream, I remain haunted for hours. Since I've been told that 'dreams are a message from you to you', I endeavour to untangle them. In this dream there was the recurring theme — losing Charlie.

Fear of losing him was the reason for invoking the cow. An impotent talisman it turned out to be.

Some healing of the soul has given me clearer, fuller vision. These days I wonder: 'Had I been able to combat the premonition and embrace Charlie's appointment confidently, as an opportunity for him, how different it might have been. He might have come home!'

And he might not.

The Name's Still Charlie (1993)

KATHARINE SUSANNAH PRICHARD

(1883–1969)

Writer. Katharine Susannah Prichard helped to found the Communist Party of Australia in 1920, was a lifelong member, and wrote several political works, including Why I am a Communist *(1957). 'Her last novel,* Subtle Flame *(1967), was a manifestation of her increasing desire for world peace', according to* The Oxford Companion to Australian Literature *(second edition, 1994), 'and centred on a middle-aged newspaper editor who suffers a personal and political crisis during the era of the Korean War which causes him to leave both family and job to crusade for peace and nuclear disarmament.'*

'A FILTHY, BLOODY TAKEDOWN'

Rain had fallen during the night; gusty showers sweeping the house and garden. Mist rose from the ground. The house looked stricken and desolate in wan moonlight drifting from behind clouds: as stricken and desolate as everybody within its walls had been all day.

An old-fashioned house, with narrow, white verandahs and plum-coloured slates on the roof, it slumped among dark trees: a relic of the early days. Claire's grandfather had built it and called it 'Elouera', the pleasant place: David bought the house for her in the first flush of unexpected affluence. It stood derelict then, in an abandoned orchard with choked drains and a patriarchal gum tree at the gate. Repairs and painting cost no end of money. Claire had installed all the fixings and furnishings to make a comfortable home there for him, herself and their young family.

So many tragedies it had hugged to itself, that old house; but none more poignant than this which had struck it today, David thought, his mind too heavy to move far from the grief racking him.

He had come into the garden, an hour or so before dawn, to find some relief from his anguish in the clear air. It kept him pacing the garden path: a restless, intolerable pain gnawing at his body and brain. The cry of another father surged in him, though he could not utter it.

'My son! My son! Would to God I had died for thee!'

A yellow telegraph form flashed and faded before his eyes: 'Regret inform you … Lance-Corporal Robert Evans … Third Battalion Royal Australian Regiment killed in action on February fifteenth.' His mind gripped only those words. They were enough to shatter a man —and a woman like Claire, so wrapped in her family that she was not interested in anything beyond the garden fences. She had hated to see Rob in uniform: begged him not to go to Korea.

'What's it got to do with us, Rob?' she queried. 'Let these people manage their own affairs. It's so silly for us to butt in. I can't bear to think of you hurting other mothers' sons, or of them hurting you.'

How he had laughed at her futile and illogical pleading. So young and sure of himself! A sturdy, red-faced lad, with bright gingery hair like her own, proud of the stripe on his sleeve, and filled with excitement about the heroic adventure before him. Now he was dead, and she prostrated by sorrow.

This was the first break in the family. It had been united by careless affection and amused tolerance of each other's idiosyncrasies. They were so different, the children, Neil, Myffanwy, Rob and Gwen, each going a different way with the characteristic obstinacy and independence, common to all: Neil, a young doctor, doing his first year as resident in a public hospital: Myffanwy, secretary to a trade union official on the waterfront, and Rob had suddenly turned from journalism to soldiering. Gwen liked her work in a kindergarten, but was determined to get what she wanted from life: a good time, whatever that meant.

As editor and general manager of *The Daily Dispatch* and *The Weekly Budget* David had been able to offer Rob an opening on *The Dispatch*. Rob had taken to journalism like a duck to water, quickly accepting views of the paper as his own.

Myffanwy and Rob clashed frequently about them; and what she called his 'obliquity of understanding'. Rob was no match for Myff in argument. He had not been able to brush aside her opposition to his fighting in Korea as easily as his mother's. To be sure he enlisted before he told the family what he was going to do. Myff and he quarrelled furiously about it, with lover-like reconciliations afterwards.

David had not faced the situation, he realised. He had been too busy writing leaders in support of the Security Council decision, ignoring evidence that it was contrary to the terms of the Charter of the United Nations Organisation: intervention might have been premature, gerrymandered and ill-advised. He knew now. That was what stung him. Why had he not given the lad a clearer understanding of the causes of this war? He admitted to himself, it was because he was reluctant to recognise the situation for what it was — a crisis faked to serve the interests of United States foreign policy.

For this his son's life had been sacrificed. He felt morally to blame. He could not escape a sense of responsibility for Rob's death. There was that in his grief: the knowledge he had shirked investigating and exposing the truth about this war in Korea.

Rob's letters from Korea had aroused David to make a closer study of events leading up to United States intervention in a skirmish between the North and South; and United Nations procedures to endorse American intervention. He was astounded to discover that United States military forces were in action before the Security Council had been committed.

The lad knew nothing of this, of course, though he had heard something of the background of Korean affairs from Myff. After the first month or so of marching and fighting through the devastated countryside, his heroic adventure had become 'a filthy, bloody take-down'.

Fragments of his letters scattered, like leaves on the garden path, through David's brain.

'It's more awful than you could imagine, all hell let loose. Troops retreating, troops slogging up to the front, blasting villages, dead and wounded lying all over the place, corpses rotting in the paddy fields, burnt-out tanks by the roadsides, homeless and starving peasants cluttering the roads, lines of nearly naked prisoners driven along the snow by armed guards ...

'The worst of it all the gooks don't seem to want us. They don't like us any more than we like them. The Yanks say, "The only good gook is a dead one"! …

'This morning a bird sang in a bush near my hootchie. God, how could it live, much less sing in the suffocating smoke and the stink of the dead all round …

'Reckon this country must've been beautiful once. On patrol, sometimes, we sight a valley the guns haven't got, thatched roofs huddled together, green patches of crops, fruit trees with yellow leaves. But mostly it's a shambles, blasted trees, burnt out villages …

'Blue sky today made me feel homesick …

'The stars at night, wonderful just now. Gazing down on you, so calm and peaceful: the stars make you ashamed of what you're doing, a stranger creeping through this country, killing and destroying wherever you go …

'Beginning to think you were right, Myff. I should have known what this war's about before I came here. Tell dad, I'll put on the gloves and have a go with him when I get home for not giving me the oil. A bloke ought to know why women and children are skinned alive by napalm bombs …'

David thrust the memory of Rob's letters from him. It was unendurable to dwell on what the boy had suffered. His father groaned inwardly. There was nothing he could do about it now. Yet he remembered, a few months ago, he had been able to throw some light on what was really happening in Korea. He had dared to re-publish the report of an American war correspondent from the battlefront. John Osborne told what he called 'the ugly story of an ugly war', referring to it as 'sorrowful and sickening'.

David suspected that the article which impressed him by its honesty had broken the barrier of censorship imposed by the High Command.

The Dispatch correspondent had sent him little more than official hand-outs. But he gathered from men who had got messages through, accredited war correspondents were cursing because their reports had been so mutilated and delayed in transmission, they were stale beer before they reached exasperated editors.

Old war horses, men with famous names, who had covered other campaigns, could not tolerate the way they were being hamstrung in Korea. They took advantage of any means to evade a ridiculously blighting censorship and get their stuff away. So that, gradually, information about what was happening on the Yalu began to leak through. A disastrous retreat could no longer be camouflaged by flowing official accounts of a strategic withdrawal and glorious victories. Military bungling was exposed: the whole administrative machinery of the campaign thrown open to criticism.

David had leafed through the papers Myffanwy brought home: papers and pamphlets which published information and reports from 'the other side'. At first he was irritated by their partisanship, tossed them impatiently aside. But his interest grew in the reports of an Australian war correspondent, Wilfred Burchett, and of Alan Winnington, an Englishman. They gave a pretty clear idea of the organisation and indomitable spirit which had enabled the North to outwit and withstand the onslaught of United States forces; the weight of equipment in tanks, transport and commissariat vehicles which supported the 'liberators'.

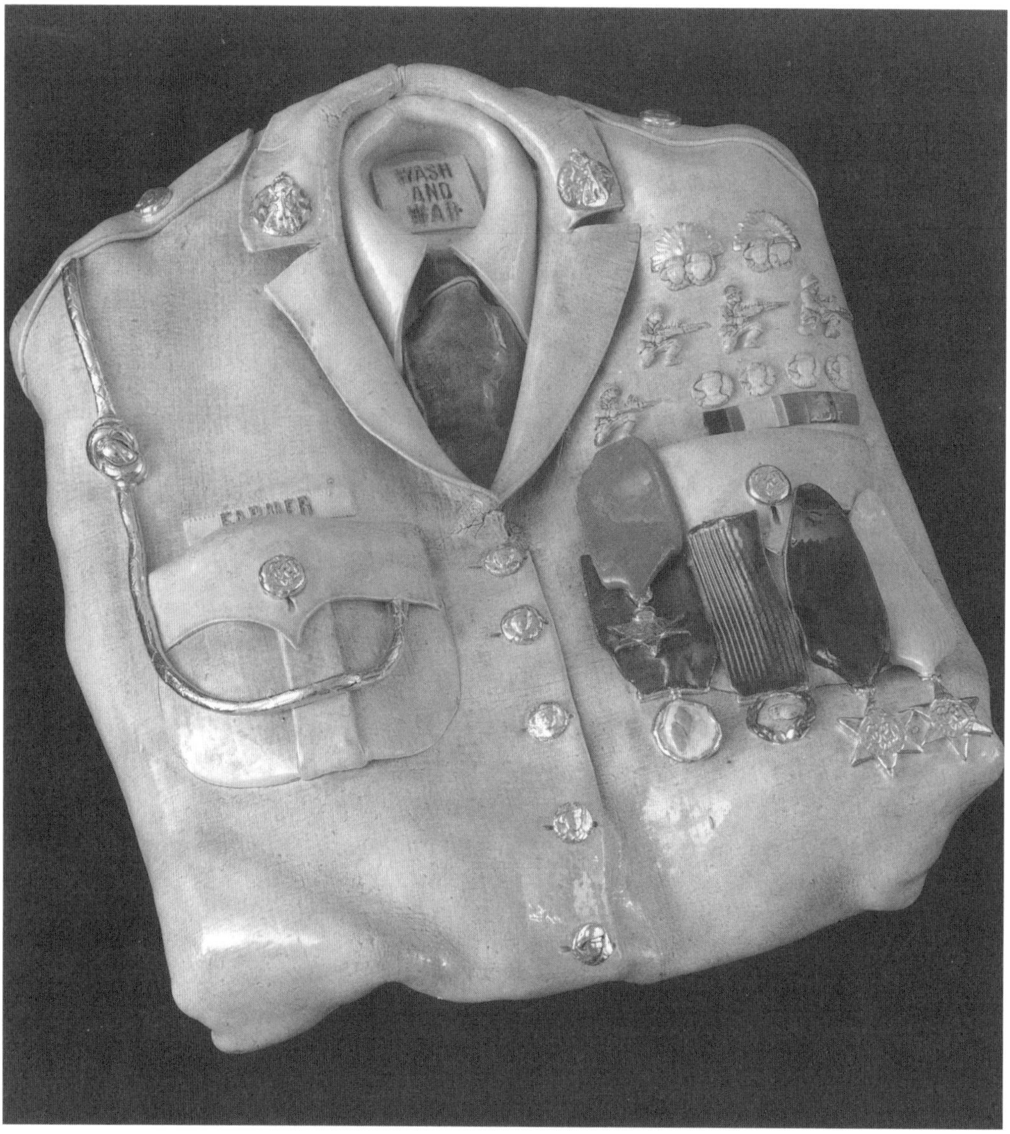

Olive Bishop (1941–), *Wash and war, General*, 1978, painted and glazed ceramic, 48.1 x 42 x 9.7 cm. Purchased in 1979. (AWM 40871)

It was an incredible story of men against machines, of the mighty laid low by tactics, faith in a cause and incredible valour.

Myff knew more about it than he did, David conceded. She had always maintained the people of the North could not be defeated because they were fighting for something they believed in. Their strength was the strength of ten because their hearts were pure. Hard on the pure-in-heart who perished in their thousands because their strength was not equal to the strength of high explosives! But then the Chinese had come to the aid of their neighbours, provoked, no doubt, by MacArthur's threat to their own territory. Myff had not reckoned on their support for her pure-in-heart. Or had she?

Such a starry-eyed idealist, his elder daughter; but well-informed and logical enough. She had made a study of Korean history after reading *Grass Roots* years ago, she said — a book by a Korean writer who described the pacifist revolution organised by patriots to put an end to Japanese occupation of their land. The Japanese massacred the pacifists. The revolution caused scarcely a ripple in the rest of the world.

He had taken a delight in arguing with Myff, David admitted to himself, treating her as a silly girl though he loved and admired her. Myff loved him, he was sure, but he doubted whether she admired him. She treated him with indulgent forbearance, as if she were much older and wiser than he: could make allowances for his absorption in *The Dispatch* and *The Budget*, his pose of good-natured insouciance. Nothing of that was left today. The only one in the family able to understand the chaos of his mind and emotions, would be Myff.

As if his need of her had reached Myffanwy, she came towards him, swaying like a shadow from the house. She stood beside him.

'You must get some sleep, dad,' she said.

'How is your mother?' His eyes rested on her. So quiet and controlled, she was, this daughter of his, straight and strong despite her lithe slenderness: her eyes held depths he could not fathom. Her face was taut in the wan light.

'She's sleeping now,' Myffanwy said. 'Neil gave me a tablet for her.'

'Has he gone?'

'Yes. He was on duty.'

'And Gwen?'

'Sleeping too ... Its hard on her, poor kid. Rob and she were such chums. I wish I had not been so cross with him ... about going.'

'You've got nothing to reproach yourself with.'

Myffanwy caught the bitterness in his voice.

'Neither have you,' she said.

'You don't believe that.' His voice broke, the words forced from him. 'I'll reproach myself till the day I die, Myff. You did what I should have done at the time — tried to prevent his going. You knew what I didn't know — didn't want to know, or believe. I feel like a murderer. I let my son throw his life away for something utterly worthless.'

'You couldn't have stopped him,' Myff said sadly. 'Rob liked opposition ... to stand on his own feet. The adventure appealed to him. He had to see for himself to understand.'

'That's the worst of it,' David groaned. 'My God, when he knew there was something wrong with what he was doing, he had to go through with it! His letters ...'

'They're the best of Rob.' Myffanwy spoke slowly, steadily. 'We knew him as a lovable, irresponsible boy; but these letters show the stuff he was made of—your stuff and mother's—the way we were brought up: to be honest, kind, and think for ourselves.'

'You shame me, Myff.' David turned away to hide his face.

Myffanwy took his arm. 'Come along,' she said, firmly. 'You must get some sleep. I'll make tea, and give you one of Neil's tablets.'

She knew the day's work would claim him, and that, inexorably, he would go through with it. Bringing out *The Daily Dispatch* was so much part of his life that it would not occur to him to fail in his duty towards it. No personal disaster would be allowed to interfere. It was true, he took a fortnight's holiday each year; but only after he had made meticulous arrangements for the efficient carrying-on of every job. Even then he fussed and fumed when he saw a copy of *The Daily Dispatch* he had not shaped, noting the way the news was handled, details of slackness, sloppy writing. He looked happier going back to work than leaving for his holidays, though he pretended to enjoy loafing on the beach at Phillip Island, reading; or watching the penguins while Claire sat beside him, making little water-colour sketches of the sea and rocky headlands.

'How about you?' David asked as she led him to the house. 'You must try to get some rest too.'

'I'm taking the day off,' Myffanwy told him. 'There'll be time to rest during the morning.'

Subtle Flame (1967)

MARY McFADZEAN

(1928–)

Army nurse. Mary Joyce was born and educated in Deloraine, Tasmania. Her father was a farmer, her mother a teacher. After having trained at hospitals in Launceston and Adelaide, she was working at the Repatriation Hospital in Hobart when she decided to join the army. She served with the Royal Australian Army Nursing Corps (the successor of the Australian Army Nursing Service) from 1951 to 1954, during part of which time she worked in Kure, Japan, and Seoul, Korea. Many years later, she recalled 'a very interesting part of my time in Japan' during the Korean War.

'THE HOSPITAL TRAIN'

To be posted to the hospital train was a plum assignment, because you were your own boss. It was only for 3 months and was a big responsibility, but you were away from the hierarchical system of the Base hospital and the formality of the British.

The staff of the hospital train consisted of: one trained nurse, one male orderly, sometimes a female nursing orderly and Japanese–American train boy for an interpreter.

The train, as it was called, was one or, if casualties were heavy, two railway carriages, equipped as small hospital wards. It was attached to an ordinary Japanese train and each morning left Kure, where our Base Hospital was and went down to Iwakuni, the RAAF base where the medical evacuation planes landed. I think it took about 3–4 hours.

On the way down we checked over our gear. Each morning we picked up a basket of food supplies — sandwiches, tea etc. We had a spirit stove and I had a medical kit with drugs and dressings.

When we got to Iwakuni we went by jeep to the Air Force hospital where we had lunch and waited for the plane from Korea. When the plane arrived the casualties were brought to the Air Force hospital, where they were given a meal if they wanted it, dressings were changed, and medication given.

After a short rest they were put back into the ambulances and taken to the train.

These patients were mainly all men from the Commonwealth troops who had been wounded or had some serious illness. The first treatment they had received at the Field Ambulance and the MASH had been mainly to stabilise them for travel and they would be going to surgery the next day or that night if urgent. During the train trip to Kure I would do any treatment or give any medication that was needed. Before leaving Iwakuni, I would ring through to Kure the details of the trip — 18 stretchers, 20 walking, ETA 1800 hours, so we would be met by ambulances and a bus as required.

I had a supply of books and magazines and a wind-up gramophone with the latest hit tunes (very cheap in Japan then).

But mostly the men slept or just rested. Many were very ill, all had been through a traumatic experience, friends killed or wounded, and I think that to be lying quietly on clean sheets with a cup of tea and a cigarette and to know that you were one step nearer to going home, was all that they wanted.

❧ ❧ ❧

The train was also used for a much happier occasion every few weeks. That was when we picked up the patients at the Base Hospital and took them down to Iwakuni for a Med Evac plane back to Australia, or in the case of the UK patients, down to the docks in an ambulance for a sea voyage back to England.

Just before the end of the Korean War there came operation 'Little Switch' [which] was an exchange of a small number of prisoners of war. I was still on the train and I can remember being called into the office and warned that I was not to question the patients about their experiences, and I was not to repeat to anyone anything the patients might tell me. No one wanted to jeopardise the peace talks or the POW exchange with stories of POW camps or atrocities.

We did not know what to expect, it was not so long ago that we had seen newsreels of Japanese POW camps and their victims so we went off prepared for anything.

Happily the Commonwealth troops who had been exchanged were not so ill. They were very quiet and they all wore gauze face masks, several said that they had developed TB. There were 4 Australians, from I Bn RAR, the rest were from the UK. Anyway without asking any questions I accompanied them in the ambulance to the door of their special ward and that was the end of their war.

McFadzean Notes

Part Five

VIETNAM WAR

SUSAN TERRY

(?–)

Civilian nurse. Susan Terry was born in Bathurst, New South Wales, educated at MacRobertson Girls High School, Melbourne, and trained at the Melbourne School of Nursing. In 1964 she went to South Vietnam with a small, civilian medical team from Australia, to join what Weary Dunlop described as an 'international brigade', to care for civilian victims of war. For a year she worked at Long Xuyen Hospital, on the Mekong Delta. After her return from South Vietnam, she wrote a book about life in the Vietnamese hospital. House of Love *(1966) takes its title from the Vietnamese word for hospital.*

CHILDREN

There are, of course, no Government social service benefits in South Vietnam, nor are there for average people any facilities for the rehabilitation of the maimed or blind. There are no hospitals which provide specialist care for the paralysed or deformed. There are no physiotherapists, no occupational therapists, no speech therapists, and no people trained in the care of the mentally handicapped. Any person in need of such specialist attention, whether the disability is due to a congenital condition, disease, or the result of traumatic injury, must take his chance on the care that relatives and the village social system can give. I am not disparaging the care and attention Vietnamese families lavish on their sick; there can be no more loving care given anywhere in the world, and we saw many very wonderful examples of whole-hearted devotion to ailing or injured relatives; but it is, in the main, unskilled care, inadequate to the needs of many cases which in Western societies would not only continue to live, but to live comparatively normal lives.

In this country where children and young adults have never known the meaning of peace, where war has gone on longer than twenty years, thousands are limbless and deformed and paralysed, condemned to spend their lives without artificial limbs on crutches or lying on straw mats waiting to be carried from place to place. Theirs is the continuing tragedy of a burden that shows no sign of lifting, that goes with them from childhood into adult life and on to the end of their days. Surely the only tragedy greater than this, is the still growing number of young people whose lot is cast into these ranks, still more are being left homeless and parentless, still more are losing their chances of proper care.

An attractive Cambodian boy came alone to us one afternoon after a mine explosion had shattered his right leg. He was only fifteen years of age but we had to amputate the leg from above the knee. The wound was slow to heal for it had been infected, but after he had learnt to walk on crutches he begged us to give him an artificial limb. Another patient had told him of an American technician who made artificial limbs in Saigon and nothing less would satisfy him; he had to have a new leg, he had to be taught to walk again.

We grew terribly fond of that bright and happy boy and after a time our surgeon decided that since he was fairly well grown it would be worth trying to fit a prosthesis. He spent several nights drawing and re-drawing designs and paid numerous visits to the market with Bach [one of the hospital's interpreters] to find a local carpenter who was willing to make the attempt. When at last our surgeon was satisfied with the prospective design, material and manufacturer, we measured the young boy and told him the good news. His happiness knew no bounds. While the limb was being made he would follow me about the hospital grounds on his crutches. He had a beautiful smile and winning ways. He would carry stores from the pharmacy with a load in each hand banging against his crutches as he hopped along. Would I, he said, when he got his new leg, take him home with me to Australia? 'He would be my houseboy and brother and would do everything I wanted him to, for as long as he lived.'

Another small boy came to us with a shattered lower limb. It was late in the evening when he arrived but he had travelled most of the day to reach us. He and two mates had got up early to go fishing; while they were out in the sampan someone had shot at them from the bushes at the side of the canal. One of his friends was killed instantly, the other had dived into the river and got away, he had been left with his dead companion and a bullet through his leg. He was eleven years old. He did not cry when I pricked him for a blood test or put an intravenous infusion into his arm. He did not whimper when we told him he was going to lose his leg, but 'Aunty' wept loudly and had to be taken outside. While he was recovering and adapting to a new life on crutches I got to know him well, because he among the other youngsters of Ward 3 was teaching me to play a Vietnamese parlour game something like Monopoly. At times he became very sad and depressed and begged for an artificial leg. Why couldn't he have one like the Cambodian boy? Time and again I explained about growing, that limbs were inefficient if they became too short and expensive if they had to be replaced. Finally I could only assure him that when he did finish growing he could come back to the hospital and someone would help him to get a new leg. How would he know when he had stopping growing? Oh, he would be able to tell by his clothes, and he would be coming back to see the doctor anyway, quite often. First after a few months, then every year, and the doctor would tell him when the time had come. 'Aunty' thought this was highly satisfactory and was very pleased, but my young friend looked at me and demanded, 'Will you still be here?' No, I wouldn't be, but someone else would be. I hope it was not a vain promise.

These wonderful children often had wonderful parents. I shall never forget the mother of a two-year-old child who came to us with appendicitis-peritonitis. Our surgeon explained that the child must have an immediate operation to have even a chance of recovering. The mother said she understood, her husband was a schoolteacher, and she understood about things like surgery. The operation went smoothly but the child did not wake up from the anaesthetic. He had an underlying brain disease which caused epileptic-type fits and he remained in a coma for weeks. Throughout this period he stayed in recovery room, his mother with him. I have never seen such tender and loving care as that child received. Lien and I came to love her and often talked to her as we went about our work.

She would tell us in great detail of any slight change in the baby's condition and of anything he started doing for himself. She never lost patience or hope, and at times when he was waking up he was very noisy and difficult to handle. Strangely, even when I was on my own, she would speak in rapid Vietnamese and stranger still, perhaps partly because of her faith, I often understood the general trend of her words. Strange, too, was the fact that she always called me 'Bac Si'. I asked Lien to explain that I was not a doctor. The lady had said she knew this but continued to call me 'Bac Si' for reasons of her own.

When the little boy woke up properly he had a severe weakness in his right limbs, and when his mother took him home we had barely got him on to his feet. They lived in Thot Not, a large village about twenty kilometres away, and whenever she came to shop at Long Xuyen market she would call in. Lien usually met her and then would find me, 'the lady who calls you Bac Si is here.' I remember the wonderful Saturday morning when she brought me the news that he was able to run about on his own and play with other children. She would bring him next time, she promised, so I could see for myself.

Next time they did come together and he truly was as well and as strong as she had said. It seemed like a miracle. We were soon to leave Long Xuyen then and they had come to say goodbye. The little boy kissed me and his mother kissed me. As they went off she said with tears in her eyes, 'I shall never stop telling him about Bac Si.'

When Bach first came to work with us at Long Xuyen he was sixteen years old; very intelligent but with the brashness and self-assurance that very young people often display in their first jobs. It was wonderful watching him change and grow, a little wiser, a little finer every day. I have the highest respect for Bach because it could not have been easy.

At first I did not like to use him to break bad news to patients or relatives for I felt he was too detached, even off-hand. He failed to realise that a loss of the moment to him or to us, was a loss for a lifetime to others, a tragedy to be lived with over every following day. Time and experience changed him, for Bach was a tender-hearted boy with a lot of intuition, and the day came when he could tell us what tragedy meant to this person or that person, and his assessment of a person's need or suffering could safely be relied upon. He grew to love his work, the hospital, the patients, the relatives, the rest of the staff, and us.

Once, in a period of 48 hours we completed thirty-seven operations, mostly emergencies. In Ward 3 Mr Anh and I counted fifty-eight patients in twenty-eight beds and in Ward 5 Bé had to put extra beds on the verandah. Bach and I were walking back from the pharmacy when we noticed a young woman carrying the whitest looking baby, Vietnamese or Australian, I had ever seen. One tiny leg was a splint of bare wood and a bloody bandage, and the other leg was covered with another bandage just as dirty. A blood-soaked dressing was wound around the babe's chest and incompletely covered a gaping hole in its neck.

Wasting no time Bach talked to the young woman and related the tragic tale to me. The babe was an eight months' old girl, the sole survivor of a family of six children from a small hamlet the Viet Cong had mortared somewhere in the Seven Mountains. Her mother was killed, the neighbour told us, and her father, who had been away at the time, was insane from grief and shock. Poor Bach was almost crying as he told me the story, as I was as I listened. It was 36 hours since she had been injured, the kind neighbour said.

The baby lay so white and still in my arms I was terrified she was going to die. Her blood count was extremely low and even when we must have hurt her she remained passive. I nursed her until the surgeons operated because she whimpered softly every time I put her down. The neighbour said she would stay at the hospital overnight. She could then take back news to the poor demented father.

After operation and blood transfusion the pretty little babe soon became much better. Indeed she was everyone's darling, but especially Bach's and mine. I was nursing her one afternoon and Bach came in and kissed her while he thought no one else was looking. Afterwards he said to me, 'I love our baby, Susie.'

The story did not end there. About a week after her operation the baby had a high temperature and wouldn't take her milk. We had just finished lunch at the White House when Bach came flying in and literally cried as he called to me, 'Susie! Susie! Our baby is very ill now. Come at once.' And she was very ill. She was having convulsions every few minutes and her temperature had soared. Our doctors thought she probably had septicaemia, blood poisoning.

Again I thought she was going to die and I prayed wildly, not only for her own sake and her poor father's, but for Bach. Again all my anger and resentment against the war rose within me. The terrible, useless, terrifying, hopeless waste — waste of everything, but most of all waste of the young and good, the bright and the hopeful, the joyful and beautiful, just squandered as though worthless. And thus all Vietnam lives, I thought, from day to day, never in peace, always in fear. How could children be brought up like this?

We watched and waited for several days and at last 'our baby' won her right to live. Her father came for her, a courteous peasant in typical black pyjamas no different from the hundreds we had met, and an 'Aunty' who was going to look after her for him. She was a happy, playful baby, once she was well again, and even when she had left recovery room and 'Aunty' was caring for her in Ward 5, we still took our turns to feed and nurse her. When she went away, her little leg still in a plaster but otherwise healthy, Bach and I saw her off. 'Susie,' he said as the cyclo drove off. 'Whatever happens to me in the future I'll never forget our baby.'

House of Love (1966)

DOROTHY AUCHTERLONIE

(1915–91)

Poet, writer, and reviewer. Dorothy Auchterlonie was born in Sunderland, England, and educated at Sydney University. Married to H. M. Green in 1944, Dorothy Green was a journalist, then reader, and later lecturer. An influential critic herself, she published a revised version of her late husband's magisterial two-volume work, A History of Australian Literature *(originally published 1961), in 1985. She also published poetry under her family name, including this poem, which was included in the special Vietnam retrospective issue of* Overland *(1973).*

DOROTHY AUCHTERLONIE

'QUESTIONS FOR KASPAR'

'Why are the soldiers off to war?
O grandsire, tell me please.'
'They fight to right their wrongs, my dear,
And ward off enemies.'

'And these men that we fight, grandsire,
Have done us injuries?
They wish to take our land from us,
And rule us as they please?'

'Well, no, my child, the men we fight
Have never caused us sorrow,
I cannot think they want our land,
Today, nor yet tomorrow.

'We fight them, child, because their friends
Have filled us with unease,
And might, we think, in time to come
Do us great injuries.'

'But have they done so yet, grandsire?
And do they want our land?
And if they have, and if they do,
Why fight them second-hand?

If Peterkin might like my doll,
Or covet my ginger-bread,
Is it quite right for me, grandsire,
To fight his friend instead?'

Old Kaspar shook his head: 'It's plain
Maids cannot understand
How high affairs are carried on
By the elders of the land.'

Now up spake Peterkin: 'Grandsire,
If I wish to fight another,
Should I not then take arms myself,
And not send my baby brother?

'If, as you say, our land's at stake,
Why are not grown men fighting?
Are not these soldiers much too young
To know which wrongs need righting.

'If they're too young to choose the men
Who send them into battle ... ?'
Old Kaspar frowned: 'You go too far,
Children should learn, not prattle.'

Said Wilhelmine: 'One question more,
And then I shall have finished ...
If, as they say, this war be long,
Shall we not be diminished?

'If you should slay the flower of your flock
Each year for ten years more,
Will it then be as good a flock,
As ever it was before?'

Old Kaspar rose and shook his stick:
'My little Wilhelmine,
Children, in an Old Man's world,
Should neither be heard nor seen.

'Be off with you and spin your wool,
You've work to do in plenty—
And Peterkin, I'll deal with you,
As soon as you are twenty.'

R. H. Morrison (comp.), *Vietnam Voices* (1973)

GAYLA REID

(1945–)

Writer and editor. Gayla Reid, who was born in Armidale and educated at the University of New England, has lived mainly in Canada since 1967. She began writing fiction in the late 1980s, and has published short stories in various journals and anthologies. This excerpt is from the title story of her collection To Be There With You *(1994), a book in which 'Reid writes about women and men who grow up Catholic and come to adulthood during the turbulent decade of the 1960s'.*

GAYLA REID

FROM 'TO BE THERE WITH YOU'

Vung Tau was easy to write about: details piled up without effort. I visited the orphanage the soldiers were restoring in a nearby village; I interviewed the surgical team at Le Loi Hospital; I wrote about Villa 44, the rest and convalescence centre; I mentioned the Grand, the main watering hole. The town, I claimed, had 'a crumbling French ambience.' The young Vietnamese women in their *ao dais* 'seemed to float along the boulevard.' That gave me particular pleasure, using the word, boulevard. Me, a kid from Australia.

I produced these lying, partial stories and at first I was happy enough to do so. I believed I was getting somewhere. I wrote the way the soldiers wrote letters home. Only they knew what they were censoring, and I did not.

Once that fact became clear to me, I became preoccupied with it.

Back home, it was a Liberal prime minister who said, 'You are right to be where you are and we are right to be there with you.' They wanted to suck up to the Yanks.

But I liked the soldiers. They were nice and ordinary and scared. I knew what their homes were like on Saturday afternoon: a radio would be blaring the races. If they were Sydney boys, I knew what football teams they cheered for, what beaches they went to.

How they'd eat fruitcake and drink beer on a hot December afternoon.

What Mum would cook for tea and where she'd hang her apron, how Mum had made that apron herself and trimmed it with a bit of rickrack.

What sort of tin Nanna kept her biscuits in. What kind of biscuits they'd be, how they'd taste.

It was just as well I knew something about the soldiers, I reassured myself. Because they told me nothing. Nothing at all.

I am up at the lines at Nui Dat. I am talking to men just back from the bush. I stand in front of them in my miniskirt, with my long young legs. I ask them to tell me all about the war.

Before Ron, I'd had one other lover, and considered myself experienced. With him, love had been an overwhelming project, constructed out of words. I would rehearse the words, analyse and revise them, finding them ill-suited to the huge task.

With Ron there was silence. His body understood. We could sit in two separate chairs and feel whatever it was, humming back and forth.

Because the soldiers told me nothing, I had to make do with geography.

Leaving Nui Dat, one sees the red soils of the dry rolling hills with their rubber, banana and coffee plantations give way to a brief flowering of tender green paddies which are, as we approach Vung Tau, suddenly usurped by the salt marshes and mangroves in their drab army colours.

I tried again.

Nui Dat, which means 'small hills,' is actually located in a rubber plantation, I chirruped. Above the camp one sees the Nui Thi Vai, the mountains that the soldiers have dubbed the Warbies, after the Warburtons, in the state of Victoria.

I even managed quotes: 'Conditions are fair enough, really. You don't expect the Ritz.'

We had been lovers in a past life, I decided. In some smoky Celtic cottage, in a valley full of mild rain, I had waited quietly for him.

Even in that life, he'd been married.

There wasn't any question of my mucking things up with Shirl.

I am sitting with Ron in the courtyard of the hotel at Vung Tau. We are reading the *Sydney Morning Herald*.

Ron is reading about what some of the Labor politicians are saying about the war. He looks cranky. Ron's been a Labor man all his life.

I am reading the review section. It is quoting famous writers on the US involvement in Vietnam. (There's a new book out.) I like the Pinter quote: 'They were wrong to go in, but they did. Now they should get out, but they won't.'

Might come in handy some day, I think. I copy it into my diary.

'What's that you're writing?' Ron asks.

'Nothing,' I say. 'Nothing.'

What does he do out there in the war? I picture him: he is in a VC village. He takes a grenade from his body, pulls the pin out, and chucks it down the well. (Is that what they do? They do use a hand grenade for something like this, don't they?)

I can see him walking away, through the village, away from the ruined well. He has now grown very tall; he walks in giant boots.

These images come to me when I am moving my hands over his body.

I wonder if Shirl reads my pieces. Shirl is sitting in her kitchen, in the Sydney suburb of Bexley North. Her kitchen smells of white toast and Vegemite and kids. The neighbours are proud of Shirl, coping on her own with the two kiddies. Shirl is proud of Ron, her soldier, her man.

It is, after all, no more than a year since the Battle of Long Tan. And at Long Tan we won by 245 to 18. We Australians excel at outdoor activities of all kinds.

I dream of writing something like that, especially for Shirl.

Everyone had a camera; cameras were all the rage. There was this photo of Ron and me and his best mate, Johnno. We are in the courtyard of the hotel at Vungers. Ron has his arms around my shoulders. Johnno is beside him, holding up a beer, putting on the big bronzed Anzac act. Ron is looking at me, sort of smiling.

I swear, if you had seen that photo, you would have said he loved me.

At first it seemed that there was Ron with me and the war on one side, and Shirl and the kids back home on the other. As the weeks went by it felt different. On the one hand there was Shirl at home and me in Vungers. On the other hand, there was the war. At this rate, I told myself, I'd never be *bao chi*, a proper journalist.

Beer left Ron as tightlipped as ever, so I got my hands on some marijuana. Ron agreed to give it a go.

It made him completely paralytic. He sat rooted to his chair, unable to move. From time to time he said, 'Ratshit, mate. Ratshit.'

It was a profound truth. But I was no further ahead.

Sometimes after sex he did get a tiny bit talkative. Like this:

'We were going down this bloody hill and we walked straight into the noggies. Right on top of them.'

'And, and?' I urged.

'Felt a bit sorry for them really. Poor bastards. Having their smoko.'

'I love you,' I say to Ron.

Ron was older than the man I'd been with before and his big heavy body pressed down upon me without apology.

(Do I love him, do I, really?)

Having been brought up Catholic I believe in the power words can have, particularly when repeated.

'I love you, Ron.'

He gives a short, tight laugh.

Being there, I am forced to consider the camouflage of language: how much, in the attempt to conceal, is revealed. At the briefings, the favoured line was, 'Contact was made.' Not even, 'We/they made contact.'

I listen to what Ron says about the Yanks. They were a piss-poor lot, really. Went crashing around like a mob of bulls in a china shop. Sat on their backsides waiting for Sunday dinner to be flown in. Cranberry bloody sauce, mate, in the middle of the jungle. Translated: Ron liked the Yanks; he liked their clumsy bigness. He was happy enough, in his own way, to be there with them.

Ron had only one word for the Vietnamese. All the Aussies did.

In a bar it would be, the noggy waiter. The VC were bloody noggies. It was a nog mine, a nog taxi, a nog ambush. The good guys we had come to save and the bad guys we had come to save them from both went by the same name.

I sat in my room and I tried to think about that.

One night I am giving him a back rub and he says: 'I deny everything.'

I stare at my hands, in surprise.

He lies still, letting me make my discoveries. (And I think: this desire in me, to find such things in him; how different is that from how he feels, at the well?)

Then he takes me and fucks me in a hard, impassive way I find dazzling.

There was a South Vietnamese military training centre in Vung Tau. Some of the kids there, I decided, must be highly disciplined cadre from the other side.

I considered the phrase, highly disciplined cadre. It suggested a staggering confidence of belief.

In Saigon — this was before Tet — one could pretend that the Vietnamese you came in contact with were pro-US (pro us). In Vungers you just knew it wasn't true. Here were Vietnamese people serving you food, washing your underwear. Just down the road was Hoa Long. And Hoa Long was VC by night and had been for years.

In Vung Tau I thought about that more: a double life.

It is raining. We are in the hotel room. Since Ron was here last, his best mate, Johnno, has been killed by a mine.

Ron stares out at the balcony. He is smoking. He says: 'We'd just come out into the rubber. It was lighter, in the rubber.'

He says: 'Bits of him. Hanging from the trees.'

He has never said anything this explicit before.

I look at his grey face, his hunched shoulders.

I go over to him, kiss him, press my breasts against his back. After a while, he is lying down and I am moving on top of him. I feel, as I am doing this, that I have become someone completely ancient.

A woman is pushing her soft body against a man's, trying to make war go away. She is powerful. And ambitious. And definitely pleased with herself.

We'd start off drinking at the Grand, then go on to those makeshift places that had sprung up along the beach front — little round huts, they were. I'd try to get Ron and the others to talk about the war. What about Dak To? (Dak To was where the main US fighting was going on.)

What about it? They spoke of the cricket scores back home.

Sometimes in one of these bars you saw a soldier crying his eyes out. 'Ratshit,' his mates would say. Then look away.

We are in a bar. It's not long since Ron's best mate, Johnno.

A chap called Ian comes up. He's young and he's really handsome. Ian starts slapping Ron on the back, in a familiar way that is part friendly, part hostile. 'Zip 'em right down the middle, mate,' Ian says. 'Whaddya say, mate? Zip 'em right down the middle.'

He's very drunk.

'Beauty, mate,' Ian goes on. 'One for you and one for me.'

Ron, who's quite a bit older, says, 'Take it easy, mate. Just take it easy, eh.'

But Ian keeps on keeping on.

'One for you and one for me. What do you say? Ripper, mate.'

Ron gets up and punches him in the stomach, hard.

That shuts him up.

I didn't see it as any big deal — Ron's punching him. They were all pretty physical men.

What interested me was what Ian had said.

I'd heard it before.

After the drinking and the fucking had been pushed to the limit, and Ron was almost asleep, out of it, he'd mumble, under his breath but loud enough for me to hear: 'One for you and one for me.'

He could have been back home coaxing his kids to eat up their peas.

But I didn't think so.

Hair brushed, perfume fresh, I open the door, expecting Ron. We are going to the Beachcomber to eat hamburgers and drink that weak Yank beer.

It isn't Ron. It is some other soldier I know vaguely. Awkward, not looking at me.

A tunnel, he says. Ron went down the tunnel. Then he says something about what kind of bunker system it was.

I think, quite without anger: The technical details are so terribly important to all of them; why is that?

What was he doing down a tunnel? Wouldn't he be way too big?

Three column inches on the front page of the *Sydney Morning Herald*. Australian Task Force troops ... Operation Dingo ... Phuoc Tuy province.

At home, the neighbours will be coming to Shirl's door, carrying food.

Shirl opens the door and the neighbours come in and sit down in the lounge room, feeling slightly elevated, on stage. Shirl is holding up like a trooper. Shirl's the widow.

She has that.

The soldier took me drinking. Some of Ron's mates gathered round.

'Good bloke, Ron,' they said. 'Good bloke.' And drifted off.

They were pissed and miserable and it was just one of those things. They did not, they did not, any of them, say it had been worthwhile.

I walked back to the hotel and the night moved like water.

I had been looking forward to the weight of Ron, upon me.

To Be There With You (1996 edition, first published 1994)

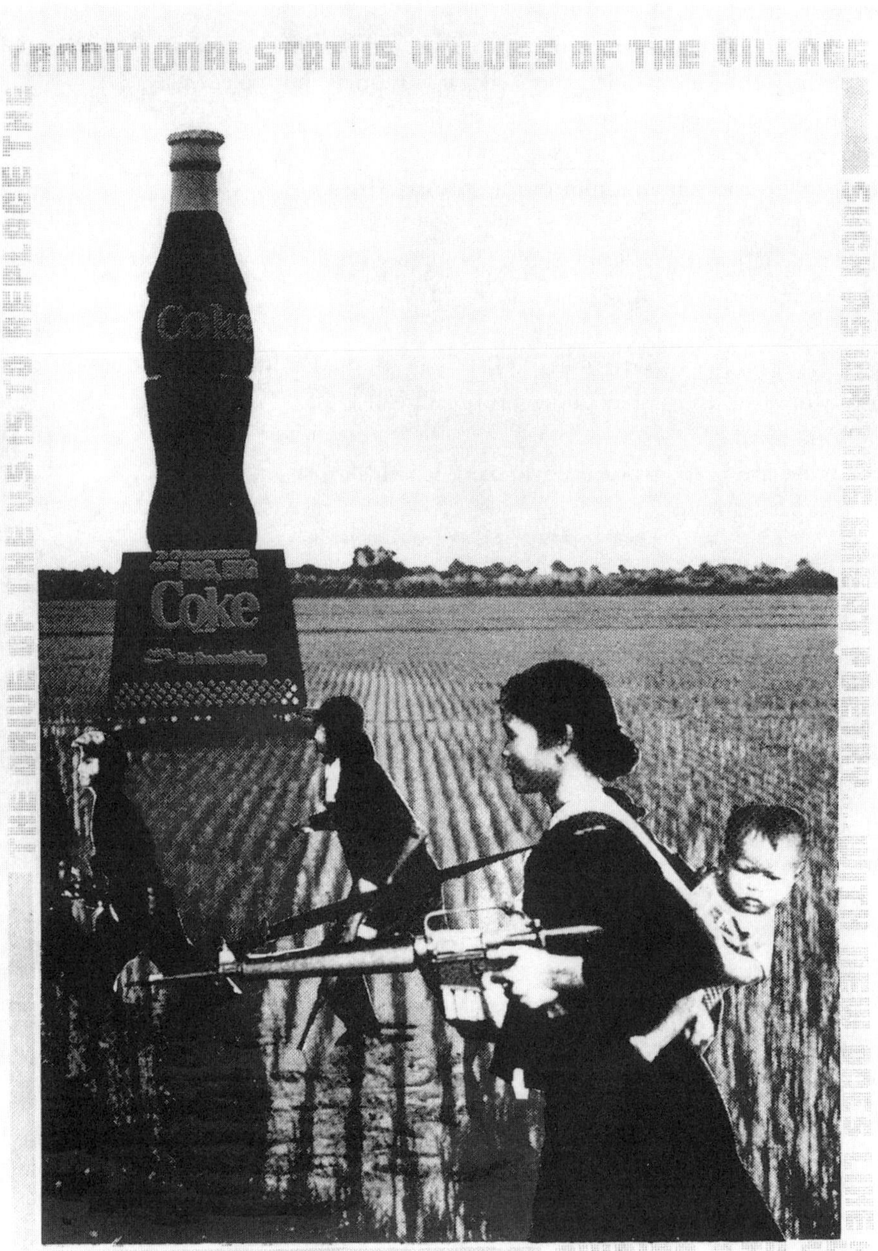

Mandy Martin (1952–), *Vietnam*, 1975, photoscreenprint, 76 x 55.9 cm. Presented in 1978. (AWM V7368)

JUDITH WRIGHT

(1915–)

Poet. Like Dorothy Auchterlonie, Judith Wright contributed two poems to the special Vietnam retrospective issue of Overland *(1973). Here is one of them. It had previously been published in Wright's* Collected Poems: 1942–1970 *(1971).*

'CHRISTMAS BALLAD'

Then they retrieved the walking dead,
wiped his eyes clear of blood,
replaced his heart with a nylon one
and dry-cleaned his uniform.

Now, Son, we'll send you home.
With your hair brushed over the crack in your head
you look as good as ever you did.
You're the luckiest bloke was ever born.

Home he came and on the wharf
in her best bri-nylon stood his wife.
Darling you look well she said;
only the children ran and hid.

He went out walking down the street.
Outside the pub his state-school mate
said, Christ, son, where you been?
Come and paint the old town red.

Things have changed since you been gone.
I turned my last-year's Holden in.
You wasn't here when the Cup was run.
You don't say much. Cat got your tongue?

Mercy, pity, peace and love,
shop in our department-store,
the Muzak angels sang above.
A long way off was the napalm war.

Love, mercy, pity, peace,
pluck us from the jungle mud.
Give a nylon heart and a metal head—
it's the newest gift for Christmas.

R. H. Morrison (comp.), *Vietnam Voices* (1973)

JANE ROSS

(1947–)

Researcher. Jane Ross was born in New South Wales and educated at Sydney University. As part of her research into the digger tradition in Australia, she spent a month in Vietnam in the summer of 1971, in the company of another postgraduate student. After completing her doctoral thesis, which forms the basis of her book The Myth of the Digger *(1985), she has worked variously as a researcher, lecturer, and writer. Intriguingly, Kenneth Maddock, who edited* Memories of Vietnam *(1991), says of Ross that her 'later experience as an air force wife has not rid her of a feeling that there is something ridiculous about service life'.*

FROM 'A HOLIDAY AT THE WAR'

Many of the thousands of foreigners in Vietnam, both soldiers and civilians, had difficulty coming to terms with being in a war zone but seeing so little of the war. It was like this at Vung Tau. There were few signs of the war in the immediate vicinity. Occasionally there were distant booms as the American B52s attempted to destroy the bunkers in the Long Hai hills; the window ledges would shake a little and some more of the ubiquitous sand would lodge on the floor. The main noise in the nurses' quarters, where I stayed, was from another American product, AFVN Channel 11 in Saigon and Can Tho. The TV played loudly all day and until midnight. As the nurses' quarters did not boast partitions to the ceilings, life there was noisy and unprivate.

Surprisingly, though, the nurses seemed reluctant to leave their quarters and go to the hospital officers mess, a pleasant, airy room on the hill decorated in standard SE Asian military style. (For those unfamiliar with this decor, it relies heavily on bamboo, unit crests, polished wood and ceiling fans.) And, of course, the whole mess centred around the consumption of that balm of stress, alcohol.

There was certainly plenty of stress to be relieved. The hospital, more perhaps than any other unit, saw the actual toll that the war exacted both physically and mentally from its soldiers. There was a continuous flow of more-or-less routine admissions (malaria, URTI, minor accidents, etc.); then there were the bad days when the dustoffs arrived at the hospital helipad, the medical staff ran to their duties, and the surgeons returned white-faced and exhausted many hours later.

To see even the photos of the sorts of wounds that high explosives can cause is to be revolted, sickened. To be working with this level of trauma, week after week, was apparently considered by doctors to be very good training, but was also a disheartening and sad way to meet so many young men. The hospital could be a depressing environment.

In fact the whole of the ALSG had little to recommend it as a place to live. Like all military camps it abounded with ugly buildings, unrelieved by any greenery. It was surrounded by wire and observation pill-boxes, and the resort town of Vung Tau seemed a long way away, although no doubt many of the long-term residents at ALSG had made second homes for themselves there. I only once went into the town, to dine at a hotel, and found the atmosphere almost unbearably tense. As in most civilian areas of Vietnam, one did not feel that the Western presence was a welcome intrusion.

By contrast, the Task Force base at Nui Dat was pleasant. I travelled to Nui Dat most days on the Wallaby Caribou flight or, if possible, on the helicopter run. It was a short trip over the rivers and marshes of Phuoc Tuy, sometimes with a brief stop at the Horseshoe base.

My first and most lasting impression of the Task Force base was the colour: green, green and more green. Green uniforms, green tents, green trees and vegetation, green vehicles. The green machine indeed. The colour lent a misleadingly cool aspect, because it was in fact stiflingly hot and dry, very like summer in inland Australia. The countryside, too, was incongruously like home. Could there really be a war in those familiar-looking hills?

Nui Dat, as I was constantly reminded, was unable to cater for female visitors (though I was told that Ainslie Gotto, as Gorton's aide, had stayed there). Even my daily presence at the base was made to seem an inconvenience. I had to use the VIP toilet block, located in the centre of a quadrangle, and each visit there meant a trip (escorted) to the orderly room, a request for the key, then go to the toilet block, then back with the key, meet up with escort ... Why the toilet block was kept so secure I never did find out.

Home base at the Dat was the Psyops Unit, a small group who were part of the winning-the-hearts-and-minds side of the war. Their task included encouraging *chieu hoi* (ralliers to the Saigon Government) by such unlikely means as broadcasting Buddhist ghost music from choppers, dropping anti-VC leaflets and generally trying to make *them* see the virtues of siding with *us*. The Psyops people were unfailingly cooperative and good-natured in their task of looking after me and arranging my itineraries, only ever growling when I accidentally mislaid my escort and got lost somewhere in the camp (the layout of both ALSG and Nui Dat remained totally mysterious to me).

We began our familiarisation with the war environs by doing a small tour of nearby villages in the province, courtesy of the civil affairs unit. Also in the party was Peter Collins, since risen to prominence as New South Wales Health Minister, then doing an assessment of the war for the Young Liberals.

We saw, first, the village of Ap Suoi Nghe. It was a showplace of sorts, having been moved in 1970 from its previous location, Slope 30, to a more secure location. The move was depicted years later in the TV series *Vietnam*. The villagers were engaged in unfamiliar agricultural activities such as charcoal burning, and lived in what could only be described as extremely simple circumstances. Like everywhere in Vietnam (or in all poor countries), use was made of any available material for building or fuel, so that sheds and houses of second-hand packing cases, aluminium cans and other cast-off military goods were common. It gave the villages an untidy look.

Behind the village — which was out in the open — we saw our first defoliated hill.

Although I cannot now remember the sequence of our journey, we went that day to several other villages. At Binh Gia, the 'good' village of Catholic refugees from the north, the market was in full swing, and it was village life anywhere in tropical Asia: women squatting over baskets of chooks, pigs, fish and vegetables, people haggling over prices; and grubby but cheerful barefoot children smiling in curiosity at the strange whitefaces.

We sped through the village of Hoa Long, a mean-looking place which never responded to Australian overtures, perhaps because the inhabitants remembered the complete destruction in 1966 of nearby Long Phuoc, where many of them had lived. We saw an Australian civic action project at Baria, the dispensary and maternity ward at Long Dien, and overall perhaps got some sort of look at if not feel for the villages of the province. We saw soldiers from our side and we met Saigon Government officials.

What we didn't, and couldn't, see of course was the politics of the situation, and nor did we see the other part of the province, the part controlled by the NLF. Somewhere out there were the enemy command posts and bunker systems, and the Government which held legitimacy in at least as much — or more? — of the population as did the more visible RVN. But we couldn't even begin to see that side of the story.

Later in my stay I saw more of the area, during a wonderful flight in a small Bubble Sioux chopper from 161 Recce Flight. From the air Phuoc Tuy was a spectacularly beautiful place, with shining waterways, white beaches and extraordinarily dense, bright green jungle turning immediately into bare rice fields, with the Vietnamese farmers and their animals standing in conspicuous relief on the brown stubbles.

The seaside villages to the north of the Long Hai hills provided more contrasts, visually, and their solidity even more strongly conveyed the impression of strength and durability. Here was a society which had survived in its environment for hundreds of years, so how could the unwelcome, foreign soldiers in their trucks and choppers — here today, gone tomorrow — ever have more than a briefly destructive impact? We were only ever on the outside.

Being with the Australian forces in Phuoc Tuy was to live in a relatively familiar landscape if one overlooked the strange military culture. The really foreign part of Vietnam was encountered when Frank and I travelled to the old imperial city of Hue.

We had returned to Saigon after two weeks at Nui Dat/Vung Tau, and decided to see a little more of Vietnam before Frank spent some time in Saigon doing research at various US agencies.

We hoped to be able to hitch rides to either Hue or Dalat, but even our approaches to Air America failed. So we bought our tickets and flew to Hue in an unsafe-looking Air Vietnam plane.

The trip was worth it for the view alone, and dispelled any doubts about the later claims that defoliants had been used very extensively. Flying to the north over the mountains of central Vietnam was to see thousands upon thousands of hectares of bare, lifeless ground and huge craters, surrounded it is true by jungle but nevertheless giving an idea of the huge amount of ecological destruction.

Hue remains my most vivid memory of Vietnam, if somewhere so lacking in colour and warmth can be called vivid. It was an overcast, wet, brooding ruin of a city, off limits now to American forces but largely destroyed by their firepower in 1968. During the Tet offensive that year the Citadel had been captured by PAVN forces, who held on until some of the bloodiest fighting of the war managed to recapture the city for the southern forces; but in the process, most of the once-elegant city was reduced to rubble. Along the Perfumed River were the overgrown stumps of the villas, and on the outskirts was the forbidding skeleton of the bombed cathedral.

The old part of the city, the imperial palace, was damp, sombre and deserted. Everywhere seemed cold and wet, and there was little feeling of splendour even looking across the moat to the river. The throne room, which once must have been luxurious, was now dark and neglected. A small group of cheery ARVN soldiers lived in a tin shed on the citadel, now its only guard.

In the inhabited part of town people went about their modest lives and had little time for travellers. For the first time in Vietnam we experienced open hostility and were spat at by passers-by. We secured a room in a repulsive hotel, with water all across the bedroom floors. At midnight we were raided at gunpoint by the SVN police, who were somewhat amazed to find two Australian passports in their haul of ID documents.

We were not sorry to leave Hue; it was a deeply depressing town even without a visit to the mass graves of those killed in 1968. However, we did not escape immediately. While waiting at the airport for our plane, which was late, we engaged in conversation with a GI from the nearby Phu Bai Combat Base (Phu Bai was pronounced by the southerners as Poo Bah). He suggested that we visit the base, have a drink and watch for the plane from there. If this unlikely plan failed, as it seemed certain to, then we could stay the night and catch one of the many US transport flights back to Saigon the next day.

Phu Bai was far from Nui Dat, and the US Armed Forces seemed as if from another planet. They, too, found us a little strange and our accents were mutually unintelligible. Our hosts were black NCOs from North Carolina, who — when they weren't consuming vast amounts of alcohol — were responsible for maintaining the aircraft used by the 101st Airborne. Things were busy, as they were preparing for the ill-fated Lam Son invasion of Laos; but the top sergeant began the day at 6.30 a.m. with a full twenty-six-ounce bottle of Scotch. Others there were users of many other substances too, and were disappointed that we refused all their offers: opium, cocaine, heroin, even hashish. We did go on the run to the cathedral for the regular pick-up of these basic necessities.

Unlike at the Australian bases we didn't have escorts, but I always had a guard. Sergeant Pepper slept on the concrete floor while I slept fitfully on the bunk, and visits to the almost open air latrine and ablutions block were a real trial. The base seemed to be riven by racial tensions, but the rules of behaviour were so unfamiliar that I was never sure exactly what was going on.

We did finally leave the delights of Phu Bai, and managed with some difficulty to get on a flight which returned us to Saigon via the immense US base at Danang.

Back to the Tan Loc hotel, which seemed almost like home, and then a few very boring days for me while Frank did his work at the agencies. I should have spent the time ensuring that my visa was in order; when we went to board the plane for Bangkok, I found that my visa (we had always looked at Frank's) had only been for two weeks and I had been without a valid visa for the past fortnight. A tense day was spent at the police headquarters and Australian Embassy before we did finally fly out the next morning.

Kenneth Maddock (ed.), *Memories of Vietnam* (1991)

Part Six

GULF WAR

JAN PEARCE

(?–)

Journalist. This piece by Jan Pearce appeared in the Melbourne Age *a week after the beginning of the Gulf War, fought in early 1991 between Iraq and a United States-led coalition of countries, including Australia.*

'DEATH ON A BALCONY'

There are some experiences that you have anticipated so often that when they come you don't know how to respond. After too many years of dreaming about the place, I found myself in 1983 walking the streets of London, and all I could think, over and over in a stunned way, was — so this is London, this shabby city.

So this is war, perhaps the war we of the post-war generation have dreamt about, not with longing but with terror. This thing that has happened so many times in the ghastly theatre of one's imagination is now happening in the real theatre of conflict. Not nuclear, but with all the signs of spreading, and drawing in enough others to make it a war that will run out of control.

Like London, so far it is not as I had imagined.

Each morning since last Thursday I have woken to a blank, then to the sickening memory that something has changed irrevocably. It's the feeling you have after you have committed some personal folly which has led to an irredeemable loss.

I never imagined war would give me a feeling like this.

Each morning I have reached immediately for the radio switch, then lain in a stupor while the commentary goes on, unable to do or think of anything else.

I heard one commentator say that this media coverage was a danger in itself, a narcotic that could immobilise people, make them unable to tear themselves away from the radio or television set.

I never in my wildest dreams imagined a war that started as television spectacle.

So far, every Tom, Dick and Harry but few Sallies have had their say about this war. When a woman does speak she is expected by some to say 'this is a man's war, the boys unable to restrain themselves from trying out their lethal toys'. And there is some truth in this. Yet there are many women among the US troops at the front — one in 12, according to reports. In the months before Christmas there were wire service photos of American woman soldiers weeping over their children as they left for the Middle East. To do her duty was why she was going, one wept to a reporter.

I never imagined a war where there were women fighting at the front.

Then there is Margaret Thatcher, whose uncompromising gung-ho attitudes after the invasion of Kuwait are now being seen as one of the important factors that catapulted the world into this fight.

I never imagined being led into a war by a woman.

Historians are rarely if ever satisfied with a single-cause explanation of events. So it would be too easy to say this is an oil war. More likely it is a poisonous mix of the long-term results of the European colonialism that carved up the map in the interests of divide and rule, the centuries-long clash between two world philosophies (Christianity and Islam), the obsessions of a despot, and the re-establishment of the Jewish state after the last war in a hostile region.

And then there is the factor of human folly. It is not hard for me to imagine that.

It is too easy simply to blame the US. This is why I will not be joining any peace rallies unless they direct their complaints equally to the Iraqis. (In fact, I find myself being irritated by those demonstrators with their flowers and ribbons and chants. This is an imperfect world, and if we had let Saddam continue even with sanctions, who knows what he might have done once he had nuclear weapons.)

Most of all this war seems to me the inevitable result of human nature, that unpredictable mix of emotion and reason. Koestler attributed human destructiveness to the coexistence of two brains, the new and rational, and the old and primitive 'crocodile' brain. Because of this, any world settlement, like most human arrangements, seems unable to last for more than 50 years. Then the power struggle starts again. Add to this the horror of modern technology and it was always a matter of when.

In the first episode of Robert Hughes's survey of modern art, 'The Shock of the New', showing again on television, there were scenes of the dead earth of the Somme Valley where, says Hughes, 'our fathers and grandfathers tasted the first terrors of the 20th Century' in the First World War. There was a pause before the writers of that war (those who survived) found their voice, since this 'mass-produced industrialised death' the specialty of our century, was so awful as to be at first indescribable.

How much more terrible (yet seemingly so clinical) have our weapons become at the other end of this peculiar century.

Yet the result of a single bullet is really enough to bring home the meaning of war. On Sunday night ABC radio news reported that a Palestinian woman in the occupied territories had been killed by Israeli fire as she stood on a balcony feeding her baby. She had apparently ignored the curfew.

That is war. That I can imagine — the warm and intimate tension of sucking broken by the terrible metallic blow.

Perhaps all you need to understand war is a single image, such as that one, or the terrified face of an Iraqi child in a bomb shelter. Or a lone voice, the sad, stilted voice of a captured American pilot mouthing enemy propaganda.

In that way war has never changed. Neither has the human heart.

Age (23 January 1991)

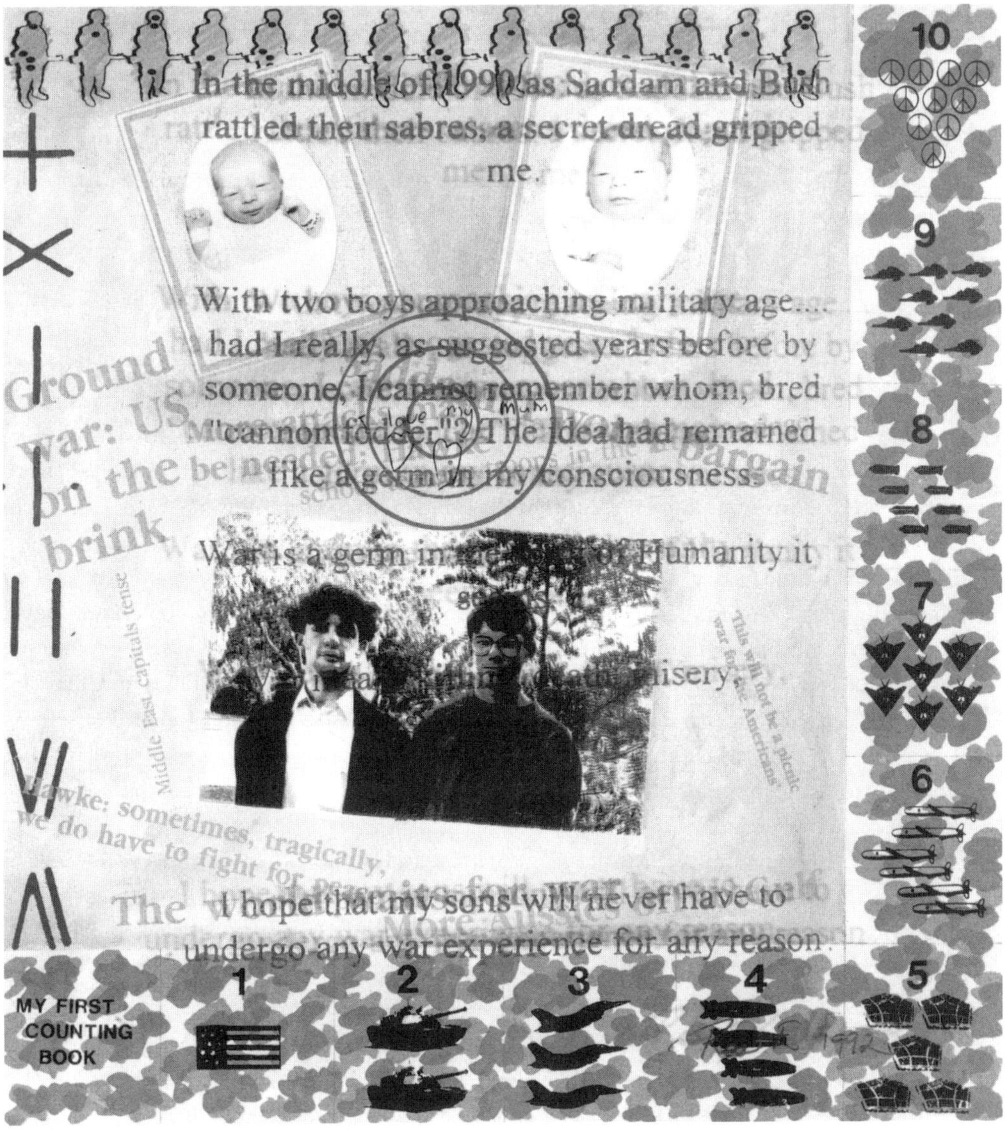

Roslyn Evans (1950–), *All the fine young men: In the middle of 1990 as Saddam and Bush rattled their sabres*, 1992, photoscreenprint and wash over pencil, with collage, in jarrah frame with etched glass and graphite, 46.6 x 42.5 cm. Purchased in 1992. (AWM 29767.06)

PAMELA BONE

(1940–)

Journalist. Pamela Bone was born and grew up in the Riverina, where her family moved around because of her father's work as a foreman on the Mulwala Canal. She had various jobs, including one as a journalist on the Shepparton News, *before joining the Melbourne* Age *in the early 1980s. Bone is the mother of four children and grandmother of several others. This article was published ten days before the 1991 war ended in Iraq's defeat.*

'AUSTRALIA'S MUSLIM WORLD'

Close up, they are hard to hate, these 'enemies'. They are the Lebanese-born greengrocer, the Pakistani-born tram conductor, the Egyptian-born engineer, the Iranian–Australian high school students, the Turkish-born footballer. They are Layla, an Iraqi-born academic, who has very direct brown eyes and who says, in a quiet, puzzled voice: 'Arabs are not from another planet. We are just people. We live, we laugh, we love our children. We are Australian citizens. What do you expect from us?'

But in war it is necessary to hate the enemy, and to the ignorant and prejudiced, anyone of Middle Eastern or Muslim appearance is the enemy and is therefore to be hated. Never mind that most Muslims living in Australia are not even Arab, let alone Iraqi. Never mind that at least half of the Arabs who have migrated to this country are not Muslim, but Christian. Never mind that most of the Iraqis living here have good reason to hate Saddam Hussein.

It was not Muslims who burnt an Australian flag in the city square after Australian ships left to join the Western forces in the Persian Gulf, as was reported in some media, but members of an anarchist group.

Australian Muslims, unlike Muslims in Britain and some other countries, have been extremely restrained in their reaction to the Gulf War. While British imams preach fierce denunciations of 'infidel aggression', while British Muslim youth burn British flags and scream for vengeance against the West, Australian Muslim leaders preach, and Australian Muslims practise, moderation.

Dr Stephen FitzGerald, the chairman of a committee [inquiring] into Australia's immigration policies in 1988, said in his report that Australia had been 'a very healing home' for migrants. Migrants seemed to perceive in Australia an innocence that was to be respected, that the ancient feuds of their countries of birth were not welcome here. Could it be that Australian Muslims feel that innocence?

For many people, Islam is the stumbling block of multiculturalism. Long before this Gulf crisis, opinion polls showed that Middle Eastern Muslims were the least welcome of any migrant group in this country. For many in the West, this war is, at its most basic, a struggle between the forces of 'civilised' Christendom and 'extremist' Islam.

And it is sorely testing our notion of ourselves as a tolerant society. Almost daily there are reports of attacks on Muslims, on non-Muslim Arabs, on mosques and Islamic schools, as well as on Jews and Jewish synagogues.

The secretary of the Islamic Council of Victoria, Mr Bilal Cleland, calls these attacks the actions of a 'minority of morons' and says we should not over-react to them. Australians, he said, do not give themselves nearly enough credit for the fact that we have absorbed millions of migrants from all over the world, with very little racial strife. Muslims can and will continue to be a peaceful part of Australian society, and Australia has nothing to fear from Islam, he says.

According to the recently released census on religion, there are 110 000 Muslims in Australia. Muslim leaders believe the figure is more like 300 000, and that the disparity is due to the fact that many Muslims are reluctant to state their religion on a census form. It is the biggest non-Christian religion in Australia, and the fastest-growing; there are more Muslims than Jews, Buddhist, Salvation Army or Church of Christ members. Muslims are younger, have bigger families, and are more likely to be in unskilled occupations than other Australians. A considerable number of Lebanese-born Muslims are small shopkeepers, a lot of Pakistani-born Muslims are doctors, many Malaysian and Indonesian Muslims are students, and a good proportion of Middle Eastern Muslims are academics.

No Muslim I have spoken to expects that Australia will ever become an Islamic state, although most say they would like Australian law to recognise the laws of Islam in relation to such things as family law and the burial of their dead. Most Muslims are opposed to the involvement of Australia, and the West, in the Iraqi invasion of Kuwait. It is, they say, a purely Arab problem.

There are few Iraqi Muslims in Australia, and those that are here are anxious not to be identified. One, who asked to be called Tariq, says he does not think Australia is the tolerant society he was told it was before he came here. Even before the war there was some discrimination but now it is much worse, he says. Because Muslims don't drink, he finds it hard to mix at office parties, and had been chided by his boss for not joining in.

Tariq has 'no love' for Saddam Hussein, and says he was not a popular leader with most of the Iraqi people he knew. But he believes Saddam would have won a lot of popularity among ordinary people of Iraq because of his invasion of Kuwait, because most Iraqis firmly believed that Kuwait really belonged to Iraq. 'Our parents told us so. I learned as a small boy from my mother about this land that was unjustly taken from us. Many would just say, "Thank God, we have Kuwait back." ' As well, Iraqis living in Kuwait were treated very badly, so there was little sympathy for Kuwait, he said.

Tariq said he had not intended to go back to Iraq, but now he feels he has a moral duty to go and help rebuild the country after the war. 'I fear that my family and friends in Iraq are suffering and I am living here in comfort. It makes me feel selfish and guilty. It is hard, you watch the bombardment of Bagdad on the news, you can even see buildings and bridges that you knew have been destroyed. Of course I am loyal to Australia, we live here, our children are growing up here, I work here. I teach my children that they are Australian Muslims. But people can't understand that we have a different understanding of this issue, and the Palestinian issue. There is a deep sense of grievance that people in the West just don't give any importance to.'

The Lebanese-born, Christian man who runs a fruitshop in my suburb looked steadily into my eyes with his own sad brown ones and said, 'My dear, I hate 'em so much.' Muslims, he was talking about. Then: 'I don't wish any harm to anyone, but I hope the Jews get in there and bomb the hell out of them.' He said he supported the Israelis, but couldn't understand why they were holding back. Who could work out, in the tangle of Middle Eastern politics, why a Lebanese Christian praises the Israelis, unless it is on the principle that 'my enemy's enemy is my friend'?

Fundamentalist Islam, as it is practised in countries like Iran, Saudi Arabia or Pakistan, is a punitive, puritanical religion that is totally at odds with Australian liberal democratic attitudes. But not all Muslims are fundamentalists, as all Christians are not. Muslims are not 'from another planet'. In this society, they might seem old-fashioned, like Catholics or Methodists were 30 years ago. It is wrong, in their religion, for unmarried men and women to have sex with each other, or even to be unchaperoned in each other's company.

Mrs Hind Daghistani, who was born in Lebanon, has been in Australia 18 years and has four sons born here. When her mother came out from Lebanon and saw the easy way her children joked around with her she was shocked.

But change is inevitable, Mrs Daghistani said. 'They can't grow up the way we grew up. We will follow the Australian way of life in some things but not everything.' She thinks it is too easy in Australia for women to break up their marriages. 'A woman who has a small quarrel with her husband can go to a social worker, and before she knows it she has a form for a social security pension and a form for a Housing Commission house. Next week she might have forgotten all about the quarrel but it is too late.'

It is also disgraceful that Australian school teachers tell children they can sue their parents if they hit them, Mrs Daghistani said.

Mrs Daghistani believes Australia should not be involved in the Persian Gulf. She thinks it is 'disgusting' that all the Western countries are interfering in Arab affairs, and that as a result thousands of innocent people are being killed. Asked whether she believed Saddam Hussein was wrong to invade Kuwait she said 'I can't say whether Saddam had the right to do what he did but it is an Arab problem.'

Muslim women insist that Islam is very liberating for women. It is difficult for Western women to reconcile this with the fact that Islamic law allows men four wives but does not allow women four husbands; that Muslim men can marry non-Muslim women, but Muslim women are forbidden to marry non-Muslim men, in case they are influenced to leave their religion. If a Muslim woman married a man who agreed to become a Muslim, divorce is granted automatically if he lapses from Islam. The same rule doesn't apply to men who marry converts.

Muslim women in Australia say that when they go out in their cars, people yell at them at traffic lights, and try to pull off their headscarves in the street. Mrs Afshan Mantoo, who was born in Kashmir, India, says that if she goes out to a restaurant, people turn around and make unpleasant comments to her. 'I am an Australian citizen. I have chosen this country. When the cricket is on I say "Come on Aussies." Yet people are swearing at us, grabbing our scarves. Why this hatred? What else do they want us to do? Go over there and fight Saddam Hussein ourselves?'

Layla, who grew up in Bagdad, said it was extremely distressing to her to see television footage of injured and dead Iraqi men, women and children, and to wonder if any of them were people that she had known.

She believes there was no possibility that last week's bombing by the United States of an air raid shelter packed with civilians was a mistake. 'It was in the middle of an area of houses, schools and mosques. There was no way they could have thought it was a military area.'

Who does she blame for the war? 'I blame both sides. We didn't want war. We have just finished eight years of war. There should have been another solution. I feel angry that there is no consideration whatever to the innocent people who are dying, I have nightmares every night. I hope it will just stop.'

Age (18 February 1991)

JENNIFER MAIDEN

(1949–)

Poet. Jennifer Maiden was born in Penrith, New South Wales, and educated at Macquarie University. Since graduation, she has been a writer, tutor, and lecturer. Her many books of poetry include Tactics *(1974),* The Trust *(1988), and* Acoustic Shadow *(1993). She has also published novels. The following taut poem is the last in a series of sixteen poems entitled 'Keeping the Lid On: A Gulf War Retrospective'.*

'PREMATURE BURIAL'

(13/9/91. On the 6-month-delayed news item that the US buried thousands of Iraqis alive in the sand with tanks at the start of the Land War.)

We've buried the war. It always was
bad taste to mention it, even
when it happened, unless one
made jokes about Saddam or CNN.
We've buried the war. It always was
a matter of a soldier in the sand,
on his belly, not believing where he was

and seeing a tank as big as the US
—whose movies he loves, where his cousin
still lives—arrive on top of him and take
his air, his air, and fill his lungs with earth.
We've buried the war. It always was
a suffocated mouth, a word not said.
Before the Land War, the Republican Guard
in their bunkers choked on sand bombed down
ventilation shafts. The children
Smart-bombed to bones in Baghdad suffered less.
We've buried the war. It always was
something the good journalist expects
who knows his side will win, who does
understand the wisdom in delay, that good
journalist who always felt a bit
cheated that we lost in Vietnam, who has
now found how easy patriotism is
when you bury the war in you, which always was:
how easily that seems to let you breathe.

Acoustic Shadow (1993)

BIBLIOGRAPHY

Adelaide, Debra, *Australian Women Writers: A Bibliographic Guide*, Pandora, Sydney, 1988.

Australian Literary Studies, vol. 12, no. 2, October 1985, special issue, *War in Australian Literature*.

Bassett, Jan, ' "Preserving the White Race": Some Australian Women's Literary Responses to the Great War', in *Australian Literary Studies*, vol. 12, no. 2, October 1985, pp. 223–33.

——, ' "Untravelled Minds": The War Novels of Mabel Brookes', in Dorothy Goldman (ed.), *Women and World War I: The Written Response*, Macmillan, Basingstoke and London, 1993, pp. 113–27.

Cadogan, Mary & Craig, Patricia, *Women and Children First: The Fiction of Two World Wars*, Victor Gollancz, London, 1978.

Cass, Shirley, Cheney, Ros, Malouf, David & Wilding, Michael (eds), *We Took Their Orders and Are Dead*, Ure Smith, Sydney, 1971.

Damousi, Joy & Lake, Marilyn, *Gender and War: Australians at War in the Twentieth Century*, Cambridge University Press, Cambridge, 1995.

Doyle, Jeff & Grey, Jeffrey (eds), *Australia: Representations and Reinterpretations of Australia's War in Vietnam*, special issue of *Vietnam Generation*, vol. 3, no. 2, 1991.

Fussell, Paul, *The Great War and Modern Memory*, Oxford University Press, New York and London, 1975.

Gerster, Robin, *Big-noting: The Heroic Theme in Australian War Writing*, Melbourne University Press, Carlton, 1987.

——, 'War Literature, 1890–1980', in Hergenhan, Laurie (gen. ed.), *The Penguin New Literary History of Australia*, Penguin, Ringwood, 1988, pp. 337–52.

Goldman, Dorothy (ed.), *Women and World War I: The Written Response*, Macmillan, Basingstoke and London, 1993.

Green, H. M., *A History of Australian Literature*, 2 vols, Angus & Robertson, Sydney, 1961.

Harrison-Ford, Carl (ed.), *Fighting Words: Australian War Writing*, Lothian Books, Melbourne, 1986.

Hartley, Jenny (ed.), *Hearts Undefeated: Women's Writing of the Second World War*, Virago, London, 1994.

Laird, J. T. (ed.), *The Australian Experience of War*, Mead & Beckett, Darlinghurst, 1988.

—— (ed.), *On All Fronts: Australian Stories of World War II*, University of Queensland Press, St Lucia, 1989.

—— (ed.), *Other Banners: An Anthology of Australian Literature of the First World War*, The Australian War Memorial and the Australian Government Publishing Service, Canberra, 1971.

McHugh, Siobhan, *Minefields and Miniskirts: Australian Women and the Vietnam War*, Doubleday, Sydney, 1993.

Manuel, Jacqueline, ' "We are the Women who Mourn our Dead": Australian Civilian Women's Poetic Responses to the First World War', in *Journal of the Australian War Memorial*, issue 29, November 1996.

Morrison, R. H. (comp.), *Vietnam Voices: A Retrospect*, special issue of *Overland*, no. 54, Autumn 1973.

Page, Geoff (ed.), *Shadows from Wire: Poems and Photographs of Australians in the Great War*, Australian War Memorial, Canberra 1983.

Reilly, Catherine W. (ed.), *Chaos of the Night: Women's Poetry and Verse of the Second World War*, Virago, London, 1984.

—— (ed.), *Scars Upon My Heart: Women's Poetry and Verse of the First World War*, Virago, London, 1981.

Rutherford, Anna & Wieland, James (eds), *War: Australia's Creative Response*, Allen & Unwin, Sydney, 1997.

Walker, David, 'War, Women and the Bush: The Novels of Mary Grant Bruce and Ethel Turner', in *Historical Studies*, vol. 18, no. 7, October 1978, pp. 297–315.

Walker, Shirley, 'The Boer War: Paterson, Abbott, Brennan, Miles Franklin and Morant', in *Australian Literary Studies*, vol. 12, no. 2, October 1985, special issue, *War in Australian Literature*, pp. 207–22.

Wallace-Crabbe, Chris & Pierce, Peter (eds), *Clubbing of the Gunfire: 101 Australian War Poems*, Melbourne University Press, Carlton, 1984.

Wilde, William H., Hooton, Joy & Andrews, Barry, *The Oxford Companion to Australian Literature*, 2nd edn, Oxford University Press, 1994 (first edition published 1985).

SOURCES AND ACKNOWLEDGMENTS

Patsy Adam-Smith, *Goodbye Girlie*, Viking, Ringwood, 1994, pp. 41–2.

J. A. [Julia Anderson], 'Some Experiences of a Victorian Nurse in South Africa', in *Una*, Melbourne, vol. 1, no. 2, July 1903, pp. 31–3.

Anonymous extract from Ann Howard, *You'll Be Sorry!*, Tarka Publishing, Sydney and Melbourne, 1990, p. 113.

Dorothy Auchterlonie, 'Questions for Kaspar', in R. H. Morrison (comp.), *Vietnam Voices: A Retrospect*, pp. 26–7, special issue of *Overland*, no. 54, Autumn 1973.

Margery Ruth Betts, *Remembering and Other Verses*, Australasian Authors' Agency, Melbourne, 1917, p. 46.

Pamela Bone, 'Australia's Muslim World', *Age*, 18 February 1991.

Lily Brett, 'Possessions', in her *The Auschwitz Poems*, drawings by David Rankin, Scribe, Melbourne, 1986, p. 15.

Mabel Balcombe Brookes, *Broken Idols,* Melville & Mullen, Melbourne, [1917], pp. 91–8.

Mrs Norman Brookes, *Old Desires,* Australasian Authors' Agency, Melbourne, 1922, pp. 199–202.

Mary Grant Bruce, *Back to Billabong*, Ward, Lock & Co., London and Melbourne, n.d. given for this edition, pp. 119–21 (first published 1921).

Mary Grant Bruce, *Jim and Wally*, Ward Lock Limited, London, 1981 edition, pp. 22–5 (first published 1916).

Ola Calderala, piece in Annette Potts & Lucinda Strauss, *For the Love of a Soldier: Australian War-Brides and their GIs*, ABC Enterprises for the Australian Broadcasting Corporation, Sydney, 1987, pp. 49–50.

Caroline Ethel Cooper, *Behind the Lines: One Woman's War 1914–18: The Letters of Caroline Ethel Cooper*, edited and with an introduction by Decie Denholm, Collins, Sydney and London, 1982, pp. 24–6.

Mrs G. R. Coxhead, *Lost a Continent! Heroes of Anzac and Other Verses*, Modern Printing Company, Melbourne, [1917], pp. 11–13.

Zora Cross, extract from her *Elegy on an Australian Schoolboy*, Angus & Robertson, Sydney, 1921, pp. 19–23.

Dymphna Cusack & Florence James, *Come In Spinner*, Angus & Robertson, an imprint of HarperCollins Publishers, Sydney, 1994 edition, pp. 377–81. This complete edition was first published in 1988. An expurgated version was published in 1951.

Eleanor Dark, *The Little Company*, Collins Bros. & Co., Sydney, Auckland, 1945, pp. 219–23.

Mary Edgeworth David, *Passages of Time: An Australian Woman, 1890–1974*, University of Queensland Press, St Lucia, 1975, pp. 93–7.

Alice Davies, letter to her daughter, Evelyn Davies, 20 March 1918, in Australian War Memorial, 3DRL 3398, Davies, Evelyn, Papers, World War 1, Folder 5.

Evelyn Davies, letter to her mother, Alice Davies, 15 January 1916, in Australian War Memorial, 3DRL 3398, Davies, Evelyn, Papers, World War 1, Folder 2.

Jean Devanny, *Bird of Paradise*, Frank Johnston, Sydney and Melbourne, 1945, pp. 197–201.

Joan Dugdale, *Struggle of Memory*, University of Queensland Press, St Lucia, 1991, pp. 206–9.

Emily Dunbar extract, from Irene MacDonald & Susan Radvansky (eds), *Arthur and Emily: Letters in Wartime*, McPhee Gribble/Penguin Books, Ringwood, 1984, pp. 53–7.

'M. Barnard Eldershaw', *Tomorrow and Tomorrow*, Georgian House, Melbourne, 1947, pp. 363–5.

Dorothy Elmes, AWM, PR 88/108, Elmes, D. G., Records, World War 1939–45. Letter to S/N J. Smithenbecker. By consent of C. Jean Neal (née Smithenbecker).

Gertrude Fletcher, *Some Memories and Extracts from the Life of a Nurse*, privately published, no details given, pp. 94–6.

Miles Franklin, *Cockatoos*, Eden Paperbacks, an imprint of Angus & Robertson, Sydney, 1989, pp. 148–50 (first published by Angus & Robertson, 1954).

Hilda M. Freeman, *An Australian Girl in Germany: Through Peace to War (January–October 1914)*, The Specialty Press, Melbourne, [1916], pp. 232–5.

Katherine Gallagher, '1942', from *Times Literary Supplement*, 20 December 1996, p. 26.

Mary Gilmore, *The Passionate Heart and Other Poems*, Sirius Quality Paperback edition, Angus & Robertson, Sydney, 1979, pp. 13–14 (first published by Angus & Robertson, 1948). *The Passionate Heart* itself was first published by Angus & Robertson, Sydney, 1918. Also appears in *Selected Poems* (ETT Imprint, 1996).

Vida Goldstein, from 'Workers of the World, Unite! Women of the World, Unite!', *Woman Voter*, 11 May 1917.

Olwyn Green, *The Name's Still Charlie*, University of Queensland Press, St Lucia, 1993, pp. 237–9.

Gladys Hain, *The Coo-ee Contingent*, Cassell & Company, London, New York, Toronto and Melbourne, 1917, pp. 93–9.

Geraldine Halls, *The Last Summer of the Men Shortage*, rev. edn, Wakefield Press, Kent Town, 1995, pp. 35–8 (first published by Constable Books, London, 1976).

Lesbia Harford, *The Invaluable Mystery*, McPhee Gribble/Penguin Books, Ringwood, 1987, pp. 109–16.

Gwen Harwood, *Blessed City: The Letters of Gwen Harwood to Thomas Riddell, January to September 1943*, edited by Alison Hoddinott, Angus & Robertson, Sydney, 1990, pp. 102–4.

Shirley Hazzard, *The Transit of Venus*, Macmillan, London, pp. 34–6.

Dorothy Hewett, *The Man from Mukinupin: A Musical Play in Two Acts*, rev. edn, Fremantle Arts Centre Press, Fremantle, Currency Press, Sydney, 1996, pp. 93–4 (first published by Fremantle Arts Centre Press, Fremantle, Currency Press, Sydney, 1979). Reproduced with permission of Currency Press.

Mary Kent Hughes, *Matilda Waltzes with the Tommies*, Oxford University Press, Melbourne and London, 1943, pp. 11–12.

Betty Jeffrey, *White Coolies*, Angus & Robertson, Sydney and London, 1954, pp. 23–5.

Elizabeth Kata, *Child of the Holocaust*, Collins, Sydney and London, 1979, pp. 7–12.

Gwen Kelly, *Always Afternoon*, Collins, Sydney and London, 1981, pp. 215–21.

Olive King, *One Woman at War: Letters of Olive King, 1915–1920*, edited and with an introduction by Hazel King, Melbourne University Press, Carlton, 1986, pp. 56–61.

Ramona Koval, *Samovar*, Minerva/Random House, Melbourne, 1996, pp. 3–6.

'R. E. Leake' [Mollie Skinner], *Letters of a V.A.D.*, Andrew Melrose Ltd, London, [1918], pp. 68–74.

Helen Light, untitled memoir, in Betty Goldsmith & Beryl Sandford, *The Girls They Left Behind*, Penguin, Ringwood, 1990, pp. 13–18.

Mary McFadzean (née Joyce), 'The Hospital Train: Kure, Japan', unpublished notes, sent to Jan Bassett by Mrs McFadzean, 9 November 1987.

Louise Mack (Mrs Creed), *A Woman's Experiences in the Great War,* T. Fisher Unwin, London, 1915, pp. 130–6.

Meta Maclean, *The Singing Ship: An Odyssey of Evacuee Children*, Angus & Robertson, Sydney and London, 1941, pp. 43–5.

Jennifer Maiden, 'Premature Burial', in *Acoustic Shadow*, Penguin, Ringwood, 1993, p. 55.

Kathleen Mangan, *Daisy Chains, War, then Jazz*, Hutchinson of Australia, Melbourne, 1984, pp. 19–24.

Mary Marlowe, *That Fragile Hour: An Autobiography*, Angus & Robertson, Sydney, 1990, pp. 137–42.

Grace Ethel Martyr, *Afterwards and Other Verses*, 2nd edn, Australasian Authors' Agency, Melbourne, 1918, pp. 32–3.

Elyne Mitchell, *Towong Hill: Fifty Years on an Upper Murray Cattle Station*, Sun Books, Macmillan, Melbourne, 1990, pp. 24–7 (first published by The Macmillan Company of Australia, 1989). Permission granted by Curtis Brown (Aust.).

Gertrude F. Moberly, *Experiences of a 'Dinki Di' R.R.C. Nurse,* Australasian Medical Publishing Company, Sydney, 1933, pp. 103–4.

Nettie Palmer, 'Their Peace', in *Melbourne University Magazine: War Memorial Number,* July 1920, p. 81.

Adela Pankhurst, *After the War — What?* The Socialist Party of Victoria, Melbourne, 1917, pp. 21–4.

Ruth Park, *Swords and Crowns and Rings*, Sphere Books, Thomas Nelson, Melbourne, 1977, pp. 46–8. Permission granted by Kemalde Pty Ltd c/- Curtis Brown (Aust.).

Jan Pearce, 'Death on a Balcony', *Age*, 23 January 1991.

Katharine Susannah Prichard, *Golden Miles*, Jonathan Cape, London, in association with Australasian Publishing Co., Sydney, 1948, pp. 246–50.

Katharine Susannah Prichard, *Intimate Strangers*, Arkon edition, Angus & Robertson, Sydney, 1981, pp. 21–5 (first published by Jonathan Cape Ltd, London, 1937).

Katharine Susannah Prichard, *Subtle Flame*, Australasian Book Society, Sydney, 1967, pp. 3–7.

Katharine Susannah Prichard, *Winged Seeds*, Australasian Publishing Company, Sydney, in association with Jonathan Cape, London, 1950, pp. 286–91.

Gayla Reid, from 'To Be There With You', in her *To Be There With You*, Allen & Unwin, Sydney, 1996, pp. 67–74 (first published by Douglas & McIntyre, Vancouver and Toronto, 1994).

Faith Richmond, *Remembrance: A Daughter's Story*, William Collins, Sydney, 1988, pp. 28–30.

Jane Ross, from 'A Holiday at the War', in Kenneth Maddock (ed.), *Memories of Vietnam*, Random House, Sydney, 1991, pp. 223–9.

'Neilma Sidney', *Beyond the Bay*, F. W. Cheshire, Melbourne, Canberra, Sydney, 1966, pp. 118–22.

Jessie Elizabeth Simons, *In Japanese Hands: Australian Nurses as POWs*, William Heinemann, Melbourne, 1985, pp. 34–8 (first published as *While History Passed*, Heinemann, Melbourne, 1954).

Jean Sims, letter to 'Dear Mum and Dad', 23 April 1944, in Sue Hardisty (ed.), *Thanks Girls and Goodbye!: The Story of the Australian Women's Land Army 1942–45*, Viking O'Neil, Ringwood, 1990, p. 76.

(Lady) Jessie M. G. Street, *Truth or Repose,* Australasian Book Society, Sydney, 1966, pp. 222–4.

Kylie Tennant, *Ride On Stranger,* Sirius Edition, Angus & Robertson, Sydney, 1988, pp. 288–91 (first published by Angus & Robertson, 1943).

Susan Terry, *House of Love: Life in a Vietnamese Hospital*, Lansdowne Press, Melbourne, 1966, pp. 185–9.

Angela Thirkell ('Leslie Parker'), *Trooper to the Southern Cross*, Sun Books, Melbourne, 1966, pp. 170–7 (first published by Faber & Faber, 1934).

May Tilton, *The Grey Battalion,* Angus & Robertson, Sydney, 1933, pp. 233–40.

Jessie Traill, 'A Visit to the Devastated Areas in 1925', in State Library of Victoria, Jessie C. A. Traill Collection, MS 7975, Box 795, env. 6, a.

Ethel Turner, *The Cub*, Ward, Lock & Co., London, Melbourne and Cape Town, undated reprint, pp. 143–4 (first published 1915).

Ethel Turner, letter to her son, in Philippa Poole, *Of Love and War: The Letters and Diaries of Captain Adrian Curlewis and his family, 1939–1945*, Lansdowne Press, Sydney, n.d., pp. 206–7.

Susan Varga, *Heddy and Me*, Penguin Books Australia, Ringwood, 1994, pp. 134–6.

Nancy Wake, *The Autobiography of the Woman the Gestapo Called the White Mouse*, Macmillan Company of Australia, Melbourne, 1985, pp. 130–5. Permission granted by Curtis Brown (Aust.).

Judith Wright, 'Christmas Ballad', in R. H. Morrison (comp.), *Vietnam Voices: A Retrospect*, p. 4, special issue of *Overland*, no. 54, Autumn 1973. Also appears in *A Human Pattern: Selected Poems* (ETT Imprint, 1996).

Judith Wright, 'The Company of Lovers', from her *Collected Poems, 1942–1985*, Angus & Robertson, an imprint of HarperCollins Publishers, Sydney, 1994, p. 7. This poem is from her *The Moving Image*, 1946. Also appears in *A Human Pattern: Selected Poems* (ETT Imprint, 1996).

Aileen Young narrative, Australian War Memorial, AWM 41, Butler Papers, 6/69. Reproduced by permission of The Australian War Memorial.

INDEX

Adam-Smith, Patsy 157–8
Alexander, Alison 106
Anderson, Julia 7–13
Anzac Day 122
Anzac landing 30–2
Auchterlonie, Dorothy 212–14, 221
Australian Army Massage Service 104–5
Australian Army Medical Women's Service 157–8
Australian Army Nursing Service 69–72, 97–9, 139–40, 140–2, 142–5
Australian War Memorial xiii, 140
Australian Women's Army Service 182–3
Australian Women's Land Army 169–70

Banka Island 140–2
Barnard, Marjorie 183–5
Belgium 24–6, 28
Betts, Margery Ruth 54–5
Bishop, Olive 202
Board, Ruby 136–7, 139
Boer War x, xiii, 1–13
Bone, Pamela 232–5
Bowen, Stella 165
'Brent of Bin Bin' *see* Franklin, Miles
Brett, Lily xiv, 188–9
Brisbane 40–2, 131–2, 162–4
Britain 51–4
British Army Nursing Service Reserve 5, 8
Brittain, Vera ix, xii, 51
Brookes, Mabel xi, 36–9, 46–9
Brookes, Norman 36
Bruce, Mary Grant xiii, 49–51, 106, 108–9
Bullwinkel, Vivian 140–2
Butler, A.G. 104

Calderala, Frank 166–7
Calderala, Ola 166–7
Cape Colony 5, 7
Cass, Shirley ix
Chapman, Evelyn 101
Cheney, Ros ix
Children's Overseas Reception Board 129–31
Conscription issue 28, 82–3, 91–4
Cooper, Ethel xii, xiv, 20–2
Coxhead, Martha 29–32
Craig, Sybil 190
Cross, John Skyring 113
Cross, Zara x, 72, 113–16
Curlewis, Adrian 164, 166
Cusack, Dymphna 178–9, 181–2
Daniel, Helen 40
Dark, Eleanor 158–62
David, Edgeworth 51
David, Mary Edgeworth 51–4
Davies, Alice 32–6, 96–7
Davies, Evelyn 32–6, 96–7
Deane, William xiv
Denholm, Decie 20
Devanny, Hal 174
Devanny, Jean 174–8
Dugdale, Joan xiv, 40–2
Dunbar, Arthur 42
Dunbar, Emily xi, 42–3, 45–6
Dunlop, Weary 209

Egypt 36–9, 46–9
Eldershaw, Flora 183–5

'Eldershaw, M. Barnard' *see* Barnard, Marjorie; Eldershaw, Flora
Elmes, Dorothy xii, 139–40
England 72–4, 76–7, 78–82, 104–5, 127–8
Evans, Roslyn xiii, xiv, 231

First World War *see* Great War
Fletcher, Gertrude 5, 7
Forde, Frank 137–8
Forward, John 170
France 49–51, 69–72, 77–8, 116–17, 170–4
Franklin, Miles xiii, 3–4
Freeman, Hilda xiii, xiv, 22–4

Gallagher, Katharine 162
Gallipoli, evacuation from 32–3
Gantner, Neilma 132–5
Garner, Helen 55
Germany 20–2, 22–4
Gerster, Robin xi, xii, xiii
Gilmore, Mary xii, 77–8
Goldsmith, Betty 125
Goldstein, Vida xiii, 82–3, 88
Grafton 197–8
Great War ix, x, xi, xii, xiii, 3, 5, 15–122, 136
Green, Charles 197–8
Green, H.M. 109, 212
Green, Olwyn 197–8
Gulf War x, xiii, xiv, 227–36

Hain, Gladys 78–82
Hain, Rex 78
Halls, Geraldine xi, 167–9
Halls, John 167
Hanrahan, Barbara 120
Hardisty, Sue 169
Harford, Lesbia xiv, 55–8, 60–1
Harford, Pat 55
Harrison-Ford, Carl x
Hartley, Jenny ix
Harwood, Gwen 162–4
Hazzard, Shirley 121–2
Healesville 32, 96–7
Hewett, Dorothy 102–4
Heysen, Nora 180
'Horner, Marian' *see* Fletcher, Gertrude
Howard, Ann 182
Hughes, Billy 82–3, 91–2, 97
Hughes, Mary Kent 127–8
Hungary 191

India 97–9
Industrial Workers of the World 55, 93

James, Florence 178–9, 181–2
Japan 204–6
Jeffrey, Betty xi, 139, 140–2

Kata, Elizabeth xii, 185–8
Kelly, Gwen xiv, 84–8
King, Kelso 64
King, Olive x, xiv, 64–9
Korea 197, 198, 204
Korean War 195–206
Koval, Ramona xiv, 192–4

Lahey, Vida 75
Laird, J.T. ix, x
Lawrence, D.H. xi, 62
'Leake, R.E.' *see* Skinner, Mollie
Lemnos 32–6
Light, Helen 125–7
Loch, Joice NanKivell 20

McCubbin, Frederick 17–20
McFadzean, Mary 204–6
McInnes, Graham 109
McInnes, James Campbell 109
Mack, Louise 24–6, 28
Maclean, Meta 129–31
Maddock, Kenneth 222
Maiden, Jennifer xiii, 235–6
Malaya 139–40
Malouf, David ix
Mangan, Kathleen 17–20
Mannix, Daniel 97
Marlowe, Mary xii, 72–4, 76–7
Martin, Mandy 220

Martyr, Grace Ethel 94–6
Meeson, Dora 89
Melbourne 125–7
Midgley, Ann 6
Miller (Aldor), Christine 152
Mitchell, Elyne 150–1, 153–4
Mitchell, Tom 150
Moberly, Gertrude 97–9
Morrison, R.H. x
munitions 53–4, 174–8
Myer, Merlyn 132
Myer, Sidney 132

National Council of Women 136
Niall, Brenda xiii
Nicholas, George xiii
Nicholas, Hilda Rix xii–xiii, 44, 107
Niland, D'Arcy 99

O'Reilly, Dowell 158
Osborne, William 128
Osmond, Warren G. 42

Page, Geoff x
Palembang 142–5
Palmer, Nettie 105–6
Palmer, Vance 105
Pankhurst, Adela xiii, 88, 90
Pankhurst, Christabel 88
Pankhurst, Emmeline 88
Park, Ruth 99–100, 102
'Parker, Leslie' *see* Thirkell, Angela
Paterson, Banjo xi, 36
Pearce, Jan 229–30
Phelan, Nancy 24
Pierce, Peter x
Poland 125–7, 188
Poole, Philippa 164, 166
Prichard, Katharine Susannah xiv, 90–4, 117–19, 146–50, 199–201, 203–4

Queen Alexandra's Imperial Military Nursing Service 62

Rae, Iso 27, 59
Rankin, David 188
Red Cross 24, 72, 149
Reid, Gayle 214–19
Reilly, Catherine W. ix
Remembrance Day ix, xiv, 122
Richmond, Faith 131–2
Riddell, Thomas (Tony) 162–4
Ross, Jane 222–6
Royal Army Medical Corps 127–8
Royal Australian Army Nursing Corps 204–6

Salonika 65–9
Sandford, Beryl 125
Scottish Women's Hospitals 3, 64
Second World War ix, xi, xii, xiii, 52, 65, 123–94
Serbian Army 65–9
'Sidney, Neilma' *see* Gantner, Neilma
Simons, Jessie xi, 142–5
Sims, Jean xi, 169–70
Singapore 139, 140
Skinner, Mollie xi, 61–4
Smith, E. Hilmer 97
Smith, Grace Cossington 138
South Africa 5, 7, 8–13
South Yarra 17–20
Street, Jessie 135–7, 139
Sumatra 142–5
Sydney 55–8, 59–61, 121–2, 158, 164, 166, 166–7, 167–9, 175–7, 178–9, 181–2, 183–5

Tamworth 182–3
Tennant, Kylie 154–7
Terry, Susan 209–12
Thirkell, Angela xii, 109–13
Thirkell, George Allnutt 109
Throssell, Hugo 117
Tilton, May x, 69–72
Towong Hill 150–1, 153–4
Traill, Jessie xii, xiv, 116–17
Trial Bay 84–8
Turner, Ethel xiii, 28–9, 164, 166

United Associations of Women 136–7, 139
United States of America 132–5, 185–8

Varga, Susan xiv, 191–2
Vietnam 209–12, 215–10, 222–6
Vietnam War x, 207–26
Voluntary Aid Detachments ix, 62–4, 72–4, 76–7, 157–8

Wake, Nancy 170–4
Walker, Shirley 3
Wallace-Crabbe, Chris x
Walsh, Adela Pankhurst *see* Pankhurst, Adela
White, Osmar x
'White Mouse' *see* Wake, Nancy
Wilding, Michael ix
Wilkins, Lola xiii
Wobblies *see* Industrial Workers of the World
Women's Army Auxiliary Corps 51–3, 136
Women's Auxiliary Australian Air Force 146–8
Women's Legion 51, 53–4
Women's Peace Army xiii, 82, 88
Women's Political Association 82–3
Wright, Judith xii, 145–6, 221–2

Young, Aileen 104–5

Zoeller, Carl 40